WAITING   FOR THE

COOL   MOON

STUDIES OF THE WEATHERHEAD EAST ASIAN INSTITUTE, COLUMBIA UNIVERSITY
The Studies of the Weatherhead East Asian Institute of Columbia
University were inaugurated in 1962 to bring to a wider public the results
of significant new research on modern and contemporary East Asia.

WAITING FOR THE COOL MOON

ANTI-IMPERIALIST STRUGGLES *in the* HEART *of* JAPAN'S EMPIRE   WENDY MATSUMURA

Duke University Press   *Durham and London*   2024

© 2024 Duke University Press. All rights reserved

Project Editor: Livia Tenzer
Designed by Courtney Leigh Richardson
Typeset in Portrait and Quadraat Sans
by Westchester Publishing Services

Library of Congress Cataloging-in-Publication Data
Names: Matsumura, Wendy, [date] author.
Title: Waiting for the cool moon : anti-imperialist struggles in the heart of Japan's empire / Wendy Matsumura.
Other titles: Studies of the Weatherhead East Asian Institute, Columbia University.
Description: Durham : Duke University Press, 2024. | Series: Studies of the Weatherhead East Asian Institute, Columbia University | Includes bibliographical references and index.
Identifiers: LCCN 2023015820 (print)
LCCN 2023015821 (ebook)
ISBN 9781478025696 (paperback)
ISBN 9781478020950 (hardcover)
ISBN 9781478027829 (ebook)
Subjects: LCSH: Caste-based discrimination—Japan. | Buraku people—Japan—Social conditions. | Women—Japan—Social conditions. | Koreans—Japan—Social conditions. | Discrimination—Japan. | Marginality, Social—Japan. | Caste—Japan. | Japan—Social conditions. | BISAC: HISTORY / Asia / Japan | SOCIAL SCIENCE / Ethnic Studies / Asian Studies
Classification: LCC HT725.J3 M375 2024 (print) | LCC HT725.J3 (ebook) | DDC 305.5/680952—dc23/eng/20231113
LC record available at https://lccn.loc.gov/2023015820
LC ebook record available at https://lccn.loc.gov/2023015821

Cover art: Satoko Nema, Untitled, from the *Paradigm* series (2014-15). Chromogenic print mounted on acrylic. By permission of the artist.

To those fighting

SO THE LAST SHALL BE THE FIRST

CONTENTS

Acknowledgments • ix

INTRODUCTION • 1

CHAPTER ONE   EMPIRE AND OIKONOMIA • 17

CHAPTER TWO   ENCLOSURE AND
THE COMMUNITY OF THE COMMONS • 37

CHAPTER THREE   BURAKU WOMEN AGAINST
TRIPLED SUFFERINGS • 60

CHAPTER FOUR   HOUSEWIFIZATION,
INVISIBILIZATION, AND THE MYTH OF
THE NEW SMALL FARM HOUSEHOLD • 83

CHAPTER FIVE   INTERIMPERIAL KOREAN
STRUGGLE IN FERTILIZER'S GLOBAL CIRCUIT • 108

CHAPTER SIX   EMPIRE THROUGH THE
PRISM OF PHOSPHATE • 134

CHAPTER SEVEN **WATER STRUGGLES IN A COLONIAL CITY • 161**

CONCLUSION WAITING, WITNESSING, WITHHOLDING • 185

Notes • 193   Bibliography • 241   Index • 261

ACKNOWLEDGMENTS

Like many spaces built to perpetuate settler colonialism and imperialism, academia often feels like a shallow pool of fire where some enthusiastically feed the flames while others are sacrificed as kindling to keep them alive. Even as I perform my work duties, I carry deep anger and resentment at technocrats, financial managers, and leaders of my own institution who, under the cover of an immense bureaucracy of their own making, created the conditions under which a graduate student, in the middle of a pandemic, was forced to continue working in order to maintain their health insurance to undergo a serious medical procedure. The uneasiness I feel about my complicity in this structure of exploitation and routinized, normalized cruelty is magnified as I prepare the long list of people without whom I would not have been able to complete this book.

I am fortunate to have found people in and around University of California, San Diego (UCSD), who are committed to collectively carving out spaces that not only are safe, albeit temporarily, from this pool of fire, but also might one day extinguish it. In addition to Shaista Patel (who, in calling out the university as "white colonial Zionist Brahamanical property," has been subject to casteist violence in banal and extraordinary ways), Katie Walkiewicz, Shannon Welch, Amie Campos, Simeon Man, Zach Hill, Rhianen Callahan, Kevin Aguilar, Niall Chithelen, Essence Carrington, Thomas Chan, Sal Nicolazzo, Muhammad Yousuf, Andrea Mendoza, Jessica Graham, Kerry Keith, and many, many others whom I have been lucky to meet while working outside of formal university structures, have my deepest respect. The most important lesson that organizing with them in multiple spaces has taught me, as it pertains to this book, is that our so-called activism against the settler colonial university cannot be an alibi for unethical research practices we engage in elsewhere. The difficult lessons we learned along the way have provided me with a clarity that I wouldn't trade away—the clarity to see that attempts to pull ourselves out of our shallow pool of fire through collective acts of place making, if undertaken without extending such care to the communities that we involve in our research, are nothing more than a deferral of crisis—that is, a colonial act par excellence.

In addition to my named and unnamed coconspirators at UCSD, I would like to thank Huma Dar, a fierce scholar and activist fighting for the liberation of Kashmir, her home, for being such a generous teacher. Huma has patiently taught me about Kashmir and has gifted me invaluable lessons about the importance of intellectual honesty as the weight we carry as teachers, mentors, and colleagues. It has also been an honor to meet Zainab Ramahi, without whom I would not have survived this past year as the university weaponized its discrimination policies, institutionalized in the aftermath of the so-called Black Winter of 2010, against those of us on the Critical Gender Studies Program's executive committee who decided to disaffiliate a scholar whose research practices in Kashmir were antithetical to our shared vision of the program. The institutional procedures mobilized against us, particularly against Shaista Patel as the only Dalit Muslim and untenured scholar in the UC system, have interrupted important work. It remains necessary to rethink, as a program and a community of scholars, the standards that we adhere to and teach our students to adhere to as they relate to our research practices. If there is a silver lining, the entire ordeal—most of all, witnessing the powerful role that the language of civility and collegiality plays in punishing those of us who shed light on the coloniality of research practices—has taught us the futility of appeals to justice. I now understand the urgency of systematic and broad-based political education around the invisiblized issue of caste discrimination in US higher education and around the way that the Indian state's settler colonialism in Kashmir is bound up with issues of caste and religion. Meeting Dia Da Costa, Diyah Larasati, and Fuifuilupe Niumeitolu in the course of my learning on these issues has been an honor. While it is not my place to write about Kashmir or caste, thinking about how I, as part of the Okinawan diaspora, living and working on the stolen lands of Native communities, can connect Okinawan struggles against US and Japanese (neo)colonialism to freedom struggles in Kashmir has shaped, and will continue to shape, where I choose to devote my energies.

I am grateful to, in addition to those named above, interlocutors old and new who have helped me think critically about the kind of work it is appropriate for me to do as a researcher based in the United States, the country that continues to rule Okinawa militarily. The work that Mayumo Inoue, Kaori

Nakasone, Satoko Nema, Shinjō Ikuo, and the rest of the las barcas collective have done to dismantle the shallow representations of Okinawa and easy analyses that derive from them, which do little more than legitimate liberal policies of inclusion, continues to be an inspiration. I continue to think with and about the uncompromising, yet generous, political vision they have expressed through prose, poetry, theory, photography, and other art. I thank Satoko Nema for allowing me to use an image from her photo book, *Paradigm*, published on June 23, 2015—the seventy-year anniversary of the end of the Battle of Okinawa, also known as Okinawa's Day for Consoling the Spirits (*Irei no Hi*)—for the cover.

Many others whom I've met over the years in Tokyo, Kyoto, and Okinawa have, through their work and our conversations, shaped the questions I bring to my research on Japanese imperialism, including the ways people living under it organize themselves against and beyond its violences. In Tokyo, Okamoto Koichi, Gabe Masao, Katsukata-Inafuku Keiko, Uechi Satoko, Umemori Naoyuki, and many others provided great company and institutional support, especially in my early years as a researcher. I also thank the archivists at Hōsei University's Ōhara Institute for Social Research for access to their vast collection of movement documents. In Kyoto, I would like to thank Tomiyama Ichirō and his former students Mori Akiko, Asako Masubuchi, Asato Yōko, Okamoto Naomi, Kiriyama Setsuko, and Mairead Hynes for many years of often intense engagement. I am grateful to have met Ariko Ikehara at one of the weekly seminars run by Professor Tomiyama at Doshisha University. The research year that I was able to spend in 2017–18 as a Japan Foundation Research Fellow at Kyoto University's Faculty of Agriculture through the support of Adachi Yoshihiro and Itō Atsushi allowed me to think alongside their students about how bureaucratic instruments, such as the Farm Household Survey ledgers that appear in this book, served as counterrevolutionary instruments able to transform small farmers into conquistador humanists. I thank them, as well as the Faculty of Agriculture, for allowing me to take part in their seminar and for granting me access to the ledgers, which are held in the Faculty of Agriculture library. I would not have been able to do my work in Okinawa without the support of the archivists at the Okinawa Prefectural Archives, in particular Nakazato Kazuyuki; the librarians at the Okinawa Prefectural Library; Nakamura Mika at the Ōhara Institute for Social Research, Hōsei University; Ayano Ginoza at the Research Institute for Islands and Sustainability, based at the University of the Ryukyus; and Narisada Yōko at Okinawa University.

My relationship to Okinawa has shifted quite a bit since I published my first monograph, *The Limits of Okinawa*, in 2015. Ever since my colleague Michael

Provence insisted that I join him on a panel at UCSD called "From Japanese Internment to the Muslim Ban" in 2016, I have been grappling with the history I uncovered: that my paternal grandmother, Hideko Matsumura, was from Naha, the capital of Okinawa prefecture, and moved to Hawai'i following her eldest sister, Tamayose Shizue, who arrived there in 1926 with her husband to establish a Buddhist temple. Prior to seeing my grandmother's FBI file, which I found in the course of preparing for the panel, I did not know that our family had deep roots in Okinawa. I have been thinking about the ways my grandmother's silences around her hometown have shaped my scholarly relationship to Okinawa, and how learning about this history will bring with it new, perhaps more difficult, questions around complicity and obligation. Tze Loo, Shō Yamagushiku, Sam Museus, Sam Ikehara, and Wesley Ueunten have listened to me process what all of this means and have shared their own stories with me. Shō's insight, that what I experience as a severed connection is actually a deeply submerged one, has changed the way I think about relations that some definitions of diaspora occlude or frame as losses. The thinking and writing that Tze and I have done together for close to a decade sustain and challenge me.

The support of mentors, colleagues, and friends has made the publication of this book possible. I sent an early draft to my longtime mentor Harry Harootunian in February 2021. Since then, with the swiftness that is legendary among his students, he not only read the full draft but also shared it with Carol Gluck, who also responded with enthusiasm and generous advice. In addition to Harry and Carol, Louise Young, Keith Camacho, Tze Loo, Simeon Man, and Sharad Chari read full drafts of the manuscript through a University of California Humanities Research Institute–funded manuscript workshop. I thank the five of them not only for enduring what was probably an extremely painful read, but also for providing me with feedback from their specific areas of knowledge, which I have tried to address in this final version. I also want to thank Rebecca Karl, someone I deeply admire as a Marxist scholar and mentor, for providing me with extensive feedback as one of Duke University Press's expert readers. At Duke, my gratitude extends to a second (anonymous) reader, Ken Wissoker, Ryan Kendall, Livia Tenzer, Courtney Berger, and everyone else who brought this book to publication. I also thank Laura Keeler for their careful edits and Sophia Massie for compiling the index. For opportunities to present parts of the chapters at other institutions, I thank Tom Lamarre at Duke University; Michael Bourdaghs at the University of Chicago; William Marotti at the University of California, Los Angeles; Hyun Ok Park at York University; and Yukiko Hanawa at New York University. Thanks to Kōta Kimura of the *Against Japanism* podcast for allowing me to share my work with his audience.

My admiration for the work that Léopold Lambert has been doing at *The Funambulist* to make visible the connections between seemingly disparate places and communities, without losing the specificity of struggles that arise from them, has allowed me to think about Okinawa in new ways. I thank him for publishing my earliest public-facing pieces on Okinawa. I also want to thank Allison Hurst, the only good thing that came out of my years teaching at Furman University, for her friendship and example. Finally, I thank Youngoh Jung for providing generous feedback on the entire manuscript, Inga Kim Diederich for providing translations of Korean language materials that enabled me to write about interimperial circuits of anticapitalist, anticolonial struggle in chapter 5, and Jin-kyung Lee, who, with Andrea Mendoza, provided generous feedback on earlier drafts. The Japan Foundation, the Association for Asian Studies, the University of California Humanities Research Institute, UCSD's General Campus Research Grant, and UCSD's Office of the Dean of Arts and Humanities provided funding for this project.

I got into the rather obsessive habit of checking in on my mom three times a day during the pandemic. I thank her for putting up with my only-child anxieties of needing to know she was okay from across the ocean and for trying to understand why I became so interested in tracing the roots of my grandmother—someone I know was the source of much difficulty for her. My sweet but embarrassingly territorial Rosa is my constant writing companion. My final thank-you is reserved for Paul, for whom all the words in the world are not enough.

INTRODUCTION

The Longue Durée *of White Supremacy*

Worlds are burning, but that, too, is becoming normalized.[1] Liberal forms of recognition that drove the discourse of human rights during much of the last century have revealed themselves to be useless, even as a political tactic.[2] Entire communities are left to die without any true claim to life, and this is considered a necessary condition for the continued prosperity and self-actualization of others. That mass racialized killings are the result of nothing but the obvious, predictable, and devastating manifestation of historically rooted, layered, and complex modes, structures, and relations of the logics of capital, colonialism, and white supremacy is an uncomfortable truth. However, this truth is infrequently taken seriously as a problem that implicates *all of us*. The inability to connect mass death and genocide *over there* with the modes of sociality and kinship that must be honored *over here* is a product of modes of rationalization and extraction that persist through the ongoing, relentless erasures of the knowledges, arts, and ways of life of those people deemed expendable in each site, though differently.[3]

As Lisa Yoneyama teaches us, to insist on a humanism that gained its place as liberal apologia through the denial of the *longue durée* of white supremacy and its accomplices gets us nowhere close to abolishing the foundations of our daily violence. Abolishing these foundations requires that we understand both the way that liberal humanism blunts the political demands of those whose lives are torn apart through ongoing colonial violence, particularly in its heteropatriarchal forms, and, crucially, the way that people refuse these conditions through their rejection of the politics of inclusion in the rights-based regime.[4] Different weapons have to be sharpened to destroy what Alexander Weheliye calls, in *Habeas Viscus*, "our extremely uneven global power structures defined by the intersections of neoliberal capitalism, racism, settler colonialism, immigration and imperialism."[5] These structures render regimes of state-mediated killing—by medicine, law, surveillance, flooding, industrial pollution, language, the barrel of a gun, or a signature on a sheet of paper—natural and therefore not prosecutable. In addition to making these scenes visible, a more capacious ability to apprehend, and therefore learn from, moments when political communities coalesce to draw blood from their oppressors is needed.

Historical narratives crafted by scholars of bourgeois and Marxist persuasions alike that pursue narrative closure through their belief in the possibility of archival mastery reinforce rather than free us from murderous structures, processes, and grammars. This is not least because closure is closely tied to (social) scientific assumptions about historical transformation that fail to reckon with the implications of narrating change over time in ways that, as Michel-Rolph Trouillot explained over fifty years ago, are circumscribed by the positivism-constructivism dichotomy.[6] The inability of historical narrativization to unsettle this moment of mass global death is related to the fact that dominant conventions of academic history writing, broken into fiefdoms and subdisciplines, have not seriously reckoned with the logics and structures of white supremacy that implicate us all—even those of us whose institutional homes orient us to the so-called non-West.[7] Black radical intellectual genealogies offer a comprehensive critique and guide against structural, willful ignorance.

The main theoretical problem that animates the current project, *Waiting for the Cool Moon*, is informed by these critiques. I ask, what of Walter Benjamin's historical materialism can remain intact if we accept as theory, thought, and praxis that anti-Blackness is inextricably linked to the way that we conceptualize relations between pasts and presents?[8] Christina Sharpe's *In the Wake* teaches me that the suture of the world brought forth by the Middle Passage is an epochal and ongoing event that poses an unbearable challenge to the discipline of history, in all its versions, including historical materialist ones. The method and project of historical materialism I problematize here is defined by Benjamin in "Theses on the Philosophy of History":

> The tradition of the oppressed teaches us that the "state of emergency" in which we live is not the exception but the rule. We must attain to a conception of history that is keeping with this insight. Then we shall clearly realize that it is our task to bring about a real state of emergency, and this will improve our position in the struggle against Fascism. One

reason why Fascism has a chance is that in the name of progress its opponents treat it as a historical norm. The current amazement that the things we are experiencing are "still" possible in the twentieth century is *not* philosophical. This amazement is not the beginning of knowledge— unless it is the knowledge that the view of history which gives rise to it is untenable.[9]

Sharpe's formulation poses a challenge. It insists that for those who grapple with the world-shifting implications of the Middle Passage, the ongoing state of emergency—fascism—that Benjamin calls the norm under modernity is not the only or most important condition of oppression for everyone. In fact, what Benjamin recognized as a state of emergency might be better understood as an enduring condition since slavers, accountants, navigators, kings, planters, priests, and philosophers set out to conquer distant lands—much earlier than he acknowledges and continuing still today. Sharpe insists that recognizing an epochal break in the fifteenth century must take precedence over debates on shifts, for example, to the organic composition of capital, or even of processes that led to the revolutionary overthrow of regimes. That break continues to overwhelm, structure, and shape our present—in other words, anti-Blackness remains the weather.[10] Put more concretely, the "we" who accept Benjamin's exhaustion with people who continue to be surprised that atrocities are "'still' possible in the twentieth century" have to contend with our own ignorance about how the conditions that made the Middle Passage thinkable in the first place are the yet-to-be-broken grounds upon which contemporary fascisms, colonialisms, imperialisms, and genocides (as well as our understandings of them) continue to thrive.[11] Studies of the politics of knowledge production in modern Japan have to contend with anti-Blackness, as well as anti-Indigeneity, not as additive context but as the very grounds on which our understandings of imperialism, colonialism, and total war must stand.[12]

In order to trace the ways that units of analyses that Marx identified as building blocks for his critique of political economy, including surplus value, the commodity, and labor power, are imbricated in knowledge structures, production regimes, and discursive representations of the human that are reified through the erasure of their embeddedness and indebtedness to capital's bloody encounters with noncapitalist worlds and relations, I draw on a rich tradition of scholarship that has theorized capital's use and production of racialized and gendered regimes of accumulation in its ceaseless drive to overcome its own limits. Sylvia Wynter's writings on the *pieza* conceptual frame are indispensable for understanding the ways that colonial and metropolitan disavowals of Blackness as a category that was forged during the Middle Passage infused categories of work that Japanese thinkers and policy makers invoked to differentiate themselves from their early modern predecessors and Asian neighbors from the late nineteenth century. I discuss this in detail in the first chapter.

This project is also indebted to the scholarship of Saidiya Hartman, Shona Jackson, Denise Ferreira da Silva, and Lisa Lowe, who have shown how the building blocks of bourgeois and Marxist categories of analysis like land, capital, and labor are always already burdened by assumptions about place, wealth, and people that efface the dehumanizing violence wrought through the enslavement of people of African descent through the Middle Passage. Jackson's linking of the specific relations among the genocide of Indigenous peoples, the labor performed by enslaved and indentured people in extractive industries, and settler claims on land and nation as a condition of "nineteenth-century economic humanism" is particularly important for my understanding of the way that the first generation of Japanese settler scholars' disavowal of the state's colonization of Ainu Mosir and the Ryūkyū Kingdom was the foundation upon which they authorized genocidal practices in the Pacific Islands.[13] Situating the formation of the Japanese nation-state qua empire as part of this shared context of nineteenth-century economic humanism opens up lines of inquiry that can aid in unearthing the tangled roots of our monstrous presents.

Waiting for the Cool Moon asks why coevalness has yet to figure meaningfully in analyses of Japanese capitalism qua imperialism even though the historical record is replete with trenchant critiques and militant action against the consequences of imperialism for and by racialized, gendered, and colonized people in the Japanese empire.[14] This is not a problem of paucity of evidence, but rather, as Yoneyama argues, an indication of the need to clarify "through what structural access, and under what personal, social, and historical conditions" we understand and assign value to particular narratives of the past.[15]

Japanese Grammar and the Social Sciences

Harry Harootunian argued in *Marx after Marx* that Japanese Marxists of the 1920s and 1930s did take seriously the inability of Marxism to fully capture the meaning of dizzying transformations to social and economic life that were unfolding before them. They did not, however, respond to the interwar spectacle of unharnessed development on the one hand and the persistence of forms of extra-economic compulsion on the other by proposing fundamental reworkings of the genealogy of bourgeois revolution to center the Haitian Revolution, as C. L. R. James did in *Black Jacobins*. Nor did they link the establishment of the Japanese nation-state to a chronology that highlighted the interconnectedness of Spanish genocide of Indigenous peoples, capitalist encroachment in Latin America, and the consolidation of Peru as a modern nation-state offered by José Carlos Mariátegui in *Seven Interpretive Essays on Peruvian Reality*.

Uno Kōzō, Inomata Tsunao, Yamada Moritarō, and other Marxist thinkers did grapple with the dilemma of how to reconcile paths to revolution imaginable in what they called "latecomers" to capitalist development, such as Japan, through faithful readings of Marxist theory available to them at the time. They filtered their reading practices through their understandings of Japanese realities, which, they believed, took some of those strategies off the table, at least for the time being.[16] However, their focus on debates over what constituted empirically sound diagnoses of the present conjuncture that relied on state-produced data sets made them unable to see what Cedric Robinson called revolutionary attacks on culture that were taking place before their eyes.[17] Their collective inability to see the anticolonial, anti-imperialist, and feminist critiques within and outside of organized labor and peasant struggles that people were waging in the heart of empire was tied to a shared conceptual limit: their belief that the Japanese worker and his vanguard was ultimately the protagonist of revolutionary struggle. In other words, their understandings of what constituted reliable empirical data were informed by and reinforced a methodological nationalism whose clearest and most enduring consequence was colonial studies scholars' disavowal of the colonialism at the roots of Japanese nation-state formation.

Labor, Subjectification, and Colonial Commonsense

Dionne Brand's writings play an indispensable role in the way I understand colonial violence, its erasure, and my own task as a witness to these realities. Brand's work shows that there are many ways to communicate what Wynter also explicated theoretically—that colonial violence is embedded in the narrative structures of texts, in language, and in the velocities of imperial time that cohere as commonsense.[18] K'eguro Macharia's explication of the concept of sociogeny, as articulated by Frantz Fanon and Wynter, allows them to examine the way that heteropatriarchal anti-Blackness grounds commonsense notions of the self in modernity. Macharia emphasizes that the concept, which "directs how family, society, and nation are experienced," exposes the difficulty of uprooting structures of racial and colonial domination precisely because they take hold as commonsense:

> The commonsense experience of whiteness is as a generic human while the commonsense experience of blackness is as defect in relation to whiteness, which is, then, defect in relation to humanness. Commonsense is not only intellectual ... but also the whole ensemble of how the senses experience the world, especially how ideas and experiences of pleasure and unpleasure, beauty and ugliness, good and bad, are framed.[19]

As aesthetic experience, Macharia explains, commonsense is "marked by the fractures created by colonial modernity."[20] In the context of modern Japan, commonsense as aesthetic experience, expressed through print, philosophy, art, literature, history, surveyors, soldiers, and storytellers, naturalized the state's denial of its genocidal beginnings and shaped peoples' understandings of who was fully human and who was not.[21] This, as much as conditions we understand as structural, has to be accounted for in our examinations of the entrenched nature of white supremacy and its accomplices as they took hold in the heart of Japan's empire.

It is not surprising, given the thickness of colonial commonsense, that the struggles of groups like the Suiheisha fighting for buraku liberation, the Japanese branch of the Korean feminist organization Kinyūkai/Kŭnuhoe, and a group of activists in Okinawa affiliated with the Labor Farmer Party, who all fought to dismantle grammars of social analysis that legitimated their oppression, went largely unrecognized by radical intellectuals who were brought up in the imperial university system and saw the colonies and colonial struggle as qualitatively different from antagonisms in the metropole. The conceptual gulf was even wider in their analyses of the agrarian question, where they treated colonial and national spheres as separate due to their acceptance of the boundaries that state authorities drew and tirelessly adjusted between "Japan proper" and places like Taiwan, Korea, northern China, and the Pacific Islands.[22] Assumptions of territorial fixity that accompanied Japanese Marxists' acceptance of the concept of the imperial division of labor structured their delimitation of agrarian struggle to Japanese small farmers in the metropole. Japan studies scholars have yet to fundamentally challenge these assumptions.[23]

Franco Barchiesi and Shona Jackson's introduction to a special issue of *International Labor and Working Class History* addressing "Blackness and Labor in the Afterlives of Racial Slavery" offers a starting point for thinking about the relationship between colonial erasure and the valorization of certain kinds of struggles against capital. Their essay problematizes how labor historians, in their placement of "changes in the status of work at the core of the very meaning of captivity and freedom, their epochal watersheds, and institutionalized or unintended overlaps" unwittingly serve as apologists for colonialism.[24] Barchiesi and Jackson argue that rather than accepting the establishment of waged labor relations as evidence of a step that a society has taken on the path to freedom, labor historians would do well to contend with the "fundamental antiblackness of labor itself, its categories, and its forward motion in history."[25] That recognition allows for an interrogation of the field's valorization of organized, working-class resistance over refusal, escape, play, or waiting, which are considered passive acts that ultimately do not produce the class antagonism required for transformation to a higher stage of capital. Barchiesi and Jackson's critique of political economy's bestowal of "ontological prominence on work as the terrain from which something globally essential, not just situationally contingent, can be enunciated about the meaning of freedom, indeed on the very definition of the human"—resonant with Lisa Lowe's assertion in *The Intimacies of Four Continents* that "the social inequalities of our time are a legacy of these processes through which 'the human' is 'freed' by liberal forms, while other subjects, practices, and geographies are placed at a distance from 'the human'"—helps me understand why an analysis of how anti-Blackness and anti-Indigeneity are inscribed and reproduced in the grammar of Japanese political economic critique is indispensable to making sense of the way that trenchant critiques of colonialism, racism, and patriarchy issued by the aforementioned organizations and others failed to register in the minds of most Japanese intellectuals and activists as indispensable to their own struggles.[26]

The Post-World War I Agrarian Question

The state, in contrast, understood the destabilizing force of interwar anti-imperialist struggles organized through alliances between tenant farmer unions and radical labor unions, especially those with feminist or anticolonial divisions. The Ministry of Agriculture and Commerce (after 1925, the Ministry of Agriculture) worked with the Home Ministry to combine policy with physical repression to bring order to an empire in crisis. A central component of the former's counterrevolutionary project was its promotion of protectionist policies whose primary objective was to transform the head of the small farm household into a conquistador humanist—a figure who successfully overcame a lowly position in the chronically undercapitalized agricultural department through training, hard work, and the ability to manage other peoples' labor time.[27] The ministry's enthusiasm for this project makes clear that, by the 1920s, policies that relied solely on inculcating a pioneering spirit in the hearts of embattled and heavily indebted Japanese small farmers could not resolve the structural and spiritual problems of agrarian crisis. It had to dig deeper into the organizational form of the small farm household and enact policies that political theorist Angela Mitropoulos calls *oikonomic*—those that promote the actualization of unequal household relations as the fulfillment of a primordial, authentic relationship that "made the extraction of surplus labor possible by the affective registers and architecture that legitimated the implied contractualism of the *oikos* [household] . . . as species of unbreakable covenant."[28] Within the ministry's ideal small farm household, surplus labor was to be offered freely by members of the family—especially women—as "obligation, indebtedness, and gift."[29]

Writings by Black radical thinkers alert us to the way that feminist critiques of state oikonomic policies need also to attend to the fact that major transformations to notions of family as they are tied to nation are always already racialized. This analysis in turn alerts us to how normative categories of the family work to reinforce white supremacist norms as commonsense. Angela Davis, for example, exposes an irreconcilability between the kind of woman and family form assumed to be the object of struggle and the protagonist of a revolution-to-come in *Women, Race and Class*. Pointing to the enduring effects of the history of enslavement to explicate the way that Black families' gender dynamics were not comparable to those of white families, Davis writes, "As a direct consequence of their outside work [during slavery] . . . housework has never been the central focus of Black women's lives. They have largely escaped the psychological damage industrial capitalism inflicted on white middle-class housewives, whose alleged virtues were feminine weakness and wifely submissiveness."[30] Hortense Spillers explores the consequences of this history in "Mama's Baby, Papa's Maybe," arguing that feminist analyses that do not recognize that (white) womanhood and the (white) family are predicated on the denial of womanhood to Black, Indigenous, and colonized peoples reproduces a universal woman whose primary purpose is to uphold the logic of domination that Wynter calls "Man-as-human."[31] In short, the abstract category of woman, as well as hegemonic definitions of family, exist in antagonistic relation to, and are maintained by, the labors and lives of people who are excluded from theorizations of this purportedly universal category.[32]

Also illuminating are works by historians such as Jennifer Morgan, who argues in *Laboring Women* that the reproductive labor of enslaved women was central to profit calculations of slaveowners in the early English colonies that shaped both men's and women's experiences of enslavement and understandings of kinship, family, and distinctions between private and public spheres. Additionally, Sarah Haley argues in *No Mercy Here* that late nineteenth and early twentieth-century formations of the "gendered-racial-sexual order" were shaped by white supremacist ideas about "white feminine sexual vulnerability" and associations of imprisoned Black women with "sexual antinormativity."[33] The calcification of the gendered-racial-sexual order in the New South was inextricably linked, argues Haley, to societal fears in the United States around white women's entry into the wage labor market.[34] One question beyond the scope of this project that emerges from these works is how the entry of a larger number of migrant workers from various Asian countries (including Japan) to the United States and to areas that Southern plantation owners also sought fortunes in globally (thinking with Gerald Horne's *The White Pacific*, for example) impacted the dynamics that Haley traces. As chapters 6 and 7 will show, sociopolitical configurations into which Okinawan migrant workers entered starting in the first decade of the twentieth century significantly altered the way that Okinawans abroad and at home were positioned within the Japanese empire's gendered-racial-sexual order.

This project is indebted to these scholars, who have given me the depth of perspective required to understand the Japanese Ministry of Agriculture and Commerce's interwar oikonomic policies as more than just a shoring up of small farm households suffering the effects of chronic recessionary conditions after World War I. I trace the hardening of new boundaries between communities within the agrarian village who were deemed worthy of protection and those classified as expendable and think about how the categories of the small farm household came to operate in service of Japanese supremacist ideas. That is, I tie state protectionist policies toward these units to the entrenchment of colonial commonsense in the metropole's agrarian villages. This perspective helps me make sense of my findings in chapters 2 and 3, that consensus, not state policy, drove the expulsion of racialized burakumin households from their village communities. In later chapters, I trace how this commonsense that small farm households honed at home helped to legitimate genocide, including military sexual slavery throughout Asia and the Pacific. In clarifying the relation between the ministry's oikonomic policies at home and Indigenous genocide on an ever-expanding scale, which coincided with the securing of the borders and financial foundations of the early Meiji regime and were rooted in (settler) colonialism and its disavowal, I expose the Japanese empire's side of what Haunani-Kay Trask, in "Setters of Color and 'Immigrant' Hegemony," described as the denial of Japanese settler ascendancy in Hawai'i, "made possible by the continued national oppression of Hawaiians" through the ideology of the "local nation" after statehood.[35]

Japanese Humanity and Anti-archival Praxis

In addition to clarifying the relationship between the state's enactment of oikonomic policies in the metropolitan countryside and its dispatch of conquistador humanists to the Pacific islands, *Waiting for the Cool Moon* makes visible multiple forms of struggle that people who were rendered disposable in new ways after World War I waged. Despite their violent expulsion from the body politic, which was authorized by the law, enabled by sensibility, and enacted through consensus, the people and organizations whose stories I share here insisted on radically different relations that rejected their expulsion from village community but did not pin their political hopes or desires on state recognition.[36] Their most devastating critique—that "Japan" is a fantasy shored up through the disavowal of colonial relations at the heart of empire—continues to be politically relevant today, not least because the field of Japan studies continues to operate as though it is a stable unit of analysis. In other words, their critiques shed light on our complicity as scholars who have not managed to obliterate the fantasy of Japan as only temporarily and uncharacteristically a perpetrator of colonial genocide.[37]

Struggles against concrete processes and logics of enclosure that were tools of racialized and gendered expulsions took the form of strikes, petitions, and other recognizable actions, but they also appear in more amorphous, hard-to-trace moments of world making like refusal, play, flight, and waiting.[38] I view each instance as a revolutionary attack on the state's cultivation of the national subject's fascistic interiority, packaged in a grammar refined from the Middle Passage, its acquisition celebrated as a hallmark of successful transformation into a protagonist in the forward march of Japanese history. While collective struggles for freedom rarely make their appearance in the vast archives of imperialism, their traces are nevertheless abundant.[39]

As Lisa Lowe illuminates in *The Intimacies of Four Continents*, seeing and attributing what states do not want us to see takes creativity, as archives tuck away and classify challenges to the unholy triad of capital, nation, and family in ways that occlude interconnections between numerous, often small, but meticulously organized wars against colonial barbarism across nations and empires.[40] I also recognize, however (as Lowe does), that illuminating the structures and enactments of a dominating Japanese social grammar through a promiscuous reading of and across state archives is inadequate for understanding the power of these experiences of world making and refusal. Without attending to the violence of our own imperial gaze, we risk reinforcing colonial logics that inform archival production and excavation.

Brand's *The Blue Clerk: Ars Poetica in 59 Versos* guides my skepticism toward freedom dreams that scholars locate in archives of struggle.[41] Her proposal for opacity, multifocality, and flux, which I expand on in chapter 7, cautions us from devoting too much of our energies to describing liberatory projects, as they are always at risk of being co-opted by ever-accommodating imperial projects.[42] Secrets, Brand's blue clerk suggests, have to be guarded in order for acts of world making that lie beyond the reach of the logic of European Man-as-human to cohere, evade reabsorption, and sharpen their blades. Brand's clerk is constantly preparing, making room for, waiting, guarding, and resuscitating the bales of papers that contain secrets (and green aphids) still very much alive. They demand acknowledgment, emitting the "the sharp, poisonous odour of time."[43] Careful readers will notice that the blue clerk is multiple women who make appearances in photographs, diary entries, and the clerk's memories—subject and safekeeper of the continually shifting line that separates the cargo's right- and left-hand pages.

I approach the women (and some men) who appear in the archives I read as keepers of secrets who cannot rest even in death because vultures are constantly circling, and acknowledge that neither right- nor left-hand ledgers are mine to excavate, collect, claim, or consume. What is visible to me as a reader of texts to which I have varying degrees of proximity limit and shape the form and content of this text.

The Refusal of Representational Violence

The methodological and ethical challenge I came up against repeatedly while writing about acts of refusal against colonial commonsense concerned representational violence. I wanted to avoid making the named and unnamed buraku, Korean, and Okinawan people who appear in the text into what Sharpe calls a metaphor: a figure that "appears only to be made to disappear."[44] While neither the place from which I write nor the people about whom I write are the same as Sharpe and her interlocutors in *In the Wake*, the communities I write about also appear in some studies simply to move forward a narrative of suffering or resistance or to clarify the character of the Japanese imperial formation. That is, they are made to appear without any apparent authorial commitment to dismantling those violent structures or grammars.

In the Wake is concerned with breaking this commonplace, anti-Black representational logic that cannot apprehend the suffering of a young Black woman, Aereile Jackson, who appears in a 2010 film by Allan Sekula and Noel Burch, *The Forgotten Space*, in its specificity.[45] Linking Jackson's erasure to the structure of a world that places Black people as its constitutive outside, Sharpe reiterates the importance of writers, poets, and artists who have taken up the task of bringing people with "no bones to recover" to the surface for air.[46] Sharpe proposes that, while the logic of anti-Blackness is all-encompassing, there is something that haunts the screens, the texts, and the photographs where recognition takes place, but only between those who are engulfed by the ecological terrain in ways that are legible to each other. Sharpe writes, this time upon encountering a photograph of a little girl with the word *ship* on her forehead in a collection of materials following the 2010 earthquake in Haiti, "I had to take care."[47]

In untangling the logics that made actually existing struggles waged by Okinawan, Korean, and buraku women unseeable in different ways to colonial intellectuals and activists, my own place in the world sets limits on my ability to share the stories of ordinary women in the archives of Japanese imperialism who haunt and shape the text. I write about what I am meant to see, what my own position in the world demands that I see.

My paternal great-grandmother, Tamashiro Kama, is from Haebaru, Okinawa, and her daughter, my grandmother Hideko Matsumura, was born in Wakasa, Naha, where her father was the head priest at a Buddhist temple. I was not aware of even the faint outlines of this family history until I accessed my grandmother's FBI file from the US National Archives while researching the reasons for my father's repatriation to Japan from Honolulu as a small child in 1943. It has been a strange experience doing academic work on Okinawa before and after this knowledge, a condition I know will continue to bring me waves of discomfort and joy. My alienation cuts deeper the more that archival records illuminate all of the things I was never privy to as family stories. The main proposition I laid out in my first monograph, *The Limits of Okinawa*—that tracing the complex and antagonistic relations that accompanied the emergence of a reified category, Okinawa, is a necessary part of honoring the intense battles over living labor that took place as the former region became a site of capitalist extraction and exploitation—stands. Still, I often think about how much that line of argumentation contributed to, or obstructed, ongoing struggles for freedom in Okinawa. That is, I wonder how much of the analysis I offered there unwittingly naturalized colonial commonsense, including the silences that run through my own family's histories. I continue to position myself primarily as a researcher from the United States—a country that continues to exercise colonial rule in Okinawa and one that is responsible for massacres carried out in the name of democracy throughout territories the Japanese state and capital ruled until surrender—whose work can easily become extractive and mobilized to violent ends even as I try to operate from a place of solidarity. Still, I remain untethered by this new knowledge. Reading the transcript of a conversation between R. A. Judy and Fred Moten published in *boundary 2* over the question of the relationship between the "I" and the "we," I ask myself, Where is the ensemble, or the collective, that I hold myself accountable to, and that shapes and holds me? Still in the process of arriving at a satisfying answer to this question, I work unsteadily with what I am certain about: since academic work does not have to be directly funded by the Department of Defense to be an effective tool of counterinsurgency, when in doubt, restraint is preferable to narrative abundance.[48]

Structure

Waiting for the Cool Moon is divided informally into four parts. Read together, they invite the reader to see the depths of the colonial violence and struggles to live otherwise at the heart of an empire in crisis. The first part, chapter 1, examines the relationship between Wynter's *pieza* conceptual frame—which refers to the mode of domination composed of philosophies, logics, and practices that made the unit of the *pieza* possible as a standard of exchange for enslaved peoples from the fifteenth-century slave trade onward—and concepts such as laboring capacity (*rōdō nōryoku*) and labor efficiency index (*rōdō nōritsu*) that emerged in Japan in the early 1920s as additional tools for the violent abstraction of labor and were utilized by the Japanese Ministry of Agriculture and Commerce.[49] While I do not trace a straight line between these concepts, Wynter's *pieza* conceptual frame helps me think through how understandings of the human embedded in the conceptual building blocks formed in the wake of the Middle Passage were baked into categories like those that enabled Japanese thinkers and policy makers on all sides of the political spectrum to understand the economic calculations they were making about wages, labor power, and productivity as entirely separate from compulsion. The second half of the chapter introduces an apparatus developed by the Ministry of Agriculture and Commerce called the Nōka Keizai Chōsa (Farm Household Survey), which many social scientists, then and now, have unquestioningly used as a reliable data set for understanding class differentiation in the countryside. I argue, in contrast, that through its differentiated use of laboring capacity and labor efficiency to ascribe values to labor performed in the farm household, the survey actively produced participating small farm households as conquistador humanists in ways that establish a genealogical relationship between the *pieza* as an instrument of dehumanizing accounting during the slave trade, the imposition of colonial rule over territories that became Hokkaido and Okinawa, and the remaking of small farm households into apparatuses through which fascism instantiated itself in the body politic of Japan.

The second part comprises chapters 2 and 3, which examine how conflicts that erupted between burakumin and ippanmin communities following the state's enactment of a new round of enclosures produced and reinforced colonial sensibilities in the Ise region of Mie prefecture. While these new enclosures destabilized many agrarian communities through the contraction and privatization of vast tracts of communally held and managed lands, they also produced new distinctions between racialized farm households. Chapter 3 argues that when buraku communities and organizations refused to accept their collective erasure, they were not simply or even primarily fighting for inclusion in the rights-based system of common lands (*iriaiken*) but were refusing a sensibility that figured them collectively as a threat to the nation.

The third part, chapters 4 and 5, illuminates the relationship between the housewifization of Japanese women in small farm households, the employment of Korean migrant workers who were denied the resources to guarantee the reproduction of their own families, and the erasure of non-wage-earning Korean women from the Japanese economy altogether. Chapter 4 argues that despite their small numbers, Korean men and women agriculturalists were indispensable for the self-actualization of the Japanese small farmer as conquistador humanist in the metropole. Chapter 5 traces the imperial fertilizer circuit of Taki Seihi, one of the country's leading fertilizer companies whose product aided in the transformation of Okayama's small farmers into fruit producers. Korean workers that the company recruited to expand its operations created spaces of solidarity throughout the very same imperial circuit that rendered them disposable.

The fourth part, chapters 6 and 7, considers the consequences that the mode of the Ryūkyū Kingdom's incorporation into the Japanese empire as a prefecture had upon the people of the region. It takes as emblematic of these violent processes the recruitment of Okinawan workers into the phosphate industry in the Pacific prior to the Japanese state's colonization of the northern Mariana, Marshall, and Caroline islands. By starting with the over three hundred workers from Okinawa who were transported to Banaba Island between 1908 and 1910 to toil as semi-skilled workers for the Pacific Phosphate Company (PPC), chapter 6 rejects prevailing understandings of mainland Japanese and Okinawan workers as merely differentially privileged agents of settler colonialism in the Pacific.[50] Highlighting the latter's historical role as a disposable, colonial workforce allows me to read the extension of the Farm

Household Survey project to Okinawa in 1930 as an instrument of colonial rule rather than as evidence of national inclusion. Chapter 7 directly engages Brand's work and reads the colonial ledgers as repositories of contestation and refusal rather than faithful assimilation. In this chapter, as in the rest of the book, I pay close attention to the importance of what people withheld from the colonial gaze as a necessary part of building spaces of retreat, sites of mourning, and repositories of joy while living through counterrevolutionary terror.

CHAPTER ONE   EMPIRE AND OIKONOMIA

In *Beyond a Boundary*, C. L. R. James discussed cricket as an avenue for Trinidadians to become socialized into the manners and sentiments of their British colonizers, as well as a path to entry into low-level colonial bureaucracy. Sylvia Wynter, in her reading of what she called the Jamesian poesis, explains that even if James could never completely free himself of the manners and sentiments he so meticulously adopted through school and sport, he had a decision to make. She writes, "He would, however, have to free himself from the master conception that underlay the [public school] code, the conception that effected the separation of the 'native' elite from the native masses, binding the loyalty of the former not to their own reality but to that of these colonizers."[1] Whereas James gained access to the colonial bureaucracy through his mastery of the "public school code," freedom from it required a recognition and disavowal of his place within it. That is, there can be no innocent telling of his story outside of the analytical categories chosen to narrate it.

Wynter argues that James's novel *Minty Alley* made clear his commitment to understanding and ultimately undoing the colonial reality at hand—a move reflected in its clarification of the infrastructure of global accumulation in which Trinidadian society existed, as well as its embodied effects on the daily lives of different segments of the population. The novel illuminates the deeply rooted nature of the subjugation and dehumanization with which its characters (like Matthew Bondsman and others who might otherwise be defined as colonial lumpenproletariat) were imbued. These conditions required more than a critique of the capital-labor relation from which many would have been altogether excluded.[2] For James, clarifying or resolving the so-called labor question in the colony was not sufficient as a decolonizing call. Rather, liberation required undoing the global mode of racial domination inaugurated by the slave trade, transformed with the commencement of "free trade," and extended with the new round of colonization of Africa in the later nineteenth century.

Wynter's category, the *pieza* conceptual frame, derives from James's method of seeing the colonial and metropolitan disavowals of Blackness as a category forged during the Middle Passage's transformation of enslaved persons from Africa into *pieza*, or an abstract unit of measurement "based on the estimated productive capacity of an able-bodied, usually male, slave of a certain height and size."[3] According to Demetrius Eudell, the disavowal of how chattel slavery infused the pores of categories of work associated with freedom reveals to Wynter that the value of a commodity is always already based on a *"societal* definition of the value of that labor according to the *social value* ascribed to the bearers of particular variants of labor power."[4] She explains that "Man's overrepresentation of its 'descriptive statement' [Bateson 1969] as if it were that of the human itself"—what she calls "the struggle of our times, one that has hitherto had no name"—depends on an ability to claim the position as the bearer of free, as opposed to enslaved, labor.[5] That is, they claim supremacy by benefiting from, while at the same time naturalizing, chattel slavery.

This chapter argues that the *pieza*, a standard of exchange that figured enslaved people as fungible units of labor and whose beginnings can be traced to the fifteenth-century Portuguese and Spanish slave trades, must be engaged as a conceptual framework that endures in other forms, including in parts of the world not usually discussed in conversations about the transatlantic slave trade or its wake. This is important if we are to understand the global mode of racial domination that underpins and enables capital to overcome its constant crises through intensified forms of extraction and justifications thereof in liberal humanist discourse.[6] The philosophies, epistemologies, logics, and practices that made the *pieza* and its naturalization possible are what Wynter and James explored in their writings. This problematic is shared by Cedric Robinson, who clarified in *Black Marxism* that the deep though disavowed racisms were "rooted not in a particular era but in the civilization itself."[7] The fundaments of all capitalisms bear this naturalized frame.

By the time the modern Japanese state commenced its own imperialist projects in the second half of the nineteenth century, the *pieza* conceptual framework and the related notion that colonialism brought civilization and development was shared and articulated by a wide range of European thinkers, including Hegel, Smith, Locke, and Mill, and put in practice by enterprising men, particularly those who looked to islands in the Pacific, to Asia, and to Africa for new frontiers to colonize.[8] Lisa Lowe's *The Intimacies of Four Continents* provides a model for the work that remains to expand the spatiotemporal scope of the *pieza* conceptual frame. Of the presence of Asia and Asians as labor and fantasy for liberalism, Lowe writes:

> One does not observe a simple replacement of earlier colonialisms by liberal free trade, but rather an accommodation of both residual practices of enclosure and usurpation with new innovations of governed movement and expansion. The new form of imperial sovereignty expressed by nineteenth-century "free trade" in India and China consisted in the power to adapt and improvise combinations of colonial slavery *with* new forms of migrant labor, monopoly *with* laissez faire, and an older-style colonial territorial rule *with* new forms of security and governed mobility.[9]

Ideologues of the Meiji state as well as their critics depended on these categories, concepts, and models of value and accumulation that operated in European political thought and philosophy—land, labor, and capital—and that had required and then effaced centuries of enslavement, genocide, expropriation, patriarchy, and exploitation, though they would bring their own grounded insights to their analysis.[10] As Robinson outlined, these categories worked precisely because by the time they were adapted and adopted by national (and colonial) bourgeoisies outside of Europe, local contexts mediated by methodological nationalism allowed differences to float as abstractions free from particular histories. Specificity could be read as evidence of *national* belatedness—a narrative that was hegemonic in interwar Marxist debates over the character of Japanese capitalism and encapsulated in endless debates about feudalism or feudality.[11] Not only did Japanese intellectuals and bureaucrats *not* situate the significance of "older" forms and relations as they were mobilized in service of the construction of a new socius within regimes of accumulation that extended globally; they also adapted and translated the conceptual logics that underpinned Wynter's Western-bourgeois Man-as-human and that constituted the Matthew Bondsmans of the world as "useless and therefore expendable" into something akin to a Japanese Man-as-human—an abstraction of an abstraction that supported mid-nineteenth-century justifications for Japan's imperial expansion.[12]

Japan and the White Pacific

It is useful to engage what Gerald Horne calls the formation of the "white Pacific" in the postbellum world to understand the degree to which Japanese ideologues, policymakers, and settlers were imbricated in global histories of domination and, beyond space, what Bedour Alagraa calls a repeating structure of catastrophe that Wynter's *pieza* conceptual framework illuminates.[13] Because of the importance that the Pacific comes to hold in Japanese empire-building projects, an examination of the ways that white supremacist ideals and practices extended their reach to the Pacific Islands through imperialist competition and cooperation is vital to understanding how the *pieza* conceptual frame took on new life in this place and moment. In *The White Pacific*, Horne traces the relationship of the end of the American Civil War to the enactment of what he calls "a new kind of slavery" by white men like William "Bully" Hayes and Ben Boyd. He explains that they played pivotal roles in extending the frontier from the United States (particularly the West Coast) and Britain to Hawai'i, Australia, New Zealand, and Fiji. In these sites, they established plantations worked by bonded Melanesians and Polynesians in a practice known as *blackbirding*. The word *white* in the title of his book highlights the shared affinities that exceeded the bounds of nation-states, which enabled vanquished Confederates in the US South to establish white (supremacist) settler colonies in the Pacific with varying degrees of support from their home governments. Japan enters Horne's story as an emerging state that advocated for its nationals who emigrated to these locales, Hawai'i in particular, to be treated as equal to their European and American counterparts.[14]

In her study of Western racial constructions of Polynesians, *Possessing Polynesians*, Maile Arvin demonstrates that while the settler colonial project to turn Polynesians into "almost white" as an expression of what she calls a logic of possession through whiteness took place in earnest beginning in the early nineteenth century, European racial mappings of the Pacific had begun over two centuries earlier. Her work, which illuminates the mutually constitutive relation between Western constructions of the Polynesian race as almost white and Melanesian people as Black, allows me to understand how white supremacist ideals and practices were embedded in Japanese aspirations to lay its own claim to the islands and peoples of the Pacific as policy makers and intellectuals began debating what forms of labor contracting befitted a modern nation-state qua empire.

This debate began in earnest in Japan in 1872, just four years after the establishment of the Meiji regime, during what came to be known as the Maria Luz incident. Distinctions between chattel slavery, indentured servitude, and contract labor played out in the courts in Kanagawa in response to the escape of Chinese indentured workers who fled a Peruvian cargo ship, which had stopped in Yokohama for repairs.[15] By the first decade of the twentieth century, when blackbirding in the Pacific was outlawed, and contract and "free" Japanese immigration commenced, racialized discourses that had justified a slave trade of Pacific Islander people were fully ingrained in the way that Foreign Ministry authorities discussed the place of Japanese migrant workers in the extractive economies of the Pacific, Latin America, and North America.[16]

Writings by the late historian Tracey Banivanua Mar highlight the responses to the enactment of a new slave trade, coterminous with the intensification of colonial rule over Polynesian and Melanesian people and the connections they forged with each other through and beyond the French, British, German, Japanese, and US empires. *Violence and Colonial Dialogue* is a study of how blackbirding on the sugar plantations of Queensland, Australia, around 1863 took place in tandem with the dispossession of Aboriginal people from the same lands. A posthumously published essay, "Boyd's Blacks," is a treatment of the same Ben Boyd whom Horne discusses. In it, she asks what stories of Ni-Vanuatu men and boys from New Hebrides who were transported to Boyd's plantations can be told through limited archival sources. Quito Swan's *Pasifika Black*, which, like Banivanua Mar's writings, is focused on tracing the way that racialized Indigenous peoples created rich connections, political networks, and cultural practices as they became imbricated in these interlocking global imperialist systems and processes, argues that the colonization of the Pacific, as an enduring condition, was justified by European officials as a response to the end of what blackbirding provided—easy access to and control over large flows of bonded, racialized workers.[17]

This chapter, though not exclusively focused on the formation of early Japanese colonial policy in the Pacific, demonstrates the importance of situating the Indigenous genocides that the Meiji state commenced after its own founding in 1868 within this larger story of the creation of new plantation regimes in the midcentury white Pacific.[18] The immigration schemes that commenced in the late 1860s in mainland Japan have to be linked to these interimperial global, regional, and national histories of settler colonialism, Indigenous dispossession, and the continued exploitation of racialized workers, as well as struggles against them. This framing allows me to better appreciate the critique that Shona Jackson makes in *Creole Indigeneity*: that scholars of the modern period must attend to the way that Black peoples' enslavement, foundational to European modernity, is "complexly intertwined with the subordination of Indigenous peoples," and that this relationship is crucial to understanding the emergence of the figure of the proletarian subject.[19] Insisting that the (Japanese) conquistador humanist qua worker was present from the moment of the modern nation-state's formation keeps anti-Blackness, Indigenous genocide, and colonial expropriation at the forefront of my own thinking as I write bearing witness to the consequences of colonial erasures past and present.[20]

Colonialism at the Heart of Nation-State Formation

In his dissertation, "No Man's Land," Michael Roellinghoff argues that the Japanese, US, Russian, and British empires were co-imperialists in transforming Ainu Mosir into a Japanese settler colony, Hokkaido. He traces the activities of Hokkaido Colonization Office (Kaitakushi) officials, a trio of hired American liberals, the Meiji state, and scholars who enacted the settler colonial project from the 1870s as defeated US southerners shifted their settler energies to places like Queensland, Australia. For Americans Horace Capron, Benjamin Smith Lyman, and William Clark, upholding whiteness was essential to the project: "They not only carried pioneer discourses of the American frontier with them to Hokkaido and 'Indianness' to the Ainu, but also saw their developmentalist mission as transferring their own whiteness and with it, rights of sovereignty and property to the Japanese."[21] Their unwavering belief in the norms of white bourgeois society, founded on a worship of property, industriousness, and proselytizing—in other words, conquest—had deadly consequences for the Ainu and other Indigenous communities.[22]

Settler colonialism requires enclosure, a process that commences and then accelerates conquest as states repeat and refine its methods. By treating Ainu Mosir as terra nullius through the passage and enactment of the Hokkaido Estates Regulation in 1872, which allowed it to claim all Ainu land as belonging to the crown, the Meiji state began laying the foundations of colonial development the same year it began its land tax reforms in mainland Japan.[23] Its completion required other mechanisms of violence, since massive infrastructural development and reclamation projects could not be completed without controlling the land and mobilizing the labor of people who were not free in Marx's doubled sense.

Sakata Minako's work introduces the key role that imprisoned people played in the economic development of the region. From 1855 to 1907, a system of penal transport that had initially been imposed by the Tokugawa regime brought thousands of criminalized people to five designated prisons to engage in preliminary work needed to establish a settler colony peopled by former samurai called *tondenhei*. They cleared dense forests, worked in mines, constructed roads and railways, built settler towns, and performed tasks that remained invisible to entrepreneurs and writers who arrived in Hokkaido seeking fortune and adventure.[24] While the penal transport system officially came to an end with the passage of a revised penal code in 1907, the deployment of imprisoned people to perform arduous labor in forestry, mining, construction, and other extractive industries continued well beyond the Meiji period. In fact, convict labor was so productive that the Naval Ministry sent imprisoned people to join workers from Japan's colonies to build bases in the Pacific from the late 1930s.[25]

In these ways, the state, monopoly capital, and settler colonialists mobilized criminalized populations to clear Indigenous lands that they declared, in Roellinghoff's words, "ownerless or unoccupied."[26] This description made the people and other living beings there vulnerable to the slow violence of militarism and genocide by polluting their waters, lands, and relations.[27] The products of industries established through Indigenous dispossession were, and continue to be, systematically deployed against other Indigenous communities in and beyond the Japanese empire in a global cycle of unceasing interimperial genocidal violence.[28] Since much of the labor that accelerated Indigenous genocide was performed by criminalized people whose numbers were considered insignificant in the overall balance sheet of labor inputs, the value of their work, the impact that this labor had on their bodies and minds, and the violent outcomes of their dehumanization were effaced or exceptionalized as minor fragments of a larger story of the Meiji economic miracle that starred more noble actors.[29]

Okinawa, the focus of chapters 6 and 7, was subject to its own enclosure processes immediately following the overthrow of the Ryūkyū Kingdom. Resource-rich parts of the newly annexed prefecture fell under the control of relatives and political allies of governor Narahara Shigeru and other Meiji elite based in Tokyo prior to the land reorganization project of 1899–1903 that transferred the "profitable parts" of Okinawa's forestlands out of community control and into state or settler jurisdiction.³⁰ This prehistory meant that Narahara (who was also the architect of Okinawa's immigration policies), his cronies, and the state had already expropriated the most fertile lands long before the start of the reorganization project. Their machinations left local common use rights holders to fight with each other, their village communities, reclamation associations, and the prefectural government over crumbs that were misrepresented as major concessions.³¹ In addition to enclosing the commons, the state eyed the former kingdom as a potential site of industrial sugar production that could alleviate its trade deficit with the United States in particular.³² We see in Narahara's policies a clear link between imperialist enclosure and the ascent of Okinawa as a dependable supplier of workers abroad from the first decade of the twentieth century.³³

Japanese settlers, intellectuals, and policy makers who played key roles in the naturalization of conquest as development or national integration did so through acts of translation that transformed lands and peoples into territory and labor. As Sidney Lu and Eiichiro Azuma have traced, neutralizing verbs like *shokumin, ishokumin, takushoku,* or *kaitaku* reveal the way that Japanese and non-Japanese people were socialized sociogenically.³⁴

Because land surveys undertaken in regions that were colonized and came to be regarded as national frontiers like Okinawa and Hokkaido resembled, at least in form, acts of enclosure that were taking place around the same time in parts of the archipelago that had been incorporated through the surrender of feudal authority, Marxist theoreticians retroactively read state policies in these territories not as colonialism but as a manifestation of Marx's so-called primitive accumulation. In other words, they understood colonial enclosure as a *national* moment of transition from feudalism. They rarely acknowledged the colonial character of turning common lands in Hokkaido and Okinawa into state-owned and then private property for development even as they critiqued the large-scale enclosure and dispossession that authorities enacted in places like Taiwan or Korea as examples of colonial violence.

Central figures in what came to be known as Japanese colonial studies, such as Nitobe Inazō, Yanaihara Tadao, and Yamamoto Miono, laid the foundations for this denialism by distinguishing the establishment of state control in places like Ainu Mosir and the Ryūkyū Islands from contemporaneous "new colonialisms" on the African continent, in the Pacific Islands, and in Central Asia. In so doing, they crafted the foundations for the now commonplace story that the Meiji regime only commenced its own imperialist policies in response to Euro-American imperialism that arrived on Japan's shores with Commodore

Perry and his warships.[35] The field, which was institutionalized in the 1890s, defined the conquests of Ainu Mosir and the Ryūkyū Kingdom as part and parcel of the process of national unification as they crafted solutions for the state's "real" colonies in Taiwan and Korea. As Roellinghoff notes, Nitobe, who trained at Sapporo Agricultural College to become a colonial bureaucrat, characterized Japanese policy in Hokkaido as internal colonization—a description that treated the region and the Ainu as "an always-already natural extension of the Japanese national polity."[36]

Despite this disavowal, it is difficult to distinguish between state policies toward Hokkaido and Okinawa and those it imposed in territories it labeled formal colonies, starting with Taiwan. In Okinawa's case, immigration policy functioned as a lever to alleviate the negative impacts of the region's transformation into a sugar monoculture. It also gave many Okinawans a taste for life as Japanese subjects.[37] While the actuality of life in diaspora was never complete acceptance or parity, the conversion of Okinawan migrant workers into Japanese settlers somewhere between port, ship, sea, and plantation performed the important work of muddying their colonial status. Even as they became, in Hyun Ok Park's words, displaced from nation and capital in different ways, they were represented by colonial apologists as full-fledged Japanese workers— what Yamamoto Miono explained in his 1920 book *Shokumin Seisaku Kenkyū* (Research on colonial policy) as neither "native" or enslaved and therefore, with dignity.[38] He defended the colonialism of his present by noting that at least it did not rely on the labor of enslaved peoples.[39]

Successfully transformed into Japanese workers, Okinawan people who were recruited to work in extractive industries all over the world from the first decade of the twentieth century could serve as proof that Japan was not morally depraved no matter what their actual experiences were like. Consistent with his times, Yamamoto defended settler colonialism by explaining that Japanese settlers were only present because "natives" (*domin*) regrettably had not yet developed the desire to work.[40] It was only natural, he claimed, that people from the "mother country" (*bokokumin*) be called over to spread civilization and to provide the labor power required for wealth accumulation at least for the time being.[41] Yamamoto wrote himself into a puzzle that he never bothered to resolve when he added the caveat that, for extractive colonies, the labor of "natives" or "coloured races" (*yūshoku jinshu*) was still needed because they were most suited to working in harsh climates.[42] Migrant workers from Okinawa, who in these cases were conveniently turned into something in between "native" and "settler," allowed Yamamoto and other colonial studies scholars who wrote about Japanese settler colonialism in the Pacific to keep this contradiction of their own making unresolved.

Autarky and the Boomerang Effect

Aimé Césaire's assertion in *Discourse on Colonialism* that "the colonizer, who in order to ease his conscience gets into the habit of seeing the other man as *an animal*, accustoms himself to treating him like an animal, and tends objectively to transform *himself* into an animal" is helpful for thinking through some of the repercussions that the disavowal of the colonial foundations of Japanese nation-state formation had on people who came to believe in their own superiority as they transformed themselves into conquistador humanists without setting foot outside of their hometowns.[43] The securing of one's home(town), celebrated by politicians and writers as unchanging time-space of the Japanese nation, was enabled by the same logics, grammars, and operations of enclosure that the Meiji state enacted throughout its growing empire. That is to say, conquistador humanist logics that inaugurated colonial violence in Ainu Mosir and the Ryūkyū Kingdom, as well as Taiwan, Korea, Sakhalin and the Kuril Islands, northern China, and the Pacific Islands, took the metropolitan countryside as their target in very specific ways.

Japanese Marxist theoreticians were hard-pressed to find the language to protest these processes because their preoccupation with the question of feudalism or feudality in the Japanese capitalism debates of the interwar period required their acceptance of the premise that a smoothly functioning capitalist society was one that was free of all forms of unfree labor. This, combined with their stagist descriptions of Japan as a "late-developing nation," meant that many forms of state-directed development, coerced labor, and racism were read as exceptional characteristics rather than part and parcel of the perpetual manifestation of difference that was necessary to capitalist valorization processes in general. Uno Kōzō, a contemporary Marxist economist and theoretician who has been most influential to my understanding of Japanese capitalism, accepted these assumptions.

In his writings on the agrarian question, Uno argued that Japanese agriculture was caught in an irresolvable dilemma after the World War I agricultural recession. Capitalist countries with large agrarian populations, including Japan, had to reform "all aspects" of agricultural life because the global turn to autarky was "embedded in the political necessity of securing the fate of agriculture in the metropole."[44] He observed that imperialist competition required states to carefully coordinate agrarian spaces throughout the empire rather than rely exclusively on an imperial division of labor. While his writings on autarky highlight the Japanese state's efforts to reconfigure social relations in agriculture throughout its empire, his theorization downplayed the depths of domination that were required in order to realize the policy of small farmer protectionism in the metropole that state authorities deemed necessary for containing the crisis of legitimacy. In other words, in his effort to develop an analysis of the relationship between class differentiation and revolutionary consciousness, he failed to recognize that an important aspect of the state's postwar agricultural policy was inculcating conquistador humanist logics into the new core of the Japanese nation—the metropolitan small farm household.[45]

This failure had consequences for Uno's understanding of revolutionary strategy. We see this in his treatment of Japanese small farm households' use of hired labor in an essay titled "The Structure of Agriculture" (*Nōgyō no Kōsei*), which focused on the category of "extrafamilial labor" (*kazokugai no rōdō*).[46] Uncritically utilizing data compiled by the Imperial Agricultural Association (Teikoku Nōkai) in its 1935 Agricultural Management Survey (*Nōgyō Keiei Chōsa*) as well as records compiled by the Tōhoku regional office regarding extrafamilial labor, Uno concluded that because small farm households could not overcome agriculture's seasonal surpluses or labor shortages on their own, but also could not afford to abandon agricultural production, they had no alternative but to rely on temporary paid and unpaid extrafamilial labor.[47] Many thus increasingly relied on "helpers" (*tetsudai*), a category of extrafamilial labor that was part of a system of village mutual aid that preceded the modern era. The problem with this for Uno was that while the communal work (*kyōdō sagyō*) required of the farm household intensified, it changed shape from a passive, reciprocal relationship that prioritized reproduction of village relations to an aggressive labor-saving technique that increasingly atomized farm households relied on for survival. He argued that these new conditions were rooted in a feudality that remained intact in thought, sentiment, and custom in Japan's agrarian villages and that would not disappear through simple changes to the law. Feudality, not imperialism, structured his thinking on the way that the creation of difference was necessary for Japanese small farm households to survive in a time of chronic recession.

Uno's presentation of extraeconomic compulsion in the labor process is puzzling, considering his writings on autarky. In those, he posits that the central dilemma for imperialist powers was that they had to enact agrarian policies that were economically impossible but politically necessary—first and foremost new policies that propped up Japanese small farm households. If we connect this understanding of the current conjuncture to his observation that small farm households had to rely increasingly on unpaid extrafamilial labor to survive, a question that should follow is, How did the state facilitate the acquisition of this labor force without relying on the power of large landlords, which it sought to weaken in order to shift the balance of power to industry?

As the following chapters will show, making possible the economically impossible required the expulsion of people from the existing village community and, at times, the temporary incorporation of workers from outside of it. Boundaries of newly negotiated village communities between those who fit the bill as potential conquistador humanists and those who did not were enforced by newly crafted instruments of terror that cannot be labeled feudal remnants. These instruments, as well as the revolutionary consciousness of those who suffered its blows, went largely uninterrogated in Uno's work as well as in contemporaneous debates on the Japanese agrarian question that worried so much about the small farmers' orientation to a fascism that was kept analytically separate from the problem of colonial commonsense.[48]

Crisis and Oikonomics

Despite their erasure from theorizations of the post–World War I agrarian question and attendant discussions about revolutionary strategy, organizations like the Suiheisha (for buraku liberation), Kinyūkai (for anticolonial feminist demands), and the Okinawa Labor Farmer Party (discussed in the chapters that follow) issued forceful critiques of new mechanisms of expropriation and expulsion in the countryside. The anti-Japanese boycotts in 1915 that sparked an anti-imperialist May Fourth movement in China, struggles for independence on the Korean peninsula that culminated in the March First movement in 1919, the formation of the Japan Farmer's Union, the founding of the Japanese Communist Party, the organization of the Suiheisha, and the rise of anarchist and socialist women's organizations and journals throughout the empire collectively ushered in an era of radical, sometimes interethnic political organizing and imaginaries.[49]

Ishiguro Tadaatsu, an official in the Ministry of Agriculture and Commerce who became minister in 1940, grasped the seriousness of the militancy that developed in the interwar period.[50] As he explained in a lecture to regional tenancy officers about the "problem of tenancy" in 1925, he was gravely concerned that tenant farmers had secured strong negotiating positions because they had a superior grasp of the costs of agricultural production compared to their parasitic landlords, thanks to the political education provided by the JFU and other tenant farmer organizations.[51] Ishiguro shared Uno's belief that winning tenant farmers to the side of capital was a politically urgent matter—69 percent of all of Japan's farming households were either pure tenant farmers or half-owner cultivators who borrowed at least a portion of the land that they cultivated and managed. He was aware of the disaster that would strike if a significant percentage of them joined with proletarian organizations or radical tenant farmer unions.

This fear drove the ministry to a politics of the household (or oikonomic politics), which was an attempt to secure and develop gendered, unequal household relations as the fulfillment of a primordial, authentic relationship that made the extraction of surplus labor "possible by the affective registers and architecture that legitimate the implied contractualism of the *oikos* . . . as a species of unbreakable covenant."[52] This could never be fully realized, but its pursuit through seemingly neutral mechanisms like surveys and the creation of new categories of work through these social scientific instruments impacted how people imagined their place within structures like the family(-nation). The Farm Household Survey, which I introduce next, was an oikonomic tool that the ministry wielded to repair cracks in the state's legitimacy in the ailing countryside. Its counterrevolutionary instrumentalization signaled the appearance of what Aimé Césaire calls the *boomerang effect*—the dehumanizing effects of colonial rule coming home to roost.[53]

The Farm Household Survey mandated meticulous record keeping in daily household ledgers. As I show next, it resembles an extension of the public school code that C. L. R. James was forced learn and unlearn in the most intimate spaces of shared existence. In addition to requiring participant households to meticulously record their own income, expenditures, and labor time in increasingly compartmentalized ways, the survey introduced two distinct modes of valuation for familial and nonfamilial workers: laboring capacity (*rōdō nōryoku*) and labor efficiency (*rōdō nōritsu*). Ostensibly used to reduce waste, maximize productivity, and create baseline standards for output in small-scale agricultural production, these categories served as tools for rationally measuring the relative rather than absolute amount of labor time individual agricultural workers contributed to the farm household. The ministry's use of these as measures of rational economic behavior signaled its acceptance of neoclassical economic assumptions about human behavior that, as scholars like Nancy Folbre, Michael Greenberg, David Blaney, and others have argued, condensed centuries of enslavement and colonialism into the seemingly eternal category of human nature. Such assumptions vacated any critique of capital or the state's reliance on force to extract the kind of labor that produced the wealth that allowed philosopher-kings, intellectuals, and colonial bureaucrats to rest on the laurels of their own civilizational prowess.[54]

Success was evaluated by metrics that began from the presumption that women, the young, the elderly, and the infirm in the family unit were inherently substandard workers: according to the definition of laboring capacity, they were 70 percent, 40 percent, 20 percent, or noncontributing members of the farm household economy compared to fully contributing, healthy, adult men.[55] Nonfamilial members of the small farm household—people like Uno's helpers or agricultural workers—were measured according to their labor efficiency, a term that appeared less frequently in the survey and applied solely to people who were classified as part of the farm household but not part of the family. Both tools of labor management were systematically incorporated into the small farm household economy in a manner that invisibilized and naturalized the racist, sexist, and ableist—that is to say, eugenicist—assumptions upon which determinations of the value of human labor rested. The category of labor efficiency extended the fiction that compensation for labor performed by nonfamilial members of the farm household was based on a fair (i.e., labor market based) exchange. It effaced the way that the value of labor was always societally defined "according to the *social value* ascribed to" its bearers, as Wynter reminds us in her presentation of James's *pieza* conceptual frame.[56]

The Creation of a New Family-Household Nexus

Despite the ministry's efforts to transform the small farm household into the material and ideological core of the nation, the category has escaped many of the negative connotations associated with, for example, the family in critiques of patriarchy and nationalism. It has been rather uncontroversially defined as a group of people who shared a dwelling or consistent workplace that was dedicated to the production of agricultural commodities and the reproduction of people and animals who were engaged in that production. The survey reveals the dual structure of the farm household, with the family, its privileged kernel, comprising members whose function vis-à-vis society was not exclusively, but centrally, to ensure genealogical continuity. That is, while the family was significant for its ability to mobilize a powerful anticapitalist fantasy that, in philosopher Tosaka Jun's words, "blur[red] the essence of today's developed monopoly capitalist system" by invoking a timeless, horizontal community of people united in the family-nation of the emperor, the farm household satisfied the state's need to control the time of the present and to legitimate its regime of private property.[57] Securing the countryside after World War I required the family, which conjured a transhistorical, organic tie to the mythic past, and the small farm household, which unified people territorially (in the shared space of the residence and paddies) and temporally (in the rhythms and practices of the everyday). Each was to perform their respective function to reproduce itself and, by extension, the nation.

The Farm Household Survey demonstrates how this dual structure operated in practice. It was just one of the many surveys, reports, and census forms that various ministries and research institutes administered after World War I in response to massive socioeconomic transformation in the metropole.[58] The 1921 revision to the survey had three parts. First was the comprehensive Farm Household Survey, which compiled national averages based on three types of farming households that participated: owner cultivator (*jisaku*); half owner cultivator, half tenant farmer (*jikosaku*); and tenant farmer (*kosaku*). Second was a longitudinal analysis of the conditions of farm household economies spanning two decades, and third was a batch of ledgers that participating households recorded about their own activities during the course of one fiscal year.[59] The comprehensive nature of the third part indicates the degree of intimate self-management that state authorities deemed necessary for transforming farming households into productive units through new modes of affection and accounting.

The set of ledgers I analyze here in order to illuminate their value as an oikonomic tool was submitted by one farm household out of the 180 surveyed in 1921. It was a half-owner, half-tenant farmer household that cultivated a total of 6.62 tan of a combination of paddy, fields, and forests.[60] The majority of their agricultural production was in rice but they also cultivated barley, soybeans, vegetables, and tea. The household consisted of eight family members, listed here with their ages: the head of household (49), his wife (46), their eldest son (25) and his wife (24) and two children (1, 4), their second son (20), and the father of the head of household (80). In addition to these family members, the household relied on the assistance of three unnamed workers who were paid in kind to perform babysitting, tea picking, and seed planting duties. The survey required participants to keep six different ledgers over the course of one year: a property ledger, a work diary, a daily notebook, a price list, a daily cash account book, and a daily record of noncash items. Read together, these provide a snapshot of the socioeconomic life of a single farming household that the Ministry of Agriculture and Commerce acknowledged as economically faring slightly above average compared to peers who shared the same relationship to landownership. A critical reading of the three ledgers through an oikonomic lens illuminates the discursive and material work that they performed to facilitate social reproduction in a manner that explicitly differentiated between family and nonfamily members.

A. THE WORK DIARY

Survey participants were expected to keep records in the work diary of the number of hours that every member of the household, including hired workers and animals, expended on tasks that were divided into agricultural work, housework, and work in subsidiary industries. This provided ministry officials with a fairly good sense of the way that labor time was distributed among members of the household. It also provided them with data that they later used to calculate national averages of total number of days worked per farm household.

In the work diary kept by the family surveyed in 1921 (see figure 1.1), the breakdown of labor time in the household is recorded as follows: the head of household worked a total of 330 hours, of which 93 percent was dedicated to agricultural work; his wife worked a total of 291 hours, of which 81 percent was devoted to housework; their eldest son worked a total of 305 hours, of which 91 percent was dedicated to agricultural work; his wife worked a total of 352 hours, of which 72 percent was dedicated to housework; their second son worked a total of 262 hours, of which 66 percent was dedicated to agricultural work, 24 percent to work performed in subsidiary industries, and 10 percent to housework.[61] The amount of work that nonfamilial household members performed was quite low—a woman hired as a caretaker for the eldest son's young children worked 19 hours over forty days. The work diary also recorded 72 hours that a cow worked during these forty days.[62]

The ministry mandated a conversion of these hours into a total number of days worked based on the aforementioned labor capacity (*rōdō nōryoku*).[63] This category, whose early use in Japanese was the translation of Austrian economist Nicolaas Pierson's "zeal and efficiency in the workman," was later rendered as "laboring capacity" by Ōtsuki Masao of the Faculty of Agriculture at Kyoto University, in his *Book Keeping System for Family Farm* (1958).[64] The category assigned different values for the laboring capacity of each member of the household based on their gender, age, ability, and the region where they resided and was an index used to convert the real labor time performed by each member of the household into the adjusted figure of the total number of days worked. In the 1921 survey, this conversion was made to obtain average measures of labor compensation per day per type of farm household in relation to net agricultural assets.[65] The recording of all labors using the empty unit of the hour flattened the quality and intensity of the variety of work that

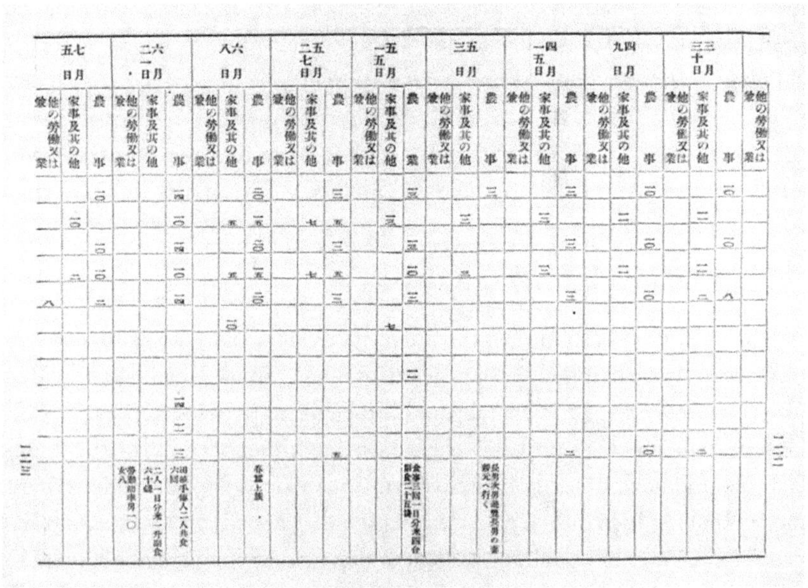

FIGURE 1.1. These pages from the work diary (*nisshi*) section of the 1921 Farm Household Survey record the number of hours spent by each farm household member on different tasks, divided into the categories "agriculture," "housework and other," and "other labor or subsidiary work." The wife of the head of household and the wife of her eldest son are listed as performing the majority of work classified as "housework and other." Nōshōmushō Nōmukyoku, *Nōka Keizai Chōsa: Taishō 10-nendo* (Tokyo: Nōshōmushō Nōmukyoku, 1925), 120–23.

members of the household performed, but the category of laboring capacity established valuations of labor times according to a household member's sex and age. The work diary reveals that Japanese women, who performed a disproportionate share of the work of social reproduction that included the financial management of the household (classified in the survey as housework), were not credited in the same way as their male counterparts. The method of calculation articulated in the survey declared that her laboring capacity was, at best, 80 percent of her male counterpart's.

B. THE NOTEBOOK

The notebook was a place where respondents could briefly describe important activities that members of the household took part in. The example completed by the family surveyed in 1921 listed 122 entries that provided the ministry with insight into the social and economic transactions that peppered the

EMPIRE AND *OIKONOMIA* • 33

lives of these respondents. [66] We see, for example, that the family paid for the rice they cultivated to be polished, purchased sweets for their youngest grandchild's first visit to a Shintō shrine, borrowed money to purchase wood charcoal, took their own firewood to town to sell, hired a babysitter on occasion, sold eggs from their hens (quite regularly), hired two women to help pick tea leaves, lent their cow to a neighbor, purchased mulberry leaves for their silkworms, and purchased a "western-style" rope-making machine on installment.

C. THE DAILY CASH ACCOUNT BOOK

The daily cash account book required participant households to keep detailed records of their daily cash expenditures and inputs, which were divided into those related to agricultural work, those related to housework, or miscellaneous. These entries provided the ministry with an account of the financial ebbs and flows of the household during one year as family members spent money on gifts for visitors, paid electricity bills, handed out sweets as favors, deposited savings into multiple bank accounts held by the head of household's two sons, purchased cigarettes, submitted taxes, sent mail through the post office, received cash for helping to transport rice, handed out cash gifts to neighborhood children and domestic helpers, received returns on investments in the fisheries industry, and so on. The household of the family surveyed in 1921 recorded a total of 478 entries over 222 days. [67] This detailed tracking of cash inputs and outputs gave officials unprecedented access into the daily lives of different members of these households and leveled all financial transactions—whether it was 20 sen given to a neighbor's child or 8 yen to pay the village taxes—into the same category, "cash transactions."

The daily cash account book lacked a category for wages or its equivalent. Instead, the compensation that family members received for the work that they performed in the paddies, fields, or at home was recorded as *kozukai*, or allowance. During the calendar year, the total allowance that members of the household received was 78.5 yen, of which 41 yen, or 52 percent, was given to the twenty-year-old second son. The eldest son received 25 yen and his wife received 11 yen, 10 of which she received as a one-time allowance right before she returned to her natal home for the January holidays (*yabuiri*). The head of household received a 1.5-yen allowance one time in August to attend Buddhist festivities called *tōkamairi*. Recorded as miscellaneous expenses and dispensed not in exchange for work performed but as one-time gifts from the household coffers, the very existence of this category downplayed the idea that work performed by members of farming households should be thought of as waged labor at precisely the moment that tenant organizations were basing their struggles on this claim. The state took advantage of and exacerbated conditions of overwork and underconsumption by designating all work time spent by family members as unpaid and potentially available for extraction.

The activities of nonfamilial members of the household were also recorded in the daily cash account book. Labor time and payments to yearly hires, seasonal workers, day laborers, and live-in caretakers are meticulously recorded, but their spending activities appear nowhere in the ledgers.[68] While they formed an indispensable part of the farm household, their consumption, daily activities, and well-being were not matters of concern to the ministry. The Farm Household Survey forwarded the notion that those who worked for families other than their own were not rational economic actors but mere inputs, like the cattle and other animals that played a supporting role in someone else's household. Their stories remain even more out of reach to us because the survey form did not require any information but their labor time, classification, gender, laboring capacity, and mode of compensation to be recorded.

Total War and the Disappearance of Housework

The category of housework, whose precise definition was clarified during the interwar period, disappeared completely from the fifth phase of the Farm Household Survey revisions, which commenced on March 1, 1942. The two-ledger system was amended that year to a single ledger called the Agricultural Management and Farm Household Survey Tally Card (Nōgyō Keiei Narabini Nōka Keizai Chōsa Shūkei Kādo). This format condensed the information that participant households were required to keep and got to the core of the information the ministry wanted to collect from farm households during total war. It confirms that, in just two decades, the surveys helped the state turn agrarian villages into sites of extraction to fuel the war machine whose end was either total victory or total annihilation. As I mark this boomerang effect, I note that the oikonomic project of small farmer protectionism was only possible through the hyperexploitation or expulsion of racialized, gendered, and Indigenous people in the Japanese empire. Their stories do not even have a small place in postmortems on essays on "Japanese fascism in the countryside" because they were, and continue to be, ignored even as they held a meaningful place in national agriculture.

How can we read this disappearance of housework in the context of total war mobilization in a manner that brings these erasures to light? What, for example, is the relationship between the disappearance of housework from these ledgers, the Japanese military's establishment of military sex venues for sexual gratification of its soldiers (worked mainly by women from the empire's "formal colonies" as it pillaged and occupied new parts of Asia and the Pacific), and the intensification of other forms of mass labor expropriation that took place throughout the empire? How did Césaire's respectable bourgeois and SS member converge through the state's project to establish autarky by making, in Uno's memorable words, the economically impossible but politically necessary a reality? Who had to be discarded in the process? How did people who were deemed refuse in—but also outside of—the metropolitan countryside refuse that label? How can I narrate their stories as collective refusals of the public school code that helped entrench colonial commonsense in the heart of the nation even if they did not coalesce into something that we label a revolutionary or anticolonial movement? I consider these questions in the next six chapters.

CHAPTER TWO **ENCLOSURE AND THE COMMUNITY OF THE COMMONS**

A decades-long struggle against the exclusionary logics and practices of Japanese conquistador humanism took place in Asama, one of five districts that constituted Shigō village, located in the Ise region of Mie prefecture. The district was unofficially split in half by the Asama River, the southern part occupied by self-proclaimed "ippanmin," a term that people who considered themselves the only legitimate members of the village used, and the northern side occupied by "burakumin," a category that gained political meaning following the 1871 Edict Abolishing Ignoble Classes and that ippanmin used to label their neighbors as outsiders.[1]

This chapter illuminates the power of consensus exercised by ippanmin in ensuring that the financial, social, and political burdens of state enclosure of common lands would be borne exclusively by their burakumin neighbors. The declaration that burakumin were outsiders, a claim supported through ippanmin representatives' destruction of official property and registration records that would have proven otherwise, made it challenging for state authorities to enact corrective policies even when they acknowledged the seriousness of charges of discrimination levied by burakumin. The force of consensus, which lay in ippanmin's ability to turn the disavowal of shared generational existence into the capture of political power and which made it acceptable to destroy historical records, was not exclusive to Asama or to Mie prefecture. However, the Asama struggle highlights the farcical nature of claims people made about enduring, unchanging, and therefore immutable relations in the countryside. It also illustrates the way that the modern legal regime established by the Meiji state, which granted a place for customary law to operate, is, as Petero Kalulé writes in their explication of its policing function, "still imbricated within precalculated legal-juridical limits and unilateral coercions that engender quotidian instances of violence."[2]

The enthusiasm with which self-declared ippanmin participated in the dispossession of their neighbors by deploying the law and the police was shaped by the state's creation of burakumin as a social-scientific object of study, a process which began in the decades following the passage of the 1871 edict. As historian Kurokawa Midori argues, the devastation that many buraku communities suffered during the Matsukata deflation of the early 1890s and their radicalization during the early phases of the Buraku Liberation Movement made them targets of state scrutiny well before the struggle I trace here. Led by the prefecture's governor, Arimatsu Hideyoshi, who was also a former official in the Home Ministry's Police and Social Affairs Office, Mie became a central node in social science research about buraku communities. Arimatsu entrusted Takeba Toraichirō to develop a survey of conditions in Mie's buraku neighborhoods. His report, published in 1907 as "An Outline of Special Buraku Improvement" ("Tokushu Buraku Kaizen no Kōgai"), became a model for similar studies nationwide.[3] According to Kurokawa, Takeba's study was significant because it proposed the term "special buraku" (*tokushu buraku*) to merge existing connotations of feudality with data-driven evidence of buraku criminality into a single object of inquiry.[4] This, combined with research on the racial origins of the burakumin by anthropologists such as Torii Ryūzō, made the notion that they were objects to be studied and reformed commonplace. Even when presenting examples of successful programs of buraku reform, the reformed were described as "newly released prisoners" (*shinjukeisha*) who benefited from a state-directed rehabilitation process.[5]

State and societal scrutiny over the figure of the burakumin intensified after the 1918 Rice Riots. In Mie, the riots took place from August 12 to August 15 in Tsu and nine other areas and led to the arrest of 277 people. Concerned observers responded by pontificating about the dangers that were latent in buraku neighborhoods.[6] They were especially disturbed that women seemed to be at the center of these riots—their high rates of participation confirmed that something was seriously amiss in the buraku family. State officials and the media doubled down on an existing narrative of burakumin as untamable people who had to be subdued through a combination of constant observation, sexual education, increased state surveillance, and the implementation of reformist solutions to immiseration.[7]

A series of articles published in the newspaper *Chūō Shimbun* in the aftermath of the riots explains the moral degradation of buraku family and gender relations in social-scientific terms that would make any eugenicist proud. In a multipart piece titled "Unmoved by Adultery, etc. (6)" published on September 13, 1918, the author described the conditions of buraku communities, beginning with a concern for their health. It explained that the propensity of burakumin to fall ill was the result of their weak physical constitution, stemming from poverty and inbreeding. Earlier ages of marriage—young men of seventeen and eighteen and girls thirteen and fourteen years old having children together— led to the birthing of children who were, in the author's words, "simply incomplete" (*tonikaku fukanzen*). In what emerges as a recurring theme throughout the series, the article problematized sexual promiscuity, which, it claimed, afflicted both men and women.[8] For this author, it was likely easier to attribute riotous conditions to pathology than to confront the conditions that nurtured the spread of increasingly militant collective action, much less take seriously the radical aspirations it carried.

People who participated in the Rice Riots did so in part because they had difficulty finding affordable sources of rice due to discrimination. Buraku studies scholar and labor historian Ōyama Shunpō explains how *yamayatoi*, day laborers, cargo transporters, longshoremen, and flower sellers who took to the streets had already been surviving on very small quantities of rice in a manner described colloquially as "one shō living" (*isshō-seikatsu*).[9] These working people considered rice merchants' refusal to sell to them a threat to their lives. As Kurokawa warns, however, the perception that people from buraku households disproportionately participated in the riots was a misperception and reflected stereotypical beliefs in their lawlessness.[10]

One outcome of the Rice Riots as it concerned the state's treatment of burakumin was its inauguration of a new mode of confrontation that pitted so-called harmonization (*yūwa*) policies aimed at reform against concrete struggles that newly formed organizations fighting for buraku liberation, like Suiheisha, waged, often in solidarity with peasant and labor organizations like the Japan Farmer's Union (JFU) and the General Federation of Labor (Sōdōmei).[11] In Mie, the center of Suiheisha-affiliated movements was Hino Nichōme, a small neighborhood in Matsusaka city; neighboring areas in Suzutome village like Higashi Kishie, Nishi Kishie, and Yagawa were also particularly sympathetic to the cause.[12] Hino Nichōme was a vibrant neighborhood close to the Matsusaka train station—an important transportation hub that linked Mie to Nagoya in the north and Osaka via Wakayama city to the west. The connections that Suiheisha organizers built between their urban hubs, rural branches, and across prefectural lines concerned state authorities, who tasked prefectural police with keeping an eye on their political activities. Suiheisha-led organizing in the prefecture tied growing immiseration in the countryside to anti-burakumin discrimination in villages and factories.[13] Mass roundups of those who were accused of spreading "dangerous thought" were periodically carried out during the late 1920s and the 1930s.

Enclosure of Forestlands

The Asama struggle took place as these new antagonisms coalesced in and around Mie. At first glance, Asama seems an unlikely site of intense, multiyear confrontation. But behind its peaceful veneer are many ghosts who were sacrificed in the process of making a space sacred for the nation. The district is part of the Ise region and is approximately six kilometers from the Ise Grand Shrine complex, which historian Tze Loo calls the "apex of the prewar shrine system"—the most important institution for legitimating state Shintō.[14] Railway companies and prefectural authorities aggressively developed and marketed the entire region for religious tourism beginning in the 1920s. Ise's successful development into a destination for religious tourism required planners to craft and maintain pristine landscapes for visitors traveling by rail or cable car through lush, still mountains that heightened the spiritual experience of pilgrimage. Asama, and Asama's Kongōshōji Temple complex, was (and remains) a key node in this route.

The work of making the route to Ise appear unsullied by human activity required the destruction of many relations. This crafting of landscape, which transformed Ise into the apex of religious tourism in the metropole, required that the state tighten its grip over land that had escaped its scrutiny during the early years of nation-state formation.[15] It was in the spirit of reassessing the

FIGURE 2.1. Postcard with a photograph of the Ise-Asamadake cable car to the Kongōshōji Temple, built by Asama Tozan Railway Company; ca. 1925–27. Asama Meisho, Asamayama Kenzan ni Kakaru Kēburukā; courtesy of Mie Prefectural Museum.

fragile balance that had been maintained since the first decades of the twentieth century between conservation and development, community and state management, and privatization and communal ownership that the state embarked on two interrelated projects that created the conditions for the expulsion of buraku residents from Asama in the late 1920s.

The first was a project to reorganize commonly held lands. The Home Ministry and the Ministry of Agriculture and Commerce jointly pursued this through a directive, "On the Reorganization and Development of Publicly Owned Forestlands (Forestry Order no. 4927)," issued in October 1910.[16] This directive commenced the transfer of management rights over publicly owned, common use woodlands to a new bureaucratic unit called the administrative village.[17] Despite the state's characterization of this process as a simple jurisdictional transfer, enactment required repeated negotiations over several years that included rewriting old property titles and demoting some temples and shrines to lesser status in the national religious hierarchy, all to create space for a new system of local management whose smallest bureaucratic unit in the increasingly vertically integrated political structure was the administrative village.[18] This transfer of publicly owned forestlands to the administrative village was a bureaucratic nightmare for impacted communities because forestland boundaries often defied existing administrative borders and forests were often comanaged by members of multiple villages or districts that did not fall under the jurisdiction of a single office. In the chaos of this process, some members of the local elite enriched themselves by rewriting history in ways that stripped their burakumin neighbors of the ability to access or manage lands they had worked for generations.

The second project, also overseen by the Ministry of Agriculture and Commerce, reclassified lands that had been designated "protected forestlands" under the 1897 Forestry Law in a manner that was responsive to new needs and changing land conditions. While many of these forestlands were also publicly owned, much of the land was already in the hands of individual landowners, small corporate bodies, or large corporations. Regardless of ownership status, all forestlands came under the purview of the Forestry Law, which underwent a major revision in 1907. The law governed the state's relationship to the country's vast forestlands and empowered the ministry to determine which lands would remain subject to strict usage restrictions and which could be managed and developed freely by stakeholders. A variety of reasons, including landslide prevention, fisheries protection, landscape preservation, and national defense, were listed as criteria for determining which lands would remain under protected forestry status.[19] Individual petitioners, municipalities, interest groups, corporations, and state ministries were periodically given the opportunity to make their case for certain forestlands to be granted or released from protected status. Mie prefecture's records concerning this land category show that most requests for the reconsideration of protected status came from municipal authorities who had been entrusted with completing small portions of much larger infrastructural projects that spanned multiple administrative units, such as major road repairs, the construction of new railway lines, the laying of water or sewage pipes, the expansion of ports, and other measures that accompanied capitalist development.

The stakes of these enclosure projects were particularly high in the Ise region, which was not only an important religious center but held over half (174,813 of 333,522 chō) of the prefecture's forestlands.[20] The Mie branch of a semigovernmental organization called Chihō Shinrinkai, whose members included the prefectural governor as its head, forestry experts, and representatives from prefectural Imperial Agricultural Associations, was placed in charge of evaluating requests for release or inclusion that interested parties submitted prior to the final decision by the minister of agriculture and commerce. Forestlands in Ise came under the organization's purview beginning in the mid-1920s, when the prefecture's plan to promote religious tourism along the Shingū route that connected Kongōshōji Temple on Mount Asama, Ise Shrine, and Futami on the coast necessitated a coordinated strategy to preserve and develop landscapes that tourists would be moved by as they traveled from one pilgrimage site to the next.[21]

For religious tourism, protecting areas from unmitigated development was just as important as freeing up land for infrastructural development. Governor Yamaoka Kunitoshi was a central actor in advocating that Ise's pristine beauty not be threatened by deforestation. He began conservatively, submitting an application to the minister of agriculture and commerce, Takahashi Korekiyo, requesting permission to incorporate 21 chō 2 bu of land (out of an area of forestland that was 69 chō 3 tan 7 se 15 bu) that the Imperial Household (*Goryōrin*) held in Asama as protected forestland.[22] Yamaoka made his case on behalf of the Nagoya branch of the Kyūshū Imperial Household Forestry Department (Kyūshitsu Rinyakyoku, Nagoya Shikyokuchō) on May 28, 1924, arguing that this area of imperial forestland had to be placed under state protection so that the Isuzu river and its drainage basin would remain intact (see map 2.1). This was key, he explained, because the river fed directly into the forestlands of the Ise Grand Shrine complex that were adjacent to the plot's southwestern edge.[23] Minister Takahashi's approval of this request in October ensured that the scenic views from Kongōshōji temple on Mount Asama would not be obstructed

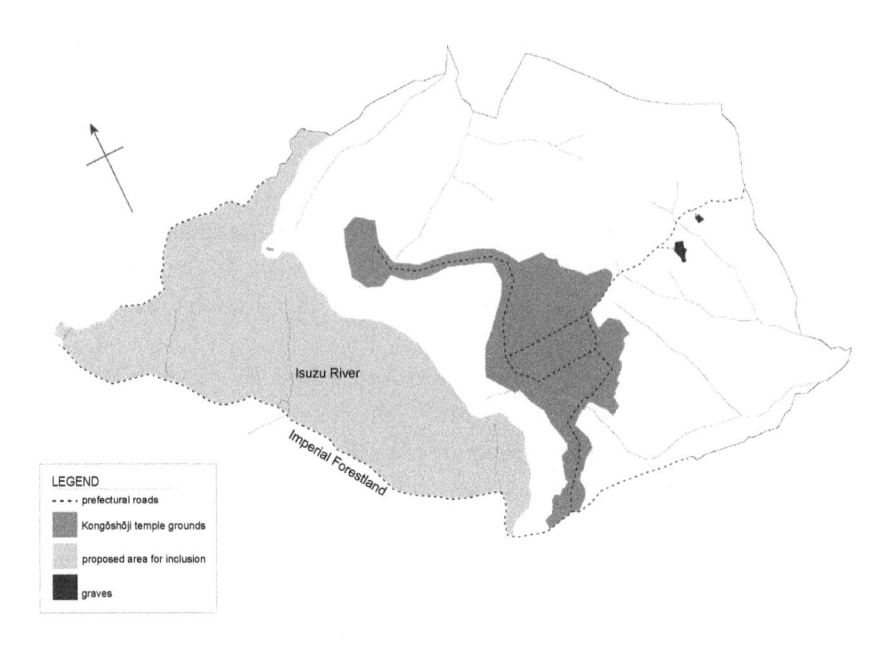

LEGEND
- - - - prefectural roads
▇ Kongōshōji temple grounds
▇ proposed area for inclusion
▇ graves

MAP 2.1. Map of the area in "Asama, Dake 547-1" (Asamadake) that was the target of Governor Yamaoka's "protection" request. Map by Paul Yu. Adapted from Hoanrin Kaijo Mieken 1928; National Archives of Japan, record locator 昭47林野00124100.

and that the forests surrounding the shrine would remain lush by virtue of continued access to the Isuzu river.[24]

Two years later, Governor Yamaoka used the Forestry Law as an even blunter instrument, also for the state's monopolization of sacred space in Ise. On April 9, 1926, he issued prefectural notice no. 156, which echoed the intention of his earlier request but extended the ask to cover an additional 600 chō of land throughout Shigō village in preparation for the construction of an auxiliary shrine for the Ise Shrine complex.[25] Of the five districts of Shigō, Asama was most directly affected by this order, since most of the village's forestlands lay within its jurisdiction.[26] In total, notice no. 156 approved the designation of 617 distinct plots in Asama encompassing 72 neighborhoods (*ko-aza*) as well as 635 other plots in three other districts (*aza*)—Kitanakamura, Kusube, and Ichiuda—as protected forestlands.

The size and ownership relation of these plots varied greatly but the swiftness with which local residents organized their responses to notice no. 156 offers an indication of the grave threat that Yamaoka's order posed to their livelihood.[27] A group of forestry workers and regional elite submitted two separate petitions on April 29, 1926, requesting that he reconsider the scope of the order. One was signed by 313 people who identified themselves as "Watarai Province, Shigō Village Yamakaseginin," or forestry workers of Shigō village.[28] While acknowledging the importance of protecting the scenery for the auxiliary shrine, they pleaded with the governor for mercy:

> We only have two to three tan of arable land nearby upon which to engage in agricultural production. Thus, for us, the cultivation of paddies and fields are merely subsidiary occupations and our main work takes place in the mountains (*yamakasegi*). . . . If we are unable to perform our work there, we will have to switch occupations from what we have been doing for many years. There are very few opportunities to make the change. . . . Over three hundred of us will become unemployed and we will be placed at the edge of life and death.[29]

Given the necessity of access to forestlands for their survival, petitioners requested that Yamaoka reconsider whether all 600 chō really had to be "protected." The petition ended on an ominous note: "The government surely does not believe that they can threaten the lives of many people, without regard for necessity, on behalf of the shrine or the imperial household and think that this will be celebrated without the degradation of thought."[30]

A second petition, signed by 112 "Watarai province, Shigō village stakeholders" and delivered on the same day as the first, expanded the opposition beyond local forestry workers. Among the signatories were representatives of regional railway capital such as Noma Kunihiko, Sakaguchi Shiemon, Ōi Kōtarō, Sakaguchi Yoshitarō, Azuma Tōjirō, and Nakai Isokichi. They were all shareholders of the Asamadake railway company, which had received permission from the Ministry of Railways to begin construction on the rail line that linked Shigō village's Kusube and the top of Mount Asama in November 1922 (see figure 2.2).[31] Noma was one of the executives of the company. Signatories also included representatives from four major religious establishments in the area: Keidenin temple, Kongōshōji temple, Bokaiin, and Donkaiin (both part of Kongōshōji complex). Also signed by three local elites from Asama district, Ogawa Chōshirō, Nishino Yasutarō, and Hashimoto Hideo, the second petition followed much of the same language as the first and implored Yamaoka to pare down the scale of enclosure.

Railroad company representatives, local elites, nearby temple complexes, and workers who relied on forestry work to make a living rallied against Governor Yamaoka, who had unilaterally decided which lands would be taken out of commission.[32] The existence of two separate petitions suggests that the parties

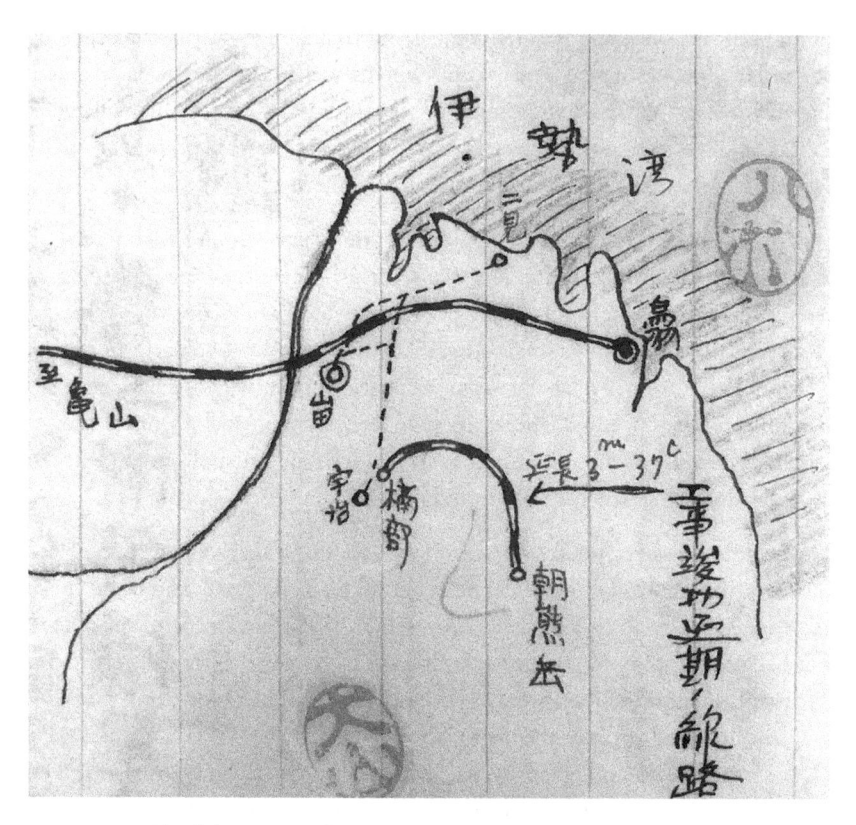

FIGURE 2.2. Hand-drawn map from a 1924 petition requesting a postponement of the construction of a portion of the Asama Tozan Railway Company rail line (the horizontal black-and-white line). Kongōshōji Temple (at the south end of the curved black-and-white line) sits along the Grand Ise Shrine pilgrimage route, which includes Futami and Toba on the coast near Ise Bay (diagonal lines, shaded). The construction that eventually took place damaged a village road that runs through Asamadake. Shigō villagers petitioned the railway company to build a suspension bridge so that they could regain their ability to transport lumber and other forestry products. *Tetsudō Menkyo, Shintō Kōtsu (Tōhō Denryoku) (Moto Asama Tozan Tetsudō) Zen Taishō 8 nen–Shōwa 4 nen*; National Archives of Japan, record locator 01536100.

did not share identical interests but their coordinated submission indicates that they found their objectives on this matter compatible.[33]

These constituencies were able to organize themselves quickly in response to the governor's order because many had already been tracking the matter of negotiations over Asama's publicly owned forestlands closely. Negotiations over their reorganization had been underway since January 1925. These talks had attracted attention because any resolution to how these lands would be managed first had to address the disproportionate amount of land that was currently under Asama district's control. Satisfying Asama's residents, who held the vast majority of common use rights, had challenged local officials since 1908.[34] Shigō village head Nishino Kōkichi, a signatory to the stakeholders' petition, informed prefectural authorities on April 10, the day after Yamaoka issued notice no. 156, that representatives of the districts had reached an agreement after fifteen months of intense negotiations that would place all publicly owned forestlands under the management of his office.[35] The absolute area of land held by the Asama district fell by 40 percent as a result, but the settlement gave 141 Asama residents who were recognized as having "proper lineage" the opportunity to purchase as their personal property 215 chō of what remained.[36] In addition, three signatories of the April 29 stakeholders' petition, Nishino, Ogawa, and Hashimoto, obtained the right of superficies to an additional 13 chō. These concessions to local elites were announced just two months after they signed their names to the petitions to Governor Yamaoka opposing his plan to bring 617 plots of forestland in Asama into protected status.[37]

Enclosure of the Family

Maria Mies's analysis in *Patriarchy and Accumulation on a World Scale* teaches us that the enclosure of the commons is historically and necessarily linked to violent transformations of social relations that diminished women's financial and sexual autonomy. Marxist economist Inomata Tsunao said something similar, briefly, in his 1934 record of field investigations of forty-three agrarian villages, *Kyūbo no Nōson*. There, he outlined the gendered repercussions of infrastructural developments that accompanied enclosure and capitalist development. As a result of the ability of trucks to easily access the forestlands on newly built roads, he explained, women who had supplemented their household incomes by earning small amounts of cash called *temachin* (a word that marked the casualized nature of their labor and harkened back to an earlier economic structure) in exchange for transporting materials from the mountains by foot lost access to this work.[38] Describing a trajectory that materialized in forestry regions throughout the empire, Inomata explained that improved and expanded roads also invited large forestry capital to construct modern milling facilities. With mechanization, "two people can complete all of the work."[39] These developments took jobs away from male villagers who had supplemented their household economies by engaging in seasonal work like sawing.[40] While Inomata did not spell out the broader societal implications of these changes—in particular, how they influenced the division of labor within farm households—he provided readers with enough material to draw their own conclusions.

Inomata's insights allow us to understand the consequences that the 1925 Asama forestry settlement had on the district's farming women beyond what appears in the archival record.[41] Mie prefecture's Farm Household Survey ledgers help as well. As the previous chapter outlined, the survey defined housework (*kaji*) as an unproductive category of work because it did not produce income for the farm household. Despite being defined as nonproductive in the ledgers, the tasks that fell within the scope of housework grew in range and quantity because the Ministry of Agriculture and Commerce defined the category as primarily women's work from around World War I. Tasks that people performed that did not fall into the category of housework because they were not seen as essential to the reproduction of the domestic economy, like socializing with extended family or the broader community, fell into the realm of care, obligation, or, at times, waste. Because the ministry used the Farm Household Survey to naturalize these categories of work and nonwork that had gendered implications, I treat it here as an oikonomic tool that the state used to inject its accounting practices into the most intimate of relations. These were naturalized in large part through repetition.

The survey ledgers I briefly turn to next were kept by the Sasaki and Honda families.[42] Both resided in Nyū village, also part of the mountainous Ise region. Together, they confirm that, for the Ministry of Agriculture, successful household reproduction, and at times even the accumulation of material wealth, were signs that a farm household had attained the skill of intimate self-management—a characteristic that distinguished villages and populations that were worthy of relief from those that could be sacrificed for the sake of national survival.[43] This was a valued characteristic, as the ministry was making it much harder for small farm households to survive through policies (like those outlined above) that reduced their access to the commons. The ledgers offer a glimpse of how farm households managed to survive under these state-imposed conditions of austerity.

The Sasaki farm household (no. 251), a part-owner-cultivating farm household, faced many obstacles during the eleven years that they participated in the survey. Sasaki Toranosuke, the head of household and respondent to the survey, was thirty-seven years old when the family was recruited to take part in the survey in 1931. His wife, Sasaki Sae, was thirty-three. She gave birth to her daughter, Mieko, in 1932 and third son, Shōtō, in 1934. They lived with Toranosuke's parents, Kiyohachi and Tora. Their living arrangements allowed them to supplement their own landholdings with land that was in Kiyohachi's name until his death at the age of seventy-nine on July 8, 1939.[44] If we accept the ledgers' ability to reveal and at times shape broad tendencies in the household economy, we can conjecture that the Sasakis survived the agricultural recession through a combination of relatively good health, access to opportunities to earn cash by working a variety of side jobs, private ownership of small slivers of forestland and wasteland (*genya*), the village's participation in the economic rehabilitation movement (which brought in funding for public works projects), and renting from landlords who provided rent reductions during natural disasters.

The Sasaki farm household's good standing in the village also meant that when Sae gave birth to two children during the survey years, they were able to pay a midwife four and five yen to assist in delivery. They were also able to hire a babysitter for their young children several times per year—a luxury that not all farm households could afford at the time. Their participation in the survey, which yielded them twenty yen in cash annually, helped them to expand their total area of arable land to just over 1 chō at the start of the 1935 survey year to over 1 chō 2 tan by its end.[45] While their lifestyle, inferred from ledger entries related to entertainment expenses, food expenses, and income, was by no means extravagant, cash they earned from working on road construction, repairing waterways, participating in the firefighter's association, and holding leadership positions in the village allowed Toranosuke and Sae to support their four children, send them to school, occasionally take them to the theater, feed them fish and eggs, and provide them with medicine when they fell ill.

In contrast, the Honda farm household (no. 276), also from Nyū village, did not own any forestland or wasteland. Land registration (*tochi daichō*) records show that head of household Honda Hiroshi only came into land of his own after the post–World War II land reforms redistributed agricultural land to cultivators.[46] The tenant farm household consisted of Hiroshi; his wife, Mitsu; and his father, Saichi. They borrowed 8 tan 6 se of mostly paddy land on which they cultivated rice, grains, and some vegetables. They produced just enough to pay their rent, eat, and participate in some savings and mutual aid organizations. They supplemented their agricultural income by working in the mountains—weeding, cutting grass, and transporting trees. They hired seasonal agricultural workers to help them prepare their paddies for planting rice.

Their reliance on waged work made them vulnerable in 1937–39 when a series of family disasters took place: Saichi was hospitalized in late July 1937 and died on August 2, 1937. The following year, on September 10, 1938, Hiroshi was drafted. This left Mitsu in charge of completing the survey and keeping the farm household above water. She was able to get through the year through a combination of gift income, additional work, and assistance from agricultural helpers who did not receive any compensation (at least not recorded in the ledgers). Regular distributions of lumber and other forestry products for heating from the commons helped keep electricity costs down.

The Farm Household Survey's active devaluation and intensification of tasks classified as housework, the bonds that farming women who trekked the hills and walked the riverbanks of Nyū village developed as they collected the firewood and the water that their farm households needed each day to complete the mundane tasks required to stay alive, are only visible in their conspicuous absence from the mountains of data that the ministry collected.[47] The joys, sorrows, and frustrations of women like Sae, Tora, and Mitsu in these small farm households have no place in these ledgers.

The information we are able to gather from these extremely detailed ledgers about non-buraku women agriculturalists—the way that the forms flatten them into ideal types—make the difficulties we face when trying to understand how their burakumin counterparts survived the effects of the new enclosures that swept the region even clearer. Further, because ippanmin status was so normalized in the Farm Household Survey project, the way that the survival of women like Sae, Tora, Mitsu, and others may have been aided by the expulsion of their buraku neighbors in Nyū village is obscured. Suiheisha-led struggles like the one in Asama that spread throughout the Ise region and prefecture shed light on this connection.

Buraku Struggles against Enclosure

Asama district contained approximately 280 farm households. Half were labeled by ippanmin as burakumin households. What quickly came to be called the Asama struggle erupted in early 1927 because negotiations overseen by Nishino, the village head, to complete the reorganization of the commons had expressly excluded burakumin. In addition to being left out of negotiations, they were deemed ineligible to receive any of the privatized lands that the prefecture offered up as concessions to impacted farm households. They were also excluded from current and future access to publicly owned forestlands that remained under Asama's collective management. The struggle waged by Asama's residents in response to these expulsions from the village community is one of the longest-lasting fights buraku communities waged in the metropolitan countryside during the first half of the twentieth century.

By the late 1920s, prefectural branches of Suiheisha, a national organization founded in 1922 to achieve buraku liberation, and the Japan Farmer's Union, representing tenant farmers, had both been in existence for several years and were ready to lend their support. The reorganization of publicly owned forestlands was not the central pillar of either organization, but it was an issue that activists understood to be an important point of antagonism. By 1925, local branches of the JFU with strong Suiheisha connections had compiled detailed records concerning the disproportionate impact that enclosure had on buraku agriculturalists.[48] For example, in its publication "Ichishi gun Tsūshin," members of the Ichishi branch of the JFU flagged the problem of the unequal distribution of forestlands by village and district.[49] They implored other activists to keep an eye on how the 605 chō 4 tan 3 se 1 bu of common land held in the province was doled out to each district. Providing breakdowns by district rather than by village allowed the union to pinpoint which communities received privileged distributions and which were shut out.[50] Their structural analysis focused on the way that existing segregation of burakumin from ippanmin neighborhoods affected how the reorganization of common lands was implemented. It was an invaluable resource for members of Mie prefecture's JFU and Suiheisha branches as both model and recruitment tool.

The Ichishi branch's study was republished in the organ newspaper of the Mie Suiheisha, called *Aikoku Shimbun*. It appeared alongside an update to an ongoing tenant farmer dispute in Nakahara village in Taki province over the cancellation of tenancy rights by a landlord named Aoyama Fusakichi. The fact that it was published next to a series of updates concerning landlord-tenant disputes suggests that the branch was keenly aware of the importance of continued access to the commons to the well-being of tenant farmer households generally and particularly to buraku farm households, which were even more dependent on securing labor in the mountains than their ippanmin counterparts. The republication of local JFU newsletters in *Aikoku Shimbun* reflects the close coordination of these organizations, an outcome of substantial overlap in the membership and leadership of the two groups in the prefecture. It was within this sociopolitical milieu that the Asama struggle was sustained for over a decade.

The major daily newspaper of the region, *Ise Shimbun*, hinted at the brewing conflict in an article titled "Fight over the Distribution of Asama District's Publicly Owned Forestlands" in its February 26, 1927, edition. It reported that representatives of 140 or so farm households "north of the river" from a neighborhood called Kaito attended and made demands at a district assembly meeting that was convened on the evening of February 16, 1927, to decide the upcoming year's budget.[51] They crossed the bridge that separated the two neighborhoods and demanded to be allowed to participate in the deliberations.

This was a breach of an informal but increasingly impermeable boundary that had been hardening as buraku families were increasingly pathologized in the wake of the Rice Riots.

Kawamura Zenjirō explains that despite the fact that buraku and non-buraku residential areas were not distinguished as such on any official map, Kaito's residents had never been invited to participate in these meetings. Their plans to attend it so alarmed authorities that they requested police forces come down from Uji Yamada to keep the peace. The seven demands issued by representatives from Kaito included a broad call for elections for important district posts, a demand that neighborhoods north of the river (including but not limited to Kaito) be allowed to elect their own representatives to district meetings, that they be included when profits from the reorganization of the commons were paid out to residents, and that they be allowed to participate in the bidding process the next time that district-held forestlands were sold off (*haraisage*).[52] In a discussion that preceded the dispersal order issued by the Uji Yamada police, assembly members refused Kaito residents' demand for inclusion in the profit distribution structure by insisting that it would violate the freedom of current rights holders to decide who would be included—a freedom, they explained, that was protected as it was "based on precedent."[53]

In response, a flyer published by the Shigō village branch of the Labor Farmer Party's "Committee Concerned with the Asama Communal Property" titled "The Truth of the Asama Communal Property Issue" appeared less than two months later, on April 10, 1927. It was distributed to all Asama residents and reiterated a position that Kaito residents first expressed at the assembly meeting in February: there was a fundamental problem with the settlement that Nishino had brokered because he had failed to consult them. The flyer also objected to their exclusion from the profit distribution plan. They feared that, in addition to being shut out of any distribution of profits from the leases and sales of land that Asama had made with other districts, they would no longer even be permitted to enter the mountains to collect lumber, leaves, or other materials—a de facto right which they had enjoyed for generations. It accused district officials—all of whom were ippanmin from the southern side of the river—of rewriting land ownership records, denying them access to old ledgers, and holding closed district assembly meetings in order to monopolize claims to Asama's remaining communally held resources.[54] It explained that these officials held no legal authority to exclude them but operated in a manner that parlayed their power into an even more entrenched financial position by taking advantage of new laws. In other words, they recognized the way that the law buttressed the power of those who were recognized as full members of the community. The flyer summed up what its authors believed drove their collective expulsion from Asama as a political and social unit: "The genesis of the problem is not simply the profit motive or greed; its cause is a discriminatory perspective that sees us as nonhuman humans."[55]

The charges of discriminatory treatment leveled against ippanmin by the committee were so serious that the prefecture's Ministry of Agriculture had to investigate. Its findings, published three months later, on July 15, 1927, confirmed the claim made by district assembly members in February: that legal recourse was not possible because custom ruled over all decisions regarding the commons.[56] The report regretted that the ministry had no active mechanisms for settling this kind of conflict and explained that residents north of the river were not entitled to make legal claims to the state because pre-Meiji forms of recognition were granted legitimacy in modern property law with regards to use rights. Further, tacit permission for entering the commons in order to collect fuel and firewood was defined within the system as falling under villagers' customary rights. Claimants had to demonstrate their generational existence in Asama in order to be granted these rights. It added that they were free to submit supplementary materials like old ledgers and property records to prove these claims but final decision ultimately depended on consensus.

The ministry's report thus confirmed that Asama's self-proclaimed ippanmin residents had not acted illegally in settling the matter of access to the commons and affirmed the primacy of consensus—assumed to be determined by ippanmin residents—in determining membership in the community of shared generational existence. It concluded with a pithy echo of the district assembly's response in February 1927: "It is not possible to restrict the freedom of the rights holders, which is based on precedent."[57] This decision highlights the northern residents' prescience when they proclaimed that their expulsion from the commons ultimately rested on a denial of their very existence, an erasure of generations of living together. As long as the world that allowed ippanmin consensus to operate remained intact, the law would remain an instrument to inflict violence upon them.

Enclosure and the Shōwa Emperor

Asama's example suggests that there was no hope for what might be called class solidarity between buraku and non-buraku tenant farmers despite the existence of a close relationship between the prefecture's Suiheisha and JFU and shared conditions of impoverishment. It leads me to ask, were things especially hopeless there because the region held such important symbolic, spiritual, and political importance, as it was the site of the Ise Grand Shrine complex? What happened to relationships that had been mediated by local *ujiko* and shrines after those institutions were absorbed into a national hierarchy overseen by the Bureau of Shrines through the enclosure process? While these changes surely mattered to the way that solidarities and conflicts were both imagined and enacted, this wholesale expulsion of burakumin from Asama's community cannot be adequately explained through ready-made concepts like structure or ideology that framed contemporaneous debates on the emperor system.

Struggles that buraku residents in Asama and Maemura, considered next, waged in response to their expulsion from the commons highlight the inadequacy of Rōnō and Kōza factions' Marxist attempts to describe the obstacles that the imperial system posed to the emergence of a revolutionary subjectivity in Japan. Neither ideology (Rōnō) nor structure (Kōza) could fully explain the perniciousness of community that was constantly recalibrated through consensus and legitimated by the modern legal regime. Inomata studies scholars address this issue as it concerns anti-buraku discrimination, arguing that it is not enough to talk about the imperial system as ideological or as a feudal remnant; it became deeply rooted in everyday practices in the countryside.

Tsumura Takashi, who wrote for the journal *Inomata Kenkyū*, published a series of essays beginning in August 1975 that discussed the prewar relationship between the JCP and the Buraku Liberation Movement. Reflecting on the effects of the Comintern's 1927, 1931, and 1932 "Theses" on this relationship, as well as on national Suiheisha policy, Tsumura makes two points: First, he reiterates the point made by Matsumura Chiichirō that "the buraku exist because the emperor exists," noting the importance of reflecting on the spiritual and religious links between the two. Then he asserts that, when discussing the relationship between state and capital, it is important to include in that analysis the way the most impoverished classes of society (of which many buraku communities were a part) were interpellated or expelled from revolutionary struggles against capital. In other words, our understanding of anti-buraku discrimination must account for the way that organizations like Suiheisha were positioned in understandings of revolutionary struggle at the time.[58] I argue that, as relationships were rooted in praxis, the most entrenched sensibilities that emerged as consensus were always in flux, and our analysis should try to capture this instability.

A series of conflicts that erupted in a district called Maemura, part of Sana village in Taki province, northwest of Asama, suggests that small openings for solidarity were created by those who fought against their expulsion. As we will see, the basis for this solidarity largely deferred the question of the family-nation and focused instead on a common enemy: the power that landlords exercised to parlay their existing privileges into legal protections that, in turn, enhanced their socioeconomic position in the village. Inomata described that position in *Kyūbo no Nōson*: "Landlords, who were only the owners of the land of the sharecropper, nominally obtained individual ownership rights in name and in reality by taking advantage of their new strengths in the law and using their superior position in the patriarchal system and economic strength that they had from the past."[59]

Being excluded from the mochi-pounding ceremony, the centerpiece of Daijōsai celebrations to commemorate the enthronement of the Shōwa emperor, sparked the collective outrage of burakumin residents of Maemura.[60] This cannot, however, be dismissed as their desire to be included in the emperor-nation. It was in the process of contesting their exclusion from the mochi-pounding ceremony that they learned that their expulsion from village affairs ran much deeper than they had initially thought.[61] Maemura's incorporation into the orbit of the national railway system and the attendant transformations of space had provided lucrative opportunities for local elite, much like land reorganization had done in Asama.

The Kise railway project overseen by Kobe-based conglomerate Suzuki Shōten, which began in December 1920, was one example of local elites enriching themselves by parlaying their political influence into economic gain. In exchange for their cooperation, a group of ippanmin affiliated with the nearby Kōyasan Shingon Buddhist temple, Amida-dera, received ownership rights over land that the Kanagawa-based subcontractor for the railway line, the Tōkai Kōgyō company, had donated to the district.[62] The company's president, Imaizumi Fukuji, transferred the titles to land he purchased in 1921 along the planned rail line to three men in late 1922 after the first phase of construction from Oroka to Tochihara stations was completed. They parlayed these gifts into the accumulation of even more wealth and influence in their communities by dispensing small but transformative favors to other residents. In the process, what had been largely informal boundaries between eastern and western parts of Maemura that separated ippanmin and burakumin neighborhoods hardened.

Several years later, in the summer of 1930, the Maemura dispute came to a head. While the August 5, 1930, *Suihei Shimbun* newspaper reports that buraku residents of the Higashi neighborhood had already succeeded in securing an apology for discrimination and had won access to a portion of common use lands, a written petition submitted to the Sana village assembly dated August 28, 1930, reveals that Higashi residents, with the help of activists, sought to broaden the class aspect of their struggle against local elites by working with impoverished farmers who had also experienced great suffering as a result of the post–World War I enclosures:

> The murderous recession has lowered prices of our agricultural products while fertilizer fees have not gone down. Taxes and electricity costs remain high. One of the only subsidiary industries we have access to, *ise omote* [straw sandals] production, pays very little—around one third of the previous year. We only earn ten to fifteen sen per day as day laborers. There is no summertime grass-cutting wage labor available. We have already eaten into this year's rice because the price has fallen to six to seven yen in what can be characterized as a bumper crop starvation. We also have to pay eight thousand yen in rebuilding costs.[63]

The analysis provided above shaped the demands that over three hundred people from five districts who attended the meeting agreed to issue in one voice. These included the reduction of the electricity bill by 30 percent, cuts to the salaries of highly paid village officials and teachers, the establishment of a free medical clinic, halving the 8,000 yen of proposed Sana shrine rebuilding costs, an extension of the term for debt repayment on loans issued by the Nōkō Ginkō, abolition of the Imperial Agricultural Association as an institution, and the extension of repayments that usually came due during Obon (July) until October.[64] These wide-ranging demands rejected the legitimacy of state-sanctioned organizations and institutions that were focused at the time on transforming small farm households into rational actors capable of intimate self-management.

While the concrete demands that farmers issued to the village are available in written form, how consensus was reached, what relationships were transformed in the process, and who performed the ongoing labor of organizing on the ground are not questions that I can answer. The Maemura story is one fragment of a larger set of stories we can tell of Suiheisha-affiliated organizations mobilizing against enclosure processes that were enacted by their expulsion from their village communities. It is an important instance of solidarity between buraku and non-buraku tenant farmers built atop their shared animosity toward large landlords and anger at local politicians for not providing them with adequate economic relief, but nothing about that solidarity was guaranteed.

As the Maemura dispute neared a resolution due to this strong show of solidarity, the conflict in Asama seemed also to be reaching its end. Over three years after the initial conflict between residents north and south of the river began, the feuding sides came to an agreement on August 6, 1930. It was concluded in response to heavy pressure from village head Nishino, who was backed by Ueda, the chief of Uji Yamada city police. The settlement gave the 140 households of northern Asama a total of 1,000 yen and management rights over 4 chō 5 tan 8 se of forestland.[65] In addition, southern residents agreed to pay for expenditures to "improve public morals" (*fūki*) on the buraku side. The northern residents' acceptance of these terms was taken as their agreement to not pursue further claims.[66]

Among the eleven people who signed the agreement as representatives from south of the river were several familiar faces: Fukuzumi Katsuzō, Kamimura Shōtarō, Iwamoto Yoshizō, Nishino Yasutarō, Hashimoto Hideo, and Ogawa Chōshirō. The first three were forestry workers who signed the first petition filed against Governor Yamaoka's notice no. 156. Nishino and Hashimoto had signed the second petition as local elites. Ogawa was a signatory to the second petition and was one of three recipients of over 13 chō of the right of superficies for fifty to ninety-nine years.[67] Not only did the new arrangement uphold the expulsion of buraku from Asama's commons by paying them off with a special onetime gift, it reinforced the state-crafted language of harmonization that blamed buraku (im)morality for their dire economic conditions.[68]

Representing the Asama Struggle

The Asama, Maemura, and other conflicts over the commons that erupted in Mie prefecture in the late 1920s were, on their surface, over access. But they were also broader struggles that people marked as burakumin waged against their collective erasure from shared generational existence, enacted through the language of precedent and custom that was given a prominent place in the modern legal regime. Kawamura characterizes the exclusion of the buraku communities north of the Asama River from the entire process of negotiating common use rights as a manifestation of fascism for this very reason. He interprets the tightening control over the commons by the central government and the destruction of local autonomy in managing these lands as, on the one hand, a process that secured the economic foundations of the imperial system, and on the other, the very thing that enabled landlords to strengthen their control over tenant farmers in local communities. This is echoed in an interview that a participant in the struggle, Yamamoto Heijū, gave to Imai Hiroko, published as "I Think It Is Precious." In it, Yamamoto emphasized that the class differences in the south also put poorer southern residents at a disadvantageous position vis-à-vis wealthy landlords in securing access to common lands—southern residents who needed to borrow money would pawn their rights in exchange for cash and ended up not ever being able to gain those rights back.[69]

Contrary to Nishino's expectations, the struggle did not end in the summer of 1930. On September 5, 1935, *Suihei Shimbun* printed a supplement titled "News on the Struggle against Political Customs of Asama Discrimination" that reported that the struggle had recently been reignited through the efforts of a man named Nakanishi Chōjirō, a farmer and forestry worker who had been one of the signatories of the 1930 arrangement from the buraku side. After getting out of prison following his arrest in the March 13, 1933, roundup of suspected communists, he returned to Asama, established a consumer cooperative, and began to rebuild local buraku activism.[70] In addition to Nakanishi's return to Asama, discrimination by a schoolteacher who had uttered the slur "eXX" against an elementary-school-aged daughter of a Buddhist priest named Ueki Tetsunosuke reenergized residents north of the river to resume their fight against their expulsion from the commons.[71] The seventeen-article list that Nakanishi and other organizers submitted to Shigō village and Asama authorities, with the backing of Mie Suiheisha, included a broad slate of demands that emphasized transparency in the political process and improved resource allocation. It also included demands for financial reparations for their suffering since their entry into the commons was now criminalized as theft.[72]

"News on the Struggle against Political Customs of Asama Discrimination," published two months after these demands were submitted, narrated the events leading up to the struggle's resumption. It emphasized that burakumin provided labor that was integral to the reproduction of communal life in Asama:

> Despite being on the receiving end of status-based discrimination, they continue to participate in Asama village's activities like providing labor service for religious ceremonies, *ujigami, yamayaki*, and *inoshishi-oi*, under the watchful eye of authorities. In other words, due to their status, they were subject to a cruel corvee, and had to absolutely subordinate themselves to it. They were villagers without any rights or freedoms, and had, like their comrades, been driven into the darkness.[73]

The problem, the piece continued, was that, despite the passage of the Edict Abolishing the Ignoble Classes nearly sixty-five years earlier, southern residents who dominated politics in Asama converted their economic and patriarchal power into law, thereby monopolizing the entirety of whatever communal rights over publicly owned forestlands remained after the reorganization had been concluded in April 1926.[74] This was especially devastating to residents north of the river because 80 to 90 percent of them made ends meet by performing forestry work on Mount Asama, compared to 20 to 30 percent of southern residents.[75] The difficulty of their position, acknowledged in the Ministry of Agriculture's July 1927 report, was that conflicts over the commons could not be resolved through modern rights-based discourse.

Organizations for buraku liberation like the Suiheisha understood the impossibility of legal recourse and recognized the need to control the terms of their relationship to the state, capital, and Japanese radical organizations. The collective work of imagining a world outside of one that could be settled through consensus began from a recognition that the former was only realized through their expulsion as burakumin from the plane of commensurability. Still, we are left with questions. Were the indignities of all burakumin residents fully captured by the seventeen demands to ameliorate them? Whose voices were included in shaping a vision of a world to come, and whose voices fell through the cracks?

As the next chapter shows, these questions cannot be answered by sticking faithfully to the documents of the Asama struggle. Analyses produced by Suiheisha and Suiheisha-affiliated groups teach us how the local connects to the global and how the abstract family-nation was tied to intimate and everyday forms of violence that barely register in grand narratives explaining the rise of Japanese fascism.[76] Engaging the critique developed by Suiheisha-affiliated women who rejected the entirety of the Japanese grammar that rendered them particularly exploitable on the one hand and incapable of domestication on the other makes narrative closure impossible. Their articulation of the concept of tripled suffering (*sanjyū no kurushimi*) was an immanent critique of Japanese fascism that reveals new imaginings that flowed as they fought ever-changing forms of violence rooted in antiburakumin sensibility. I turn to some of these imaginings next.

CHAPTER THREE BURAKU WOMEN

AGAINST TRIPLED SUFFERINGS

Self-proclaimed ippanmin in 1920s Asama erased their burakumin neighbors from the past, present, and future of their village community as they struggled with the impacts that state policies of enclosure had on their ability to access and manage communally held resources that were essential to their survival as small-scale farm households. The previous chapter clarified that while there were places like Maemura where agriculturalists came together as impoverished tenant farmers to find common cause against landlords, in Asama and many other places in and outside of Mie prefecture, the state's second round of enclosures bore down heavily on burakumin in the countryside. Ameliorations for community exclusion, if they were offered, were stingy and legitimated the Japanese grammar that made buraku erasure via consensus a foregone conclusion. In Asama, this erasure took the form of a proposal, passed by the village head under the watchful eye of the police, that required burakumin to participate in a program of harmonization (*yūwa*) that was in truth nothing more than a project of further criminalization.[1] In Asama and elsewhere, the growing immiseration and criminalization of burakumin at the hands of state and society kept the social wage down and drove ippanmin to transform themselves, in Aimé Césaire's words, into animals qua conquistador humanists.

The processes that expelled burakumin from history (shared generational livelihood) and the present (the national body) were especially devastating to women. Not only did their burdens of social reproduction grow heavier as their communities were systematically denied access to the commons, the small measure of financial autonomy they had been able to exercise from income they earned collecting firewood, gathering leaves, and selling *shikimi* (tree branches placed as offerings on graves) was a casualty of the post–World War I enclosure.[2] Most egregiously, the redefinition of entry to and collection from historically communal lands as trespassing and theft following the reorganization of the commons meant that buraku women were criminalized for continuing to perform the subsidiary work that was indispensable to their survival. According to Yamamoto Heijū, a participant in the Asama struggle, those who went into the mountains carrying their children on their backs were called "small thieves" by landowners.[3]

The way that the Asama struggle was taken up outside of the district is a testament to the power of buraku-led organizing in Mie. The September 1935 report "News on the Struggle against Political Customs of Asama Discrimination" allows us to see how their organizing connected seemingly disparate struggles in the prefecture. The report included seventeen demands that called for full inclusion and representation in Asama's political and economic life. The author presents archival and oral testimony proving that the south-north divide was far less inviolable than ippanmin made it out to be. In response to the ippanmin's assertion that burakumin were not part of the village's shared generational existence, the report countered with genealogy to demonstrate the fictitious nature of the current boundary. It emphasized that people currently separated by the Asama River were actually related by invoking the family history of an elderly buraku man—"buraku XX jīsan"—as evidence.

The value of "buraku XX jīsan" to the report lay especially in his family documents.[4] In his possession were records that could confirm that he was the descendant of someone who was originally from the southern side of the river. His ability to produce these records had the potential to shatter any self-image that ippanmin held about their purity. The old man's words, which open the report—"We were born into the abyss and grew up in darkness, but we do not want to die in the darkness"—seem to mark his hope that these documents could provide a ticket for him, and by extension all of Asama's burakumin, out of their present darkness.[5]

We cannot know the meaning behind the old man's words, but it should be noted that the author of the report did not disavow the ippanmin sensibility that made differentiating people in this manner possible in the first place. In fact, the report's appeal seemed to hinge on the old man's ability to prove that he could claim shared generational existence. Reading the report in relation to other buraku struggles, which this chapter does, complicates an interpretation that fixates on an apparent desire for inclusion in the community of consensus through a recitation of kinship relations. I start by placing his utterance in relation to critiques that women writers made in the organ paper of Suiheisha, *Suihei Shimbun*, in the early 1920s about their collective position in Japanese society.

Suiheisha Women's Analysis of Tripled Sufferings

Suihei Shimbun, records of the local JFU branches, and other archival materials contain numerous accounts by women from buraku farm households who fought to be seen and heard. By 1935, they had been in conversation with Japanese feminist criticism for over a decade. They contested the reification of the very category of woman that many Japanese feminists took for granted and argued that Japanese feminists' critiques of the family were inadequate because they failed to understand how the family form was realized only through the material and discursive expulsion of buraku communities. Reading the report's deployment of the old man's words in the context of these critiques and a string of textile factory strikes led by buraku women in Mie in the mid-1920s allows me to understand the abyss in which he felt mired as a sociogenic condition that, perhaps to the disappointment of the authors of the report, could only truly be alleviated by dismantling the structures and sensibilities that kept him in the darkness.[6] Women who organized within and outside of Suiheisha recognized that reforms and inclusion were not adequate responses to the darkness that engulfed their lives. Instead of appealing to ippanmin sympathies, they cultivated spaces of solidarity and mutual aid that connected struggles in Asama's forestlands to those in the factories in which many of them toiled and the domestic spaces where they worked long hours with little compensation, all while being portrayed as sexual deviants who needed to be shamed, policed, and reformed.

Many Suiheisha-affiliated struggles drew attention to a point later theorized by feminist economists and social reproduction theorists: that the universal basket of goods that formed the basis of workers' wages was determined by constant political struggle and that even the basket of goods that constituted the national average required the existence of racialized and gendered others for whom "need" was not something that the state was interested in guaranteeing. Feminist social scientists like J. K. Gibson-Graham have explained that in capitalist societies where the heteropatriarchal family form is hegemonic, peoples and communities that were not recognized as capable of constituting familial units on their own were not included in calculations of the living wage.[7] They were also deemed ineligible for receiving anything but a supplementary wage. Similarly, Suiheisha-affiliated writers and activists publicly criticized the fact that buraku workers' living standards were not included in a generalized understanding of need, a highly contested category that was tied to the concept of necessary labor time.

Several women who wrote for the Women's Column in *Suihei Shimbun* and the Women's Page in *Suihei Geppō*, the monthly organ of Suiheisha's Kyūshū branch, set the early parameters of this conversation.[8] Their analyses of the conditions that working-class buraku women faced did not completely reject the possibility of solidarities between buraku and non-buraku women or between buraku people but pointed out the need to specify the interlocking nature of the oppressions they faced as proletarianized buraku women.

An essay that appeared in the August 20, 1924, Women's Column titled "Buraku Fujin no Tachiba Kara" (From the standpoint of buraku women) positioned buraku women in the following manner:

> We Buraku women should not forget that in today's society we are subject to a tripled suffering [*sanjū no kurushimi*]. 1. Because we are Burakumin (we endure many more insults than men); 2. Because we do not have freedom of livelihood (our freedom of occupation has been taken away and [we] are usually proletariat and are economically exploited); 3. Because we are women (we are treated more like slaves than men [*doreiteki atsukai*]).

Following this explanation, the author, "Kei," calls on buraku men to reflect on their complicity in relegating them to this tripled suffering:

> I do not think that men who see the way that we are insulted as burakumin understand the pain of being persecuted, and who participate in movements extolling humanism or love of humanity but regard their mothers as being of lower intellect than men because they are women or look down on them as being parasites who live through the strength of men, or insult us, have any value associating with the Suihei movement.[9]

In part two of the essay, published in October, "Kei" directed their gaze toward "ordinary women" (*ippan fujin*):

> We do not understand in detail the living conditions of ordinary women, especially those of the bourgeoisie, since we only see and hear about it through newspapers and magazines. Those people appear to live at the hands of men and believe that the work of women is to bear children, to adorn themselves, and to gracefully bow to their husbands with the knowing look of old manners. In extreme cases, they entrust the important work of women like housework (*kaji*) and child rearing (*ikuji*) to someone they hired and simply adorn themselves like peacocks.... These people are respected as ladies.[10]

After pointing to the invisibilized labor of hired domestic workers that enabled bourgeois women, ostensibly living the most progressive form of womanhood, to reproduce their households, Kei turns to their hypocrisy. While they secure idealized familial relations for themselves free from the extended family form that was still common, especially in the countryside, their views of buraku communities betray their ignorance:

> In recent years there are a lot of people who are awakened—they call themselves new women—or those who talk about economic democracy, the liberation of women, or equality between men and women. Don't they discriminate against us burakumin or ostracize us though.[11]

Notably, "Kei" ends the piece with language that is quite close to that of "buraku XX jīsan." She implores her sisters, "We have finally found our star at the dawn that follows the long and dark night." Her goal is not inclusion in the village community through genealogy but the liberation of 300,000 of her fellow burakumin, with her sisters leading the way.

The organization of Suiheisha-affiliated women continued through the decade in direct defiance of police surveillance. In her study of the women's Suiheisha movement as it developed within a broader proletarian women's movement, *Suiheisen o Mezasu Onnatachi* (Women who sought the horizon), Suzuki Yūko traces the hotbed of this activism to Kyūshū (mostly Fukuoka), where dynamic women activists and orators congregated.[12] Suzuki's work provides a model for what becomes visible if we expand the scope of our analysis beyond Asama to other centers of Suiheisha life and activism in Mie during the 1920s and 1930s, such as Hino Nichōme. What appears is a rich tapestry of open rebellion and beautiful experiments among women who heeded this early call to fight together.[13] Reading the archival silences and willfully misreading extant textual sources allow me to appreciate the undeniable force that proletarianized buraku women exercised to counter the disciplinary impulse embedded in calls for inclusion in a society that was wholly unprepared and unwilling to undo their conditions of tripled suffering.[14]

Kanbe's Matsusaka Momen Dispute

Around the same time that the Women's Column began running in *Suihei Shimbun*, a group of women (many of them from buraku communities) who worked in a textile factory in Kaibana, a district of Kanbe village just south of Matsusaka city, began to organize against their treatment by the Matsusaka Momen Company (est. 1886). They rejected the company's expectation that they engage in intensified levels of work at the same level of pay because of recessionary conditions in light industry. *Ise Shimbun* reported that thirty women workers from the factory's cloth weaving section gathered at nearby Buddhist temple Kaieiji at 5 p.m. on May 30, 1924, in order to discuss the company's reduction of their real wages.

While the local paper was rather blasé about this action, reporting that workers were coaxed by company officials to return to work the following day, the act of gathering together outside of company grounds was a serious transgression of the physical and mental barriers that the factory placed on their ability to move about freely in the world. The company was notorious for not even allowing their workers to leave their dorms unless they were on their way to work. Congregating to discuss actions against their employer was punishable as an illegal act of assembly.[15]

The courage that it took for thirty young factory workers to make their discontent known so publicly is not contemplated by the reporter who penned the short piece. The article does not tell us what promises (or threats) were made by whom or what procedures, spontaneously invented or meticulously plotted, led to their decision to return to work the following evening. Answers to these questions, which are invaluable for understanding the formation, duration, and strengthening of this political community, do not appear in the bounded archives of this (non)event. After all, an action by a group of unnamed women workers without a concrete victory or defeat barely registers in historical narratives of struggle. The relationships built, compromises made, trust nurtured; the common language drawn upon and invented as each person processed the repercussions that the company's policies would have on their material well-being and possibly their safety; how they came to the conclusion that they would act together; and how their relationships were tested as they placed themselves in direct confrontation with factory managers in the open air of Kaieiji temple were of no concern to the author of the *Ise Shimbun* article.

The point of the brief report was not to acknowledge that the women's actions were transgressive. Rather, it covered the gathering as one vignette that could enliven the larger story the reporter sought to tell of the recession that plagued light industry in the prefecture. The walkout was narrated as a manifestation of the plight of "factory girls" and used the language of economic rationality to lightly rebuke the company's practices. In the end, the article described their actions according to the same logic that it used to discuss the difficulties facing light industry: that the layoffs of over half of the company's two hundred employees and the intensifying working conditions for the remaining workers were misleading and illegal, and that the women had expressed discontent about their mistreatment. It could only end with a warning to its readers that small to medium textiles factories would simply not survive these recessionary conditions.[16] The thirty young women were merely a narrative device to propel a larger story of an industry in crisis.

By treating workers and the company as both operating according to the logic of capital, the piece minimized what it took for these thirty women to decide to take this action, which I read as one that sought to break open the world that kept them triply dominated. Illegality—a word that indicates an uncritical acceptance of the world that the legal structure maintains—was the only register in which the writer could understand the actions of Matsusaka Momen's cloth weavers as legitimate.[17] Writing about their actions as factory worker discontent kept the struggle in Kanbe isolated from the struggle over the commons in Asama. Important connections between seemingly disparate manifestations of refusal that took place in a society that was structured by buraku women's tripled suffering remained uninterrogated.

Rōdō Shimbun, the organ paper of the Zenkoku Rōdō Kumiai Hyōgikai, or Council of Labor Unions (hereafter Hyōgikai), which split from Sōdōmei in 1925, provided a slight corrective to this mode of analysis.[18] Its coverage began by stating that company executive Shiratsuka Daisaburō was one of the largest capitalist landlords in Matsusaka. It reminded readers that many of the tensions in Kanbe village, where the Kaibana factory was located, were linked to the transformation of Matsusaka city and surrounding regions as railway-based infrastructural development accelerated after World War I.[19] While Shiratsuka benefited from rising land prices, residential tenants and tenant farmers who could not keep up with these increases formed renters' unions and flocked to existing tenant farmer unions. In early 1922, ninety-three tenant farmers in Matsusaka demanded a 50 percent reduction of the rents Shiratsuka charged.

The matter was eventually resolved following mediation by various officials and the police chief, but the antagonism did not disappear.[20] Shiratsuka continued to line his pockets, including through commercial advantages gained by his railway company, Matsusaka Keiden, which facilitated the transport of cloth woven in his factory in Kanbe to Matsusaka station so that it could be delivered to customers in Tokyo, Osaka, Kyoto, Nagoya, Korea, and Manchuria.[21] As the analysis published in *Rōdō Shimbun* reveals, Shiratsuka's position as railway developer, large landlord, and factory owner makes it impossible to separate the factory workers' demands for improved working conditions in the factory from demands championed by tenant farmers, including the demand for access to the commons that was echoing throughout the region. The main organizers behind each of these demands were men and women from buraku communities who were members of their local Suiheisha branches. As industry moved into Kanbe village and land prices increased, Suiheisha, Nichinō, and the Hyōgikai-affiliated Mie Gōdō Rōdō Kumiai (Mie Amalgamated Labor Union, established January 1925) began to organize.[22]

The thirty weavers who walked out of the factory on May 30, 1924, resumed their duties the evening following their action, but the tensions that prompted their action intensified with the establishment of these organizations. An article in *Rōdō Shimbun* titled "The Company That Hesitated Keeping Its Promises Finally Yields" describes how a dispute between the company and its workers at the Kaibana factory in December 1925 escalated into a two-day strike in late March the following year.[23] Like the media coverage of the meeting at Kaieiji temple in May 1924, published accounts of the strike's unfolding in March 1926 are sparse, even in articles and reports from Mie Rōdō Gōdō Kumiai, the union that provided organizational and material support for the strikers.

Most of the demands that strikers made and ultimately won concessions to in late March 1926 were those that the weavers had issued two years prior. This was an impressive accomplishment, especially given that it was resolved before the Suiheisha branches in Kanbe village were fully activated. I have not been able to find out if any of the thirty women joined in the Suiheisha assembly held in nearby Uekawa district to mark the revitalization of its branch on October 16 or if the strikers had been inspired by the success of the recent tenant disputes that won rent reductions from landlords (including their boss, Shiratsuka).[24] We also do not know if any of the women (thirty out of three hundred factory workers) who went on strike had been at the initial meeting in spring 1924. What we know is that the 1926 strike was the outcome of at least four months of negotiations with the company, spurred by broken promises of better meals and higher wages, the firing of two workers, and a public statement by the company's president that his machines were more valuable than the workers. The strike was also preceded by constant harassment by the factory manager, Sahara, whose firing was one of the nineteen demands that the women presented to the company at the start of the strike on March 27.

The statement issued by the strikers described their action as a fight against "the capitalists who exploit workers and try to keep us eternally in subservient positions." It continued, "We embarked on a strike with nineteen demands in order to fight the company and for our right to existence."[25] Their demands completely rejected the company president's statement, made during negotiations that his machines were more important than the bodies of the workers he employed. Improvements to meals including the addition of snacks two times a day, the establishment of entertainment facilities and worker's compensation, and the firing of an abusive supervisor, were not only about shifting the way that necessary labor was calculated, but provided them with more time to breathe, to heal, and to nourish mind and body. They expressed a wholesale rejection of their treatment as suppliers of interchangeable units of labor power to run the other machines, all day and all night.

No less than six organizations from around the country provided moral, physical, and financial support to the strikers.[26] Newspaper articles in *Rōdō Shimbun* and the Mie Suiheisha–affiliated *Mie Nōmin Shimbun* provide descriptions of how local organizations mobilized their members to support them. The latter mentioned that the nearby Hino-chō branch of the Japan Farmer's Union immediately sent two barrels (120 kg) of rice. Members of tenant farmer unions in neighboring villages also sent material support.[27] *Rōdō Shimbun* reported that members of the National Proletarian Youth Union (Musan Seinen Dōmei), once they learned that negotiations had broken down, rushed to Kaibana and set up a temporary strike headquarters in front of the factory gates, where 800 people, including 120 women from the Proletarian Youth Union's Women's Committee (Musan Shojokai), stood guard as talks resumed. Their numbers provided protection, which empowered the strikers to present their demands to the company, make a speech inside of the factory, and declare victory on the second day of the strike.[28] Solidarity from Suiheisha and Suiheisha-affiliated groups in and around Kanbe (including Matsusaka city) that converged in front of the closely guarded company gates allowed strikers to transform the factory from a place of exploitation, abuse, and confinement into a platform from which they could address their fellow workers and other supporters as sisters and comrades.

The victory at Matsusaka Momen's Kaibana factory was short-lived—the company was repeatedly found to be imposing wage reductions and violating factory laws prohibiting night work in subsequent years. However, the message that it sent should not be underestimated. It fueled a vibrant universe of organizing throughout the decade by workers residing in and around the district where the factory stood.[29] Between 1926 and 1930, tenant disputes, school strikes, May Day demonstrations, factory strikes, and other forms of direct action blurred the boundaries between residents, rank-and-file members, and leaders of labor and tenant farmer unions, political parties, and organizations like Suiheisha that represented them. People who participated in these struggles understood, just as their siblings in Asama did, that the law—even the tenant arbitration law that was ostensibly set up to give them a fair shot in the courts against richer and more powerful opponents—existed to reinforce the status quo. They mobilized accordingly.[30] By the end of the decade, a new political category, the unemployed, emerged as a figure that signaled a collective rejection of the terms through which capital exploited them as workers, women, and burakumin.

Alliances of the Unemployed

The prefectural branch of the Alliance of the Unemployed (Shitsugyōsha Dōmei, hereafter Alliance) was founded in Matsusaka in the summer of 1930. It was part of the new world that Matsusaka Momen's strikers, organizers, and supporters opened up.[31] It advocated mainly for tenant farmers from buraku communities who had recently been evicted from their homes and did not have income because their family members had been laid off from their factory jobs.[32] It also countered the discriminatory discourse that undergirded the state's harmonization policies, which focused on buraku shortcomings rather than addressing structural discrimination or entrenched anti-buraku sensibility. Finally, its activism was informed by the critique that Suiheisha women made several years prior—in particular, that their exploitation made the reproduction of Japanese bourgeois households materially and ideologically possible.

Branches of the Alliance quickly spread from Matsusaka to other areas with substantial buraku populations. The category of the unemployed that formed the basis of their solidarity represents their understanding of the interconnectedness of city and country and the impossibility of delinking class exploitation from buraku discrimination, the oppression of women, and the plight of impoverished farmers. Their pamphlets and reports reveal the close communication and coordination between groups that were formed expressly to organize, often around single issues. They worked with local branches of tenant farmers' unions to fight landlords' efforts to revoke tenancy rights, articulate collective demands for access to public works projects, form consumers' associations to combat high food prices and low wages outside of the formal market, raise emergency funds to support people whose family members were arrested for participating in tenant disputes, and so on.[33] They pooled information through handwritten publications they shared as they attended each other's meetings and convened study groups. We see, for example, that Sata village's Alliance chapter won eight hundred yen worth of construction work by mobilizing at the village assembly meeting in early 1930, and that in Matsusaka Nichōme, Higashi Kishie, and Nishi Kishie, consumers' associations (*shōhi kumiai*) were organized so members could purchase miso, soy sauce, sugar, and sake directly from producers at approximately half the retail price. These consumers' associations planned to open a storefront in Matsusaka in cooperation with other local branches to make goods as accessibly priced as possible for their members.[34]

The nuanced understandings that Alliance members developed of the interrelatedness of struggles over wages, housing, social welfare, and discrimination can be seen in the documents of the Toyota village branch, which was centered in Toyota's Niiyano district, northwest of Matsusaka city and between the Meishō and Kise Honsen railway lines. Its formation followed the tenant farmers' defeat by a large landlord named Yamada, who was authorized by court decision to evict one hundred tenant farmers for not submitting their rents.[35] The very fact that one hundred tenant farmers had borrowed 1 chō 3 tan—an area slightly larger than what an above-average small owner-cultivating farm household needed to reproduce itself—from a single landlord illustrates the dire conditions in the district.[36] Antagonism came to a head in October 1928 when the words of the elementary-school-aged daughter of Niiyano's district head sparked a school strike that lasted for three days.[37] She had described the buraku neighborhood as "the dirty *eXX* village" to her friends on their walk home from school one afternoon, noting how different its conditions were to those of the "clean one over here." The matter escalated when the district head—the girl's father—responded to demands for an apology by claiming that his daughter had not said anything wrong. The strike finally ended after the school principal and district head issued public apologies.[38]

Tensions worsened as the global depression hit the district. The Alliance notes as much in a pamphlet that it prepared for its founding. Dated September 13, 1930, the founding document provides us with an understanding of how buraku organizers viewed their role in the village. It began by framing the difficulties Niiyano's tenant farmers faced as a result of the Shōwa panic (Shōwa Kyōkō).[39]

> Last year, the price of silkworms was seven or eight yen, but this year the summer price is one yen ninety sen. The mulberry leaves were thirty to forty sen last year but this year it is five. What about the fall in the price of agricultural products? Eggplant, cucumber, and daikon prices are dirt cheap. By the time it is our turn to sell rice and barley, the price is way down.... However, the price of fertilizer, cigarettes, sake, and soy sauce have not fallen at all.

As a result of these conditions, the pamphlet continued,

> even if we cultivate and own five or six tan of land, we impoverished farmers (*hinnō*) cannot make ends meet. In order to pay our interest and taxes and send our children to school we have to engage in home work and day laboring. However, there is no work. We send our daughters and sons to factories in order to pay our rents and loans, but capitalists talk about recession and industrial rationalization and lower their wages or extend their hours. They exploit our daughters and sons, then threaten to close the factories, refuse to pay their wages, or fire them.... We have not received any remittances from them as a result.[40]

The pamphlet criticized the village leadership for not doing anything to alleviate these conditions even though the prefecture provided them with funding for public works projects on prefectural and village roads: "We are suffering, but why do they allow subcontractors to bid for these jobs?"[41] The Alliance demanded that construction jobs created by state subsidies for infrastructure projects be allotted to them as the most impoverished members of the village.[42] Their fight inspired the formation of Alliance branches throughout the region (see figures 3.1 and 3.2).[43]

The Niiyano Alliance's organizational activities culminated at the end of 1930 with members' participation in a meeting at the village office that was called to discuss the implementation of state-managed "harmonization" measures. In a flyer issued in advance of the meeting imploring villagers to attend, the organization echoed Suiheisha's warnings that efforts to install assimilatory projects aimed at reforming buraku communities would only reinforce the prejudicial attitudes and structures that naturalized their precarity. The flyer encouraged villagers to demand that village authorities extend unemployment relief funds to all.[44] Their understanding of what demands were winnable was informed by a concession that their comrades in Matsusaka had won a few months earlier for the distribution of ration tickets for rice to every household.

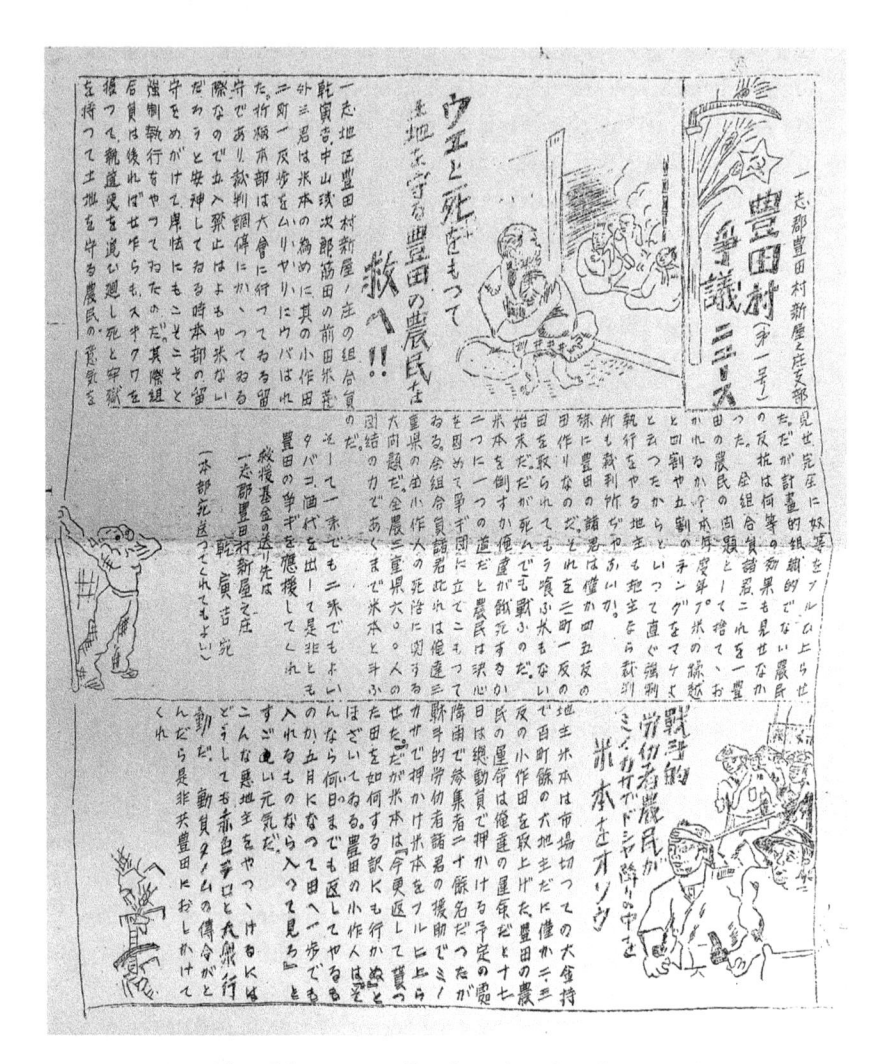

FIGURE 3.1. Pamphlet of the Toyota village branch of the Alliance of the Unemployed; *Toyota son Tōsō Nyūsu Daiichigō* (March 1931). This edition features a call for mutual aid for three farmers of Niiyano who were suffering from starvation while fighting to protect their lands from eviction by a landlord. Courtesy of the Ōhara Institute for Social Research, Hōsei University.

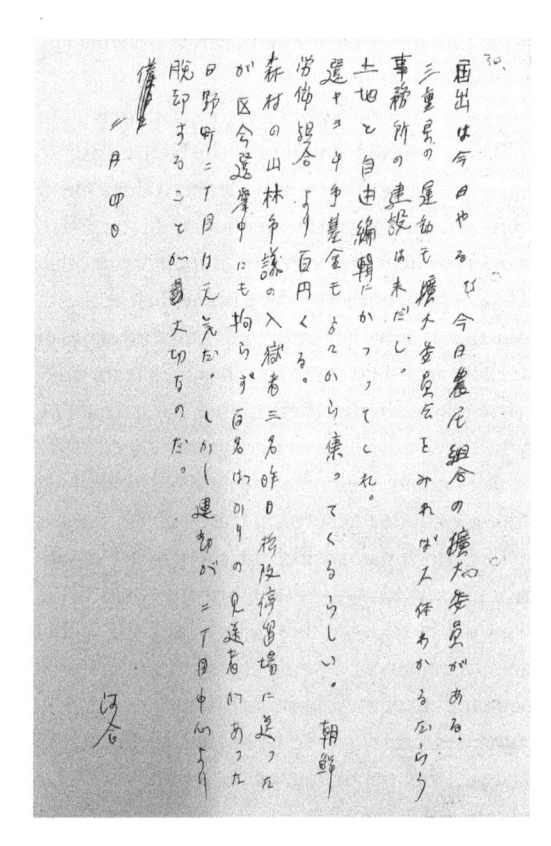

FIGURE 3.2. Note from Kawai Hideo, founder of *Aikoku Shimbun* from Mie prefecture's Sana village, who held a leadership position in Zennō (National Farmers Union); February 4, 1930. It states that one hundred yen will be arriving soon as an election contribution from Chōsen Sōdōmei, a labor union that was founded in February 1925 for Korean workers in the metropole. It also reports that, in the midst of preparations in Hino Nichōme for district elections, more than one hundred people went to provide support for those imprisoned in the recent struggle against forestry landowners. Courtesy of the Ōhara Institute for Social Research, Hōsei University.

In addition to making material demands for rations, access to employment, and unemployment relief, the Alliance called out the discriminatory attitudes of officials who crafted policies that lessened people's ability to survive the economic crisis. A pamphlet published during this struggle, *Shitsugyōsha Tōsō Nyūsu No. 2* (Alliance of the unemployed news, no. 2) describes an incident that took place as members of the Alliance engaged in negotiations with Toyota village head Suzuki, who visited Niiyano district to conduct an inspection prior to determining whether he would accede to their demands or not. The anger of Alliance members erupted after Suzuki took a cursory stroll around the neighborhood and half-heartedly reassured them that things were not as dire as residents made them out to be—they had a rope-weaving machine that could be used to earn supplementary income and the community comprised able-bodied people who could work if they wished. Suzuki's hasty dismissal of their suffering incensed the youth and women's divisions of the Alliance.

They demanded that he at least set foot inside their homes before drawing any conclusions.

This demand is quite similar to one voiced by villagers in Kanbe, who in August 1930 issued a statement, "The Ultra-Rich Should Pay the House Tax!," to protest the implementation of a regressive tax that was under consideration at the time.[45] Niiyano's activists implored the committee that had been formed to investigate the matter to conduct a thorough investigation of their "crumbling houses" rather than doing brief inspections of two or three homes before deciding that such a tax would be reasonable. If only they inspected all of the homes of the village, "they would see that there are no taxes that can be taken from us."[46]

What did their insistence that officials enter their homes before making evaluations about their ability to survive without state support signal? Was this a test to see if these authorities could overcome the stereotypical views that mainstream papers and state-sanctioned experts on the so-called buraku problem continued to print about the supposed filth of their living conditions—a prejudice that had already been clearly revealed, just two years prior, in the incident that led children from buraku families to boycott their school for three days? Alternatively, were members of a newly formed women's division convinced that a true understanding of their impoverishment was impossible without a recognition that the intensity of the work they performed in their homes was the result of the fact that opportunities for waged work were only open to non-buraku farm households?

The former is certainly plausible given the entrenched prejudicial narratives of burakumin families that were cloaked in social scientific rigor and historical nuance. A work written by Tanaka Ichirō and reprinted in *Shihō Shiryō* 4 in February 1933, titled "Research on the Suiheisha in the Mie Region," reported the conditions of buraku communities in the prefecture beginning with population growth figures, wealth and hygiene conditions, occupational roles, descriptions of character mediated by history, and concrete living conditions. Research in these areas led Tanaka to conclude that burakumin, despite being granted their freedom from "outcaste" designation in 1871, would continue for some time to suffer the depths of despair. His disdain is cloaked in the way that he describes their living conditions. He lamented their inability to conform to norms of domestic life, explaining that once one ventures beyond the storefronts of butchers, leather workers and sellers of specialty goods that might be visible to people who walk around their neighborhoods and goes into their living spaces, they will see that burakumin live in conditions that are unfit for human life. His dehumanizing description is the flip side of the coin of Suzuki's statement, which can be read as a reflection of his belief that it does not matter whether he enters their homes or not because their suffering has been caused by their unwillingness to comport themselves in a manner befitting a (civilized) Japanese family.[47] In both cases, the burden of transformation falls on burakumin rather than on dominant Japanese society.

This is not to say that Alliance members' collective ire was not also fueled by Suzuki's assertion that their conditions were actually not as bad as they said they were. Recessionary conditions in agriculture and the contraction of the commons had especially devastating effects on women in buraku farming communities, who engaged disproportionately in housework, performed home work for piece rates, earned extra income by foraging in communally held mountains for leaves and twigs, and were often sent to work outside the village in exchange for cash advances that were paid directly to the head of household. A report from the branch of the Alliance in Isedera, a village south of Toyota that became the site of an intense fight over the commons in 1931, shows that the gendered impacts of the recession were matters of grave concern for activists: "Isedera has very little in the way of arable fields and paddy land.... From day to night, mothers make *ise omote* [straw sandals] and cook gruel. The more they produce, the heavier their debts become."[48]

For groups like the Toyota village Alliance's Women's Division, demanding that local politicians learn what kind of work was being performed in their kitchens and homes and under what conditions was not an effort to be recognized as capable of, or in favor of, domestication. Rather, it was a rejection of resolutions that proposed more responsible household management as the solution to their poverty, which was perpetuated by structural discrimination. Their critique converged with a dismissal of the language of austerity that a reader submitted to the editors of *Aikoku Shimbun* on May Day 1924. Titled "Setsuyaku Day" (Day of thrift), the piece raised seven objections to the government declaring a day to raise awareness of the importance of thrift in response to a deepening recession. In response to the state's proposals, which included reducing the consumption of sake and cigarettes, refraining from throwing lavish parties, and eliminating idle time, the author pointed out that cutting consumption and intensifying labor time in the household would only enrich the capitalist class by providing them with further justification to lower wages. The resulting profits would be used, they warned, to rescue ailing companies from bankruptcy and reinvest in machines that facilitated workers' exploitation.[49]

Wholesale rejection of the state's austerity discourse, which informed the Alliance's demands, was pushed further by women, who took the lead in organizing mutual aid projects following the arrest of a member of the Alliance in April 1931.

The women's division began by organizing a branch of the Comintern-affiliated MOPR, the abbreviation for International Red Aid (Mezhdunarodnaja organisacija pomosci borcam revolucii, in Russian), which was first organized in late 1922 to provide aid to political prisoners and their families in Russia. They organized after a prominent landlord named Yonemoto responded to demands to reduce rents and guarantee lands by applying a no trespassing order to their lands.[50] This led to a physical altercation between Yonemoto and his cronies, police, and tenant farmers who were already organized as members of the village's Alliance and Zennō (National Farmers Union). One of the people whose lands came under the no trespassing order, known only by his given name, Torakichi, was arrested in the scuffle.[51] The Niiyano branch of MOPR was quickly mobilized to provide his family with support. Tenant farmers continued fighting against Yonemoto, other landlords, and the state through mutual aid they organized through the newly formed organization. They also extended solidarity to their comrades who continued to fight against their collective expulsion from the commons in places like Asama and Maemura (see figure 3.3).

Like all of the other organizations that buraku tenant farmers, unemployed activists, and workers formed in response to new needs, MOPR spurred militant organizing. It becomes clear by shifting our gaze to the Hino Nichōme branch of MOPR, which was organized just before the Niiyano branch in February or March 1930, that MOPR members had strong connections to earlier forms of organizing. A report compiled by the prefecture's Special Higher Police titled "The Special Characteristics of Matsusaka City's Suihei Buraku" traces Hino Nichōme MOPR's formal affiliation with the MOPR Japan branch in October of that year. The organization's pamphlet, *International Red Aid News No. 3* (*Kyūenkai Nyūsu Daisangō*) provides insight into what members sought to accomplish in their own words. After a brief description of the campaigns that they were supporting and the organizations that they were working alongside, it concluded with a short statement announcing the formation of a women's division. It quoted the Nichōme labor union's women's division as its inspiration: "Women who have awakened will not be shown up by men." This quote bears a striking resemblance to the words that "Kei" penned and published in her 1924 article in *Suihei Shimbun*.[52] The pamphlet authors demanded mutual aid for families of political prisoners and that violent police be fired. The threat that MOPR organizers posed to the entire infrastructure of Japanese grammar is revealed by the swift police suppression of their activities.[53]

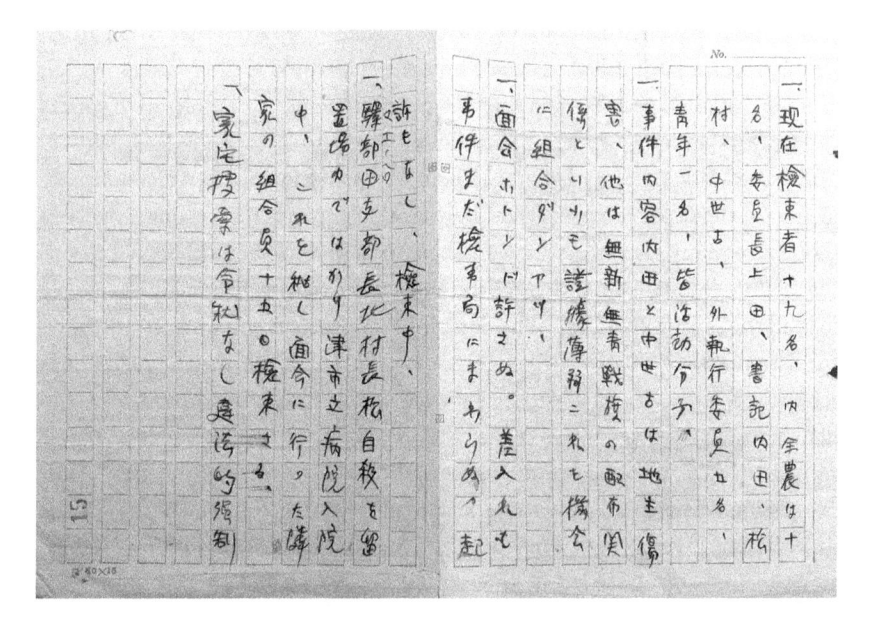

FIGURE 3.3. Report from the Mie branch of MOPR about nineteen imprisoned people it was supporting, of whom ten were Zennō members; 1931. All were activists charged with inflicting damage on landlords and distributing anarchist literature. The report states that visitation is quite difficult, that one of the imprisoned people tried to commit suicide and is currently hospitalized, that this fact has been kept secret, and that fifteen union members who went to visit were arrested. It also relays that home searches are being carried out illegally. Courtesy of the Ōhara Institute for Social Research, Hōsei University.

The Riotous Assembly of the Listening Section

Buraku women's activism, exemplified by the organization of MOPR divisions by women's departments of unions, flourished in Mie because many understood that their tripled suffering could not be addressed by easy answers based on simplistic understandings of their dehumanization through the language of discrimination, exploitation, or patriarchy. A conflict over the distribution of a fifty-thousand-yen donation that the Mitsui Hachirōemon family made to Matsusaka city reveals the force that buraku women exercised despite not having power in formal political processes. The money sent to the city on behalf of the head family Mitsui (and by extension, Mitsui Gōmei Gaisha, the headquarters of the Mitsui conglomerate) was granted as a philanthropic donation that authorities were tasked with using to commence unemployment relief projects in Matsusaka, a city in which the family had deep roots.[54]

The July 26, 1932, edition of *Osaka Asahi Shimbun* reported that when an assembly meeting was called to decide how the city would spend Mitsui's money, over two hundred people, including unemployed members of proletarian parties and farmers' unions, women, and children filled the seats of the listening section of the Matsusaka city assembly. Their presence so intimidated city assembly members, the paper reported, that they were unable to achieve a quorum. Even though assembly members who were there tried to coax their colleagues to join the session, they failed to assemble the necessary majority, making it impossible to hold the session that day.[55] The quiet force of the men and women who filled the listening section, designed expressly to differentiate those who held representational authority from those who were merely observers, drove those who held structural power into silence.[56] More importantly, the listeners' power seeped outward, into the world outside of the listening section, and grew. After the session was suspended without a word of formal discussion about how the fifty-thousand-yen "gift" from the Mitsui family would be distributed, the Internationale rang out and a clash broke out between police and activists.[57]

This confrontation in Matsusaka—after a city assembly convened to discuss the distribution of a cash gift that resembled donations that subcontractors and developers had granted to local elites in places like Asama and Maemura in exchange for their cooperation—supplied the beautiful sounds that fed the riotous energies that grew louder and louder at the center of Suiheisha-Zennō-Sōdōmei activism in Mie. So powerful was its centripetal force that Hino Nichōme came to be known as a Soviet—an organizing hub for all of the Suiheisha-affiliated organizations and activists in the region and a place where dreams of autonomous control were actualized every day.[58] The importance of young buraku women organizers in sustaining this reputation and these relationships becomes clear when we pay attention to the names scattered in the voluminous records of the Tokkō Geppō of those who violated the Peace Preservation Law (Chian Ijihō).[59]

In the pages of these secret police files are the names of people like Nakazato Hatsuno, a young woman who was arrested for organizing the Matsusaka branch of the MOPR in the summer of 1931 after it had been gutted by an earlier round of arrests, distributing Communist-affiliated publications like *Senki* (Battle flag), and for organizing the Mie branch of the Communist-affiliated Zenkyō (All Japan Teachers Union).[60] Nakazato Shizue was twenty-two years old when she was arrested for being part of the Zenkyō-affiliated Mie Gōdō Rōdō Kumiai (Mie Amalgamated Labor Union). She was also accused of distributing contraband materials. Iguchi Shina (17), Iguchi Masa (19), Kimura

Umeno (22), Kitamura Hana (21), Nakagawa Kotomi (19), Miyazaki Komatsu (22), Okada Koto (22), Shimaoka Koteru (22), and other women appear in these records for a variety of actions that the state classified as crimes, including recruiting union members in their workplaces and putting up flyers. They were affiliated with the Mie Gōdō Rōdō Kumiai, like Nakazato Hatsuno and Shizue, or held leadership positions in other local Zenkyō-affiliated organizations such as Mie Ippan Shiyōnin Kumiai (Mie General Employee Union) or Nōson Rōdōsha Kumiai Jyunbikai (Preparatory Committee for an Agriculture Workers Union). Kitamura Hana, Kimura Umeno, Iguchi Yone, and Iguchi Shina were among the women leaders of the Matsusaka MOPR branch.[61]

Confronted with the entries on these young women, whose addresses were only recorded as Matsusaka city, Hino Nichōme, we are compelled to think about how important their organizing activities were in creating connections within and beyond the city, establishing relationships between workers in different occupations, and formulating demands that carried the legacy of Suiheisha Women's Column authors' insistence that their tripled suffering had to be dismantled for everyone to be free. The organizing labor that these women performed was likely informed by the indignities they experienced as domestic, agricultural, and factory workers. As urban and rural areas were not isolated spaces of life and work, especially for many impoverished women from buraku communities who moved back and forth for survival, it is no surprise that the connections forged in Hino Nichōme would be mobilized to support struggles that took place in other parts of the prefecture and beyond.

Nakazato Hatsuno, twenty-four years old when she was arrested, along with many of her comrades, by the Special Higher Police for her involvement in radical activism on March 13, 1933, would have been a teenager when Hino Nichōme activists mobilized to support the striking workers at the Kanbe factory in 1926. While she and the others identified by the Special Higher Police are clear examples of women who were radicalized in Hino Nichōme and who played important roles in supporting the struggles waged by other buraku communities against their exploitation and dispossession throughout the prefecture, many others only appear as unnamed participants in clandestine meetings outside factory grounds, audience members in a courtroom, or bystanders watching intently as officials entered neighbors' homes with their shoes on. Although these women are nearly invisible in official records and in movement archives, the prefecture's Special Higher Police acknowledged that their collective rejection of existing gender norms made them a threat to society. A report compiled in 1934 said the following:

It should be noted that the buraku women's class consciousness is high. They do not have good feelings toward men who are not engaged in these class-based movement and there is a tendency to expel them. These women are at the helm of the Mie branch of the Japan MOPR (district one) where they provide relief to the people who sacrifice themselves to the revolutionary movement and to their families.[62]

To state authorities, perhaps the greatest crime of buraku women activists was their willingness to sacrifice themselves to class-based antipatriarchal revolution and not the nation. By ostracizing men who did not share the same commitment, they threatened the heteropatriarchal family that formed the material and ideological foundations of the nation. As such, the roundup of Hino Nichōme's most outwardly radical members during the mass police arrests of communists and activists known as the 3.13 incident was a counterrevolutionary measure intended to dull the impact of the years of work that women put into creating new spaces and relations that could withstand, circumvent, and possibly break open the metaphysical violence that haunted their lives.[63] Distributing contraband, recruiting workers to unions, putting up flyers, providing aid to dependents of those imprisoned, and all of the other activities that they were cited for were technically their crimes. But it was their willingness to transgress the unspoken boundaries of societal conventions and norms that was the real danger they posed to authorities, who had the world to lose if these rebellions went unchecked.[64]

The Difficulty of the Struggle Is One

The Japanese state responded to what was widely acknowledged after the 1918 Rice Riots as profound socioeconomic instability in the countryside with a series of measures that tried to minimize the realm of impossibilities inherent in capitalism. This effort took divergent forms (legal, social) and operated on a variety of scales (municipalities, villages, regions, families), but transformed the metropolitan countryside from a repository of the industrial reserve army awaiting employment in future factories into extraction zones. As with all capitalist relations of production, minimizing the inherent impossibilities of the valorization process did not mean simply controlling the point of production but required the constant production of difference that subjected some groups of people to racism, defined by Ruth Wilson Gilmore as "the state-sanctioned or extralegal production and exploitation of group-differentiated vulnerability to premature death."[65] This subjection was often disguised as a conciliatory measure from the Japanese state to its subjects and issued in the language of relief.

The expulsion of buraku residents from the commons through ippanmin consensus—the focus of the previous chapter—was linked to their stigmatization. They were seen as incapable of building "healthy families," a euphemism for an increasingly atomized unit that was tasked with upholding morality and engaging in self-exploitation. Those who were unwilling or unable to reform their behavior were labeled contagions—uncontainable threats to the community.[66] Criminalization was not the exclusive fate of women from buraku communities, but by the 1930s, the category of Japanese woman realized itself by denying proletarianized women from buraku communities a place within it.

The actions of young women activists like Nakazato Hatsuno—only visible in police records detailing arrests—draws us back to the unnamed "buraku XX jīsan" whose testimony opened the 1935 report on the Asama struggle. They help us to think through what he could have meant when he lamented the darkness that he lived in and the darkness that he did not want to occupy in death. This chapter considered the possibility that the collective "we" that he invoked and interpellated included, and was transformed by, women who responded to their collective expulsion from the category of "Japanese woman" by creating their own spaces of struggle in their workplaces, homes, and streets. While much of this work emanated from Hino Nichōme, it also took place in rural spaces like Asama, Toyota, and Kanbe and continued after the publication of the report.

On June 11, 1937, four hundred women and twenty men from the ring and finishing departments of Kishiwada Spinning Factory's Tsu factory no. 1, also in Mie prefecture, went on strike. According to Matsuhisa Matsuji, most of the young girls and women employed there came from buraku areas in Mie. Young daughters of ailing farm households sought employment at large textiles factories like Kishiwada to earn wages and to reduce the number of mouths their families had to feed.[67] They fought the firing of union leaders, demanded higher wages, called for equal pay for men and women, and asked for paid menstruation leave; they issued eight additional demands that they drew up in consultation with representatives from regional and national labor, tenant farmer, and buraku liberation organizations who came to support their action.[68] According to Ōyama Shunpō, strikers wrote, "The difficulty of the struggle is one. Save our brothers in Asama" on the wall near the factory entrance where strikebreakers, often hired from buraku communities, would have seen it.[69] The standoff ended after six days following an intervention by the Special Higher Police.[70] Two weeks later, on the afternoon of June 30, the

Mie branch of Suiheisha held an assembly to discuss how to bring the decade-long Asama struggle to a close.[71] This meeting was followed by a school sympathy strike that began on July 3 and lasted eight days and that mobilized all 142 elementary and higher school students from the buraku side of Asama against the discrimination their parents had endured.[72]

Reading the reinvigoration of the Asama struggle alongside the Kishiwada Tsu factory strike, whose participants were mostly buraku women over 40 kilometers away, and alongside the activity in the Hino Nichōme Soviet, allows us to expand our understanding of what participants at each of these sites may have dreamed about as they fought against their expulsion, exploitation, and criminalization. The lives of the four hundred women who worked at the factory and that of "buraku XX jīsan" whose words opened the 1935 report in Asama were economically and politically enmeshed. The writing on the wall shows that they understood that the fights for access to the commons and better working conditions in the factory were inextricably linked. The hope of "buraku XX jīsan" to not "die in the darkness," when tied to poor, radical women's refusals to accept their tripled sufferings, constituted a revolutionary attack on ippanmin commonsense that formed a thick fortress of consensus along the Asama River.

CHAPTER FOUR **HOUSEWIFIZATION, INVISIBILIZATION, AND THE MYTH OF THE NEW SMALL FARM HOUSEHOLD**

Approximately 125 kilometers along the Pacific coast south from Asama is Kinomoto-chō, the site of the murder of two Korean railway construction workers, Yi Gi-yun and Pae Sang-do, by Japanese residents of Kinomoto and neighboring Arai village on January 3, 1926. Zainichi Korean studies scholar Kim Chŏng-mi's essay "On the Attack and Massacre of Korean People in Mie Prefecture's Kinomoto" details these killings that took place less than three years after the massacre of over six thousand Korean people in the aftermath of the Great Kantō Earthquake.[1] A similar synergy between police, local politicians, and members of various local organizations such as the Imperial Military Reservists' Association (*Zaigo Gunjinkai*), youth groups (*seinendan*), firefighter associations (*shōbōdan*), and local vigilante organizations (*jikeidan*) produced this moment of anti-Korean terror that reverberated far beyond southern Mie.

Not long after the killings of Yi and Pae, organizations like the Zainihon Chōsen Rōdō Sōdōmei (Federation of Labor of Koreans in Japan) and the Mie prefecture branch of Suiheisha conducted independent investigations about what happened. Fuse Tatsuji, a well-known lawyer, social activist, and supporter of Korean liberation, produced a report based primarily on witness testimonies. He expressed surprise that the attack had occurred without direct provocation. The report was important because it provided a counterpoint to reporting in mainstream dailies that discussed the killings as a carryover of a turf war between competing *hanba* that were engaged in construction of opposite ends of the tunnel. Before this, on February 10, four radical Zainichi organizations, Zainihon Chōsen Rōdō Sōdōmei, Sangatsukai (March Society), Zai Tokyo Chōsen Musan Seinen Dōmeikai (Tokyo Korean Proletarian Youth League), and Ichigatsukai (January Society), issued a joint statement that situated these killings in an earlier series of events, including the Niigata massacre in July 1922, the Great Kantō Earthquake of September 1923, and the Otaru incident in December 1925.[2] They urged others to condemn these as acts of colonial and class warfare, saying, "In the end it is nothing more than yet another instance of the Japanese bourgeoisie massacring the Korean proletarian class."[3] The report concluded by praising two Japanese workers who threw dynamite at the attacking vigilantes as shining examples of internationalist class solidarity.

The organ newspaper of the Japan Communist Party, *Musansha Shimbun*, published Fuse's report on February 20, 1926. Through his investigation, he learned that approximately two hundred Korean workers and their families had moved into temporary barracks called *hanba* to engage in tunnel construction to connect Kinomoto-chō and Haku village by rail. Yano-gumi, a Kyoto-based contractor, won the bid and began construction in January 1925. Like the Asama struggle, the railway development project that spurred the Kinomoto incident was part of a larger effort to build up the Kumano Kōdō pilgrimage route, which linked the Grand Ise Shrine to Kumano Sanzan, Kōyasan, and other sites now registered collectively as a world heritage site called "Sacred Sites and Pilgrimage Routes in the Ki'i Mountain Range." Fuse confirmed that the vigilante spirit that compelled Japanese people to kill over six thousand Korean people in 1923 was replicated in Kinomoto: "Twelve to thirteen hundred residents gathered as people rang the town bell, played the trumpet, retrieved their weapons that were stored at the elementary school, and surrounded the Korean peoples' *hanba*."[4]

To many Korean men and women who continued to live and work in the metropole, neither ethno-class suicide practiced by two Japanese workers nor Fuse's meticulous investigation offered much comfort. Soon after the incident, the Korean *hanba* was shut down and workers left town. Testimony that Kim introduced in a different essay, "History of Zainichi Koreans in Wakayama," from an unnamed woman called *omoni* who was born in 1919 and first moved to nearby Wakayama prefecture in the early 1940s, confirms that solidarity and radical lawyering had little immediate impact on the lives of Korean people who lived under the threat of violence. We learn that for people like *omoni* and her husband, who were forced to move frequently in search of work, the massacre of Korean people by Japanese vigilantes and police during the 1923 Great Kantō Earthquake served as a constant reminder of the inescapable terror they lived with. Despite never having lived in the Kantō region or in Mie prefecture, both events reminded them that safety was elusive under Japanese colonial rule.[5]

The specificity of the terror that Korean men and women faced in the metropole's agrarian villages, the focus of this chapter, can be gleaned by the way that news of the massacres of 1923 and 1926 traveled from large cities to temporary *hanba* and to places like Wakayama's orange orchards, where *omoni's* husband worked as a fruit picker in the late 1920s. News traveled because people took stories with them as they fled their workplaces. For Japanese scholars, movement—a matter of survival for many Korean workers and a source of their exploitation by bosses large and small—fueled by police-backed vigilante terrorism, obscured the indispensable role that Korean agriculturalists came to play in this period as a workforce for ailing Japanese small farm households, as well as the constant danger that they endured in these spaces.

Despite scholarly inattention to their importance, particularly before the late 1930s, when mass forced labor recruitment began, Korean migrant workers were indispensable to the self-actualization of Japanese small farmers as conquistador humanists.[6] As Hyun Ok Park argues in *Two Dreams in One Bed*, immigration regimes of the Chinese Republican government, the Japanese state, and the Korean governor general's office each negotiated questions of nationality, property, and accumulation in order to secure hegemony in the contested region of Manchuria from the early twentieth century. In much the same way that racist and patriarchal bordering regimes were foundational to the formation of the United States, they were central to these states' and capital's ability to continuously deflect crisis to racialized communities.[7]

While the position of burakumin in relation to ippanmin is not the same as that of the Korean people who worked as a flexible, exploited, or indentured colonial workers in the metropolitan countryside to their Japanese employers, it is instructive to consider the two relations side by side because they reveal interlinked mechanisms of theft and terror that enabled small farm households in the metropole to reproduce themselves generationally. Expulsion and confinement were two sides of the same coin that governed the way that intimacy functioned in Japan's agrarian villages. Both were enacted through consensus and confirmed by the law, and together they constituted an important part of the Japanese grammar that operated as colonial commonsense. A critical reading of a set of Farm Household Survey ledgers of a small farm household in Okayama prefecture reveals that forced intimacy shaped the terror that many Korean migrant workers endured, particularly after World War I.[8]

Korean Agriculturalists and Japanese Conquistador Humanism

The everyday violence that Korean agricultural workers experienced in the cramped spaces of small farm households were inextricably linked to more spectacular kinds of anti-Korean terror that exploded during the Great Kantō Earthquake and the Kinomoto incident. In addition to the ways that the survey form divided agricultural workers into familial and nonfamilial members whose labor inputs were mediated either by laboring capacity (*rōdō nōryoku*) or labor efficiency (*rōdō nōritsu*), the requirement that respondents record their inputs and outputs every day routinized exploitation and violence. The mundane textuality of the ledgers produced a commonsense that was difficult for uncritical readers to detect, much less critique.[9] Because the field of agrarian economics fails to appreciate the violence in the everyday, economists did not analyze the critical position that Korean agriculturalists occupied in the Ministry of Agriculture's post–World War I oikonomic project of small farm protectionism. This erasure is symptomatic of a colonial disavowal that remains uninterrogated in these fields and in Japan studies more broadly up to today.

An analysis of agrarian transformation in the Okayama-Hyōgo region—a vibrant center of early tenant-farmer activism—that I conduct here reveals that the image of the entrepreneurial Japanese small farm household that persevered in the face of the global capitalist crisis was a myth that could only be maintained by a restructuring that depended on, then erased the presence of, a colonial workforce. Sylvia Wynter's insistence that we consider domination rather than exploitation as the appropriate frame through which to understand the weight that capital's drive for unrelenting accumulation inflicts on those who bear the highest burden of surplus value creation shatters the binary that categorically separates the Japanese farm household from the expropriated multitude in the colonies. This split persists in studies of Japanese imperialism. For example, Katsuhiko Endo argues, reading Uno Kōzō and Tosaka Jun on capitalism, fascism, and the family-nation, that the Japanese state's agricultural protectionism in the metropole was enabled by the exacerbation of exploitation in the colonies through selective forms of industrial development and enclosures that dispossessed people and subjected them to dangerous and cheaply compensated waged labor.[10]

While studies on the formation of the Korean diaspora, like Ken Kawashima's book *Proletarian Gamble* and Park's book *Two Dreams in One Bed*, complicate this schema by drawing attention to the outflow and settlement of Koreans as migrant workers throughout the empire, because their main focus is not to trace the incorporation of a colonial agricultural labor force in the metropole, they do not directly challenge the notion that Korean agricultural workers were exceptional rather than necessary for the material and ideological constitution of the Japanese countryside as the enduring foundation of the nation.[11] Studies in Korean economic history trouble the imperial division of labor narrative as it pertains to Manchuria, but this analysis has not been extended to the archipelago.[12]

An important exception is Yasuoka Kenichi, who, in *Others in Japanese Agriculture*, shows that a stratum of Korean agricultural workers formed in the metropolitan countryside. He uses statistical data compiled in the national census and other Home Ministry documents to argue that while absolute numbers of agricultural workers remained quite small compared to those of Korean workers in metropolitan industry, Korean people did become an important temporary agricultural workforce, especially in regions where their numbers were high, such as Nara, Wakayama, Osaka, and Kyoto.

The empiricism that undergirds the binary of "Japanese farm household" and "expropriated multitude in the colonies," confirmed by the voluminous data that the state's statistical bureaus, municipal record-keeping organs, police, and population departments kept on Korean workers in the metropole, provides social scientists with data to confirm that the countryside, before World War II, remained mostly empty of colonial workers. Instead of accepting these data at face value, this chapter demonstrates how ledgers and the national census actively produced their absence. Clarifying that the production of data and the compilation of statistics took place in a manner that closed off the notion that Korean and other racialized people were engaged in meaningful activity in the metropolitan countryside is important because writings that came out of these materials enabled scholars of varied political persuasions to craft narratives that invisibilized techniques of compulsion that small farm households qua conquistador humanists used to extract their labors.[13]

The Myth of Kōyō Village

Located just over three hundred kilometers northwest of Kinomoto-chō, Hikogi was one of seventeen districts in Kōyō, a farming village in Akaiwa province, Okayama prefecture.[14] According to the 1935 census, Kōyō had a population of 4,066.[15] It was designated a Model Revitalization Village (Yuryō Kōsei Nōson) in 1932, a status that the Ministry of Agriculture bestowed after village leaders proved their commitment to pursuing "spiritual and economic revitalization" through "rationalization" by successfully convincing small farm households to accept stringent austerity measures.[16] The state rewarded village leaders' initiative with national recognition and a small sum of state subsidies that they could put toward additional agricultural reforms. A survey team of eighteen people from the ministry investigated conditions for two weeks and produced a report that outlined their recommendations for even more efficient management of the village.

Kōyō's success story was turned into a full-blown myth in the hands of former "farmer literature" (*nōmin sakka*) author and Japan Proletarian Writer's League (NALP) member Maruyama Yoshiji (1903–1979).[17] His narrative traced Kōyō's successful transformation into a model village for the Cultural Section of the Imperial Rule Assistance Association (IRAA).[18] In the story *Kōyō son: Okayama ken Akaiwa gun (Mura no Chōsa Hōkoku)* (Kōyō village: Okayama Prefecture, Akaiwa Province [Report on village investigations]), published in 1942 (figure 4.1), Maruyama applauded the enlightened and self-sacrificing leadership style of the village head, Kunishiro Tatsuta, who combined hard work and moral leadership with scientific knowledge of agricultural management learned at university to almost single-handedly inoculate Kōyō from the forces of tenant-farmer activism that had extremely destabilizing impacts in other parts of Okayama.[19] He crafted a story of spontaneous communalism where residents played their parts perfectly in order to collectively overcome the impoverishment that nipped at their heels.

Reading Maruyama's description, one could be convinced of Kōyō elites' successful enactment of the "miracle and magic" of devaluation that Marxist theoretician Inomata Tsunao pointed to in his 1935 essay "Peasantry and Fascism" as crucial for bringing the petty bourgeoise masses in the countryside to the side of fascism.[20] In the piece, Inomata intervenes in debates over which strata are most susceptible to fascist mobilization. While he agrees with Uno and many others that part-owner cultivators—in this essay, he refers them as petty bourgeoisie—were most vulnerable to fascist ideology, he carefully distinguishes fascist organizations like imperial reservists' associations, industrial

FIGURE 4.1. Cover of *Kōyō son: Okayama ken Akaiwa gun (Mura no Chōsa Hōkoku)* (Kōyō village: Okayama Prefecture, Akaiwa Province [Report on village investigations]), 1942. This document, by Maruyama Yoshiji, extolls Kunishiro Tatsuta's and Ihara Toyokichi's accomplishments. National Diet Library, Tokyo, bibliographic ID 000000681645.

associations, training and educational institutes for farmers, and patriotic youth groups headed by local elite from the people these organizations were trying to mobilize. The latter, Inomata explains, are difficult to move politically against their economic interests. He argued that patriotic movements like Shōwa Shinseikai (Shōwa Divine Society), an ultranationalist paramilitary organization affiliated with Omoto-kyō (New Religion), and Rikken Yōseikai (Constitutional Development Society), influenced by the Nichiren sect, were more dangerous than the aforementioned state-affiliated organizations because they were successful in drawing the masses to their unapologetic Japanism. Japanism, Inomata argued, was key to turning the petty bourgeoisie into adherents of what

THE MYTH OF THE NEW SMALL FARM • 89

he called *kisekishugi*, a word that might be translated as "a believer of miracles," much more effectively than vertically organized state and parastate institutions that pitched themselves as neutral providers of relief to ailing farm households. It was the nation—more precisely, the articulation of a nation built on Indigenous genocide, colonialism, and heteropatriarchy—that formed the basis of the miracles and magic that bourgeoisie and petty bourgeoisie in the countryside were most drawn to even if the policies it enacted went against their economic interests. Japanism, undergirded and shaped by colonial commonsense, made Uno's "political necessity but economic impossibility" a reality.

While Maruyama emphasized the importance of good leaders like village head Kunishiro, who drew on his education and leadership skills to keep Kōyō villagers from succumbing to the radical activism for which Okayama's tenant farmers were well-known, he could not resist talking about magic, which he disguised as the entrepreneurial initiative of one particularly dedicated and skilled farmer. He credited a man by the name of Ihara Toyokichi, described as a self-made fruit cultivator from Hikogi district, with bringing prosperity to the village. In Maruyama's fairy tale, Toyokichi was a pioneer who single-handedly transformed his once-bare mountains into a jeweled tapestry of pear, white peach, and persimmon trees. His success inspired his relatives and neighbors to do the same. Maruyama noted that though he had recently passed, Toyokichi's legacy continued to live on in "Yama no Ie," a place he built after successfully opening up the mountain that towered behind his residence. As the technician Iwamoto (Maruyama's guide in the village) explained,

> He became engrossed in the reclamation of the mountain. On evenings when he could work under the moonlight, he did so and holed up in the mountain, taking a hoe to the ground.... His diligent efforts manifest in the impressive fruit orchards you see today. Seeing his example, others followed, and many others opened up their lands.[21]

Kunishiro's leadership, the initiative of enterprising men like Toyokichi, and the communal work that they inspired gave Maruyama ample content to depict Kōyō as an ideal village worthy of the IRAA's adulation. As we will see next, Japanism, though not invoked in Maruyama's story as a driver of residents' enthusiastic acceptance of village austerity policies, was not an abstract concept in Kōyō. Rather, it operated through the invisibilization of the labors of Korean agriculturalists who were indispensable to its successful conversion from an idea into embodied practice. Here, too, terror was never very far away.

Colonialism and Housewifization

Placing Kōyō village in an imperial frame can demystify how its celebrated resident Ihara Toyokichi transformed himself into a model fruit producer. Toyokichi's success story is in fact inconceivable outside of the growth of regional companies, like Mizote, Ōhara, Nozaki, Taki, and Nishi Hattori, that made their fortunes by accumulating land in Okayama and the Korean peninsula beginning in the Meiji period and parlaying those resources into fertilizer, mining, and other extractive global industries. Companies, with the full backing of colonial governments, financial institutions, militaries, politicians, intellectuals, and police, accumulated agricultural land in their historic power bases and expanded their holdings throughout the empire by using the rents they collected from tenant farmers on the archipelago to purchase large tracts of land acquired through state-sanctioned theft from colonial populations.[22] On the Korean peninsula, dispossessed peasants were often funneled to large rice plantations established by Japanese corporations, where as tenant farmers they were subject to strict control through surveillance and debt. They were forced to become consumers of commodities like fertilizer, machinery, and foodstuffs that they purchased from company stores, often through advances that were also provided by the company. Corporations reinvested profits that were triply extracted from their workers into utility, financial, and other stocks that provided them with the capital to expand their political and economic influence domestically. These interimperial circuits of accumulation, made invisible on the same ideological grounds as Inomata's miracle and magic, enabled farmers like Ihara Toyokichi to increase their own holdings as domestic markets for their agricultural products opened.

The ledgers of the Farm Household Survey that the Ministry of Agriculture and Commerce collected in Kōyō's Hikogi district allow me to highlight a direct connection between colonialism and conquistador humanism in the metropole. A longitudinal analysis of the survey ledgers of relatives of Toyokichi, the Ihara Shingo farm household (no. 229), reveals that the household's ability to transform itself into an ideal small farm household depended on kinship ties and having good standing in the village community. According to Toyokichi's land registration records, Shingo purchased a small piece of his residential landholdings in early 1930.[23] Shingo's ledgers further show that he had consistent access to temporary loans and other forms of financial assistance that aided his transformation into a stable, fruit-selling owner-cultivator who could afford to send his eldest daughter to higher girls' school. In addition to these strong ties in Hikogi, Shingo's ability to hire Korean men and women as agricultural workers at extremely low wages allowed him to expand his fruit cultivation operations even after his wife, Kimiyo, moved away from agricultural production after giving birth to their son, Eiji. These factors, not Shingo's faithful devotion to Toyokichi's example, shaped the trajectory of his farm household through the 1930s.

In 1931, the start of the survey, Shingo was thirty-eight and Kimiyo was thirty-six. Their daughter, Ryōko, was ten and in elementary school. Shingo and Kimiyo farmed a larger-than-average area of land—in 1931, 9 tan 2 se 5 bu—with the assistance of an unspecified number of nonfamily members whose work time and wages they recorded in the ledgers.[24] Their primary sources of livelihood diverged slightly from the broader pattern of Kōyō village's agricultural production, which in order of descending value was rice, fruit, wheat, livestock, and vegetables. They cultivated rice, barley, pears, persimmons, apricots, peaches, and a small quantity of vegetables. In addition to the thirty yen that their participation in the Farm Household Survey generated each year, they occasionally earned additional cash by working on paid public works projects managed by bureaucrats in Hikogi or Kōyō. They weathered financial challenges by taking on short-term loans from relatives like Toyokichi, who also resided in Hikogi, which they repaid within the year. These connections enabled them to engage in life-prolonging activities such as hiring workers; paying a midwife to assist with childbirth; covering hospital fees for all family members; subscribing to multiple newspapers, magazines, and trade journals; and spending on household expenses (*kakeihi*) that exceeded levels that the Japan Farmer's Union (JFU) set as "average" for an owner-cultivating farm household.

The ledgers reveal the impacts that broader societal currents that targeted agrarian women as objects of social policy had on Kimiyo and her daughter, Ryōko. Kōyō village's proximity to the agrarian headquarters of the Kurashiki Institute for the Science of Labor in neighboring Takatsuki village, called the Agriculture Labor Study Center, may have had something to do with what appears to be the enthusiastic adoption of many of the tools and resources seen at the time as reforms targeting women's health.[25] Established in June 1933, the center remained in Takatsuki until the spring of 1935 and functioned as a field site. The 1935 annual summary compiled by its director, Teruoka Gitō, explained that the central objective of the Takatsuki project, supported through a fund established by the Arisugawa no miya, a branch of the imperial family, and the Hattori Charitable Foundation (currently, Seikō Holdings), was to study the labor efficiency of housewives in farm households. He explained that, since 1933, these two sponsors allowed the institute to transfer some of their resources into an intensive study of the labor efficiency of agricultural work.[26]

The Agricultural Labor Study Center's on-site investigation in Takatsuki concluded after three full years on April 30, 1935, and generated twenty-six separate reports. During the investigation, researchers who lived at the center's makeshift headquarters in Takatsuki met regularly with village members and organizations in order to forge the personal bonds that they knew would be necessary to convince people to consent to some of the invasive practices they recommended. These included village-wide participation in providing blood samples for syphilis testing, a program of farm plot exchanges to reduce the time and energy that farmers expended in traveling to scattered plots of land throughout the village, and a project to make kitchen spaces more ergonomic and, by extension, to make housework safer and more efficient for pre- and postnatal women (see figures 4.2 and 4.3).

While we have no way of knowing how these social reformist approaches to improving the health of women as mothers, housewives, and agricultural workers directly affected the everyday lives of Ihara Kimiyo and Ryōko, patterns of spending in the category of "cultivation expenses" suggest that the farm household was open to testing out some of these agricultural reform initiatives. When we first encounter Kimiyo in the ledgers in 1931, she was already a member of a women's organization that provided the farm household with an interest-bearing savings account that held 63.13 yen at the end of the fiscal year—a significant portion of the 92.48 yen that was deposited into four separate savings accounts. The farm household also contributed to the Kitchen Reform Mutual Financing Group, which gave members the opportunity to pay small amounts of money into a pot that would be distributed as a lump sum when it was their turn. Each participant was expected to use the payout to complete modernizing reforms to their kitchens in a manner consistent with the Agricultural Labor Study Center's specifications.[27]

Kimiyo also had access to medical and social welfare facilities that not all women living in rural areas had access to at the time. In 1933, a 15 yen payment was recorded on the health expenditures page of the ledger with the note "gave to the midwife as thanks." The family paid 21.5 yen to a doctor for costs incurred when Kimiyo gave birth to her son, Eiji, that fall.[28] They also spent 8 yen 20 sen on a baby carriage. These entries suggest that the Iharas were imbricated in village-level initiatives that saw the betterment of women's health and implementation of more efficient work practices as keys to maintaining small-scale agricultural production. It is not clear whether participation in

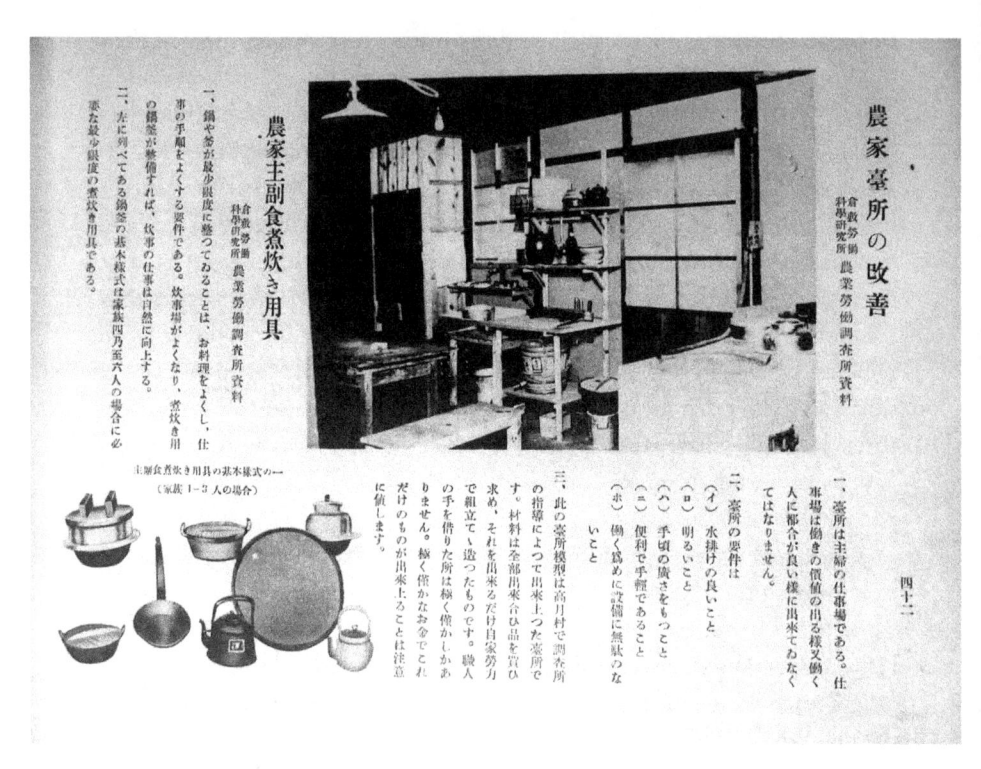

FIGURE 4.2. Photograph of a model modernized kitchen for use by a farm household, presented by the Kurashiki Labor Studies Center. From *Kōsei Tenrankai Gaiyō*, a pamphlet the center created in order to commemorate a meeting held in May 1935 and attended by representatives of various institutes and ministries committed to the reform of agricultural labor. *Kōsei Tenrankai Gaiyō*, 42. National Diet Library, Tokyo, bibliographic ID 000000759384.

these initiatives improved Kimiyo's conditions of work and life or simply led to the intensification of work and of patriarchal control over her body.[29]

Kimiyo's work ledger entries suggest that she made dramatic changes to her work patterns after giving birth to Eiji. The decline in Kimiyo's recorded agricultural labor time following Eiji's birth on September 17, 1933, is noteworthy because that was also the year that the farm household converted all 2 tan 7 se 2 bu of their forestland into fruit orchards, added more underground pipes for drainage, and dug up their grapevines in order to plant fruit trees (220 trees were newly planted). Since the familial workforce comprised only her and her husband, Shingo, the labor required to accomplish these tasks was performed by nonfamilial members, including seasonal workers who entered the ledgers

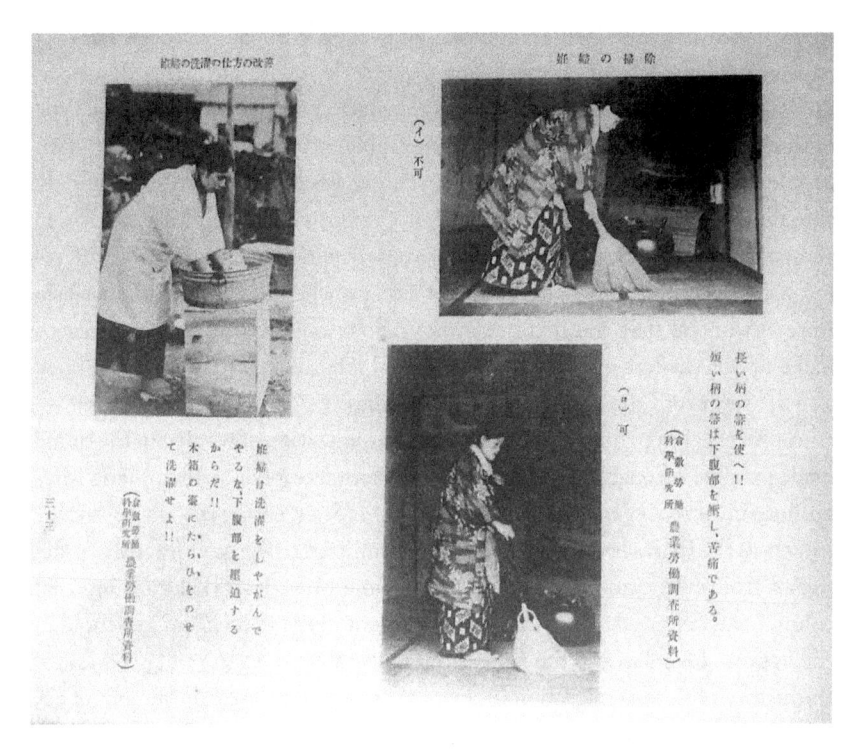

FIGURE 4.3. Examples presented by the Kurashiki Labor Studies Center of the most efficient ways of engaging in various domestic tasks. *Kōsei Tenrankai Gaiyō*, 33. National Diet Library, Tokyo, bibliographic ID 000000759384.

for the first time that year. The exact composition of this workforce eludes us, but we can see how Shingo classified them in the work table. The category "hired male" shows that this category of worker performed 1,073 of the 1,277 hours of nonfamilial work that year. We are given almost no information about the total number of workers in this category since names and tasks did not require specification. The work table indicates that the vast majority of their labor time was concentrated in July, November, December, and February and split roughly 3:7 between rice and fruit production. The Ihara farm household converted its forestlands into fruit orchards by mobilizing over 1,200 hours of labor time from nonfamilial workers for which they paid just 78.14 yen. The survey form does not provide detailed gender-differentiated breakdowns of nonfamilial workers.

A closer examination of the category "hired male" shows that Kimiyo's housewifization after Eiji's birth was enabled by the farm household's access

THE MYTH OF THE NEW SMALL FARM • 95

to the heavily exploited, barely compensated labor of Korean workers. The 1933 payment ledgers for agricultural expenses mostly record payments described as "wages paid to Korean," though no information is recorded about the type of work performed. A single entry on September 22 for payment to twenty-two people of 7 yen 70 sen, or just over 38 sen per worker, reveals the extremely casualized nature of the workforce. Though not as extreme, the total of 3.50 yen paid for the work that five Korean workers performed on February 28 reinforces this notion. The ledgers do not explain when or how the twenty-two Korean workers that the Ihara farm household employed in 1933 in order to make up for the loss of Kimiyo's agricultural labor ended up in Hikogi. They also do not record their ages, genders, or names.[30]

A process akin to housewifization, or the atomization of women in the home made possible through the exploitation of external colonies, which Maria Mies outlines in *Patriarchy and Accumulation on a World Scale*, can be read in the survey ledgers as the Iharas became increasingly committed to the cash-intensive practice of fruit cultivation. Unlike in the dynamic Mies described, the "internal colony" and "external colony" were both present in the Ihara farm household in the figures of Kimiyo and the Korean agricultural workers. A brief overview of the history of Korean migration to the metropole since the establishment of colonial rule in 1910 will contextualize the presence of Korean agricultural workers in Hikogi and illuminate the connections between housewifization and colonial labor power in ways that suggest the need to rethink the spatial distinctions between colony and metropole that Mies assumes when articulating the relationship between patriarchy, colonization, and the realization of surplus value.

The Terror of Intimacy

The 1910–18 land survey in Korea that the Japanese colonial government enacted immediately upon annexing the territory commenced the displacement of hundreds of thousands of Korean agriculturalists from their homes. While industrialization was a gradual process, because annexation provided Japanese capitalists the opportunity to enter Korea and take vast tracts of land from residents, dispossessed peasantry, particularly in the fertile southern regions of the Honam Plain, often had to find work on newly established Japanese-owned plantations.[31] Others entered mainland Japanese cities, and many struggled to stay employed as day laborers.[32] Many had difficulty adjusting to work in the factories and in construction because they had been farmers all their lives but could not find work in that department in the archipelago.

The scholarly consensus is that Korean workers did not contribute significantly to agricultural production in the metropole. However, Farm Household Survey ledgers and scattered reports and studies that I analyze next suggest a more complex reality. We learn, for example, that in the late 1920s a few prefectures formulated plans to bring Korean agricultural "trainees" to Japanese villages on one-to-three-year contracts. A report that the Fukuoka Regional Employment Placement Office (Fukuoka Chihō Shokugyō Shōkai Jimukyoku) published in 1928 titled *Working Conditions of Korean Workers in Agriculture and Quarrying* describes one such project.[33] It highlights the work of the Kumamoto Imperial Agricultural Association, which was in charge of implementing the agricultural trainee project in close coordination with the Korean governor general's office. Beginning in 1928 it brought young Korean men to the prefecture's Kamoto province as agricultural trainees who received on-the-job training from Japanese farmers who served as their employers and hosts.

This program was established in order to address the scarcity of agricultural labor power in Japan's agrarian villages as opportunities for waged employment in industrial sectors drove many people out of the countryside. In Kamoto, the project began with 20 Korean recruits as its first participants. The hope was that success would allow them to scale up the project to 600 people, or approximately one-third of the 1,800 hired agricultural workers that the province's 10,240 farm households regularly depended on to get through the busy farming season. As the current rate of 2 yen for men and 1 yen 20 sen for women per day (with meals) was too high for all but the wealthiest of farm households to afford, the entry of Korean agricultural workers was welcomed as a potential solution to a worsening labor shortage in the countryside.

The conditions of employment laid out in the report resembled the system of indentured servitude of the so-called coolie system, though its limited scale meant that it did not conjure identical forms of the racist imaginings that circulated widely in US society, which Moon Ho Jung outlines in *Coolies and Cane*.[34] It was, however, undoubtedly part of what Harsha Walia, in *Border and Rule*, called a race-making, gendering, and carceral regime that was characterized by "intense control, discipline, and surveillance of not only labor conditions or immigration status but the totality of life."[35] The Korean agricultural trainee system hardened the boundaries between the categories of citizen and colonial subject of the empire through the juxtaposition of trainees' (albeit fixed-term) unfreedom through confinement and the freedom to exploit them exemplified by the entrepreneurial Japanese farm household, which was charged with grooming young agricultural trainees in their image. Their dependence on these workers to provide poorly compensated labor power was conveniently forgotten in discussions of the program.

Eligibility criteria required that the trainees be in Japan on three-year terms for no longer than seven years and that they use their time in the program to save money, acquire new skills, and learn the self-discipline necessary to return to their hometowns as model small owner-cultivators in their own right. The years spent in Japan as trainees would make up for their "bad character" as Koreans, which, once corrected, would place them on the path to prosperity.[36] That the program's most important selection criteria was the applicant's ability to communicate in Japanese betrays its function as an unabashedly colonial instrument. Of the twenty trainees who participated in the inaugural year of the program, only a few had any prior experience in farming, but all had completed some form of colonial education.[37]

Their contracts confirmed their status as indentured servants; they were bound to their host families (which were also their employers) by method of compensation. Despite the existence of a contract, payment was left solely to the discretion of the Imperial Agricultural Association, which determined an appropriate amount of pay based on annual performance evaluations. The pay scale was set between sixty and one hundred yen per year and participants were issued an allowance by their host families of one yen per month. This admittedly low amount was offset by the fact that they would be provided with lodging, food, and work clothes. Worries that they might spend all their wages on frivolous things were assuaged by the fact that trainees did not see any direct wage payments during their entire time in Japan. These were kept in a bank account, which was to be returned to them only after they returned home.

Isolation and forced intimacy were major characteristics of the Kamoto program. The twenty young participants were sent to work for twenty different families in ten villages across thirteen districts. Some lived over twenty kilometers away from the center of town.[38] They saw each other only when their employers gave them permission to attend workshops about agricultural management that were held some evenings.[39] This isolation was by design, as part of the project was to bring forth "mutual understanding and intimacy over time" between male Korean workers, their Japanese employers, and members of farm households.[40] To further this goal, trainees shared a residence with and were given the same holidays as their employers.

The case of Korean agriculturalists in Saga prefecture, Miyaki province, introduced in the report immediately following the description of the Kamoto trainee project, is presented as an example of longer settlement in the metropole. Unlike in Kamoto, in the two villages of Kase and Mikawa, Korean workers settled in the prefecture without the Korean governor general's office or the Imperial Agricultural Association's assistance. We learn that there were six Korean dwellings containing fifty-four people who resided in Kase. Forty-four people engaged in a variety of agricultural tasks. The report described the remaining ten—a figure that included children—as *mushoku*, or without employment. Only nineteen of the fifty-four people had been in the village for over a year even though five of the six dwellings had been there for much longer. These figures, which suggested that each dwelling had taken in relatives and acquaintances who were relatively transient, were presented in order to highlight the seasonal nature of the work performed. The report emphasized that despite the small absolute numbers of Korean agricultural workers who made Kase their home, they, as well as the additional workers that their presence drew into the village during the busy months of April, May, and August, were indispensable for the reproduction of the (Japanese) community. All farm households figured the availability of these workers into their yearly management plans.[41]

The report turned next to conditions in Mikawa, where seventy Korean workers resided in three separate dwellings. Fifty of them had been in the village for over a year. Twenty worked in agriculture, while the rest worked in the local ceramics industry.[42] The report did not provide details regarding their arrival but noted that most began to settle in the village in the early 1920s. Following these sections, it reiterated the importance of projects like the one implemented by the Kumamoto Imperial Agricultural Association in Kamoto. It anticipated that similar projects would become even more important to securing a temporary workforce as industrial development on the peninsula would make "spontaneous" settlement less likely in the future.[43]

Even if we accept the report's characterization of the number of Korean men and women in metropolitan agrarian villages as miniscule, one thing that comes through clearly is that Japanese farming communities counted on their presence as a flexible, poorly compensated, and controllable labor force to overcome structural challenges. While Japanese Marxists who debated the agrarian question during the interwar period did not find these figures statistically significant enough to include in their assessments of the current conjuncture, Korean workers' flexibility and compulsion to work for low and irregular wages made it possible for families that appear in the report, as well as the Iharas, to transform themselves into success stories worthy of being celebrated as models for the rest of the nation.

The Census and the Disappearing Korean Woman Worker

The official report's narrow focus on the agricultural trainee program and dismissive descriptions of their dwellings as places where many people idled "without employment" created the impression that it was primarily men who comprised the already limited numbers of Korean agricultural workforce in the Japanese countryside. The importance of Korean women to the reproduction of small farm households like the Iharas' is especially difficult to measure because they rarely appear in official documents as a discrete category of analysis. The national census, which I analyze next, ensured that the work that Korean women performed outside of factories remained uncounted and unacknowledged in the accounting practices of the Japanese economy.[44] I treat the census as a project that shaped the political battles that were being waged over how the national community should be defined.[45] While each completed census added to the impression of empirical certitude and naturalized the categories it used, local officials forwarded hundreds of questions to the Population Department of the Cabinet Statistical Bureau in Tokyo because they did not have clear answers about who belonged or why.

A number of questions that local officials submitted in preparation for the 1930 census reflected confusion about the growing presence of Korean workers in their jurisdictions. These ranged from the practical question of how to help people who had little Japanese-language proficiency fill out the form to the existential. One issue that perplexed officials from multiple prefectures was how to record the nationality of mixed-race children. The Population Department's consistent responses to these queries reveal their commitment to establishing a clear set of principles through which the most complex familial relations and employment conditions could be reduced to the basic elements that the state cared about: maintaining the principle of patriliny and defining the category of "primary occupation" (*hongyō*) as work that was performed outside of the home.[46] The political repercussions of this become apparent when we examine moments when the question of work classification—whether a person was fully employed, partially employed, unemployed, or without employment—came up.

Unemployment (*shitsugyō*) was a topic of concern for municipalities because many local officials feared that an idle, angry, and hungry workforce would become further radicalized and organized if stopgap measures to address their conditions were not implemented. Despite financial incentives that motivated municipalities to complete an accurate count of Korean people in the census, definitions of employment and work that the Population Department utilized invisibilized much of the work that Korean residents performed. Queries submitted to the department by authorities from Kyoto clarify how this invisibilization affected Korean women agriculturalists in particular.

In questions to the Population Department, Kyoto census officials presented ten scenarios of less-than-full employment and requested that it advise if "unemployed" was an appropriate classification for each. The department's responses reveal that it considered a person unemployed if they did not have a primary job and possessed the "will and ability" to find full-time work. The gendered repercussions of its understanding of the normative worker, revealed in its clarification of who is defined as unemployed, come through in its response to a scenario posed by officials who asked, "If a factory worker has the will and ability to work but does not have any opportunities for employment and temporarily returns home to help with agricultural work, but if that work does not reach the level of a primary occupation (*hongyō*), should they be considered unemployed?"[47] The department explained that, in the case of agricultural work, if the work performed was limited to assisting others and was not their primary occupation, they should be classified as unemployed.

The department's response to a question that an official from Ehime prefecture submitted addressed another important category of work: home work (*naishoku*). When asked if it were possible to list this kind of work as a secondary occupation if the respondent was technically unemployed, the department answered in the affirmative, clarifying only that it could not be viewed as a primary or full-time occupation. Since much of the work that Korean women agriculturalists in the metropole performed was done in the home as housework, piecework, or agricultural production for home consumption, the census's treatment of this kind of work as at best a secondary occupation—even for someone who was not employed full-time outside of the home—meant that Korean women's contributions to the metropolitan labor force would be undercounted in the census. Further, if these women did not indicate a willingness or ability to engage in waged work, they would be classified as *mushoku*, a passive state of being without employment.[48]

This placed Korean women in a dangerous position. Unlike Japanese (ippanmin) women agriculturalists, who were redeemable as reproducers of Japanese-Man-as-human if they accepted their position as such, Korean women were denied entry into the heteropatriarchal nation by necessity. That is, whereas being without employment did not necessarily negate the value that Japanese women held for the state as biological and social reproducers of the family unit qua national body, Korean women in the metropole did not qualify as imagined or actual biological reproducers of the family-nation.[49] As such, their status as "without employment" made them absolute drains on the national economy from the state's perspective. While the full repercussions of this would become clear with their disproportionate recruitment into the military's system of sexual slavery, the Kinomoto massacre, which took place at a *hanba* (work site) where workers were tunneling into a mountain in order to lay crucial military and industrial infrastructure for the nation, already showed the consequences of the state's race-making practices that, combined with a public that accepted their massacre by vigilantes with impunity, was deadly indeed.[50]

Korean Agriculturalists in Hikogi

These material and psychic infrastructures of Japanese grammar operated in Kōyō village. Documents kept by Okayama prefecture record 3,075 Korean people (2,549 men and 526 women) residing there as of June 30, 1929. Of that number, 170 (158 men and 12 women) were classified as agricultural helpers.[51] Unlike in Kumamoto, no official labor policy governed Korean agriculturalists in Okayama.[52] It is not clear how many of the 170 people listed as agricultural helpers were employed by the Ihara farm household. With the exception of two named individuals, the other Korean workers appear in the ledgers in a way that makes it impossible to know their genders or names or even how many worked for the farm household. What we can infer is that their presence was not outside the bounds of comprehension for agricultural bureaucrats. The fact that their employment beginning in 1933 went completely unremarked in the notes section of that year's Summary of Results confirms as much.

Closer scrutiny of the ledgers suggests the existence of a system of recruitment that involved cash advances that bound Korean workers to the Ihara farm household for an extended period of time. An entry on December 26, 1933, shows an unspecified advance paid out by the farm household. This suggests that a relationship of indebtedness was expected to continue beyond the current survey year, and that a relationship between Korean workers and the Ihara family had been in place for a while, perhaps through an intermediary. That intermediary could have been a labor broker, a representative of a local branch of the Sōaikai (Mutual Love Society), a government official who administered a program like the agricultural trainee system in Yamaguchi and Kumamoto, or a member of the village elite who had business ties in Korea.[53]

The following year's ledgers confirm that access to a Korean agricultural workforce was an integral component of the Ihara small farm household's ability to reproduce itself daily and generationally. The page of the 1934 Summary of Results that listed the farm household composition included an entry for a yearly laborer (*nenyatoi*) for the first time. This would have been cost-prohibitive for most small farm households. The line is blank in most ledgers, but in the Iharas' we see the name of a thirty-two-year-old Korean man with just the surname Pak. The notes did not comment on Pak's country of origin and explained only that the farm household had hired a yearly laborer to accommodate the expansion of their fruit orchards. Pak recorded 2,037.5 hours of agricultural work, which was supplemented by an additional 376.5 hours of work by nonfamily members.[54] For his work, Pak was paid a total of 39.99 yen in wages—well below the going rate in the village of 233 yen for an adult male worker. Due to the distribution of his labor time throughout the year, it would have been difficult for him to split his time between agricultural work and construction or mining during off seasons, which is what Korean agricultural workers usually had to do to make ends meet.[55]

In 1937, when the second Korean yearly laborer, surname Min (male, twenty-eight years old) appeared in the ledgers, the average annual salary in the village was 270 yen. Min was also classified as a yearly laborer, though the ledger notes that he was only hired for a third of the year. It was recorded that he performed 1,104 hours of work for which he was paid 73.27 yen in wages and 1.15 yen for sake expenses. This was 83 percent of the 90 yen he may have expected to receive as someone paid for performing a third of the yearly labor but was far less than the 58 yen per month that he would have received had he been treated as a seasonal laborer. His labor time distribution reveals a similar problem to Pak's: it was impossible for him to divide his time seasonally between agriculture and construction or mining.

The final and fundamental obstacle to Pak or Min being able to constitute their own small farm households was a different manifestation of the same consensus that expelled buraku agriculturalists in Asama from the village community. In their case, even if they could have scraped together the resources to acquire enough land to sustain small farm households of their own, there was no basis for them to contest their exclusion from common-use rights and other extralegal mechanisms that were indispensable for daily and generational reproduction. Shared genealogical existence—the rule that the Ministry of Agriculture and Commerce abided by to determine access to the commons—could not be claimed by Korean migrant workers whose presence in Okayama was relatively recent, as it was the direct result of colonial conquest.

Flight as Freedom

Growing persimmons from seed to fruit is a long process. It is said that at least nine years of patience and good weather are needed. Their cultivation thus required faith that one would have consistent access to a single plot of land

and a supplementary seasonal workforce for at least several years. This did not require much contemplation for men like Ihara Shingo, who had deep roots in Hikogi and knew that he would eventually come into more land through inheritance or title transfer. But it was unfathomable for agricultural workers like Pak or Min, two Korean workers that the Ihara farm household employed between 1934 and 1938.

Like the agricultural trainees of Kamoto, who were forced to speak Japanese, take their vacation days according to the Japanese calendar, and participate in ceremonies alongside the employers with whom they lived, Korean agriculturalists in the metropole endured violent intimacies whose traces we can see in the Ihara farm household ledgers. While they were treated like fungible suppliers of a flexible and temporary labor force, they were not exempt from some of the social relations that bound the Japanese community together in the countryside. We see an example on a page of the 1933 ledger titled "Socializing Expenses, Exchange of Gifts." The June 2 entry included "condolences for funeral of 'sXXjin'" of 67 sen.[56] This amount exceeded the 50 sen that the Iharas sent their own relatives as a gift for the birth of a child on March 1. Other entries on that page include 50 sen as a get-well gift for illness, 2 yen on February 3 as a farewell gift for a draftee, and many gifts of persimmons, pears, and other fruit that they harvested.

How do we make sense of the jarring incongruities that the description "condolences for funeral of 'sXXjin'" highlights? The offering of condolences on the one hand—an act that expresses a degree of concern for the death of a Korean person in a context that does not provide any signs of connection outside of a labor relation—and the use of the racist epithet on the other exceeds my comprehension. While a fuller consideration of the possible meanings embedded in this entry follows in the next chapter, the imbrication of Korean agricultural workers into the farm household's sphere of spiritual or ceremonial exchange confirms Wynter's explication of James's *pieza* conceptual framework: when considering the accumulation regime as a whole, it is the entire value code that shapes commonsense rather than simply the labor exploitation that establishes and perpetuates relations of domination.[57] Everyday relations of intimacy were sometimes the very same violent relations that were forcibly recast as care. Perhaps we can call this a coloniality that was necessarily embedded in the ministry's oikonomic policies.

Critiques that colonial subjects who worked as temporary agricultural workers made against their own racialized and gendered exploitation in the 1930s are difficult to locate in the archives. Because their absolute numbers were small, locating their expressions or acts of dissent within the Japan Farmer's Union or affiliate associations is quite rare.[58] Demands that were central to Japanese tenant farmer struggles, even buraku tenants, could not, by virtue of the structure of Japanese village society, resonate with Korean agricultural workers.[59] The valorization of fights for access to land, such as demands for permanent tenancy rights, access to the commons, or even calls for the reduction of rent payments that were central to buraku struggles in Mie, could not fully accommodate the battles that Korean migrant workers would have had to wage against Japanese landlordism to live free from colonial terror.[60]

It is impossible to ascertain from the Iharas' farm household ledgers or related materials whether the Korean workers who appeared as line items of the household budget had their own rooms to retreat to after toiling all day, had any time to let their minds wander and dream of life otherwise, were able to communicate with those they loved, or managed to quell their longings for home. Speculative work is needed to imagine how they nurtured new relations where intimacy was not bound to the violence of confinement, the ecstasy of the nation, or even kinship.

Thinking seriously about the fleeting appearances of Pak and Min in the Farm Household Survey ledgers requires that we step outside of the field of Japanese agrarian history that prioritizes fights over land, water, and other resources rooted in the assumption that people desired settlement and inclusion in village communities. If we understand movement and settlement as outcomes of complex calculations that migrant workers made under conditions of extreme impoverishment, surveillance, the latent threat of state-sanctioned vigilante violence, separation from loved ones, and no guarantees of return, we realize the importance of recalibrating the criteria that we use to locate, identify, and evaluate anticapitalist struggle and collective articulations of freedom.

Once we acknowledge that movement between rural and urban spaces was the rule rather than the exception, we can pose questions that center the lived experiences of agricultural workers from Korea who moved frequently. Pak's appearance in the ledgers in 1934 and his disappearance in 1935, Min's appearance as a half-year worker in 1937 and his disappearance in 1938, the dozens of nameless workers recorded only as "sXXjin" in the column of wages paid, as well as the unnamed deceased Korean person whose death was marked by a cash offering from the Ihara farm household, might be read as openings into lives that refused to be coopted into straightforward stories of resistance or survival. Approached from the problematics of Zainichi Korean studies, which center the lives and experiences of people from Korea who settled in the metropole from the late twentieth century, rather than Japanese peasant studies, moving on can be read as a rejection of conditions of forced intimacy that could flip into terror at any moment.[61]

Dozens of interviews that Zainichi Korean studies scholars like Kim Chŏng-mi conducted with men and women who came to the metropole during the colonial period underscore the importance of considering forms of relation that do not assume kinship, settlement, or shared residence. What did radical dependency look like and how was it pursued by people for whom living together was not guaranteed even when family members all resided in the metropole?[62] What would it mean to take this fact as a starting point from which to think about the ways that Korean people who lived in the metropole imagined and practiced freedom?[63] The next chapter explores how their efforts at collective survival and care for the living and the dead reverberated in the places they passed through. I end this chapter with a fragment of a story—it could be friendship, mutual despair, comradeship, or maybe even true love. It may have been all of these things or none at all.

I am referring to a short article that appeared in the June 11, 1930, edition of a major daily newspaper, *Osaka Asahi Shimbun*, titled "Same-Sex Suicide: By Korean Women"—easy to miss since it was buried in the middle of page five.[64] The piece reported that the bodies of two Korean women around the ages of thirty and twenty-four or twenty-five were discovered at around 10 p.m. the previous evening a short distance from the tracks of the Yōdo station of the Keihan railway line in Osaka. Upon investigation, it reported, they were much younger than they appeared (eighteen and twenty-two years old) and had committed suicide together. Prior to their deaths, both had resided with their Korean husbands in Kyoto's Fushimi city, less than seven kilometers from the place they were found. Whether we find the police's determination that this was a love suicide credible or not, or whatever we think of the paper's decision to report on it in this manner, the deaths of two young married women by suicide, seven kilometers away from their residences, provides an opening for the kind of critical fabulation that Saidiya Hartman proposes to "convey the aspiration and longing of the wayward."[65]

Whatever the nature of their relationship to each other, their decision to wander from home and to die together in the open air was difficult to ignore for the disruption it caused to the daily routine of commuters and cargo that the Keihan line transported in service of empire. It also disrupted mourning practices that otherwise might be unthinkingly absorbed into a narrative of (post)colonial tragedy that grieved for colonial subjects' failure to fulfill their desires for a love that confirmed heteronormative ideals of kinship and intimacy. This record of their deaths reminds us of the importance of imagining lives and relations of Korean women in the metropole that extend beyond dehumanizing characterizations like "without employment," which official reports, surveys, census materials, and ledgers create to mask the state's and capital's dependence on their existence. This and other fragmentary records are traces of how Korean women may have stolen away moments as they breathed the suffocating air of empire despite the erasure of their aliveness from these archives of colonial brutality. Who mourned the deaths of the two young women? Who recognized their lives as their own?

CHAPTER FIVE   **INTERIMPERIAL KOREAN STRUGGLE**

IN FERTILIZER'S   GLOBAL CIRCUIT

A short article titled "Koibito wa Sxxjin" (Lover is a Korean) appeared in the major local daily *Kobe Yūshin Nippō* on August 14, 1933.[1] Under 150 characters long, it reported that twenty-one-year-old Matsuo Shina, second daughter to a resident of Befu-chō, Hyōgo prefecture, was tempted into running away from home by a twenty-seven-year-old Korean man, Kim, who was employed at the factory of a locally headquartered fertilizer company, Taki Seihi Kabushikigaisha (hereafter, Taki Seihi). A fair bit of investigative journalism had gone into the piece, as it concluded that Matsuo's disappearance with Kim was part of a love affair that had endured an ocean's distance. How Kim met Matsuo or how he found his way back to her was not covered by the piece, which was focused on depicting the dramatic reunion of two lovers through the coded language of a young woman who fell victim to temptation. It ends by noting that the two probably fled to Himeji city.

What each thought they were leaving behind as they fled Befu-chō remains an open question. Would there have been any interest in their purported romance or any concern about locating the couple if the gender roles were reversed, or if both parties were Korean? The analysis provided in the previous chapter explains why the story as it was narrated by the paper was imaginable, and perhaps even tolerable, as a love story for Japanese readers. Korean agriculturalists employed by the Ihara farm household in Hikogi or the agricultural trainee project in Kamoto enter the historical record as men who were able to achieve a level of intimacy with their employers that had them sharing holidays, living quarters, and sometimes even mourning practices. The compulsory intimacy required of Korean people in the metropolitan countryside created low-frequency registers of routinized violence that they endured every day. Stories in this chapter show that Korean and some non-Korean people at times imagined and enacted something completely different.

Relations of radical dependency that tore apart, if momentarily, the aesthetic experience of Japaneseness, are evident in the collective actions that workers took against Kim's employer, Taki Seihi. Before telling this story, I trace the company's growth from a small factory in Befu-chō at the start of the Meiji period into one of the empire's largest fertilizer producers by the 1930s. This growth was enabled by its president, Taki Kumejirō, who had an uncanny ability to implement and capitalize on colonialism's material and psychic violence. Korean people's experiences with the company converged with the experiences of others who were exploited along different nodes of its imperial circuit and led to multisited direct actions against its exploitative and dehumanizing treatment.[2]

Kumejirō's aspirations were global even when the reach of his company was regional. His efforts to grow his fertilizer business resulted in the extension of its tentacles to the United States (Florida and Tennessee), Algeria, Banaba, and Christmas Island.[3] In these places, a mix of mostly non-Japanese, racialized, convict, Indigenous, and colonized workers toiled in the sweltering heat to dig phosphate from the earth to fuel the global fertilizer industry. Centurieslong modes of domination and accumulation characteristic of the extraction of phosphate rock from the earth in these regions, which experienced settler colonial conquests by the British, French, German, Spanish, Americans, and Japanese, was directly tied to Taki Seihi's ability to grow its business by exploiting Korean and buraku workers at its fertilizer factory in Befu-chō.

At the Taki Seihi factory, workers transformed phosphate rock that arrived on ships owned by Mitsui Bussan into the company's much-heralded synthetic fertilizer. Bags of Taki-branded fertilizer arrived via ship or rail in places like Hikogi, where small farm households used it, in combination with Korean workers, to create replicas of Ihara Toyokichi's jewel-toned fruit orchards.[4] Here, too, bordering practices segmented the empire's labor force in ways that shaped how men like Toyokichi and Kumejirō understood their own successes.

The struggles that surfaced in each of these places, all differentially positioned within Taki Seihi's imperial fertilizer circuit, make imaginable the connections that people forged as they endured the corporal and psychic violence of the imperialist structures that underpinned and enabled the cruel confidence of Japanese conquistador humanism. By paying attention to these interlocking relations and spaces, we become better equipped to appreciate the indispensable role that Korean women residing in the metropole played in providing life-sustaining, place-making labor that produced the conditions of possibility for flight that, at times, morphed into collective action or even calls for the dismantling of empire. This chapter is best read alongside but in tension with the previous chapter, which demonstrated how the state's tools, such as the census and ledgers, made Korean women's labor invisible at the very moment that Japanese women agriculturalists like Ihara Kimiyo and Ryōko transformed themselves into housewives and daughters capable of fulfilling their world-historical mission as reproducers of Japanese Man-as-human. I focus here on moments of world building by Korean workers and workers from buraku communites that rejected false promises of acceptance through assimilative intimacy, which, as I argued in the previous chapter, was nothing more than a form of terror.

Freedom Dreams in Confinement

Korean women who found work in the metropole built many of the Korean neighborhoods that stand today, despite official classifications of their status in the national census and other tools of state bureaucracy as without work or unemployed. Take, for example, the mother of interviewee Pak Su-yŏn, who moved to Japan in 1927.[5] As relayed by Pak to the interviewer, Zainichi studies scholar So Pok-hŭi, her mother moved to Japan from a mountainous region in South Kyŏngsang province at the age of twenty-three following the death of her first husband. She joined her father-in-law, who became her second husband, in Kyoto prefecture's Fukuchiyama city and followed him as he moved from one *hanba* to the next performing construction work. Following his death, she worked as an agricultural helper digging up potatoes from the fields. She supported herself and her six children with a portion of the potatoes that she received in lieu of cash payments and clothed them with hand-me-downs provided by her employer.[6] Her widowed status, the nature of the work that she performed, and the mode of payment in kind likely established her as *mushoku* (without employment) in the census. In fact, it is not clear that her presence would have been recorded at all in Japanese state records because her inability to send her children to school may have kept her out of view of census-takers in the area.[7]

Pak's life, unlike her mother's, would have left abundant traces in official and unofficial records of empire due to the nature of Pak's work. She shared with So that, like many of her compatriots, she moved around frequently, often living apart from her family as they all tried to survive. In 1940, at the age of sixteen, she began working at a thread factory near the Heian Shrine that employed twenty or so factory girls from Korea.[8] After getting married two years later, she moved to Tokyo, supported her family, and cared for her ailing father by doing piecework at home.[9] During the war, she, along with her small children, her mother, and her younger sisters, lived in a storehouse that they borrowed from a farm household in Nagoya. They had to move again following a large earthquake that hit on July 7, 1944. She and her children fled to a different part of the city while her mother and younger sisters moved to Tokoname, also in Aichi prefecture.[10] After she fell ill, her mother supported everyone by working as a cook at a *hanba* in Aichi.

Working for free in exchange for lodging and a small plot to farm, performing unpaid domestic labor for family members, and uprooting one's life repeatedly to help loved ones survive were common experiences for Korean women who resided in the metropole. Though Pak's waged employment in a factory would have made her more legible as a worker in census records, the unwaged and unrecognized forms of labor she also performed would not have been captured in the census by design. Even if census takers had wanted to get an accurate sense of the kinds of work that Korean people performed at home, a few Korean women and children living in someone's storehouse would not have figured prominently in the demographic makeup of a village and their activities would not have been counted as meaningful levels of economic productivity. As colonial migrant workers, Korean women residing in the metropole were not, at this point, targets of oikonomic policy. While they were indispensable to their communities and to Japanese society in general as providers of reproductive and other forms of labor, this work was not understood as tied to the fulfillment of an authentic primordial relationship—that is to say, to the nation.[11] Still, these activities and relations nurtured the ground from which more recognizable forms of organization including mutual aid and revolutionary struggle emerged.

Historian Kim Chŏng-mi, who wrote about the murder of two Korean workers by Japanese vigilante groups in Kinomoto discussed in the previous chapter, published a long essay containing interviews with multiple Korean women who moved through Wakayama prefecture in the prewar period. Agriculture, mining, construction, and textiles were the main industries they worked in. Kim uses the life of a woman she calls *omoni* as a window into the preliberation world of Korean people in Wakayama. This piece, like So's, focuses on how Korean women navigated a world that could not shake the specter of the Kinomoto massacre. She suggests that the need to take cover from hostility drove their efforts to build their own communities in and around *hanba*, but that these places eventually grew into havens in which mutual aid and labor organizing flourished. Upon joining her husband, who made ends meet by working an assortment of jobs before settling on employment in a steel factory near the end of World War II, *omoni* engaged in piecework making hats and umbrellas, taking on sewing and ironing jobs, and selling bean sprouts, which she grew on the side of the road.[12] This kind of work was the starting point for the formation of the Korean market in Ikaino, which began with the informal settlement of several families next to each other in the neighborhood in the early 1920s.[13] These markets, as well as consumers' associations that initially formed in order to provide daily necessities to workers who were otherwise forced to shop at company stores, provided Korean migrant workers with alternatives to their employers' price gouging tactics.[14] Workers' night schools, communally owned vessels that carried workers between various ports in mainland Japan and the Korean peninsula, community medical facilities, labor unions, and theaters that began catering to Korean audiences became part of the fabric of cities where Korean people resided.[15] Without people like *omoni* who participated in and nurtured these spaces (even briefly), anticolonial struggles that erupted amid intense police scrutiny in the metropole and on the Korean peninsula would not have had room to breathe, grow, or find sanctuary.

Kinyūkai's Anticolonial Feminist Critique

Kinyūkai (Rose of Sharon Society), which established branches in Tokyo and Kyoto in January and February 1928, emerged from and invigorated these world-building practices. Composed mainly of Korean women who were in Japan temporarily as exchange students, metropolitan branches of Kinyūkai were radical organizations that provided what Marxist feminist social reproduction theorists today would call a unitary critique of capital.[16] Their critique, which came from their understanding of work as something exceeding the point of production and including everything that compels the worker to the factory gates, resonates with the critique of colonialism that emerges from Wynter's *pieza* conceptual frame—as something that makes visible the colonial structures and sensibilities that worked to naturalize their exploitation.[17] They were committed to incorporating the lived experiences of Korean women workers into their critique of Japanese imperialism.[18]

The Tokyo Kinyūkai branch's third meeting platform emphasized that the liberation of colonized working women was necessary for the liberation of the working class as a whole: "Unless women workers are released from their slave-like chains through the liberation of the working class, and unless the ethnic-racial (*minzokuteki*) discrimination is abolished, the working class will not be free."[19] Struggles for liberation from colonial rule could not be fought exclusively on the Korean peninsula because dispossession had driven people out of their hometowns on a mass scale: "The simple reproduction of labor power is impossible on the peninsula. The peasant masses have to go abroad. . . . Japanese imperialism merges intimately with precapitalistic exploitation and engages in even crueler forms of exploitation."[20] On the modes of domination that preceded colonial rule, the platform specified that these included Korea's "reactionary traditions" like Confucianism, ancestor worship, idol worship, and religious practices that continued to operate after 1910 as "weapons to suppress the masses."[21]

The above analysis, which brings to the fore the relationship between Korean women's work, imperialism, colonial rule, patriarchy, and ritual, provides us tools with which to reconsider the seemingly paradoxical entry in the Ihara farm household's survey ledger of 1933: the payment of 50 sen as condolences (*kōden*) to a "sXXjin," a derogatory term that was used widely in Japan to refer to a Korean person. While we have no way of knowing the specific circumstances of this payment, if we understand the sending of condolences as vital to maintaining communal relationships between kinship groups and neighbors, we might conclude that this was an instance of performative intimacy that did not fundamentally destabilize boundaries between Japanese and Korean families so long as the latter retained their mark as a "sXXjin." Moreover, it may have been an expression of dominance on the part of the Iharas—imposing their form of funerary ritual upon Korean agricultural workers.

Kinyūkai's critique of "reactionary traditions" that reinforced patriarchal relationships that sustained the imperial formation is useful for understanding this entry.[22] The gifting of condolences and other protocols for mourning, such as a policy that some Japanese companies followed of giving time off to Korean workers so that they could participate in weeks-long burial practices back home, or the port police loosening restrictions on exit and entry during lunar new year celebrations, were concessions that may have been welcomed by many Korean workers, but nevertheless aided the perpetuation of colonial rule by reinforcing ideological regimes and material practices that authorized acts of mourning and communion so long as they did not threaten Japanese rule.[23] We might think of this exercise of control over mourning practices as taking place hand in glove with the exercise of what Nozomi Nakaganeku Saito calls ossuopower, "the exercise of sovereignty as the right to control remains"—in particular, the settler colonial state's exercise of its right to control the burial grounds of Indigenous peoples.[24] I focus mainly on the way that the state's exercise of ossuopower is made possible by the colonial sensibility that appears as community consensus in determining whether outsiders are expelled, confined, or welcomed in a variety of ways, including through rituals linked to mourning.[25] The Kinyūkai's unstated but implicit charge was that activities that buttressed or reconfirmed patriarchal authority in the peninsula were granted legitimacy by corporate and state policies that appeared as concessions but were, in fact, manifestations of colonial violence. In contrast, acts of care for the living and nonliving that Korean women performed in the metropole were disavowed or viewed as subversive if they confounded normative boundaries of filiation.

The Kinyūkai platform linked this critique to a broader analysis of the Japanese empire's production of a social milieu that kept the labor power of colonized people flowing to and from metropole and colony in ways that kept Korean working women vulnerable wherever they went:

> It is a general phenomenon that labor conditions of the working class deteriorate because of capital's attack and industry's rationalization. However, even there, the persecution to which one is subject as a woman, and on top of that, as a Korean woman, means that working conditions are worsened by two or three times—the exploitation and treatment they endure are that much worse.[26]

This critique, resonant with Suiheisha women's critique of their tripled suffering, would not have been possible without Kinyūkai leaders' concerted efforts to reflect the concerns of proletarianized women in colonial and metropolitan spaces.[27] Their observation that many of the burdens of social reproduction were borne disproportionately by women, and that the colonial condition made their burdens qualitatively different than those endured by their Japanese counterparts, reflected their incorporation of insights gleaned from activists and community organizers who were working to establish facilities like daycares, schools, and hospitals in order to reduce the power of the Sōaikai and other corporate labor brokers who amassed riches by stoking nationalist sentiment while simultaneously leveraging their relationships with the Korean governor general's office for favorable contracts and access to workers.[28]

Kinyūkai branches were dissolved under police pressure in 1931 but the items included in the Tokyo branch's 1929 platform were taken up and extended by labor unions, peasant unions, and informal networks that survived into the 1930s.[29] Many of their efforts focused on how to care for loved ones in life and in death. One example appears in *Minshū Jihō*, a Korean-language newspaper published in Osaka's Ikaino by Kim Mun-jun, a labor organizer from Cheju island who founded the publication after being released from his prison sentence for his participation in a strike of rubber factory workers in August 1930.[30] What we learn from the paper, whose founding issue was published on June 15, 1935, and from oral testimonies conducted after liberation is that one of the motivations for the formation of a Korean-held shipping cooperative, Tonga (Tōa) Tsūkō Kumiai on April 21, 1930, was to alleviate the financial stresses caused by fare monopolization for sea travel between Osaka and Cheju by large Japanese interests like Osaka Shōsen, Chōsen Yūsen, and Amasaki Kisenbu.[31] Through small contributions collected primarily from Osaka residents from Cheju, the cooperative purchased a retired Nihon Kisen vessel, the Fushikimaru, and commenced the route on December 1, 1931.[32]

A reader contribution in *Minshū Jihō*, "Our Appeal, Encourage Cremation," alluded to the importance of the Fushikimaru for Cheju islanders. The author's main objective was to advocate for the adoption of cremation over burial because he believed that doing so could alleviate the suffering of impoverished islanders. He reassured readers, "Whether it is in the water or in the ground, people's remains become earth in the end."[33] Kim Ch'an-jŏng explains in the commentary to the piece that, in addition to the costs of the month-long journey to complete funerary rites on Cheju and return to Osaka, islanders often had to endure disrespect from employees of Japanese-owned shipping companies who did not want to transport peoples' bodies on their vessels.[34] The discussions that took place between communities on Cheju and in Ikaino that led to the founding of the cooperative, including debates over how one can mourn as a colonized migrant worker, stand in stark contrast to the treatment of Korean agriculturalists' deaths as a cruel line in a ledger: "Condolences for funeral of sXXjin."

Taki Seihi in Fertilizer's Global Circuits

Radical organizations like Kinyūkai and Zainihon Chōsen Rōdō Sōdōmei established headquarters and branches in locales with significant Korean populations. A close look at the way regionally based organizations brought trade unions, consumers' associations, and hometown associations together to address specific modes of exploitation and expropriation allows us to see their embeddedness in complex webs of relations that could not be easily broken. Examining one such formation in the region that spanned the eastern part of Okayama and western Hyōgo where Taki Seihi was headquartered highlights the need to go beyond city versus country, industry versus agriculture, and colony versus metropole to appreciate how Korean migrant workers created spaces from which their daily struggles for existence could emerge.[35] Struggles against its dehumanizing practices traversed regions, bodies of water, and temporalities.

After founding Taki Seihi in 1885, Taki Kumejirō took advantage of opportunities opened up by the First Sino-Japanese War to build his business. The company acquired a vast tract of land in Kimje, a region in the North Chŏlla province of the Korean peninsula that was widely recognized as one of the most fertile parts of the Honam Plain. While much of its early growth was aided by Kumejirō's close ties to Maeda Masana, one of the central architects of Meiji industrial development, its greatest success came after its expansion to the peninsula.[36] Like other Japanese landowners who made state-subsidized fortunes in Korea, Kumejirō acquired vast holdings of paddy land, forestland and other resource-rich areas by assertively participating in government-sponsored land survey trips, which were preparatory trips for land grabs. The first of Taki Seihi's plantations began operating in November 1917 in Kimje, the site of its colonial headquarters.[37] At its peak, the company held over 15,000 chō of land, which made it the leading private landowner on the peninsula.[38] Their holdings were nowhere near the scale of semigovernmental corporations like Fuji or the Oriental Development Company, but placed it on a different plane from other landowners in the Hyōgo-Okayama region like Nishi Hattori, which owned less than 1,000 chō of land on the peninsula at its peak.[39]

The company's expansion into North Chŏlla took place alongside its efforts to acquire more land in and around its factory in Befu-chō. Anticipating the need for improved transport and production facilities to keep up with territorial expansion in the peninsula, Kumejirō began to purchase land along the southern part of the factory that allowed him to build several piers along the Befu River to facilitate the loading and unloading of goods.[40] By 1911, the company owned most of the coastal areas in Ae village's Furiko, where Kumejirō planned to develop a branch factory to keep up with expanding operations. After numerous setbacks including a petition that residents of Befu-chō submitted to the Ae village assembly in the spring of 1914 that demanded an end to environmentally destructive construction, the branch factory finally opened its doors on May 26, 1931. In the meantime, the company oversaw the construction of a light rail system, including a minecart that connected its main fertilizer factory in Befu-chō to the extensive Sanyō railway system.[41] It also built its own vessels each year to keep up with increasing production. This allowed the company to transport its own cargo to and from Befu port and places like Kobe, Wakamatsu, and Moji.[42]

The two sides of Taki's business—the rice plantation in Kimje and the fertilizer factory in Befu—aided each other. By the late 1930s, its large rice farms employed over 1,000 Korean tenant farmers and its phosphate factories formally employed between 100 and 150 Korean workers and around 270 workers from buraku communities in the northern part of Befu and parts of Okayama and Tottori.[43] Kumejirō's ties to state politicians and his subsequent turn to a political career afforded him the contacts that allowed him to transform his company operations into a borderless interimperial zone in which Korean workers were shuffled around with little consideration of the territorial borders and checkpoints that separated colony from metropole.

Paying attention to the way that the company mobilized its workforce makes clear that its operations not only aided each other but in fact operated without much regard for borders. When the factory struggled to maintain a steady labor force following the expansion of the global fertilizer market after World War I, it lured tenant farmers from its Kimje plantation to Befu with promises of higher pay and a threat that going to Befu-chō was the only path out of the cycle of indebtedness that its company town structure created.[44] Those who took this offer joined men and some women from buraku communities that had family connections to the manager of the main factory, who hailed from the northern part of Okayama.[45] The company's ability to tap into these two racialized labor forces enabled it to keep its operations at full capacity.

Cycling Kimje's tenant farmers through to the Befu factory was not the only way the company took advantage of its ability to bypass stringent border controls within the empire. Factory workers were dispatched from Befu to Kimje to collect rents from Korean tenant farmers each autumn.[46] The company's ability to operate in this manner was a significant advantage given the government's gradual tightening of immigration restrictions on travel between the peninsula and the metropole after the March First movement for Korean liberation.[47] Freedom for the company expanded the sphere of enclosure and increased the intensity of violence endured by its Korean and buraku workers.

Taki's imperial circuit indirectly benefited from the exploitation of Korean agricultural workers like Pak and Min, whose labor power in rural Okayama enabled Japanese small farm households like the Iharas' to transform themselves into fruit cultivators (see chapter 4). A rather unremarkable entry in the ledgers of Ihara Shingo's fellow participant in the Farm Household Survey project, Fukuyama Gisuke (no. 255), alerts us to the role that Taki Seihi played in this process. The Fukuyamas were an owner-cultivating farm household that resided in Shōzaki, a district of Kōyō west of Hikogi, and cultivated rice, barley, and some fruits. They were not well-off but supplemented their household economy with cash income earned by doing a variety of waged work. The farm household earned 150.71 yen in 1938 for doing some weeding at a fruit orchard, packing peaches into bags, working at a canning factory, and working for a hat factory.[48] Their ledgers record a purchase of three bags of Taki Seihi's flagship fertilizer brand, Shikishima (see figure 5.1), for 12 yen—just under 19 percent of their total fertilizer expenses that year and just under 35 percent of their total cash agricultural expenses. The summary notes explain that they uprooted all of their plum trees and planted peach trees in their place, presumably in order to participate more fully in one of Kōyō village's flourishing agricultural industries.

While the Fukuyama farm household was the only one from Okayama prefecture that recorded the brand of fertilizer they used to grow their crops, ledgers of all ten survey participant households from Kōyō village record spending on store-bought fertilizer as a significant part of each household economy. A marker of the region's relative prosperity, this spending pattern also signals their growing dependence on the cash economy. Taki Seihi's records confirm that the company supplied a significant portion of commercial fertilizer produced in its factory in Befu to villages throughout the empire, including Okayama, through a network of credit associations and an extensive retail distribution system.[49]

Life-Worlds of Phosphate

Tracing the production process of one of Shikishima's main ingredients, phosphate, brings to light a far more expansive set of global linkages that sustained company profits. Treating it not as a raw material that went into the production process of Shikishima but (as Silva and Lisa Lowe have argued for "raw materials" generally) as something that had to be violently extracted from the

FIGURE 5.1. An advertisement for Taki Seihi company on the front cover of *Nōka no Tomo* (Farm household's friend), a monthly journal published by Okayama ken Nōkai (no. 428, March 1933). Okayama Prefectural Library.

land connects small-scale fruit cultivation in Hikogi to centuries of histories and geohistories of slavery, Indigenous genocide, colonialism, and resource extraction in places that most Japanese small farmers or Korean agriculturalists would never encounter, except perhaps as deadly battlegrounds.[50]

Demystifying phosphate thus means focusing on its appearance as rock—the material form that millennia of sedimentation took once separated from the land—prior to its final appearance as fine dust packed in bags and loaded onto vessels in order to be combined with other materials to produce Taki Seihi's flagship fertilizer brand. According to Kumejirō's biography, the phosphate rock that the company used in its fertilizers was sourced from the US South, North Africa, and islands in the Pacific and Indian Oceans. This was purchased through several Kobe-based merchant capitalists like Hunter, Gill, Kanematsu, and Jardine Matheson and was transported on vessels owned by Japanese shipping companies like Mitsui Bussan.[51] Taki Seihi's ability to procure the resources it needed to grow into one of the largest producers of superphosphate in the country was dependent on the entire structure of favorable trade terms, currency imperialism, and colonial wage markets that Japanese imperialists created starting in the Meiji period.[52] The company's exploitation of Korean and buraku workers in the factories and fields it directly controlled should therefore be seen as embedded in and constitutive of global processes of wars against Indigenous people, the exploitation of a formerly enslaved Black workforce, the leasing and subleasing of (primarily Black) convict laborers, the employment of indentured Chinese workers, and the destruction of entire ecologies in places deemed sacrificable if it meant securing the life-sustaining commodity, phosphate.[53] The layers of genocide on which Japanese capitalists depended as they pursued its global search for phosphorous, "an essential element for all life forms," becomes evident by tracing phosphate rock's transformation into Shikishima branded fertilizer.[54]

As I lay out the relations within which conflicts with Taki Seihi emerged, it is important to keep in mind Cedric Robinson's insistence in *Black Marxism* that dehumanization should not preclude us from understanding the rich reservoirs of art, culture, language, thought, and knowledge that continued to exist, change form, and shape the worlds made possible by the very same people who were treated as mere inputs of labor (power). His is an important reminder that the inter- and intraimperialist extraction and violence that made the world go round contended at every moment with flight, settlement, return, refusal, or waiting even in places where collective action and living is misrecorded or omitted in state archives.

Zora Neale Hurston and Katerina Teaiwa separately note that the magnitude of the endeavor of transforming phosphate rock into dust did not escape the people involved even as they endured hard manual labor in sweltering heat. In *Dust Tracks on a Road*, Hurston imagined what the workers of Polk County, Florida (the center of Bone Valley), might have encountered as they performed the punishing work of mining phosphate rock:

> Black men laughing and singing. They go down in the phosphate mines and bring up the wet dust of the bones of pre-historic monsters, to make right land in far places, so that people can eat. But, all of it is not dust. Huge ribs, twenty feet from belly to back bone. Some old-time sea monster caught in the shadows in the morning when God said, "Let's make some more dry land. Stay there, great Leviathan! Stay there as a memory and a monument to Time." Shark-teeth as wide as the hand of a working man. Joints of backbone three feet high, bearing witness to the mighty monster of the deep when the Painted Land rose up and did her first dance with the morning sun. Gazing on these relics, forty thousand years old and more, one visualizes the great surrender to chance and change when these creatures were rocked to sleep and slumber by the birth of land.[55]

In Hurston's telling, coming face to face with the "bones of pre-historic monsters" not only interrupted the rhythms of daily exploitation but transported workers to a spatiotemporal realm that exceeded the immediate and seemingly inescapable realities of slavery, capitalism, or the color line.

Peace River Valley, of which Polk County was a part, was decimated in this way by the forced removal of thousands of Seminole people from their lands during the first half of the nineteenth century.[56] Railroads, laid after the conclusion of the Seminole Wars and the Civil War, commenced new wars for mining rights in these lands that, as Zachary Caple notes in his dissertation "Holocene in Fragments: A Critical Landscape Ecology of Phosphorous in Florida," devastated local ecologies to enable the restoration of the South's cotton plantations.[57] Caple notes that the "huge ribs, twenty feet from belly to back bone" that Hurston writes about most likely belonged to the now extinct dugong. Hurston's insistence that "all of it is not dust," despite the destruction that the global drive to preserve the plantation regime wrought on people, lands, and waters, connects Polk County to present-day Okinawa, where activists remain embroiled in a fight to save Okinawa's dugong from extinction due to US military base construction in Oura Bay.[58]

Teaiwa enacts a similar maneuver of reminding readers of the livingness of places targeted as sites of extractive industry in *Consuming Ocean Island: Stories of People and Phosphate from Banaba*. She invokes the work of Pacific studies scholar Epeli Hauʻofa to engage in a reading of Banaba island as landscapes and seascapes—"spaces that are the products of multi-scalar processes in both contemporary and deep, geological time."[59] She proposes this narrative method as a corrective to common depictions of the arrival of phosphate mining to the island in the early twentieth century as a linear process of Indigenous dispossession and resettlement, indentured labor, and environmental degradation. It was all of those things, to be sure, but Teaiwa insists on telling a history of phosphate mining in Banaba that elevates stories of contestation—for example, of women who "clung to the trees in an attempt to prevent them from being destroyed" by the British Phosphate Commission's land surveyors. This was not simply because the women recognized the surveyors as agents of imperialism who were there to install a legal structure that would transform their island into an abstract space subject to international land and sea rights. It was because they understood that the ontological premise of their presence, *te aba*, was under siege.[60] Teaiwa asserts that the fight for *te aba* remains central to the ongoing story of Banaba's colonial conditions.[61]

In each site, the timescales of colonial and racial domination are contested by people who understand that their relations run deeper and are richer than those installed by capital. Bones, ancestors, and memories do not capitulate easily. These texts provide me with rich material to rethink and reframe labor disputes that erupted against Taki Seihi within the Japanese empire as anticolonial, anti-imperialist struggles resonant with the kinds of refusal that people in Banaba and Florida expressed in response to domination. I turn next to life-affirming struggles against the world-destroying properties of phosphate that workers waged from the early 1930s in Befu-chō, the location of Taki Seihi's main fertilizer factory and company headquarters.

The Taki Seihi Strike

Banshū Gōdō Rōdō Kumiai (Banshū Amalgamated Labor Union) a labor union affiliated with Nihon Rōdō Kumiai Dōmei (Federation of Japanese Labor Unions), took the lead in fighting against Taki Seihi from its formation in the summer of 1929.[62] Its aim was to unify various trades under a single umbrella in Banshū, a region that encompassed parts of northeast Okayama, western Hyōgo (including Befu-chō), and southwest Tottori, which had become an important site for heavy chemical industries. The union issued a report titled "The Fight to Defeat Taki Seihi after the Death of a Korean Worker" that narrated the company's treatment of its Korean workers.[63] This eleven-page handwritten report was dated October 20–21, 1931, and was penned on the letterhead of the union's predecessor organization, Takasago Seishi Rōdō Kumiai, a labor union representing paper factory workers in the area. As its title suggests, the report traced the relationship between the workplace death of a Korean worker named Paek Pong-un and the formation of a branch union by factory workers demanding better conditions.

The report opens with a discussion of what brought Paek to Taki Seihi's Befu factory in the first place: "The company also owns a vast area of plains in Korea's mountainous regions that they are making our Korean comrades cultivate. They have built vast wealth that way and are presently the leading capitalist in the Banshū region."[64] It explains the company's interimperial reach—those who could not make a living on Taki-owned farms in Kimje were employed by Taki Seihi, where they became subject to a different form of exploitation in the factory. It moves quickly to an explanation of the circumstances following Paek's death on October 8 after he was electrocuted by a high-voltage line of 220 volts at the factory's power plant. The report's central aim was to explain how his coworkers had mobilized to pressure the company to take responsibility for his death, which meant paying surviving family members compensation commensurate with the company's crime of violating workplace safety protocols. It described how coworkers began to mobilize after the company announced his cause of death as a heart attack. They commissioned an independent autopsy, which confirmed what they already knew: the company was lying about how he died. They were further incensed by the company's insulting offer to pay 500 yen to his surviving family members as a condolence payment and to cover 50 yen for funeral costs in exchange for their agreement to return to Korea.[65] A Taki Seihi branch of the Banshū Gōdō Rōdō Kumiai was organized soon thereafter, with over three hundred of five hundred total workers joining the union.

How do we understand the intensity of the mobilization and protest that took place between October 8 and the pamphlet's publication on October 20, which included a demonstration by one hundred of Paek's Korean coworkers in front of president Taki Kumejirō's mansion in Befu-chō on the evening of the October 17? What made workers follow through in a public show of defiance in a city where they were outnumbered by Japanese residents against a company that held a dominant economic and political presence there? When they staged a large rally in town on the nineteenth, why did they march from factory to city and back to the factory again? What were they trying to communicate through that action, which drew a large police escort, and to whom?

The strike that commenced in December helps us better understand what drove them to action, but the papers reveal that trouble had been brewing for months.

An article published on August 27, 1931, in the newspaper *Shakai Undō Tsūshin* explains that workers at Taki Seihi had been battling wage cuts, layoffs, and furloughs since at least July.[66] As part of a project of reorganization that began months after the company opened its branch factory (just east of the main factory) in May, the company laid off more than ten Korean workers and presented a plan where two hundred more would face wage cuts in a matter of weeks. Tensions between the two sides escalated as Zennō Rōdō Taishūtō (All Japan Labor–Farmer Mass Party), a party that had just formed in July 1931 out of a union of three proletarian parties, began organizing the factory and staged rallies in nearby Takasago-chō to object to the cuts. All of this activity had taken place the summer before Paek's death. Following unsatisfying negotiations between workers and the company at the end of November and rumors that the company was not going to renew its workers' expiring five-year contracts, the union braced itself for a direct confrontation. As they anticipated, on December 16, two months after Paek's death, the company announced its intent to fire three Japanese and sixteen Korean workers. It also stated that it would not be renewing the contracts of fourteen other (Japanese) workers. Included in this group of thirty-three who were slated to lose their jobs at the end of 1931 were several leaders of the newly formed union.[67]

According to Kobayashi Sueo's interview with some of the strike leaders and participants, there was no question that they would go on strike after the firings. Workers endured, in addition to wage cuts and firings, brutalizing production processes. While Paek's death drew attention to the dangers of working at a factory that cut corners on safety, fertilizer production was deadly by its very nature. Shikishima was a composite of sulfuric acid, superphosphate, bone meal, and bean cake. But *composite* is a misleading term that obfuscates the work required to transform each of these components into fertilizer: workers steamed the bones and carcasses of animals, crushed and ground what came out of the steamer, baked and sprayed iron pyrite to produce sulfuric acid, and mixed sulfuric acid with phosphate in order to make superphosphate.[68] The resulting mixture had to be strained, packed into straw bags, and prepared for transport. Kobayashi's interviewees recalled the stench that came out of the steamer, the white and black powder that got everywhere after the pyrite went into the furnace, and the pain they endured—especially in the winters—because their cracked skin was permanently inflamed from sweat, dust, and the cold. They explained that they would try to wash the dust off their bodies by going to the communal bath on company grounds, but the water would be too muddy to provide any respite if they arrived too late.[69] One person said that it was difficult to differentiate work from life because the twelve-hour workdays sapped all of their energy. Another told Koyabashi that he would stare at his wounded and inflamed body and wonder, "Is this what a human being is supposed to look like?" The toxic dust that stuck to their bodies, their lungs, and their living quarters connected these workers' experiences in Befu to what Black and convict workers in Bone Valley and Indigenous and Pacific Islander workers on Banaba endured as they produced a product that was celebrated as the life-giving miracle that could cure the world's hunger.

On the evening of December 16, just hours after being told that the company intended to commence layoffs, factory branch union leaders formed a strike committee. They established a command center in the company barracks, relayed the news to the headquarters of Takasago Befu Shōhi Kumiai (a consumers' association located just across the river at a paper factory, Mitsubishi Seishi), and welcomed organizers from the central union, who rushed over to provide support.[70] That this association, formed in February 1928 as a wing of the Zenrō-affiliated Takasago Seishi Rōdō Kumiai Kōyūkai, served as the headquarters of the struggle gives us insight into its organizers' understanding of the specific needs of a strike that involved Korean and buraku workers. While Takasago Befu Shōhi Kumiai made unequivocally clear in its declarations and resolutions that it was operating as part of a revolutionary workers' struggle against capitalist exploitation, its immediate provisioning of striking workers with three *koku* of white rice[71] at the outset reflected their understanding of the challenges that a Korean and buraku workforce would face while engaging in this kind of action in an area dominated by a formidable enemy. They knew that workers would not have an easy time procuring food supplies on their own, as the company controlled most matters of reproduction, including transportation networks and fields. Nearby stores would be unwilling to provide them with goods in advance because they knew that wages would not be paid until the strike was settled.[72] To counter the company's tactic of starving strikers out by establishing a police cordon around their living quarters, the union arranged for supplies and donations from workers in other company barracks nearby, including Kanegafuchi and Arai.[73] Their distribution circuit of rice, barley, and monetary donations from other company barracks, unions and sympathetic businesses in the area was no match for Taki Seihi's monopoly of resources and force in Befu-chō, but it did allow the committee in charge of providing sustenance for strikers to do its work without having to worry about running out of supplies.

Buoyed by the support provided by other unions and workers who flocked to Befu-chō, the bargaining team presented a final list of sixteen demands to the company that rejected the latter's characterization of buraku and Korean workers as fungible bodies whose ability to reproduce their lives was not the company's responsibility. This is echoed in the union's diary of events, a flyer titled "Taki Hiryō Tōsō News no. 1" (Taki fertilizer struggle news no. 1), which asked how the president expected fired workers to take care of their children. It reiterated one of their central demands—equal pay for Japanese and Korean workers for identical work.[74]

Insistence on pay equality was a rarity at the time, but historian Horiuchi Minoru explains that this was a hallmark of worker organizing in the region. Banshū Gōdō Rōdō Kumiai, which was initially formed to organize Korean textile workers who had endured layoffs, discriminatory wages, and poor living conditions in the region's chemical factories, had a large Korean membership. It established Korean committees in some branches.[75] This was replicated in the Taki Seihi branch's strike command center at the Nishishin Shataku, one of the four company barracks. A Korean worker, Pak Pok-tong, who served as the vice-chair of the entire leadership, was on the strike committee and the negotiating committee. In addition to Pak, two additional Korean strike division leaders, Ham Kil-lam and Ch'oe Gi-yŏl were tasked with organizing Korean workers who lived in company housing.[76]

Once the matter of leadership was sorted out, organizers spent the rest of the evening of the sixteenth communicating their strike call to union members and nonunionized workers who resided in the company barracks. Multiple sources report that despite the company's efforts to break it, most workers honored the strike that commenced the following morning.[77] It continued until the morning of the twenty-third, when police forcibly entered the former strike command center and barracks, Nishishin Shataku, and arrested over two hundred people whom they had surrounded and trapped inside by encircling the perimeter with gasoline. The intentions of the police, in cooperation with the local firefighter brigade, youth vigilante groups, and private security forces hired by the company, were to cut off the command center's communications with the outside world and to starve its residents. They also blocked access to medical care. By cutting off the strikers' ability to communicate with the public or their comrades who had traveled to Befu-chō to show their support, the company attempted to break the strike and monopolize how it would be remembered.[78]

Shataku as Sanctuary and Battleground

Though the actions of the entities the company assembled to break the strike made workers and residents sitting ducks in the company barracks, firsthand accounts make it clear that the strike headquarters at Nishishin Shataku was a nurturing place that workers, their families, and union leaders transformed in order to sustain their fight. Even after a new strike command center off company grounds was established at a nearby shipyard on the eighteenth, the barracks continued to function as a key site of recruitment, sustenance, care, and retreat.

Testimonies and accounts in *Shakai Undō Tsūshin* confirm that Korean women took a central role in the work of providing sustenance for the strike. While the census left little room for Korean women's work, in particular unpaid and domestic work, to be counted as such, the report on Paek's death anf interviews conducted by Kim Ri-hyang reveal that the wives of Korean men were regularly employed on the company's vast grounds, at the company president Taki Kumejirō's mansion as gardeners and farmers, and in the fields that the Taki family owned throughout Befu.[79] They may have been "without employment" according to the census, but the labor they performed was indispensable to the company's ability to maintain poor working conditions in the factories and plantations they owned. When the strike began, Korean women were well situated to understand the important though underappreciated position they occupied as workers for Taki Seihi. Those who took on the role of keeping the company barracks going during the strike rejected their poor treatment by a company that had to rely on new and more intense forms of expropriation, erasure, and exploitation to overcome the impact that the post-Depression-era decline of the global phosphate industry had on their profit margins.

Interviews and strike records show that Korean and non-Korean women from buraku communities performed the essential tasks of social reproduction that maintained life in the company barracks turned strike command center.[80] They fed everyone—a task that involved not only cooking but also procuring supplies, cleaning up, and looking after the children. Everyday domestic tasks multiplied as they prepared enough food for hundreds of strikers and their families. What stories were shared during the hours of work that continued well into the night? What was the common language of women who spoke Korean and women who spoke Japanese? How did they entertain each other, comfort each other, and ease the tensions that surely arose during those six long days and nights? What did their children hear and remember long after their homes were trampled by police and vigilante groups and their fathers were arrested?

Perhaps the children remembered their own participation in the strike. According to *Sōgi Nippō*, the strike's daily digest, Japanese and Korean schoolchildren declared solidarity with their striking parents and started a school strike on the twentieth. They refused to take part in an educational environment that, they argued, sided with the company and landlords.[81] The December 24 edition of *Shakai Undō Tsūshin*, referenced by Kobayashi, reported that around 130 students gathered at the strike command center to learn "The Internationale" instead of attending their normal classes. An enthusiastic group of 50–60 then marched to the front of the factory gates with red flags over their shoulders.[82] These children, who essentially formed their own *pioneer*, a revolutionary organization that came under the supervision of Suiheisha, were difficult for the police to deal with as they were not old enough to be arrested and taken in for questioning but threatened the legitimacy of colonial education by rejecting the promise and premise of uplift through assimilation offered by schooling.[83] This was also a direct attack on Kumejirō, whose hefty donation had funded the school buildings.[84] Students took a hammer to the public school code in Befu-chō by calling out the role that compulsory education played in facilitating the imperial project and in justifying the exploitative conditions their family members and comrades endured.[85]

In their reporting, mainstream newspapers were not interested in exploring the motivations behind the school strike or the workers' strike at the factory. Rather, they were invested in narrative closure. Three major dailies in the region, *Osaka Asahi*, *Kobe Yūshin Nippō*, and *Kobe Shimbun*, each published stories and printed photographs that focused on the end of the strike on December 23. Images of debris, broken homes, workers being rounded up en masse on trucks in front of the barracks, and, perhaps most dramatically, Korean women crying as they watched their family members, acquaintances, and comrades arrested transmitted only the unhinged sentiments of defeated strikers and the misguided tactics of a labor union that, readers were told, had resorted to violence that led to the tragic death of two of their own. Such descriptions fostered a sense of difference, not solidarity, with the Korean strikers in particular.[86]

The photographs and interviews that Kim Ri-hyang provides of life in the company barracks pierce these shallow accounts.[87] They suggest that company barracks, sites intended for confinement, transformed into school, communal kitchen, and medical facility in late December 1931 and became a place where dreams of what Kristin Ross, writing about the Paris Communards, called communal luxury were shared, sustained, and conjured.[88] In contrast to sensationalist photographs that showed Korean women screaming and crying during their husbands' arrests, or headlines that intimated that the violent acts of riotous Korean and buraku women had led to fellow strikers' deaths and injuries, photographs that Kim includes in her study enable us to rethink accounts of the strike that characterized women as bystanders. Her rich ethnographic study includes photographs that show a completely different side to life in the barracks and interviews that reveal that the relationships formed in the barracks that endured and were renewed through new forms of struggle that continued into the 1970s.[89] Images of everyday life remind the viewer that, as much as the barracks were intended by the company to be sites of confinement, they were also spaces where people raised children, celebrated marriages, mourned deaths, ate and drank in communion, dreamt of different worlds, and at times plotted their escape.

Not all of these activities were performed collectively but many could not be achieved in isolation. It was these spaces, these everyday rhythms and relations, that the leadership of the labor union drew on and promised to improve as it formulated demands in the language of workers' struggle. Dreams embedded in their demands for better wages, heftier severance packages, medical care for workers' families, and safer working conditions, all spurred by the memory of their fallen coworker, made openings for connections that went far beyond the boundaries of the company barracks, the factory floor, or the heteropatriarchal household (see figures 5.2 and 5.3).[90] Solidarity, while its demonstration was constrained by the heavy police presence that restricted movement in Befu-chō during the strike, is evident in the donations of money, food, and messages of encouragement that flowed in from the company barracks of neighboring facilities from the moment the strike was called.

Conclusion: Struggles across the Sea

On December 28, 1931, less than a week after the Takasago police conducted their mass roundup of the striking workers, the Korean-language paper *Maeil Shinbō* reported that over forty tenant farmers at Taki Seihi's Kimje plantation in North Chŏlla province had signed a petition objecting to the farm's recent increase in fertilizer fees. They demanded that the company return to them a portion of the fertilizer fees that they had been overcharged for.[91] The actual number of signatories is unclear, as the same paper reported three days later that around seventy people were now involved in the dispute.[92] The matter was settled through mediation by the head of the township (*myŏng*) and the middlemen (*marŭm*).[93] The agreement that was reached stipulated that the company would distribute millet purchased from Manchuria as compensation for the increase in fertilizer expenses, which would stand.[94] In addition, Taki Seihi agreed to grant

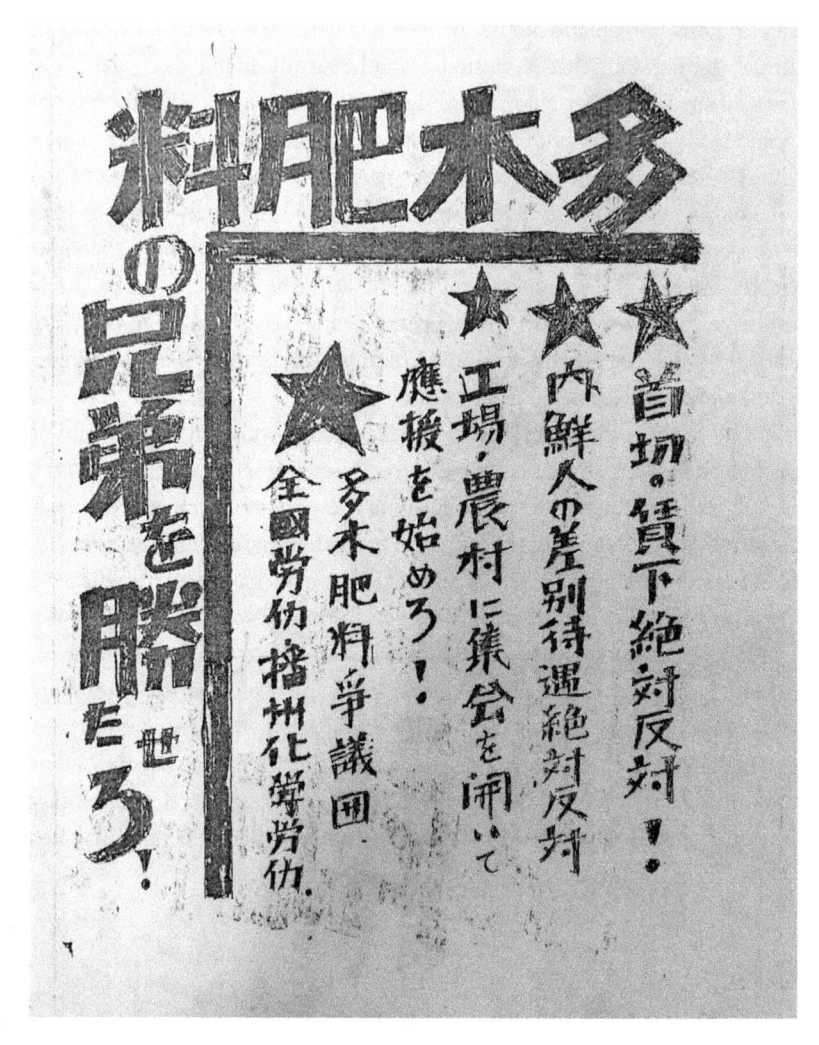

FIGURE 5.2. Flyer by the Taki Seihi strike committee that includes two of their main demands (absolute opposition to firings and pay cuts and absolute opposition to the discriminatory treatment of Koreans) and a call to comrades to start holding assemblies in factories and in agrarian villages in solidarity (December 1931). Courtesy of the Ōhara Institute for Social Research, Hōsei University.

救援米袋

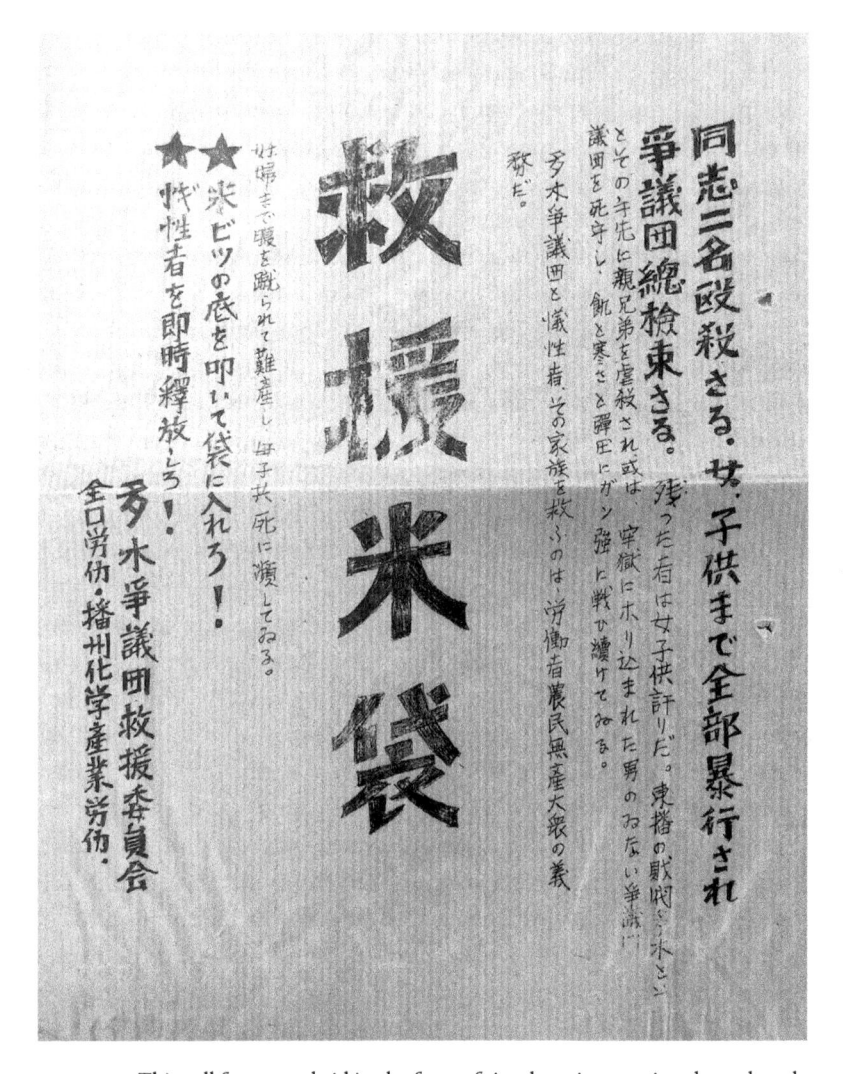

同志二名殴殺さる。女、子供まで全部暴行され争議団総検束さる。

残った者は女子供許りだ。使播の戦闘をやる水と米とその手先に親兄弟を虐殺され或は牢獄にホリ込まれた男のゐない争議団を死守し、飢と寒さと弾圧にガン強く戦ひ續けてゐる。

多木争議団と犠牲者、その家族を救ふのは労働者農民無産大衆の義務だ。

妊婦まで腹を蹴られて難産し、母子共死に瀕してゐる。

★ 米ビツの底を叩いて袋に入れろ！
★★ 犠牲者を即時釈放しろ！

多木争議団救援委員会
全口労働・播州化学産業労働・

FIGURE 5.3. This call for mutual aid in the form of rice donations—printed on a bag that can be filled with rice—was circulated after the arrest of strikers at Taki Seihi factory. It offers an account of what transpired: "Two comrades beaten to death. All, including women and children, have been assaulted and masses of strikers are in jail. Only women and children remain. The East Banshū zaibatsu Taki and its pawns have killed their parents and siblings or have hurled them into jail. The strikers, who no longer include men, are defending to the death and are continuing to valiantly fight hunger, cold, and repression. It is the obligation of workers, farmers, and the proletarian masses to save the Taki strikers, those sacrificed, and their families." It continues, "Those with child have suffered difficult births having their stomachs kicked, and mother and child are on the verge of death. Tap the bottoms of your rice bins and put it in the bag! All victims must be released immediately!" Courtesy of the Ōhara Institute for Social Research, Hōsei University.

tenants the opportunity to earn supplementary cash income by working on construction projects for Chinbong township, where Kimje was located.[95]

A Japanese-language paper published in Korea, *Kunsan Nippō*, provided its take on the start of the dispute.[96] It explained that the standoff had actually begun on December 19, 1931. Though the paper did not mention it, this was just one day after the start of the Taki Seihi strike in Befu. It took place in Kosa-ri, the same neighborhood in Kimje, the hometown of Ch'oe Gi-yŏl, who was prosecuted for the role he played as the leader of the third subunit of the factory strike committee.[97] The paper's reporting was spurred by the revival of the dispute following a meeting on January 10, 1932, between tenant farmer representatives, the middlemen, and the company to finalize the settlement. Problems emerged when the company proposed a tiered system of millet distribution rather than the promised equal distribution to all tenant farmer households. The tenant farmers' rejection of the company's attempt to institute a hierarchical payment system signaled their refusal to acquiesce to the company's divide-and-conquer labor management tactics.

While subsequent reporting stated that a harmonious resolution was arrived at in late January, attributed in large part to Kumejirō's generosity, arson reported in *Maeil Shinbō* on February 6, 1932, suggests that the claim of a satisfactory negotiation was a product of wishful thinking.[98] An article published in the January 20, 1932 edition of *Kunsan Nippō* reported that thirty tenant farmers were arrested on January 17 following a mobilization of over 1,700 people to the company office to demand a face-to-face meeting with a factory manager with the surname Yamada. After being told that he was not there, they headed to the township office, where some glass windows were broken.[99] The Kimje police made thirty arrests that day. Arrestees were charged on the twenty-second with rioting and obstructing business operations.[100] Eleven were prosecuted and their names were plastered in the papers. Beyond the revelation that workers were being charged with and sentenced for arson, the papers provide little detail about the motivations of the arrestees or of the 1,700 people who gathered at the Taki Seihi office that day. It is not possible to say with certainty that these conflicts had any connection to the Befu-chō strike.

Only the January 13, 1932, issue of *Shakai Undō Tsūshin* mentions the Taki Seihi factory strike and the tenant farmers' dispute against Taki Nōjō in the same breath.[101] Still, the parallel timelines of the two events, along with the frequency with which workers traveled to and from factory and farm, make it difficult to rule out a connection. Workers maintained familial and other networks through which they shared information and grievances about what was taking place in their respective places of employment. Stories of Paek's death in October 1931 and the ongoing threats of layoffs and furloughs would have reached Kimje through the factory workers who were dispatched each autumn to assist with the collection of rents and loans. While the tenant farmer dispute in Kimje has not occupied a central place in the history of tenant farmer struggles in colonial Korea because of its size and purported lack of ties to the red farmers' unions in the north, we should take it seriously for the possibility that it raises about the formation of a counterimperial circuit of knowledge, information, and solidarity that Taki Seihi's cruelty in both sites spurred.

Two and a half years after the Taki Seihi strike committee, Zenkoku Rōdō Sōdōmei and the Taki branch of Banshū Kagaku Sangyō Rōdō Kumiai announced on January 11, 1932, that they had reached a settlement with the company, and less than a year after seven men were sentenced to twenty-nine days of detention for inciting a riot at the Kimje plantation, *Osaka Asahi Shimbun* published the short article about Kim and Matsue fleeing Befu-chō to Himeji that opens this chapter. They may, in fact, have been comrades in the struggles that erupted across Taki Seihi's imperial circuit two years prior. Even if this were a love story that defied all odds, it can only be understood in the context of this terrain, where workers from Korean and buraku communities, union members from nearby factories, and student strikers transformed company barracks into a space where communal luxury was enacted and imagined. Their collective struggles in the winter of 1931–32 transformed what was imaginable—and therefore possible—in Befu-chō, Kimje, and beyond.

Placing these struggles that Korean and buraku people organized against Taki Seihi in Befu and Kimje alongside the stories of community formation predicated not on settlement but on the necessity of flight that Zainichi Korean studies scholars introduced as an integral part of their scholarly practice, and, finally, thinking about how we might tie our understandings of these life-sustaining activities within the Japanese empire to similar dynamics at other sites along phosphate's global circuit both highlight the refusals that emerged from within deeply entrenched global histories of domination. Racialized workers refused to be discarded because they were "useless and therefore expendable"—a designation that enabled the company to enact deadly working conditions in a factory that produced a life-sustaining commodity for the nation's small farmers.[102]

CHAPTER SIX EMPIRE THROUGH

THE PRISM OF PHOSPHATE

In total, 341 workers from different parts of Okinawa made the long trip to Banaba aboard Mitsui Bussan ships between 1908 and 1910. They did so in response to four separate recruitments starting three years after 62 Japanese workers, mainly from Osaka, first arrived on the island on three-year contracts.[1] They joined over a thousand other workers from Gilbert and Ellice and mined phosphate rock for the Pacific Phosphate Company (PPC), a multinational corporation that was formed in 1902 to manage all phosphate production on the island and Nauru.[2]

Less than two decades after the First Sino-Japanese war, which dashed the last hopes of a faction of former Ryūkyū Kingdom elites that Qing forces might come to free them from Meiji rule, farmers-turned-miners from Okinawa set to work on contracts that promised generous pay, good working conditions, and a chance to turn their fortunes around. For Mitsui Bussan, a trading company that, by then, had decades of experience filling its coffers by establishing monopolies in colonial spaces, Banaba was yet another site where it could hoard riches. They did so as a monopoly, performing the roles of merchant, shipper, and distributor of phosphate for companies like Taki Seihi that desperately needed steady sources of raw material for the manufacture of fertilizer that enabled people like Ihara Toyokichi of Kōyō village to build his jeweled mountain of fruit, seemingly all by himself under the moonlight.[3]

By going to Banaba, workers from Okinawa entered a world of phosphate that was transformed by settler colonialism, finance capital, and refusals of these structures and institutions by Indigenous people and other racialized workers. These imperialist circuits connected Florida, Algeria, Nauru, and other places that Euro-American powers eagerly colonized to feed the masses of workers for industry in their metropoles.[4] As Quito Swan argues in "Blinded by Bandung," it was not hard for white supremacist dreams of defeated US Confederates to merge with the aspirations of British colonialists and take new forms in the mid-nineteenth-century Pacific. Of the deeply rooted character of the racism that allowed white settlers to turn quickly to blackbirding once chattel slavery was outlawed, Swan explains, "The European racial imaginary defined Oceania in reference to Africa and the indigenous Americas. In 1545, Spanish explorer Yñigo Ortiz de Retez reached Papua and called it *Nueva Guinea*, as he felt that the people resembled those of Africa's Guinea coast."[5] We see here the link between slavery and colonial violence that Wynter conceptualizes as the *pieza* take a distinct shape in the Pacific Islands. Decades before Taki Seihi's growth into a company capable of operating with little regard for intra-imperial borders, phosphate helped open the door to the Japanese empire's enthusiastic participation in these scripts that reserved the label of work for an exclusive group of people who had proven themselves worthy of a place within the civilizational order of modernity.

Banaba, known to European powers as Ocean Island and commonly referred to in Japanese-language documents as Taiyōtō, was one site from which Japanese workers extracted high-grade phosphate rock in order to ship it to fertilizer factories.[6] As Katerina Teaiwa traces in *Consuming Ocean Island*, the development of the highly profitable industry in Banaba destroyed relations that Indigenous people had with each other, their lands, and their waters. It necessitated Banabans' eventual resettlement to Rabi in the Fiji islands, 1,600 miles away.[7] While Japanese involvement in these extractive processes in the early twentieth century appears only as minor episodes in studies of phosphate frontiers, the dreams of Japanese fertilizer companies like Taki Seihi to enrich themselves by exploiting the labors and lands of colonized, racialized peoples within the empire were realized through their merging with the imperialist strivings of Euro-American phosphateers in the Pacific, the United States, and North Africa.

In *Decolonisation and the Pacific*, Tracey Banivanua Mar traces how Indigenous people like her great-aunt Bubu Taka became imbricated in and at times refused a global system that dispossessed them and "systematically recast [them] as 'natives.'"[8] She describes the condition that settler industrialists reconciled as they operated in a cultural-political milieu that outlawed slavery and celebrated Indigenous dispossession: "As land was acquired, however dubiously, the resulting hunger for labour to work it was intense."[9] As "natives" who were recruited from neighboring Pacific islands to satisfy this hunger encountered each other, white settlers grew anxious about the possibility of revolt. Banivanua Mar traces the way that *kanaka* morphed into a term that colonial administrators and industrialists used to refer to Pacific Islanders following the Kanak revolt of 1878. Colonial shorthand for the rebellious Pacific Islander, this word expressed a variety of white fears that lay beneath Spanish explorer Yñigo Ortiz de Retez's linking of Oceania to Africa centuries prior. Once it entered the imperialist lexicon, *kanaka* became a marker of a shared racial imaginary that guided the way that all colonial powers formulated labor policies in extractive industries.[10]

This was the world that Okinawan phosphate workers who first arrived in Banaba in 1908 entered. They were recruited to fill PPC's demand for workers from Asia, thought to be more docile and hardworking than Banabans and workers from nearby islands. Works that the Foreign Ministry (and others) published in the late Meiji era about conditions that Japanese migrant workers faced in the Pacific reveal that Japanese immigration officials believed in the white supremacist fears of Indigenous peoples' revolt that led them to label Pacific Islander peoples *kanaka*. The only difference was that they translated the grammar within which the word's meaning was embedded into Japanese supremacist tropes that justified imperialist expansion.

An example of this cunning work of translation can be read in a report on the conditions of Banaba authored by Kobayashi Kenichirō, a Foreign Ministry official, that was published in the first volume of *Imin Chōsa Hōkoku* (Survey of immigration, 1908). Kobayashi interchangeably used the terms *native* and *kanaka* to refer to Indigenous people and Pacific Islander workers from Gilbert and Ellice that the PPC employed to extract and transport phosphate to waiting vessels. He differentiated Japanese workers from these groups while acknowledging that the latter were hired to perform the same or comparable work. His task in the report was twofold: first, to confirm to his readers that the four hundred Japanese workers who were already in Banaba had superior work abilities compared to the "natives" with whom they had to get along in order to keep the peace, and second, to remind them that they were there to convince "natives" and "kanaka" of Japan's legitimacy as a colonial power through their competence and hard work.[11] Kobayashi does not distinguish Japanese from Okinawan workers in any meaningful way.

Kobayashi's anti-Indigeneity, evident in his assumption that Japanese workers were superior to workers from Gilbert and Ellice, reaches a climax in the conclusion of part 6 of the report, titled "The Conditions of Pacific Phosphate Company." He matter-of-factly states that, given the current pace of production, "in the next seventy years or so, the mining of phosphate rock on the island will be completed."[12] A clearer expression of the Japanese government's intent to participate in the absolute, uncurbed depletion of mineral resources of an island just three years after the first Japanese workers set foot there is rarely seen.[13] Kobayashi's need to convince "natives" that Japan was a viable colonial power makes sense in this context. Once resources were depleted in Banaba, they could engage in extraction somewhere else in the Pacific, presumably under Japanese leadership.

Where did workers recruited to Banaba from Okinawa, itself a Japanese colony, fit into this relatively new world of absolute resource depletion in the Pacific? First, the Japanese government's empire-building activities in East Asia, including its strategic alliances with European powers, placed Okinawan workers in a position of relative privilege in Banaba. As Japanese, they, along with European workers, enjoyed prices that were approximately half of what PPC charged to "Kanakas, Banabans, and Coolies" at the company store.[14]

The underpinnings of the structural advantages that Okinawan workers enjoyed in these extractive colonies as Japanese are undeniable in New Caledonia, where they toiled in the nickel mining industry alongside Indigenous Kanak communities, convict workers from the French empire, and North African, Vietnamese, Chinese, Indian, and Javanese indentured workers.[15] There, Japanese and European workers were the only ones not subject to the Code de l'Indigénat, which the French applied to New Caledonia in 1887. The code, which, according to Muriam Davis, was enacted in Algeria (along with French colonies in Southeast Asia) to legally designate Algerian Muslims as "natives" in ways that "shaped discriminatory patterns of access to life, livelihood, and property" in the colony, was extended to West Africa in ways that gave colonial authorities almost unlimited policing, surveilling, and jailing powers over African people under French rule.[16] The year it was implemented in New Caledonia,

1887, was the same year it was extended to Senegal. As Banivanua Mar explains, in New Caledonia, it created "a permanent state of exception for Indigenous Kanaks, legally defined by the French as Canaques, governing them as subjects rather than citizens."[17] She clarifies its function as a tool to suppress resistance, enable Indigenous dispossession, and reinforce French domination outside of the Pacific by shaping new heteropatriarchal norms through immigration and labor practices that denied workers from Asian colonies and neighboring islands the right of familial accompaniment.[18] As Indigenous Kanaks resisted French rule and work in the nickel mines, colonial administrators had to aggressively deploy empire-wide codes to procure the necessary workforce from their other colonies and beyond to keep extraction going.

This context is important for understanding the significance of the exemption of Japanese workers (including those from Okinawa) from the code and from other laws that used immigration policy to maintain colonial domination in the Pacific. Legally, migrant workers from Okinawa were placed in a fundamentally different position compared to that of other mine workers from Asia because their exemption from the code afforded them relative freedom of movement and settlement.[19] In New Caledonia, their relatively privileged status obtained until 1919, when the French government prohibited new Japanese immigration to the island due to concerns about their rapidly growing numbers.[20]

The privileges enjoyed by Okinawans, classified as Japanese migrant workers in the Pacific, and their labeling as pioneers should not, however, be taken to mean that their colonial status disappeared once they left their hometowns. Labor contracts and recruitment strategies negotiated between the PPC and Mitsui Bussan under the watchful eye of the Ministry of Foreign Affairs reveal that immigration policies facilitated and effaced colonial violence. Take, for example, a letter that Mitsui Bussan's representative Ohno Ichitarō sent to the immigration agency responsible for the recruitment of workers to Banaba, Nippon Shokumin Gōshi Kaisha, titled "New Order for 150 Riukiu Labourers."[21] The letter, dated March 31, 1908, requested an additional 150 workers be supplied by mid-May. While an order this explicit for unskilled workers from Okinawa (or any region) only appears once in the ministry's files on Banaba during this period, it reveals the existence of a working distinction between miners from Okinawa, who were referred to as either "ordinary workers" or "coolies," and Japanese who were also employed in those categories but who were also in demand as "skilled laborers." Workers in the latter category, whose titles included engineer, technician, boatman, doctor, and cook, were paid slightly more than their "ordinary worker" counterparts and enjoyed favorable working conditions.[22] Not a single person from Okinawa was recruited to work in these skilled positions.

Recruitment thus created a segregated Japanese workforce inside of an already hierarchized workforce in Banaba. While this may seem relatively unimportant since all workers classified as Japanese were recruited as a wedge between white managers, Pacific Islander workers, and Indigenous Banaban communities, it shows that Okinawa's colonial status remained intact even as workers enjoyed relative privilege as Japanese nationals. The segregation that phosphate workers from Okinawa endured enabled the PPC to rachet up its exploitation of all "ordinary workers," Japanese or not, through industrial rationalization.

Japanese technicians, recruited as skilled workers to implement rationalization policies, made changes to the production process that allowed the PPC to drive down wages. The culmination of this process is seen in an order from January 12, 1912, that the company placed to Mitsui Bussan titled "Japanese Labourers—Ocean Island." The order communicated the company's interest in hiring replacements for fifty workers who had decided to return to Japan at the end of their contracts, but only if Mitsui Bussan agreed to an across-the-board reduction in wages for all new recruits.[23] It justified a substantial decrease in the piece rate it proposed paying to workers for mined rock by explaining that the newly installed cableways to transport phosphate rock to the railways made the current wage unreasonably high, "as they have not to wheel the phosphate at all."[24]

The PPC's wage policy was also motivated by changes to the wage rate in other parts of the Pacific. Nippon Shokumin Gōshi Kaisha had appealed to the International Trade Section of the Ministry of Foreign Affairs on August 23, 1910, asking that its head, Hagiwara Moriichi, reject a request submitted by their rival, Tōyō Imin Gōshi Kaisha, to recruit contract workers for a phosphate company in Tahiti.[25] The company explained that, if approved, the low wages offered to Japanese workers in Tahiti would drive down wages for workers in Banaba. Compagnie Française des Phosphates de l'Océanie (CFPO), which controlled phosphate mining on Tahiti, and PPC were different companies on the surface, they explained, but their leadership was closely aligned.[26] They warned Hagiwara that if his office were to approve Tōyō Imin Gōshi Kaisha's request, phosphate workers in Banaba, who had already endured a major wage cut from one shilling two pence to one shilling per ton of extracted phosphate rock would face an even larger pay cut. The aforementioned 1912 PPC order to Mitsui Bussan that offered nine pence per ton to new "ordinary workers" confirms the materialization of this warning.[27]

The rates under discussion were still considerably higher than those paid to Pacific Islanders for the same work. According to *Survey of Immigration*, the latter were paid a salary of one pound twelve shillings per month—a far cry from the approximately five pounds that their Japanese, including Okinawan, counterparts were paid when all conversions were made.[28] By recruiting Okinawans as manual laborers in the mines of Banaba, where they enjoyed significant advantages in pay and treatment compared to their Pacific Islander counterparts, the state and recruitment agencies transformed them into accomplices to the dispossession of Banabans and exploitation of other Pacific Islanders. Unless we correctly label Okinawans as colonial subjects of the Japanese empire, we miss the way that Indigenous dispossession in one part of the empire facilitated the dispossession of other Indigenous people within and outside of its borders, as well as ever-intensifying cycles of exploitation. A historical narrative that separates what should be connected obscures present and future bases of accountability and solidarity.

Immigration to the Phosphate Frontier

On July 5, 1908, the newspaper *Ryūkyū Shimpō* published an article titled "Nanyō no Sangotō" (Coral island of the South Seas) that describes Mitsui Bussan's partnership with Nippon Shokumin Gōshi Kaisha to negotiate two-year contracts with people from Okinawa to work in Banaba. Only men were being recruited, it explained, because it would be inappropriate for women to go where Indigenous people also employed by the PPC "were naked all the time."[29] While these insinuations of barbarism had been directed at Okinawans as recently as their display in the "Human Race Hall" (Jinruikan) at the 1903 Osaka Expo, the company had no qualms about turning Okinawan women into targets of protection when it came to emigration to Banaba. A reprint of an interview that *Hōchi Shimbun* did with Kobayashi Kenichirō of the Foreign Ministry, this piece repeats the racist tropes that European settlers deployed when they called for the recruitment of workers from Asia to supplement the "native" and Pacific Islander workforce. The 1916 recall of Okinawan women who had tattoos on their hands from the Philippines for fear that this "savage" practice on display would bring dishonor to the Japanese community reveals that the colonial gaze remained fixed on them at all times.[30]

New recruits from Okinawa constituted just over 30 percent of the 1,045 people classified as Japanese whom the PPC employed between 1905 and 1921. As I stated earlier, none of them were recruited as "skilled workers."[31] I am not privy to the motivations of workers from Okinawa who made up this group, but entries in the organ publication of the Kunigami Young Men's Association, *Kunigami Seinen*, suggest that the opportunity to receive remittances was an attractive concept for ailing communities, at least for local elites who supported migration. An article titled "Message to Youth Residing Abroad," published in the first volume of the publication (1909), recognized youth who sent back remittances by name, village, and amount they contributed to their communities.

Beyond immigration records that provide some information about the people who answered the PPC's recruitment call, there are few archival records that offer insight into their experiences.[32] As Ishikawa Tomonori, one of the leading scholars of immigration studies and a frequent contributor to the field's journal *Imin Kenkyū*, acknowledges, their stories, as well as those of the 17 Okinawan people who joined 63 Japanese, 1 Korean, 32 Chamorro, 311 Carolinian, and 4 Chinese people to work in the Japanese-controlled phosphate mines of Angaur, Fais, and Peleliu following the imposition of mandated rule, remain glaring omissions from studies of prewar Okinawan immigration.[33] Two photographs held at the Melbourne archives of the PPC label Okinawan people as "Japanese coolies" but provide no accompanying information about those pictured (figures 6.1 and 6.2). Many stories are buried underneath the mountains of company and colonial archives that are stored in Japan, Australia, and Britain. Others, of course, live on in the stories that families and communities pass down.

The decades-long presence of Okinawan and Japanese workers in the phosphate- and nickel-producing Pacific Islands, not to mention the thousands who settled in the abaca-producing region of Davao in the Philippines, reinforced relations of cascading Indigenous dispossession that were, as Swan and Banivanua Mar point out, rooted in anti-Black, anti-Indigenous racial imaginaries and practices.[34] The establishment of the headquarters of the South Pacific Mandate, Nanyōchō, should therefore not be seen as the start of Japan's settler colonial policies in the region, but rather as a fulfillment of Kobayashi's desire for the Japanese monopolization of profits through the total devastation of Indigenous communities. The state's imperialist aspirations went into overdrive as it became an equal partner with the United States and Australia, which brought their own carefully honed systems of legally sanctioned genocide to the world stage after World War I.

As Banivanua Mar explains, a direct line connected the mandate system negotiated at the Paris Peace Accords to earlier forms of Indigenous dispossession, genocide, and settler colonial rule. The former existed in the "conceptual legal universe created by the US Supreme Court justice John Marshall in his trilogy of the so-called Cherokee decisions" that established "effectively a permanent

FIGURE 6.1. Photograph, ca. 1908, with original caption: "Ocean Island 1-1908—First lot of 150 Japanese Coolies—Ocean Island—Mr Watanabe and Dr Matsuoka on the right." Notably, 1908 was the year an order for "150 Riukiu Male Labourers" was placed with the agency Nippon Shokumin Gōshi Kaisha by trading company Mitsui Bussan on behalf of the Pacific Phosphate Company (PPC). Photo digitized from the archives of the PPC. National Archives of Australia.

trusteeship [that] went on to enable the widespread and far-reaching processes of assimilation, land alienation and the denial of civil, political and economic rights of Native American nationals, rendering all the benign act of wardship."[35] In contrast to the promise of self-determination extolled throughout the Paris conference, the islands that were designated class C mandates were denied recognition as nations because Indigenous people were "considered too savage, untutored or remote to be afforded any kind of meaningful autonomy."[36] Banivanua Mar argues that "this system rescued the new imperial era from a period of decline" by empowering new powers like Japan, Australia,

FIGURE 6.2. Photograph, ca. 1908, with original caption: "Ocean Island 2—Japanese Coolies' Messroom—Ooma—Coolies taking their evening meal." Photo digitized from the archives of the PPC. National Archives of Australia.

and New Zealand to take greater control over these islands that thousands of their subjects had already been working as contract workers and settlers since the late nineteenth century."[37]

After being granted the keys to the mandate islands in Paris, Japanese colonial authorities deemed the approximately fifty thousand Indigenous people who lived under the control of its headquarters, Nanyōchō, too untrustworthy to work the islands' extractive industries. Instead, the state financially supported the recruitment and settlement of workers from Okinawa and other prefectures that had demonstrated success in sending out large numbers of migrant workers in the first decade and a half of the century.[38] As the militarization of their hometowns and the battles in the Pacific including the Battle of Okinawa and its aftermath tell us, the work that workers from Okinawa did to destroy the world of Banabans could not buy them or their families dignified lives or deaths.

Settler-Colonial Complicities in the Pacific

Scholars working outside the fields of Okinawan or Japanese studies have raised questions of complicity. Maki Mita's interviews with Palauans who lived through the period of Japanese rule reveals that many observed a clear difference between Okinawans and Japanese settlers.[39] For example, Mechas Ochob Giraked (b. 1928), who lived in Koror, the Japanese headquarters since 1921, recalled that the spatial segregation of the parties in the city—Okinawans and Koreans living in alleys off of the main thoroughfare where shops and government buildings stood—reinforced her awareness of the divide between the groups.[40] Rubak Santos Ngirasechedui (b. 1923), who attended colonial secondary school (*kōgakkō*) in Koror, shared that the Okinawan children he met at sports festivals and construction sites in his youth "were poor and they had to help their parents to survive like us."[41] Interviewees also recalled the pain they felt hearing words like *tōmin* ("islander," but used in this context as a derogatory term to put down Pacific Islanders both from the island and from other islands) and *kurXXbō* (a derogatory word that underscored the anti-Blackness operating within settler communities) hurled at them by their Okinawan friends, as well as the hurtful words like *Ryūkyūjin* (literally "Ryūkyūan person," but in that context, an insult intended to signal that they were inferior to Japanese) that they shouted back in response.[42] These words, meant to inflict pain, reinforced the divisions imposed on all of them by the settler colonial government and affirmed, in Wynter's words, (colonial) commonsense.[43]

Lest we neglect a discussion of the structural because of the importance of the interpersonal in shaping sensibilities, Pacific and Pacific Islander studies scholars offer crucial insights into the position that Okinawan settlers occupied in Micronesia. They contest the tendency in Okinawan and Japanese empire studies to focus primarily on the discrimination faced by Okinawans in the mandate system's labor market. For example, in *Cultures of Commemoration*, Keith Camacho expresses the need for more work that treats the Mariana Islands (and the Pacific more broadly) as spaces of contact and exchange between colonial, Indigenous, and settler populations and echoes Gary Okihiro's call to attend to colonial and Indigenous relations "across the Americas, Asias, and the Pacific."[44] Camacho's project to bring these complex geohistories together in order to understand how Chamorro people remember and commemorate war in the present at once centers Chamorro experiences and memories and situates them in a larger Pacific context. He distinguishes Japan from Okinawa but places Okinawans alongside Koreans as manual laborers without examining their differences or shared complicities. An analysis of the role that Okinawan settlers played in the dispossession of other Indigenous peoples must feature centrally if we are to fully appreciate the coconstitutive nature of the policing of cultural practices and customs that reinforced Japanese supremacy everywhere.

The overdetermined nature of Japanese discourse on Okinawa makes the unpacking of complicity practically and politically complicated. Journalists, intellectuals, industrialists, bureaucrats, and politicians feverishly discussed Okinawa's conditions as "Sago Palm Hell" in the mid-1920s as an exceptional condition borne by an island that suffered due to its isolation, culture, and circumstances, and roundly denied the impact that half a century of colonial rule played in the people's immiseration. In fact, the postannexation transformation of Okinawa's economy into a sugar-producing region made it so that small farmers could not withstand the impact that the collapse of sugar prices on the world market had on their household economies. Thousands were left with little choice but to send some family members to the newly acquired mandate territories as settlers. The 53,000 men and women from Okinawa's sugar producing regions who formed the backbone of the settler colonial economy and its vast military infrastructure—over half of the total Japanese labor force on the islands—arrived in the Pacific Islands after being expelled from their hometowns.

Supposed experts like Yanaihara Tadao, chair of colonial policy at Tokyo Imperial University and self-proclaimed Zionist, normalized the transfer of tens of thousands of people—the vast majority of whom were men—on multiyear labor contracts to the mandate islands through an understanding of migration that is almost entirely emptied of its power dynamics.[45] In an essay included in a collection titled *The Labor Problem in the South Seas Co-Prosperity Sphere*, he sidestepped the question of what forced workers from Okinawa to the islands en masse and devoted his energies to explaining why they were especially desirable as a labor force in the South Seas: "The Okinawa people are extremely energetic as workers in the tropical region and have proven their endurance and tenacity. For this reason, they are extremely well suited as settler colonial (*kaitaku*) type labor power."[46] He insisted that they, unlike Taiwanese migrant workers, were merely deficient subjects compared to ordinary Japanese from the mainland (*ippan naichijin*).

Yanaihara's prejudices come through most clearly when he qualifies his praise of Okinawan workers' ability to withstand taxing working conditions with a problem that he saw as a latent liability for the imperial project: "The people of Okinawa have a much lower standard of living than people from the mainland. They are culturally backward and partake heavily in *shōchū* and other alcoholic beverages."[47] He lamented that their behavior led locals to call them Japanese *kanaka*, *kanaka* used in this context as a derogatory term to refer to Carolinian people who had not experienced colonial rule enough to be as civilized as the Chamorro people.[48] The root cause of this embarrassing condition, he noted, was the lack of rational household management. He criticized Okinawan settlers in the mandate islands for sacrificing their own standard of living in order to fund what he judged to be wasteful practices and habits of their relatives in the prefecture: "A very large portion of their remittances are used back home in order to engage in the construction of tombstones and other unproductive expenses."[49] In his view, it was extremely problematic that the legitimacy of the settler colonial project was in the hands of a group of people whose investment in it was suspect but whose labor was necessary. The denial of the colonial violence embedded in linguistic policies, education, land reforms, and the prohibition of funerary rites and other practices in Okinawa that structured his and other experts' dismissal of Okinawans as untrustworthy settlers went hand in hand with the denial of this very same violence against Pacific Islander communities in the mandate islands. I turn next to Babeldaob island to clarify these connections.

Ossuopower inaugurated the Japanese Imperial Navy's assertion of control on Babeldaob island.[50] Its project to identify parcels of land that could be used as sites of village cemeteries commenced well before Nanyōchō began its land survey on the island in 1926. The report, "Palau Compact Road Archaeological Investigations," commissioned by the US Army Engineer District and published by the Palau Resources Institute in 2005, confirms the Japanese state's attempts to control the bones of Babeldaob's residents through its policy of discouraging communities from engaging in the long-standing practice of burying their kin in stone platforms called *odesongel*.[51] This interference with residents' funerary practices was an attack on clan and kin relations.[52] The impact of the state's destruction of these relations endures in how researchers at the Palau Resources Institute have had to carry out their work, intended to protect sacred and important cultural and historical structures and sites from being destroyed by the US Army's extension of military infrastructure on the island. Because so much was destroyed during World War II, researchers who put together the report frequently referenced the written works of Hijikata Hisakatsu, the first Japanese person to move to Palau, in order to survey Palauan people's myths and legends. Hijikata was motivated by a desire to find "primitive society" in Palau. His exploits were funded by the wages he was paid by Nanyōchō for teaching woodworking at *kōgakko*, the name given to the public elementary schools that were built throughout the mandate islands to teach Indigenous children Japanese customs and language.[53] Following his stint in Palau, Hijikata was hired as a civilian employee of the Imperial Army in Borneo and worked as a researcher and advisor there during the early 1940s.[54] Japanese colonial knowledge endures in archaeological investigations conducted under US domination.

The Nanyōchō's efforts to weaken peoples' existing relations of authority and kinship advanced in lockstep with land policies that culminated in the establishment of the colonial agricultural settlements Shimizu (Ngerdorch), Ringio (Ngerderar), Taiyō (Ngerbekuu), and Asahi (Ngermeskang). The "Palau Compact Road Archaeological Investigations" report succinctly notes the physical and psychic violence of settlement: "Agricultural settlements were given Japanese names although the places already had Palauan names."[55] The first group of settlers from Fukushima arrived in Babeldaob in late 1927 after having failed to succeed in a similar project in Hokkaido, Japan's first settler colony.[56]

Fifteen years later, the Asahi settlement received a fairy-tale treatment of its own in a publication by the South Seas Research Institute (Nanyō Keizai Kenkyūjo) titled *Going Upstream on Ngermeskang River* (1943). The piece begins with an account of a setback attributed to the isolation that the first group of eight settler households faced and ends with the construction of Asahi Shrine, a concrete marker of Japanese domination of the spiritual and religious sphere. In between is a section celebrating the accomplishments of Shishido Sajirō, a Japanese settler credited with overcoming near-impossible conditions to establish a pineapple industry on the island that was eventually purchased by Nanyō Takushoku, the largest Japanese state-owned enterprise in the Pacific.[57] His was the classic case of failing up. Prior to arriving on Babeldaob in 1930, he had failed in a project to reclaim hemp mountains in Davao; after that, he was involved in a failed agricultural colonization project in Hokkaido. The report notes that Shishido achieved success because of his devotion to Asahi's development. It explains that his devotion is best expressed in his declaration that he would be buried there—he had already claimed the most scenic spot in the village as his final resting place. The report expressed support for his wishes, stating, "It would be meaningful if they called that spot Mt. Shishido" to honor his contributions.[58]

Reading the report, one is left with the impression that Asahi plantation was completely isolated from the rest of Babeldaob. When Indigenous communities are mentioned, they are disparagingly called islanders (*tōmin*) who put the entire project to settle Ngermeskang at risk. The report regurgitates the explanation that the first group of settlers gave for their failure—that *tōmin* had acted irresponsibly when asked to transport the first harvest to the market in Koror. It blamed them for the settlers' early difficulties: "Islanders are extremely irresponsible so the items had spoiled by the time they reached Koror city. Since it was not widely known that there were settlers in Ngermeskang and because they were not dependent on goods produced there, people were unwilling to lend a helping hand."[59] Oral testimonies collected by Mita and members of the Palau Resources Institute make clear that people who resided in the area were not only aware of the presence of Japanese settlers; they had been conscripted to carry out much of the manual labor of port reinforcement and road construction that had made the agricultural settlements viable in the first place.[60] A settler colonial document, *Going Upstream on Ngermeskang River* reinforced the image of Babeldaob as terra nullius and diminished the dispossession, renaming, expropriation, and exercise of ossuopower in Babeldaob. It also erased the presence of Korean and Okinawan workers whom authorities deemed insufficient as settlers but on whom they relied to provide much of the labor power necessary to reproduce Asahi village's economy.

Turning our attention back to the prefecture after tracing how settler narratives erased Indigenous and colonial labor from stories of economic transformation in the Pacific Islands, we see how colonial violence and its erasure in one site reshapes the contours of domination in another. Crucially, it allows me to understand the Battle of Okinawa not as a story of the Japanese state's unique betrayal of Okinawa's residents, but as one in a series of midcentury genocidal events that Japanese authorities, soldiers, and settlers carried out against Indigenous and colonized people in Asia and the Pacific.

Customs and Enclosures

Okinawa had its own Hijikata Hisakatsu in Tamura Hiroshi, a scholar and bureaucrat best known for authoring texts like *Ryūkyū's Communal Villages* and *Okinawa's Economic Conditions*, which provided field-based analyses of agrarian village social relations. Tamura's scholarly work is even more inseparable from his career as a colonial official. He served concurrently as industrial head (*sangyō kachō*) and highest official of Kunigami (*gunchō*), the northernmost region of Okinawa island, following his arrival in the prefecture in 1922.[61] His scholarly activity was enabled by his privileged access to official records, archival materials, and the local population. It, like Hijikata's study of Palauan customs, was rooted in a colonial will to know.

In his analysis of Okinawan/Ryūkyūan customs, Tamura addressed the question of difference head-on. He argued that Okinawa's and Japan's shared primordial origins made present cultural differences acceptable. The paradox of his position was that while he asserted that the persistence of customary practices in Okinawa was an outcome of historical rather than fundamental differences with Japan and argued that practices of *gemeinschaft* (*kyōdō shakai*) that were no longer present in mainland Japan but that remained intact in the prefecture should be studied and even celebrated, his interest in them stemmed from his desire to resolve an urgent economic problem. He collected information about the practices of hundreds of farm households in dozens of villages and their internal laws (*naihō*) throughout the islands of Okinawa in order to locate the root cause of the prefecture's dire economic conditions. His 1925 work, *Okinawa's Economic Conditions*, argued that the dramatic collapse of the prefectural economy was attributable to Okinawans' lack of motivation to save money, their carelessness, and their overdependence on loans.[62]

> The people of Okinawa have respected and worshiped their ancestors, and have pure, good customs that reflect this. However, they have a high degree of dependency and tend to be jealous of other people's successes.... They should learn from the mutual aid and communalism of the previous era and ... should recover through their own hard work and effort. I deeply believe that Okinawa's people should be ashamed of their impoverishment. Lamenting their situation and asking for help will only bring forth the same result.[63]

Tamura prepared this text for publication while working his day job overseeing the implementation of industrial development policies in the prefecture. In that capacity, he coordinated the release of communally held forestlands in the northern region of Kunigami as part of a prefecture-wide effort to strengthen the region's military capacities. Without irony, he petitioned for the release of nearly three chō of protected forestland in order to advance two multivillage road improvement and construction projects. The first connected Shioya district in Ōgimi village on the western coast to Taira and Kawata districts in Higashi village on the eastern coast. The second linked the district of Iha in Misato village, one of the centers of sugar production in the central part of Okinawa island, to Nakadomari district in Onna village on its western coast. These projects were strategically and commercially significant—Nakadomari was a stopping point for Yanbaru ships and Kin Bay, off the coast of Misato, was an important landing area for the Japanese army that was stationed in Okinawa to guard against internal and external enemies.[64]

Completion of both projects required that Tamura petition the Ministry of Agriculture for the release of lands that had been designated protected forestlands during the first round of enclosures in the early 1890s. Building new economic and military infrastructures that cut across multiple villages required access to land that had been protected from development during the Meiji-era debates over the enclosure process. That period had seen plenty of debates and negotiations between members of the National Diet, high-level prefectural administrators, local intellectuals, politicians, groups of colonialists, and peasants who had previously cared for and made decisions about commonly managed lands during the Ryūkyū Kingdom era. Complicating matters for Tamura, two and a half decades later, was the fact that all but one of the eighteen plots of land that he petitioned to release were communally owned, either by the village or by individual districts. Once enacted, his proposal would completely transform social relations in these areas in what was effectively a second major reshuffling in less than a generation. While an analysis of the longer-term impacts this change had for social relations in the affected districts requires access to detailed land records that did not survive wartime devastation, hints of discord appear in the proceedings of the Chihō Shinrinkai (Prefectural Forestry Association).[65]

Tamura formally submitted his proposal for the multidistrict road construction project to the prefecture's deliberating body in 1924. He claimed that it would provide much-needed unemployment relief to imperiled farming communities and argued that building this infrastructure was necessary to realize the construction of a large sugar factory that Tainansha had announced in 1917. He described his proposal as being integral to the advancement of the public good (*kōeki*). In so doing, he revealed that the appreciation he expressed for customary practices in *Okinawa's Economic Conditions* held so long as they did not threaten his vision of a more economically developed and militarily fortified Okinawa.

Just as phosphate mining destroyed taro patches called *mesei* in Peleliu that were central parts of an existing structure of matriarchal authority overseen by Ngesias chiefs, not to mention entire lifeworlds of people in Banaba, including places that were "taboo and haunted," Tamura's enclosure proposals held little regard for the worlds his proposed large-scale infrastructural projects threatened to destroy.[66] Women's authority, especially in honoring nonreproductive intimacies, weakened in Okinawa as a result of Tamura's policies, which celebrated only the aspects of "Okinawan customs" that did not threaten Japanese rule. As many scholars have demonstrated, *yuta*, who presided over the spiritual and material lives of communities, were the first to come under attack.[67] They were dismissed as embodiments of irrationality and superstition and were chastised as standing in the way of Okinawan women's development into modern subjects. Targets of witch hunts (*yuta-gari*) periodically carried out by police, they were accused of ruining entire family fortunes and were arrested, placed on trial, and prosecuted for spreading rumors that incited others to destroy physical infrastructure following natural disasters.[68] On these occasions, suspicion converged with desire: a willful conflation of *yuta*, *noro*, women who worked in the pleasure quarters of Tsuji, women merchants who moved freely from market to market as tofu sellers, men and women who mingled too much in the mixed-gender panama hat factories in Naha, young students who met up at the movie theaters and enjoyed "secret pleasures" in the dark, and ordinary young women who met up with their friends in the outskirts of villages, underneath tunnels, and in other common places in the countryside. All were culpable for disrespecting the spatial or moral boundaries befitting a modern (Japanese) society.[69]

The witch hunts that accompanied large-scale infrastructure projects of the 1920s were part of a continuum of counterrevolutionary action against what the state intuited as a powerful libidinal economy that had to be eradicated—a war between the forces of enclosure and erotic pleasure. The state's position, established by bureaucrats like Tamura and police officers who appear frequently in literary works of the period, was sold through fearmongering tactics that exploited people's anxieties about economic devastation. In the process, nonreproductive sex was turned into a moral crime and inclusion in the national community was tied to Okinawans' ability to perform normative sexuality.[70] The types of women listed above embodied existing relations common in many parts of Okinawa that had to be broken, assimilated, or contained in order to secure the region as the southern frontier of the nation-state. This was necessary in order to transform the population into a surplus labor force that could be funneled into the expanded empire in a manner that would not morph into errant pursuits of freedom.

Survey as Counterrevolutionary Instrument

It was in the context of this intensifying surveillance and repression of Okinawan women and everyone else who did not fall in line with heteropatriarchal norms that the Japanese Ministry of Agriculture and Commerce extended its Farm Household Survey project to the prefecture. The prefecture's Imperial Agricultural Association was tasked with implementing the survey on the ministry's behalf beginning in 1930.[71] Two villages on Okinawa Island, Chatan and Haebaru, were selected as sites from which participant farm households would be drawn in the inaugural year.[72] While a direct link was not posited, the survey implementation accompanied the prefecture's fifteen-year economic recovery plan whose main objective was to provide relief from so-called sago palm hell conditions through increased production of centrifugal sugar (*bunmitsutō*).[73] The project drew its participants from regions that had been most destabilized by tenant farmers' disputes against the Tainansha, Nakagami, and Shimajiri districts. This context suggests that the attempt to create disciplined, rational, and productive sugarcane-cultivating farm households in the center of anticapitalist organizing was a counterrevolutionary project.[74]

The Yamashiro household (no. 214) was one of six farm households from Okinawa that began participating in the Farm Household Survey in 1931. They resided in Ishikawa, one of six districts that composed a single political unit within Misato village called Uekata. In the prewar period, Misato had abundant water supplies that made the village the center of rice cultivation in the prefecture. One of Tainansha's large sugar factories was built nearby for the same reason. The rapid development of infrastructure in the region produced its fair share of conflicts. A few years before the Yamashiro farm household's recruitment into the Farm Household Survey project, several teachers from Iha elementary school had been arrested or suspended for taking part in Marxist study groups that were accused of propagating dangerous thought. Though it was difficult for these teachers to continue their activities in the open, they formed mutual aid networks to support those who were arrested or lost their jobs as a result of their activism. Some worked with tenant farmer unions and factory workers to formulate a set of demands for better working conditions, higher wages, and increased autonomy for cultivators in the production process.[75] There is no record of the Yamashiro farm household being part of these struggles, but the prominence of the Ishikawa district's elementary school teachers in these radical circles was well-known.

While the farm household's reliance on agricultural production declined over time, they counted on sugar manufacturing wages to earn the cash they needed to survive. The most important crop for this farm household was sweet potato (60 yen) followed by brown rice (25.4 yen), the majority of which went to household consumption. This is not consistent with the rest of Misato village, which was well-known as a sugar-producing region and major supplier of cane to the large sugar factory in Kadena owned by Tainansha, the largest Japanese sugar company operating in the prefecture. In contrast to other farm households in the area that earned agricultural cash income by selling raw sugarcane or brown sugar on the market, the Yamashiros used their rented agricultural fields and paddies mainly for subsistence crops and relied on other forms of work to make ends meet.

The Yamashiro farm household followed the district's pattern of sending family members to the Pacific Islands as migrant workers. The majority of their cash income earned outside the household came from a combination of different remittance sources: the head of household's younger brother in Hawai'i, an unnamed relative in "Nanyō" (an imprecise, colloquial term for the mandate islands), and two people working in mainland Japan or another part of Okinawa temporarily (*dekasegisha*). Recorded in the ledger under "housework, income from gifts," these remittances were indispensable to the Yamashiro farm household's ability to survive even though the Ministry of Agriculture and Commerce considered all cash inputs recorded in this category to be irregular, unreliable, and an inessential part of the farm household economy. These types of inputs could not, in other words, sustain a conquistador humanist.

We are introduced to the composition of the Yamashiro farm household for the first time in 1932. Table 3 of the Summary of Results (*kekkahyō*) records each family member's age, title, occupation, labor efficiency index, and days spent in residence. Four contributors of labor time to the household economy were listed that year: the head of household, Yamashiro Kamekichi, aged forty-six; his wife, Tsuru, aged forty-three; their elder son, Kameatsu, aged twenty; and their second son, Zentoku, aged sixteen. Both sons worked for unnamed farm households as *nenyatoi*, or yearly hires. As a result, the elder spent 126 days outside of his residence and the second son spent 286 days elsewhere. Despite the time they spent away from home, they were included in the table as family members because the survey required that everyone who stayed at the residence at least one day of the year be included as members of the farm household. Below their names are the names, genders, and ages of the family members who were not acknowledged as contributing labor time to the household. In 1932, this included Kamekichi and Tsuru's second daughter, Sachiko, aged thirteen; their third daughter, Yoshiko, aged ten; their fourth daughter, Tsuru, aged seven; their third son, Yūshin, aged four; and their fourth son, Kenshō, aged two.

An absence immediately marks our introduction to the Yamashiro farm household. It is not clear if this omission was an act of withholding by the ledger keeper, head of household Yamashiro Kamekichi, or if it was simply an outcome of the logic of the form. Kamekichi and Tsuru had an eldest daughter but her name, age, and whereabouts are unlisted. Her absence becomes presence with her younger sister Sachiko's appearance in the table as the family's second daughter. Her conspicuous absence invites us to think about the work that the survey performs to close off certain lines of questioning.

The structural impossibility of survival as a sugar-producing tenant farmer produced conditions whereby young family members had to enter the labor market. Kamekichi and Tsuru's second son, Zentoku, seventeen years of age in 1933, completely disappeared from that year's labor time distribution table. He became a yearly hire—the only way to earn significant cash income in a farming household—for another unspecified farm household. As Zentoku left home in pursuit of cash income, his younger sister Sachiko (fourteen years old) and Yoshiko (eleven years old) took up some of the slack. They both appeared on the labor chart for the first time in 1933. Sachiko performed close to half of the 4,057 hours recorded as housework that year.

On June 15, 1934, just nine days after returning from his yearly hire job, Zentoku departed for "Nanyō" with Yoshiko. Kameatsu, the eldest son, followed on December 1, 1934.[76] After the June departure of her second brother and younger sister, Sachiko continued to balance school attendance with over 2,100 hours of housework. Tsuru gave birth to her fifth son, Zen'ei, in late August but barely took time to slow down.[77]

The quantitative measure of these life changes appeared as line items in the ledger but concealed as much as it made apparent about their collective well-being. That was the point. Sachiko's 2,100 hours of housework did not reflect changes in intensity (which is assumed) or the value of her work to the household's ability to reproduce itself, nor did it capture the way that changes to the family transformed what Sachiko and her family thought would be possible in the future. How did the departure of two working adults in the family to the mandate islands—a place so distant that it was recorded in the ledgers simply as "Nanyō"—circumscribe the futurities of everyone who remained? What language exists to articulate the changes in what each member of the household could imagine for themselves, for each other, and for those who were not technically part of the farm household? How did they cope with the space opened up by the departures of Zentoku, Yoshiko, and Kameatsu to a faraway place with no clear schedule for returning? How did these changes affect people who were not part of the farm household?

Remaining family members did become much busier. Adult members took on additional work after a 387 yen payout from a collective fund called *moai* made the purchase of some additional land possible on August 30. The land they acquired lowered rent payments from the 38.5 yen they paid in 1933 to 32.5 yen, but the loss of family members to the labor market became a problem.[78] Sachiko, now sixteen years old, began to weave panama hats.[79] Her entry into this industry coincided with the revival of Okinawa's panama hat industry due to increased demand in the markets of France and England via Kobe-based merchants.[80] Between November 1935 and the end of the survey period the following February, she recorded 419 hours of nonagricultural work and earned a total of 4.4 yen in cash income in addition to the 2,506 hours she devoted to housework. Given her location and description in the family composition table as *bōshiami* (panama hat weaver), Sachiko likely joined other young girls and women who worked in small, enclosed spaces in the evenings weaving panama hats for subcontractors or sub-subcontractors who received bundles of *adan* leaves and other raw materials from panama hat companies based in Naha. She was probably paid weekly according to a piecework system based on quantity and the intricacy of the weave.[81]

Sachiko's father, Kamekichi, also increased the amount of time he devoted to nonagricultural work following the departure of his sons and daughters to the mandate islands. In 1935, he was paid a total of 30.46 yen (25 yen of this was for filling out the ledger) in exchange for working forty-eight hours. He worked as a laborer, a recordkeeper for a *moai*, a sugar manufacturer, and a day laborer. The farm household earned 34.86 yen during the 1935 survey year in nonagricultural cash income. The substantial discrepancy in wages per hour between Kamekichi and Sachiko notwithstanding, when this total is compared to the remittances the farm household received that year, we understand the indispensability of migration to the prefecture's economy. The farm household recorded 145 yen in remittances from Hawai'i and the mandate islands—an amount that would have been impossible for Sachiko or Kamekichi to earn in a year while continuing as agriculturalists. The name "Treasure Island" that circulated among residents to refer to the mandate islands makes sense in this context. With the 1934 departures of Zentoku, Yoshiko, and Kameatsu, the Yamashiro farm household became fully integrated into a global system that drove tens of thousands of Okinawan migrant workers to become settlers in the islands. The Yamashiros were put in a position to facilitate the dispossession of Pacific Islanders as their own hometown became a military outpost and as they finally acquired what was touted as the holy grail for small farm households—their own plot of land.[82]

Petty land ownership and remittances could not save the Yamashiro family, however. The handwritten notes in the 1937 summary indicate that, despite their efforts to maintain agricultural production and obtain their own land, they became, in effect, a part-time farm household (*kengyō nōka*) in no small part due to a mongoose attack on their wheat crop. They also lost half of the land they had been renting from their landlord. What remained was not enough to sustain seven family members, four of whom were nonworking dependents. These developments affected the work patterns of each of the three family members of working age differently. Kamekichi turned to nonagricultural sources of cash income. While he devoted 48 hours to paid work outside of agriculture in 1935, in 1937 that figure increased to 320 hours. Just as notable was the decline in the number of hours he devoted to agriculture, from 1,879 to just 610. His total labor time in the work ledger fell from 2,812 to 2,229 hours.

In contrast, Sachiko's total work time increased significantly. The work ledger shows 3,440 hours worked in 1937 compared to 3,075 in 1935. Her waged working hours, like her father's, increased substantially, from 419 to 2,679, which she devoted exclusively to weaving panama hats. The hours that Sachiko recorded in the housework category fell from 2,506 to 596 over the same period. The burden of this loss in the housework category appears to have been borne by her mother, Tsuru, who divided her time (a total of 2,903 hours) evenly between agriculture and housework.[83]

The ledgers suggest that the members of the farm household who stayed behind in Misato worked tirelessly, sustained by a diet of rice, sweet potato, tofu, daikon, pumpkin, winter melon, and some green vegetables they harvested. The recorded purchases of eighteen chicken eggs per year and twenty-four pounds (listed as 12 kin) of pork reveal a kind of accounting that brings home the joyless rational management embedded in the concept of rations. [84] They consumed additional quantities of tofu, sōmen, mochi, beans, and pork during almost monthly celebrations or practices filed under the category "ceremonial occasions" (*kankon sōsai*) and labeled as spring and autumn equinox, lunar new year, anniversaries of deaths of family member, *shi-mi-* festivals to welcome back ancestors, and so on. Far from being excessive instances of overspending as Yanaihara would have accused, ceremonies were occasions for household members to reaffirm kinship and other relations and to share in food and drink that they otherwise could not afford. Each meeting created shared spaces of celebration and mourning amid state policies that transformed them into atomized farm households. These ledgers are a window into relationships that either remained intact or were revitalized in this time of colonial enclosure and migration but should by no means be taken as the only relationships that people nurtured in the countryside. Many of them are inaccessible—either because of the ledger form or because I am not in the position to see them.

In 1937, Sachiko worked 2,679 hours in exchange for 33.43 yen in wages. Though I cannot definitively conclude why she expended so many hours on piecework that yielded so little monetarily rather than leaving the farm household altogether in order to work for more wages in a factory or to join her other siblings in the Pacific Islands, her ability to move between agriculture, housework and piecework was an integral part of this farm household's survival. Working at all hours of the day and filling all of her free time with small amounts of work that could be resumed at a later moment—a condition that feminist activist, tenant farmer organizer, and writer Yamagami Kimie critiques in an essay written around this time, "Women of the Agrarian Villages and the

Family System," with an analysis that prefigured social reproduction theory—was indispensable to farm household economies like hers that lived on the edge of collapse.[85] Hurricanes, wars, mongoose attacks, or any other interruptions to scheduled operations struck often and proved in many cases to be fatal.

As it became clear that maintaining the farm household through agricultural production was unsustainable, Sachiko's mother and all three of her younger brothers left for the Northern Mariana island of Saipan on April 17, 1938. Sachiko remained in Misato with her father and her younger sister. The financial cost of the move, which is recorded in the ledgers as 139.62 yen exceeded the 104.37 yen that Kamekichi and Sachiko were paid during all of 1937. In addition to 71.3 yen in remittance payments that came from Hawai'i and "Nanyō," a 150 yen remittance that arrived two days before Tsuru's departure enabled them to make the trip. The 1938 work ledger tells us that while Sachiko's work time around their departure was primarily devoted to housework, she picked up the pace of her panama hat weaving in mid-May. By then, the farm household had very little ability to engage in agricultural production.

Sachiko's younger sister Tsuru appeared in the farm household's work ledgers for the first time this year. She was spared a heavy workload and recorded 181 hours of labor time (175 hours of housework and 6 hours of agricultural work) beginning in December. This was comparable to Sachiko and Yoshiko, who entered the ledgers at the ages of fourteen and eleven following the departures of their two older brothers in 1933. While her mother's departure was a primary reason for Tsuru's entry into the work ledgers, the immediate reason was Kamekichi's failing health. He fell ill in December and had to reduce his work hours almost entirely through February. Tsuru, as well as an unnamed woman helper who performed 73 hours of housework in January, made up for her mother's and father's absences—perhaps this was a sign of their diligence, or a reflection of their desperation for the 25 yen that would only be paid out in January 1939 if they submitted something that passed official muster.[86]

Tsuru's entry into the work ledger was undoubtedly influenced by Sachiko's death on August 11, 1938, at the age of nineteen. Until her death, Sachiko had been on pace to become the leading contributor of labor time in the family. She averaged 243.8 hours of work per month between March and July and even recorded 34 hours of work during the first ten days of August, the month she passed away. She continued to split her time between panama hat weaving and housework with some agricultural work sprinkled in.[87] The hours she devoted to weaving decreased considerably from the middle of April 1938, the same time that her mother departed with her brothers. It is not clear whether the decline is attributable to these departures or if it was a result of her worsening health.[88] Whatever help the family received, if it was not performed by a farm household member or was not waged work, it had no place to be recorded in the ledger.

Ledgers and Their Silences

There is a large blank space underneath Sachiko's name that exists without commentary in the 1938 work ledger from September 1938 until the end of the survey year in February 1939. Despite her death in August, this column remains. Combined with the blank space left by Tsuru's departure in April, Kamekichi's own blank space following his illness in December, and the persistent unaccounted absence of the unnamed eldest daughter, the absences that mark Sachiko's departure from the world, made visible through her continued presence in the work ledger, highlight the particular violence that the survey inflicted on its participants. By making daily inscription a condition of participation, those who remained were obliged to relive the deaths, departures, and illnesses of family members by inscribing them or leaving them empty in a form that was useful for the Ministry of Agriculture and Commerce but completely divorced from how they coped. It is also incapable of recording the rich life that Sachiko may have had before her death outside of her farm household. The relationships she formed at school, in the panama hat weaving rooms, or at the well she traveled to daily to collect water for her household all fall out of the frame and hinder our ability to imagine different kinds of experiences Sachiko had toward the end of her short life.

The emptiness of the 1938 work ledger gives the vibrancy of earlier tables—the way they seem almost to overflow with hours and hours of recorded work time—a sense of foreboding. It reveals itself to be nothing more than a visual representation of the overwork and exploitation directly linked to this final emptiness. I read Tsuru's entry into the survey as her older sister Sachiko's replacement as the start of another cycle of overwork, underconsumption, and undervaluation. There is no way to track her work time any further, though, since the Yamashiro farm household was removed from the survey project altogether. Its collapse was irreparable and therefore of no use to the ministry, which was only interested in collecting information from farm households that could prove their ability to intimately manage themselves at least well enough to produce reliable data sets. Thereafter, it became one piece of a mountain of statistical data that was available to state authorities and social scientists and provided evidence for them to make a wide variety of claims, including, for example, that Okinawans should not become members of Babeldaob's agricultural settlements because they lacked the capacity and desire to transform themselves into proper Japanese colonizers.

What is by design harder to see is how the valorization of a stable, atomized farm household unit went hand in hand with the devaluation of existing cooperative and communal relations and organizations that had been essential to the ability of Okinawa's small farm households to manage the growing burdens of social reproduction. Farm households were by no means expected to become nuclear families cut off entirely from others, but their core members were expected to devote their surplus time and resources to official or semiofficial organizations like patriotic youth groups, women's groups, or local agricultural associations, which directed the energies of people in the countryside to state-sanctioned entities that were lauded as forms of mutual aid necessary for full inclusion into the Japanese community. In the process, the nation was to emerge as the primary form of (af)filiation and the patriarchal family unit transformed into its privileged building block. In Okinawa, the survey project was a counterrevolutionary tool, its purpose being to eliminate ungovernable forms of social and economic organization that had been highly effective in refusing mainland sugar capital's attempts to separate producers from their means of production: not the communalism that Tamura Hiroshi celebrated, but visions of something closer to communism.[89]

Lives like Yamashiro Sachiko's were dismissed by representatives of empire such as Yanaihara and Tamura as refuse—disposable remnants of a farm household whose labor was acknowledged only as supplementary.[90] The encouragement of everyday forms of intimate self-management that required Okinawan small farm households to sharply reduce expenditures for ceremonies, socializing, and daily necessities as a means of proving their worthiness as Japanese subjects did much of the work of producing a sensibility among policy makers and colonial intellectuals that made the genocide that was the Battle of Okinawa seem like a natural, albeit devastating, outcome to a brutal war that could not be avoided in order to save the nation. As this chapter has argued, the scale of their work was global, and the naturalization of colonial rule in Okinawa was directly connected to similar processes the state enacted in the Pacific.

This colonial commonsense that deepened over time made Governor Shimada's statement in the daily paper, *Okinawa Shimpō*, on February 12, 1945—a month before the start of the Battle of Okinawa in March 1945—thinkable, utterable, and printable for all to see.[91] Straightforwardly titled "Halving the Population of the Prefecture to 300,000," it introduced his proposal to create a bureau that would be tasked with cutting the population in half over the next century. He was quoted as saying, "Generally speaking, the population density of the prefecture is a problem for the livelihood of the people of the prefecture. Unless adjustments are made, a resolution will be difficult. A reduction in the prefecture's population by half from 600,000 to 300,000 is appropriate." How the government's genocidal aspirations would be enacted, where the cuts would be made, and what a satisfactory resolution would look like were not questions that he ever had to answer. The Allied invasion of the islands the following month, a year after the United States raided Palau, spared him the effort of laying out concrete plans for his vision.[92]

Still, as I discuss in the following chapter, that some farm household ledgers included significant payments to *noro* and *yuta* suggests the persistence, or perhaps reaffirmation, of forms of relations presided over by women who held some degree of authority over community spiritual life. Their fleeting appearance in these colonial archives through the late 1930s is a reminder that archives are sites of contestation and that people are also creators and keepers of knowledge. Despite the rigidity of their form and their repetitive quality, the ledgers contain traces of fierce struggles that continued to be fought in local communities against policies that designated them collectively as refuse. Just as Taki Seihi's participation in the global phosphate industry connected colonial domination experienced by Korean and buraku phosphate factory workers in Hyōgo to its Kimje plantation on the Korean peninsula and to named and unnamed Korean workers who were employed by the Ihara farm household in Kōyō village, Okinawa's ledgers allow us to draw another line in the tangled circuits of colonial domination and refusal. This line connects the lives of Okinawan phosphate workers who toiled in the Pacific Islands alongside other colonized and Indigenous populations to the prefecture's small farm households, where poor women were transformed into an extremely flexible workforce who performed a combination of agricultural, waged, and uncompensated labor to keep their households afloat as bureaucrats crafted long-term industrial development policies that were intended to transform the region and its people into a militarized site of raw material extraction and war. What can be narrated as their refusal and how should these stories be told? I consider these questions in the final chapter.

CHAPTER SEVEN   **WATER STRUGGLES**

IN A COLONIAL   CITY

Yamashiro Sachiko's death, like the deaths of Korean and buraku women who also appear fleetingly in this book, should not be read as a tragic outcome of incomplete inclusion or self-exploitation. Rather, it reminds us that nation-state formation from the middle to end of the nineteenth century had the establishment and obfuscation of colonial violence at its core. As the previous chapter traced, Sachiko's fate and those of Indigenous Pacific Islanders who faced the destruction of their lands, waters, and relations were interconnected in ways that are obfuscated through the denial of Okinawa's coloniality on the one hand and the erasure of Indigenous communities from narratives of Japanese imperialist expansion to the Pacific on the other. Clarifying these relations enables us to attend to the ongoing nature of colonial violence that structures the

Japanese state's and capital's relationship to its current and former territorial possessions. Lisa Yoneyama's point that the end of World War II should be seen not as an end but as the start of a new colonial configuration driven largely (though not exclusively) by the prerogative of US imperialism reminds us of the importance of viewing the pre–World War II empire as also comprising multiple imperialist powers that competed at times and cooperated at others to maximize extraction from the bodies and lands of those it colonized.[1]

This chapter focuses on refusals that were part and parcel of imperialist domination in Okinawa. I read archival materials like the Farm Household Survey ledgers that recorded Sachiko's death in August 1938 as a researcher who writes from the bowels of the US educational system, which continues to churn out colonial knowledge. This position requires that I concentrate my attention on the question of what I am unable to see because of how I am situated. That is, I start from the presumption that my imperial gaze fundamentally limits how and what I can see in those ledgers. Accepting opacity in the archives is the absolute minimum for a nonextractive method.

Dionne Brand's work *The Blue Clerk* guides my reading practice. Opacity is a necessary corrective to historians' fetishization of the archives, which assumes their transparency or legibility to any trained correctly to read them. This arrogance is central to the colonial desire to know, master, and ultimately consume, which I chronicle throughout this book as a powerful impulse in intellectuals whom the state mobilized to produce knowledge about those it sought to dominate. Not only does approaching the historical record as an opportunity to gain entry into an unknown world risk replicating the worst impulses of people like Tamura or Hijikata, but it can also trick even the well-intentioned among us into replicating the atomized, individualized worlds that capital sought to create. The fetishization of proper nouns effaces the reality that even people fighting against colonial rule and Japanese supremacy live in complex webs of social relations that careful reading cannot fully grasp, especially if those communities are not our own. We may also miss the importance of the many people who are nameless and faceless in the archival record who live among those whose names appear in the very same records as colluders or revolutionaries. The former provide retreat, healing, pressure, or courage to their more visible contemporaries. Among them are people who wait, perhaps for a sign that that their dream of turning the world upside down is not theirs alone—that, actually, it is a dream shared by many.

The Blue Clerk also teaches me that some are hard at work to make sure the dreams of the many are not destroyed by being exposed too soon. Brand's opening verso points to the heaviness that the clerk, who has taken on the task of standing guard over peoples' dreams and memories, bears. She waits, Brand says, for a sign that shows her which way the weather is going to turn. She pays attention to the color of the sky, the sense of time, the smell of the air. She also waits for the appearance of the cool moon—a time when the heaviness of carrying all of those dreams disappears.[2]

The issue is, therefore, not about reading as Ann Stoler and other stalwarts of the field of empire studies have taught us to do; their approach to the archives reinforces the authority of the critical reader who is professionally attuned to the colonial structuring of the archive and who operates from the presumption that they (we) can read archives with more precision than their creators.[3] By contrast, people, insects, plants, and colors are alive in the cargo that make up the archives in which Brand's blue clerk operates. What she withholds is immeasurable. They are the "delicate and beautiful" things that need to be kept, for now, from seeing the light of day.[4]

What is so important about *The Blue Clerk* is the way that Brand reminds us of the need to distinguish between at least three processes operating simultaneously: the work that the blue clerk/I is engaged in to clarify and withhold everything that is too cruel and too beautiful to be revealed to the world; the work that the author/I performs as she works with what the aforementioned blue clerk/I has clarified and withheld, and "scrapes and scrapes" to uncover worlds that lie beneath the surface; and the work that the author/I then does to cover her own "sense-making apparatus" with tracing paper so as to not give away too much.[5] Each is a laborious, ceaseless task, never done in isolation, to manage the line that keeps the left-hand ledger contents from seeping over to the right.

My biggest challenge in this chapter is to write in a way that honors Okinawa's clerks (who are implicated in the anti-Blackness that undergirds Japanese imperialism, though they do not necessarily bear the brunt of it directly) and communicates the magnitude of what they must have deliberately and instinctively withheld from self-reported documents like the Farm Household Survey ledgers. How do I write about, and with, those right-hand pages that are the barely visible parts of a vast universe of left-hand pages and whose scope is unimaginable, especially to trained miners and dissectors of colonial archives like me? While the experiences of Okinawan people under Japanese colonial rule cannot be conflated with Brand's blue clerks, their lives and their practices of withholding, survival, refusal, and collective action shape a world ravaged by capital. Just as Brand's blue clerks lived with an acute awareness that guarding the stories contained in the left-hand pages of their archives was a matter of life or death, the keepers of ledgers in Okinawa surely intuited the same.[6]

As Indigenous studies scholars Eve Tuck and K. Wayne Yang argue, acts of reading that promise to excavate secrets are more violent than those that are simply ignorant about such secrets' existence.[7] To understand that acts of withholding and waiting are everywhere that secrets are indispensable to survival is to fundamentally challenge the practices and evaluative norms of historical knowledge production. To accept that other peoples' secrets are not mine to uncover is in many ways antithetical to our disciplinary/disciplining work of discovery. Rejecting this colonizing practice allows me to rethink the position of the designated ledger keeper of the Yamashiro farm household, Yamashiro Kamekichi, not only as a subject recruited to ensure genealogical continuity for the small farm household but also as a keeper of secrets. I extend this understanding to my reading of a struggle over water that erupted along the western coast of Okinawa island in the early 1930s. Despite previous narrations of the struggle in Ginowan as a localized fight between two old political rivals, I understand it as an extension of a struggle fought every day over who would set the terms of life and death. Palimpsests of colonial cities, riven, as Brand writes, with bigotries, reveal themselves just beneath the surface. So do traces of people who withheld, waited, and at times, collectively dreamt of destroying the world as they know it.[8]

Ceremony as Refusal

Theorist and literary scholar Shinjō Ikuo uses the word *deluge* to describe how unspeakable stories periodically demand a reckoning—an outpouring that he describes as at once a response to an intense thirst and inundation that leaves one struggling for air.[9] Shinjō's work takes up the bodily needs and wants that are satisfied by swallowing or releasing water that people experience as deluge. These uncontrollable flows of water become, in his telling, openings that at times connect their bodies with those of others who are also overwhelmed by memories that cannot be shared but can no longer be locked away as secrets. Deluge—made riskier as the water and its surrounding ecosystem become increasingly toxic due to the monuments to civilization that continue to be built as part of its forward march—collapses territory and time. It suggests a world in flux as the calculus of mourning and forgetting clashes with genealogical imperatives that necessitate total war. His work dwells on the way that Okinawa's structural and symbolic relation to Japan and the US empire are intimately linked to the deluge, but communicates through literary and other artistic genres that its arrival is neither predetermined nor controllable. It is an important intervention in a field whose limits lie in the reification of the category "Okinawa" in a manner that constantly brushes up against the risks of reinforcing colonial tropes and discourses.[10] His theorization of deluge expresses moments when the weight of the world held up by the blue clerk's labors becomes too heavy for all to bear.

Residents of Ginowan village in central Okinawa who fought against the takeover of their water sources by Naha city authorities in the early 1930s understood the power of water as healer, nourisher, gathering place, poison, conjurer of pasts, and destroyer of existing paths. Docks that were in regular need of repair and fortification as more people and cargo moved out from Okinawa in vessels that brought soldiers and materiel to the prefecture were potential chokepoints, to be sure, but they were also places that met the water and reminded people of their connections to those they longed to see again. The water that flowed beneath the docks connected the coasts and ports to inland spaces. Springs and mountain streams were gathering places, particularly for women, who were in charge of collecting water and presiding over ceremonies celebrating life and mourning death.[11] Many of these ceremonies that continued to structure the rhythms and spatial organization of village life revolved around *munchū*, or kinship groups. Everyday life was overlaid with ceremonies that were part of yearly cycles and rhythms of gatherings and worship at spiritual sites including springs, wells, trees, *noro hinukan*, and *noro dunchi* (see figure 7.1).[12] Bodies of water also appear as protagonists in stories passed down by communities as things that shapeshift into rice or other bodies of water when those who control access share what they have with a generous spirit.[13] It is no surprise that water became a central point of refusal across the western coast of Okinawa island during the early 1930s.

Before turning to the conflict that I call the Ginowan water struggle, I take a brief detour into Haebaru, a village southeast of Naha that was my great-grandmother's hometown. I read the right-hand ledgers of two additional farm households—the Teruyas (no. 77) and the Nakamuras (no. 213)—from Haebaru that were conscripted into the Farm Household Survey project in 1931. Reading these ledgers alongside those of the Yamashiro farm household and in the context of the water struggle in Ginowan gives us a sense of the meaning that ceremony continued to hold in the countryside despite the prefecture's efforts to implement austerity measures. I understand them as records of wagers they made that reflected and pushed the boundaries of acceptable expenditures as scrutiny over household spending intensified. Regulations against ceremonies, particularly those tied to mourning, were meant to assuage worshippers of civilization for whom loud or extended displays of joy or grief during weddings and funerals reflected Okinawa's backwardness. Reforming existing transfamilial

FIGURE 7.1. Woman drawing water from a well in the prewar period, Shurin. Naha City Museum of History, record locator 34541.

practices of mourning the dead and celebrating life were requirements for districts to qualify for state subsidy funds under the economic rehabilitation (*keizai kōsei*) project that began around this time.[14]

Ledgers kept by both households show that, despite the prefecture's efforts to curb what it deemed excessive and long-winded ceremonies related to births, deaths, and other occasions that brought farm households together, these practices remained important parts of village life at least through the late 1930s. Ceremonial expenditures (*kankon sōsaihi*) ledgers that recorded harvest cycle ceremonies illustrate the degree to which community and kinship ties remained central to the household economy despite the intensified policing of these relationships. Notably, both farm households made payments to *noro* (priestesses) and recorded these in their ceremonial expenditure ledgers. Head of household Teruya Kameichi's possession of the highest office (*kuchō*) did not stop him from calling on the ceremonial authority of noro during a time of unimaginable pain for the family.

The Teruya farm household more than doubled their landholdings—something celebrated by the prefecture—during the 1935–1936 fiscal year. This achievement was accompanied by devastating loss. On September 15, 1935, Kameichi and his wife, Kiyo, lost their third daughter, Shizue, who was five years old at the time. Shizue's younger sister, an infant born in late June 1934 passed away four weeks after Shizue. We learn of the death of Shizue's younger sister, whose name is never shared in the ledgers, from an entry in the ceremonial expenditures ledger for November 15, 1935: "This is the seven-week death anniversary (of Shizue) but during her four-week death anniversary, one more person passed away." Mourning for one daughter was interrupted by the need to record another daughter's death.

The ledgers offer limited information about the impact that these deaths had on the farm household. These glimpses appear in the language of expenditures: sake, incense, rice, meat, and tofu purchases are regularly recorded beginning on September 15, the day of Shizue's passing. Thereafter, expenditures for weekly memorials are recorded and interspersed with those of other ceremonies that took place annually. It was on October 16, just two days after the unnamed younger sister's passing, that we first see an entry of fifty sen paid to a noro. This expenditure reappears on November 23, this time for eighty sen. Despite the Meiji government's expropriation of noro land and the general removal of noro from positions of political authority in the government, noro continued to be important sources of comfort for grieving families.[15]

The Nakamura farm household, whose residence was in Tsukazan district, also in Haebaru village, was socioeconomically quite different from the Teruyas'. As tenant farmers who depended on the sugar economy, economic decisions they made were highly dependent on the constantly fluctuating purchase price of cane and the ability of the village-operated communal sugar manufacturing facility to accommodate their crop. What they had in common with the Teruyas was the high proportion of social reproduction costs (*kakeihi*) they devoted to ceremonial expenditures. They also experienced many losses during the 1930s.

The Nakamuras reported five family members in the 1932 survey ledgers: head of household Nakamura Masao (twenty-eight years old); his wife, Ushi (twenty-four); his mother, Kamado (sixty-four); his eldest son, Kenta (four); and his nephew Moritoku (ten). Masao's unnamed younger sister appears in later years and performed the majority of waged work along with her sister-in-law, Ushi, primarily in cloth weaving. The household's other major sources of cash income were their participation in the survey, which brought in twenty-five yen per year, and remittances from an unnamed person or persons in Hawai'i. Masao's move to newly occupied Hainan island in 1939 to work for the military brought in a one-time infusion of cash.

Like the Teruyas', the Nakamuras' ledgers reveal the heavy financial costs that accompanied celebrations of births, mourning of deaths, commemorations of unions, and participation in community-level harvests and other ceremonies. These always included meat and sake, which were welcome breaks from their usual diet of rice, sweet potato, sōmen, barley, tofu, and soybeans. These were often the only occasions when they could consume pork or goat. The household also made periodic payments to a noro and a one-time payment to a *yuta* (shamaness). While it is not possible to confirm why a yuta was consulted in February 1932, payments to noro indicate that the *munchū* system was thriving in Tsukazan. It is difficult to overstate the continued importance of munchū for cementing one's place in a kinship group and, by extension, a district. Munchū festivals or celebrations required members to gather and pay their respects to spiritual sites including tombstones, wells, springs, and trees in and beyond the district depending on where their ancestors came from. Noro payment entries, along with all explicit notations about munchū ceremonies, disappear from the ledger in 1940, the year that Masao left for Hainan as an employee of the Japanese military. They are replaced with payments to two major Shintō institutions in the prefecture, Naminoue Shrine and Okinawa Shrine.[16]

While it is impossible to conclude anything definitive from these colonial ledgers about the lives of members of either household, including their spiritual beliefs, it is notable that payments made to noro were recorded multiple times. It is not farfetched to observe that the world that valued the noro for her spiritual role in a village community that was structured in many ways by the munchū system remained intact alongside the dizzying economic and political changes spurred by infrastructural development and militarization. Whether to read this as a rejection of assimilation, an assertion of local authority, or something else altogether would require the kind of situated knowledge to which I am not privy.[17] In spite of state campaigns since the Meiji period to weaken the noro's political and material influence by eliminating their official religious functions and taking away lands over which they held a monopoly (*norokumoi*), their societal role was neither completely dissolved nor hidden, even in a set of documents that aimed to inculcate scientific rationality in Okinawa's agriculturalists. This may have been due to the importance of the ceremonies over which noro presided to chronically impoverished farmers, or, if we make inferences based on colonial bureaucrat and researcher Tamura Hiroshi's work, their existence may have even been welcomed so long as communalism did not turn into communism.[18] Whatever the reason, a world that valued the contributions of noro and yuta remained intact, even for small farm households that state authorities had deemed most assimilable to the Ministry of Agriculture's counterrevolutionary and, in Okinawa, colonial project.

Monopoly Capital in Ginowan

As representatives of empire treated the lives of young girls like Sachiko and Shizue as refuse, they reaffirmed the strategic value of Okinawa by funding infrastructural development projects that supported the military's aspirations for hegemony in the Pacific. Prefectural authorities worked with financial institutions like the Japan Hypothec Bank (Kangyō Ginkō) to build up the operational capacity of Naha port as they facilitated the migration of Okinawans as settlers to Palau, Saipan, and other Pacific islands as producers of surplus value for monopoly capital and as builders of military infrastructure for the wars to come.[19] Through repair and expansion projects, Naha port, along with ports on the island's eastern coast, joined Sakishima and Daitō islands as strategic nodes from which the military objectives of southward expansion and defense of mainland Japan could be secured.[20] These ports connected Okinawa to military installations in the Pacific mandate territories in order to support the plan to occupy Southeast Asia.[21]

Politicians began planning Naha's transformation into a culture city (*bunka toshi*) amid this aggressive military buildup.[22] The city's elevated position in the expanding empire had serious consequences for its residents. Increasing rents, neighborhood clearings, and crackdowns on pleasure quarters and their powerful women leaders accompanied road improvements, port repairs, and other capital-intensive projects that promised to transform Naha into something befitting its newly designated importance.[23] City politicians and prefectural authorities tried to quell the growing opposition to gentrification by insisting that these improvements would raise living standards for all.[24] Once completed, they promised, this infrastructure would improve the health and well-being of all residents.

The Naha city waterworks project was an indispensable component of this urban development plan. Initiated by Mayor Kishimoto in 1927, it was continued by his successor, Mayor Komine, who took over the tasks of overseeing budget creation, funding procurement, and the securing of appropriate water sources to bring tap water to the parts of the city that were most important for commerce, governance, and defense.[25] It clashed with the interests of men and women who resided in places where water would be drawn.

Ōyama, one of twenty-two districts (*aza*) in Ginowan village, was a key node in the water struggle. Gleaning the contours of prewar social relations there is challenging because war and US occupation-era base construction forced many families to settle elsewhere. According to neighborhood maps compiled in the process of completing the Ginowan city histories and occupation-era maps, the district had been divided into eighteen neighborhoods (*koaza*) and residences concentrated in six of them. The rest consisted of forestlands, fields, paddies, and other types of land that residents traversed daily. Most people lived in an area called Mejobaru to the southeast of Ōyama rail station. This neighborhood was a vibrant social hub in the district, with at least four *uganju*, two water sources, and some fields.[26] Once built, the Naha city waterworks' pipes ran horizontally and vertically through the northern part of this neighborhood and linked up to a main water line that connected Ōyama to the water purification plant in Mawashi village's Ameku district, just outside of Naha city.[27] Mayor Komine's selection of Ginowan as the waterworks project's main water source threatened existing social relations in Ōyama and obstructed residents' ability to continue to engage in their primary source of income, small-scale cultivation.

The Naha city waterworks, which identified twelve water sources for acquisition in Ōyama and the adjacent districts of Mashiki, Uchidomari, and Ōjana, was thus a colonial institution that was charged with implementing a project of resource extraction in order to take Indigenous dispossession in Okinawa (long facilitated by Indigenous dispossession in the Pacific, the Philippines, Hawai'i, and other destinations that Okinawans settled beginning in the first decade of the twentieth century) into genocidal overdrive. The bureau's plan to draw water from the rivers, reservoirs, ponds, streams, and springs of Ginowan village through underground pipes, pump it through Urasoe village's Makishi district, and store it at the purification plant in Ameku before supplying it to the city's residents and businesses required the consent of thousands of small farm households that happened to possess land along the route or could claim historical use rights to the water sources. Of all of those affected, Ōyama residents, whose well-being depended most on access to these waters, expressed the most determined opposition.

Ōyama's contested water sources were located along the western coast from Narisebaru in the northernmost part of the district, where the prefecture-owned Ōgumuyā was located, down to Kushibaru, which was the site of another abundant water source, Majikinagā. Ownership relations of this period are difficult to reconstruct since the two sources, the land registers (*tochi daichō*) and maps (*kyūzu*) that I referenced in other chapters to gain a better understanding of the changes to property relations on district and neighborhood levels do not exist in most parts of Okinawa.[28] I thus rely on the invaluable work of historians, published in *Ginowan Shishi* (Ginowan city history) volumes, who asked local residents to recall the locations of stores, residences, roads, spiritual places, and other sites that were destroyed by wartime preparations, the

Battle of Okinawa, postwar US military occupation, and post-occupation era development projects. Ministry of Agriculture and Commerce records from the 1920s and 1930s on protected forests and the Naha City Waterworks Bureau blueprints held at the National Archives in Tokyo helped me to visualize how the policies enacted in Ginowan were linked to larger long-term plans for the prefecture's transformation into a key strategic node in the Pacific.

The water struggle began when Mayor Komine issued notice no. 677, addressed to the head of Ginowan village Miyagi Takemasa, on July 30, 1929. It relayed the Ministry of Agriculture's approval of a plan in March to install tap water facilities in Naha. The *Okinawa Asahi Shimbun* dated August 16, 1929, reported that a group of politicians and technicians appointed by the mayor to the Naha City Waterworks Committee had traveled to Ginowan on August 12 to follow up on notice no. 677 and to inspect the water sources that outside experts had selected.[29] To their surprise, they were rebuffed by village authorities and were only able to inspect a few of the locations, including Ōgumuyā, which the prefecture gained control of during former governor Narahara's first round of enclosures during the first decade of the century.[30]

Despite local authorities' noncooperation with Komine's proposal, Japan's financial elite publicly backed the mayor. The president of Tainansha, Yasuda Gen'emon, declared his support in an *Osaka Asahi* article, "The Naha Waterworks Gets Underway" on October 10, 1930, the same day that Komine sent a letter to the interim Ginowan village head stating that he would be forced to apply the Land Expropriation Law as a final measure against residents if they continued to refuse to grant the city access to their water sources.[31] Yasuda's enthusiasm for the project followed a series of blows dealt to Tainansha's position as the largest Japanese sugar capital in Okinawa. For starters, its more powerful rival, Mitsui Bussan, had announced the previous year that it would begin directly importing brown sugar from the prefecture's producers in December 1929.[32] This competition, as well as worker organizing against Tainansha's exploitative tactics, had made his efforts to expand centrifugal sugar production in the prefecture increasingly difficult.

President Yasuda's declaration of support for the project came right after he announced cost-cutting measures in Tainansha's five sugar factories in Okinawa that included laying off highly paid workers and lowering the purchase price of cane.[33] As one of the leading producers of centrifugal sugar in the prefecture, any measure Tainansha deployed to maximize its own profits immediately affected social relations in Ginowan. Of the 2,375 farm households in Ginowan, 2,009 cultivated sugarcane. In addition, of the total area under cultivation, 84 percent was used as fields to grow a combination of sugarcane and sweet potato, the two primary items produced in Okinawa.[34] Yasuda's support for Komine's project as he announced these cuts did not help to ease the tensions between small sugar producers and the company.

The fight that unfolded in Ginowan was part of a new phase of the conflict between large sugar capital and small producers. In June, just months before Yasuda voiced his public support for the waterworks project, two hundred laborers hired by Tainansha to conduct land reorganization around its factory in Yomitan village went on strike. The concrete issue was the discrepancy between promised and real wages, but its leaders reframed the conflict as a broader struggle between labor and capital. Higa Kamejirō's article in the September 1930 edition of *Senki* (Battle flag), "We in Okinawa Also Fought," explained the significance of the dispute against Tainansha, which it described as "a large organ of exploitation of a colony, Taiwan." Higa called the 38,000 yen subsidy that the prefecture granted the company to cover half of its construction costs a "blood tax squeezed from the proletariat."[35]

Despite the subsidies it received and the profits it stood to earn, Tainansha decided to squeeze workers and peasants further. The company broke its initial promise of paying wages of forty to sixty sen per day and instead paid the workers twenty-seven to forty sen for their backbreaking labor.[36] Higa described the harsh conditions of the workers:

> Try working in the heat of this tropical region continuously for eleven hours at a time. Even horses will be happier in hell. Not only that, even if the factory whistle sounds, the factory's clock is set thirty minutes late. Workers found with a watch are berated, "If you factory workers have watches, stop working!" Even if it is as hot as a desert, workers are not allowed to drink water. How can we remain silent in these conditions?[37]

Yamada Kanji, one of the leaders of the Okinawa's Labor Farmer Party, helped organize the strike and compiled a set of demands that workers presented to the factory, which included a demand for access to drinking water during the workday. Their resolve, as well as solidarity from other workers, forced the company to cave.[38] Higa wrote the following about the significance of their victory: "Our demands are small. However, what we have battled for and have won is big. Our gains, even if just one sen, could only have been gotten through struggle. We were able to realize this and relay it to the workers of the prefecture."[39]

Having barely absorbed this most recent challenge to its tactics, Tainansha flexed its muscles on the water issue and other matters. On October 11, 1930, the day after Yasuda publicly backed the Naha city waterworks project, the company announced that falling sugar prices globally would force them to lower the price at which they purchased raw sugarcane from local cultivators once again. *Osaka Asahi Shimbun* estimated that losses to local sugar producers would total 200,000 yen when all was said and done.[40]

Complicities under Total War

Governor Ino had to tread carefully because further radicalization of the countryside would be antithetical to the broader project of securing Okinawa for the empire. Ino explicated the strategic value of Okinawa in a report titled "On Port Repairs": "Naha is Okinawa prefecture's foremost port. It is the gathering place for commodities. From Naha city, it is the center of shipping routes that connect to Kagoshima, Kobe, Osaka, Taiwan, South China and the various outer islands of the prefecture."[41] He followed this description with a discussion of existing communist threats and concluded the report with a plan to expand the port to accommodate larger vessels in the future.

The plan that Ishii Torao, the commander of the Okinawa regiment, a branch of the Sixth Infantry Division of the Japanese Imperial Army, submitted to the Army Ministry in 1934, "Plan for Okinawan Defense," clarifies exactly who stood in the way of securing Okinawa for the empire. Ishii approached defense from two main perspectives. First, he described the islands of Okinawa as forming a wall between the Pacific and the East China Sea that was crucial for keeping Japan's imperial rivals, the United States and China, at bay: "It would be very damaging if any one island or harbor was taken by the enemy."[42] He emphasized that these defensive capabilities could only be fulfilled if dangerous elements within the prefecture could be eradicated.

These "dangerous elements" were the second target of Ishii's defense plan. The section titled "Current Conditions" reveals Ishii's mistrust and contempt for all local residents. He explained that they could not be counted on to mount an effective defense of the islands from predators coming from the outside because their overall dependency, laziness, diseased bodies, promiscuity, and seditious tendencies were outward manifestations of their lack of self-consciousness as Japanese subjects.[43] Oozing with contempt for Okinawans, "Plan for Okinawan Defense" perfected the discourse of colonial disavowal that informed early colonial studies experts like Nitobe, who naturalized Hokkaido's colonization; was elaborated by Yamamoto, who echoed Egerton's apology for Indigenous genocide in the aftermath of the abolition of chattel slavery as an issue of labor procurement; and developed in Yanaihara's lament that Okinawans were responsible for ruining the settler colonial project in the mandate islands due to the excessive spending habits of their families back home. Ishii added his specific disdain for the people of Okinawa, whom he accused of having "no will to overcome the root cause of their suffering."[44]

Ishii proposed stationing over four hundred troops in different parts of Okinawa to counter the internal and external threats he identified as obstacles to protecting Japan from its imperial rivals. Armed soldiers would be placed in charge of coastal surveillance on Okinawa and Sakishima islands.[45] Infrastructural development would enable troops to move expeditiously throughout and between the islands and would allow them to access adequate resources while they were stationed there. Port development and fortification plans focused on the northeastern part around Kin Bay, the ports along the western coast including Motobu's Toguchi port, and the expansion of Naha port.

The discursive and material maneuvers that aimed to transform Okinawa, the territory, into a fortress against attack from external and internal enemies created the conditions for a set of complicities that Hong Yunshin raised in her book, *The Battle of Okinawa and "Comfort Stations" in Memory*. The first military comfort station on Okinawa was not built until 1941, but militarization, coupled with the notion that Okinawa and Okinawans were dispensable, created the conditions of possibility for the establishment of close to 150 military sex venues across Okinawa where approximately 1,000 Korean women and a smaller number of Okinawan women were confined and forced to provide sexual services to occupying Japanese soldiers.[46] Many of these were built in the middle of village communities and were often converted large homes, schools, and public offices in full view of residents. Hong's monograph was made possible by the work that activists, local historians, writers, and residents had been doing since the end of the war to make sense of their wartime experiences, which included their memories of Korean women who were forcibly brought into their communities. Hong's is the most explicit call for Okinawans to interrogate their own wartime complicity in perpetuating sexual violence against other colonial subjects.

Hong's query about Okinawans' complicity in wartime military sexual violence against Korean women in the prefecture can be extended to the islands of the Pacific where the Japanese state built up military facilities during the 1930s and early 1940s. This accelerated development combined the infrastructural with the intimate and occurred in parallel with similar processes that converted villages into airfields and bases and dredged harbors to build seaplane bases in places like Jaluit, Malakal, Ngerbesang, and Peleliu.[47] The transformation of the mandate islands into a battlefront required, as Mori Akiko shows, not only building military infrastructure, but converting the islands into resource procurement sites. With the declaration of total war mobilization, the Nanyō Takushoku company, which had been entrusted with developing and managing the phosphate industry in the mandate islands in addition to managing Asahi settlement's pineapple industry, became part of the military recruitment apparatus.[48] It compelled workers, predominantly from Okinawa and Korea, to begin producing food for Japanese soldiers, mainly on Pohnpei in 1939.[49] Okinawans were also mobilized, along with Korean workers, convict laborers, POWs, and Pacific Islanders, to engage in military-related construction from late 1940 on.[50] The stories of these workers (some of whom may have witnessed the military sex venues that were built on Palau and Guam), like the stories of workers who traveled to Banaba in 1908 and 1910 to work for the PPC, remain largely absent from Okinawa (or Japan) studies' narratives of life under Japanese colonial rule.[51] The ocean links these stories of wartime complicities together.

Absolute Refusal

Back to the water struggle in Ginowan. Little progress was made for months after the Naha City Waterworks Bureau first attempted to inspect Ginowan's water sources. This was because city officials could not come up with a satisfactory answer to the question that Ginowan village head Miyagi posed at the start: How would the city's proposal to draw water on which residents depended for irrigation, agriculture, and everyday life be enacted without seriously threatening the well-being of those living there? In an article, "Inadequate Explanation of Water," Miyagi reiterated his skepticism: "We would like to think more about the costs and benefits to the residents of the village.... The question remains, how much of the water is going to be taken by Naha City Waterworks and how much will be left for the villagers?"[52]

Members of the village assembly echoed these concerns. An *Okinawa Asahi* article reported the results of a meeting they held on October 20, 1930: "These water sources are not only used to irrigate fields and paddies. During times of drought, they are also used by people and livestock as drinking water. Water quality is the life-source of the villagers."[53] They countered Komine's invocation of the "public good" with the language of protecting the "health and hygiene" of residents, noting that they had already experienced diminished supplies "for over ten years," a time frame that corresponds to the arrival of Tainansha and other Japanese sugar capital to the region. They also referenced ancestor time—that is, generations of life on the land—in order to argue for their customary right to the water sources of their communities. This language would have been legible to colonial bureaucrats at the time, though Okinawa's coloniality meant that invocations of customary law and practice to oppose privatization and enclosure of communally managed resources were readily overridden by appeals to public good or interest, which did not include the general well-being of the people of Okinawa.

The stalemate between residents and Naha city could not be broken even by a prefectural order that granted authorities permission to access water sources in Ginowan in early November 1930.[54] Sensing no way out of the deadlock, Komine formally requested permission from the home minister to invoke the Land Expropriation Law for eight of the twelve water sources that remained.[55] The Home Ministry granted this permission on May 18, 1931. As a result, 120 people who owned land, 244 people who held water use rights, and 7 others who were listed in the order as "related parties" were compelled to turn over a total of 7 tan 4 se 24 bu of land valued at 2,844 yen 66 sen in Ōyama, Mashiki, Uchidomari, and Ōjana.[56] According to this order, the city's lease would begin on April 1, 1933, and would remain in place for fifty years (eventually shortened to fifteen years).

Acknowledging the fundamental unknowability of what motivated residents to continue to engage in the struggle despite the abundance of certain kinds of data (maps, petitions, orders, statements, etc.) is necessary even as we provide the context needed to argue for the significance of residents' continued refusals to allow officials access to Ōyama's water sources even after the state commenced its process of expropriation. Despite lacking powerful allies within the prefecture or prospects for change, residents defied the order and maintained their refusal even after the expropriation order went into effect in the spring of 1932.[57] The papers reported on these holdouts as though they were just a small number of greedy landowners who were delaying a project that would benefit the greater good. However, as the occupation-era landholding maps (*ippitsuchi chōsazu*) suggest, most if not all of the people who owned plots of land along the path of the water pipes refused to comply. These exceeded clan or kinship affiliations, although it is impossible to rule out the importance of these relations at neighborhood, or subdistrict (*koaza*) scales. As a result of their continued noncooperation, the Expropriation Law had to be applied to approximately three kilometers of land stretching from Narisebaru in the northernmost part of Ōyama down to Hamabaru in Uchidomari.

A map of these areas can provide us with a good indication of the scope of the refusal, but it cannot reveal much about how the collective resolve of so many small farmers was cultivated or what visions participants articulated during their opposition to the project. What knowledges and experiences were embedded in their insistence that "water is our life source"? What were the limits of community that this claim invoked and how did these reverberate at the time or in later struggles?

For one, their tactics suggest a profound distrust of the modern land ownership system's method of forcing consent, the land registration system. Rather than seeing this system as giving titleholders legitimacy over their holdings, the resisters understood it as a mechanism of enclosure whose true authority lay not in consent but in the state-capital alliance enforced by the police and the law. This system, which Brenna Bhandar calls "title by registration" to describe the way that property law naturalized racism and patriarchy by embedding it in the legal sphere, buttressed its legitimacy by counterposing the registration process to what it labeled an exceptional measure, the invocation of eminent domain.[58] The way that Ōyama's landlords dealt with the authorities' attempts to force a legal process onto them shows their recognition of regular and exceptional modes of ownership transfer as two sides of the same private property regime the state upheld through force.

An *Osaka Asahi* article published on March 25, 1932, "The Application of the Expropriation Law on Water Sources and Land," explains that Ōyama landlords refused to comply with even the procedural elements needed to begin implementation of the order: "The village's landowners refuse to adhere to the city's selling agreements and they even refuse to create a land registry (*tochi chōsasho*)."[59] A follow-up article titled "The Expropriation Law Applied as a Final Measure" provides additional details: "110 landlords from Ōyama Miyasato etc. are not complying. The city has asked them to submit their land registries to the city's waterworks bureau by the eighth but to no avail. They were eventually returned blank."[60] Returning the forms blank not only escalated their fight against the Home Ministry; it expressed their rejection of the legitimacy of the state's seizure of their land. It also declared the legitimacy of their existing relationship to the lands, the waters, and the relations that were kept alive through access to these spaces.[61] The forms that they returned blank and the forms that small farm households filled out in excruciating detail, the latter peppered with hints of time they stole away to grieve and celebrate together, are not as far apart politically as one might imagine, though it is not possible to trace any direct lines between time carved out to mourn the deaths of young girls in Haebaru and Misato and the persistent fight that Ōyama residents waged to keep their water sources in their own hands.

At stake in the Ōyama residents' fight was the ability to collectively define what was needed to live in abundance. Access to water sources had allowed small farm households to avoid becoming completely dependent on large sugar capital for their livelihoods. Within Ginowan village, Ōyama's economy was quite diversified despite Tainansha's entry. Many young women worked as peach sellers and traveled quite a distance to Goeku village (in the north, near Misato) in the mountains to procure peaches that they sold the following day at nearby villages Shuri, Naha, and at times as far south as Itoman.[62] The arrival of the railway and the development of the prefectural road (*kendō*) along the western coast of the village had already created new nodes of interaction that supplemented the Yanbaru ship ports that had provided safe harbor along both coasts of the island for merchants who transported people and commodities in and beyond Okinawa.[63] Stores called *machiya* that served each district opened their doors along the prefectural road that ran north to south across the island and at train stations.[64] Residents struggled to maintain connections with relatives and friends who had to move outside of their hometowns for survival. In these ways, Ōyama was already a vibrant part of the regional tapestry that had been greatly transformed after annexation. A project as large and extractive as the Naha waterworks was bound to be met with scrutiny.

Women in Ōyama would have been particularly affected by the loss of access to existing water sources in their neighborhoods since they performed the vast majority of the social reproductive work that hinged on daily access to the rivers, springs, wells, and other water sources abundant in Ōyama. As entries recorded in *Ginowan Shishi*'s Ethnology/Folkore (*Minzoku*) volume show, water also played a key role in many of the ceremonies that sustained and reaffirmed communal ties in Ginowan. Mendakari Hijā-gā, a spring south of one of the sources slated for use by Naha city, Majikinagā, was the clearest example of this in Ōyama. It was used not only for bathing, cooking, and laundry, but for ceremonies to welcome new lives into the community (as such, it was called an *ubugā*).[65] It also doubled as important spiritual sites called *utaki* or *uganju* that were presided over by noro, who were indispensable for maintaining these relations.[66]

In addition to their practical and spiritual importance, water sources throughout Ginowan were also openings to worlds outside of the strict confines of family: places where people exchanged information and nurtured relationships; where resources that enabled women's economic activities outside of the workplace could be accessed and where people might form bonds that transgressed the limits of what was deemed acceptable. In a moment when options seemed to be contracting, these openings could be escape hatches from the dangers, toxicities, and alienating work processes that met them in the home and in the factory. Water sources offered connections to people and places beyond their neighborhoods and produced relations that were at times completely out of sync with both the unchanging Okinawa imagined by folklorists and the homogenous empty time of capital.

If the phrase "Water is our life source" reflected a fight to collectively nurture a set of relations that could stand outside of, or at least alongside, the increasingly suffocating logic of Japanese grammar, what connections can we draw between the struggle in Ōyama and acts of withholding that I identified as the left-hand pages of the Farm Household Survey ledgers? Both might be read as acts that ordinary people who felt the colonial gaze engaged in to protect entire worlds, material and imagined, that allowed them to create openings for each other beyond the heteronormative family whose boundaries seemed to harden the more that Okinawa's position as the inner frontier of the Japanese empire solidified. Safeguarding water sources and keeping family secrets in the ledgers of the Farm Household Survey kept open connections to the departed and the living without which even a temporary reprieve from the state's violence could not be guaranteed. Much more than livelihood narrowly defined as the ability to secure the material conditions of reproduction was at stake in Ōyama and surrounding districts where residents refused to give up control of their water sources. The sustained refusal of Ginowan's residents to comply with the expropriation order meant that even the state-owned river Ōgumuyā was not available for pumping water to Naha until September 1933, close to five years after then-mayor Komine had obtained approval from the city assembly to proceed with the project.

Deluge

The water eventually flowed south. Naha and its surrounding areas were transformed by the completion of the waterworks project and the expansion of Naha port (see figure 7.2). The Ameku district of Mawashi village, where the water purification plant was built, was drastically restructured following the city's purchase of close to fifteen thousand square meters of land on which it built a filtration pond and service reservoir.[67] While the official history of the Naha Waterworks Bureau, *Naha Suidō 50 nenshi*, does not mention any problems with the acquisition of or construction on these lands, the Ministry of Agriculture's documents on protected forestlands indicate otherwise. In 1934, three different plots in Ameku near the plant had to be released from protected forest status to accommodate the construction needs of the city.[68] Because Naha city owned these lands, there was no sustained clash with residents of the kind seen in Ginowan, but the maps included with the release requests show the broader consequences that placing the plant there had on the people who resided nearby.

The release request submitted by Mawashi village head Maeshiro for plot 1401 covered only a tiny piece of protected forestland owned by Naha city, which he explained was required in order to expand the road that connected Ameku to the rest of Naha—a requirement for laying water and sewage lines. The map that situates plot 1401 in a wider area shows that it lay next to fields, a large plot of protected forestland, and nine plots of graves (plots 1402–1410) that lay side by side. These graves were surrounded by protected forestlands, unprotected forestlands, and fields. While the grave sites were not destroyed during the installation of the water purification plant, due to the plant's strategic importance, they were decimated following a major air raid that struck Okinawa island on October 10, 1944 (figure 7.3). Not only did Naha residents lose their water supply; residents of Ameku lost a direct connection to their ancestors. Allied forces occupied the facility and found its height useful in mounting attacks on the city.

The end of the war did not bring an end to colonial rule in Okinawa or the Pacific Islands under UN mandate. Occupation, which commenced in Okinawa months before Japan's formal surrender documents were signed in September 1945, was a time when countless left-hand pages were added to the docks and when over a hundred thousand ghosts joined the queue of those who waited for a deluge to come. While much of the infrastructure, as well as entire landscapes that would have been familiar to Ginowan's residents in the 1930s, were destroyed by the Battle of Okinawa and enclosed by the US Futenma air base after the war, the contours of this earlier moment were not easily expunged. The prewar railway that transported people, sugar, and lumber from the central and northern parts of Okinawa island to Naha port was decimated during and after World War II but reemerged in the form of Highway 1 (currently Highway 58) and the "pipeline," the name of a road that lay between Highway 1 and Futenma that transported oil from the naval port in Naha city to military installations in central Okinawa.[69] Water pipes installed after the lengthy standoff in Ginowan were destroyed after the battle but were rebuilt quite easily in the early occupation period because Naha city had already expropriated the land in the 1930s.[70] During Allied occupation, control over these land and water sources was shared by the US military and Naha city's Water Bureau.

One young girl who paid the price for the renewal of Okinawa's position as a keystone for the US empire in the Pacific was a second-grade student named Ōshiro Tsuneko. In the spring of 1957, a moment still heavy with the weight of the island-wide struggles against the violence of US militarism in the mid-1950s, she lost her life on her twice-daily trek to get water for her family. Tsuneko was one of many girls and women who set out daily from different parts of Ginowan morning and night to procure water. She walked for a kilometer and crossed

FIGURE 7.2. Prewar water line construction at Naminoue. Naha City Museum of History, record locator 33061.

FIGURE 7.3. Haku and Naha city following the Allied forces' attack on the area in early May 1945. Photograph taken from the Haku water purification plant. Naha City Museum of History, record locator 17383.

Prefectural Road 34, which connected Ōyama to Futenma, in order to get to Chunnāgā, Kyūna district's largest water source. Initial reports by local papers *Ryūkyū Shimpō* and *Okinawa Taimusu* in their March 9, 1957, editions included a photograph of her small, bloodied body but little other information.[71] An article, published months after her death in the July 22, 1957, edition of *Ryūkyū Shimpō*, titled "Celebrations of Water in Ginowan Village, Kyūna's Districts" added more details of her death in a piece whose main purpose was to map the locations of the district's water sources.[72] It explained that Kyūna had three communal wells that had been spared enclosure in the Futenma air base, but residents preferred to walk one kilometer out of their way and up and down a steep hill called Kābira to collect water because the depth of their own wells made it extremely difficult to draw water. It was on her daily trek to Kābira that Tsuneko was hit by a bus. Similar routines of the daily grind to obtain water were shared by women and girls in other parts of Ginowan that had been spared the complete requisition of their lands (Isahama, Uchidomari, and Ōyama) by the US military. Other districts did not even have that—entire villages, including places where so-called comfort women spent their days and nights, were swallowed up into the vast military complexes that the US declared off-limits to them, along with the tombs, springs, forests, fields, and other spaces that residents had fought so hard to keep out of the hands of capital and the Japanese state after the kingdom's annexation.

Unlike the dramatic bulldozing of the fields of Iejima and Isahama a few years earlier that sparked the island-wide struggle of 1956, Tsuneko's death did not lead to the widescale mobilization of anti-base or anti-US struggle. However, we cannot discount how her ghost, like the ghosts of other girls who died early as a result of Okinawa's colonization, joined Yamashiro Sachiko's in haunting political life and nurturing worlds whose boundaries are amorphous, multiple, and never completely closed.[73] How did newspaper readers who had, just over a decade earlier, witnessed and survived genocide in Okinawa and in the Pacific Islands, experience Tsuneko's image splashed on the front page of the paper? Did people mourn her death in the aftermath of the crashing of a US F100D helicopter at nearby Miyamori Elementary School on June 30, 1959, that killed twelve children and six others?[74] When they mourned her death, did anyone think of Korean women who were confined in homes that the army requisitioned from local elites during the 1940s as so-called comfort women to the troops? Did anyone reflect on their own complicity in the violence that Japanese soldiers committed against CHamoru and Filipino women during the war?[75] Who refused the journalistic fetishization of her bloodied body and chose instead to celebrate her life?

Residents of Ginowan who fought Naha city in the early 1930s over the latter's attempts to install tap water in its most important neighborhoods could not have anticipated the specific conditions that led to Tsuneko's death when they punctuated their refusals to provide powerful city officials permission to extract their resources with the declaration "water is our life source." However, they and women farmers understood the importance of wells, rivers, springs, and other bodies of water that connected them to their loved ones across many seas, for example, and to their ability to maintain connections that gave them moments of rest, commiseration, and joy. Whatever feelings they may have harbored about the additional duties they shouldered as performers of rites for the dead, such as the practice of bone cleaning (*senkotsu*) that came under scrutiny around that time, they also understood that the attack on their collective access to water, like contemporaneous attacks on their relationships to land, threatened life as they knew it: value systems, eating habits, rhythms of life, and practices of mutual aid were under siege as Japanese capitalism in crisis demanded that they move to faraway lands as plantation workers, maids, soldiers, police officers, fishermen, and factory workers. They took on additional hours of piecework because labor laws did not have to be followed in the home and had to give up forms of play labeled immoral or debauched.[76] Their collective disposability as women living under colonial rule was also something they would have understood, even if the building of military sex venues (*ianjo*) in the middle of their villages, in their schools, on their fields, and atop their hospitals, the incalculable loss of life during the Battle of Okinawa, their wartime experiences in the Pacific Islands, and the terror of the US military occupation that followed Japan's surrender likely exceeded their worst nightmares.

Battles against processes of enclosure, dispossession, heteropatriarchy, and containment were never fought exclusively above ground. If digging dirt and uprooting trees in order to lay pipes in the ground was capital's use of infrastructure to expropriate Ginowan's water sources and create a privileged center of accumulation and consumption in Naha, people's collective refusals to acquiesce to this colonial project are reminders of the work of countless unnamed people who imagined and enacted different relations all along.[77] Linear narrative is the expert realm of historians, not of communities created under and against conditions of colonial domination. The ghosts of Sachiko, Shizue and her unnamed baby sister, Tsuneko; the Ōyama residents who refused expropriation by one of the highest offices of the state; Korean, Japanese, and Okinawan victims of military sexual slavery who were confined in schools, barracks, and civilian homes as military defense buildup commenced on the island; and the tens of thousands of young girls and women who lost their lives to the brutal wars in the Pacific are brought together by water, at times as a deluge, demanding remembrance and collective mourning. They, as well as the living who tend to their stories, are, like the left- and right-hand pages that they safeguard, the weather: mercurial, beautiful, uncontrollable, uncontainable, and dangerous for those who carelessly project their colonial desires onto them.

CONCLUSION   WAITING,

WITNESSING,   WITHHOLDING

As I wrote this book on lands stolen from the Kumeyaay peoples, during the COVID-19 pandemic, and in the aftermath of the uprisings that followed George Floyd's murder, I kept thinking about how here, and in the places that I discuss in *Waiting for the Cool Moon*, states and capitalists rob poor, colonized, and racialized people of the time, space, resources, and energy to mourn while they enrich their own coffers and sharpen their war-making capacities. In May 2022, the fiftieth anniversary of the return of Okinawa to the sovereign rule of the Japanese state came and went with little mention of the construction that continues on Henoko using earth that journalist Maia Hibbet describes as "packed with remains" from the Battle of Okinawa for landfill in order to buttress the region's strategic capacities.[1] The trampling, retrampling, and continued crushing and drowning of the bones of Okinawans, Taiwanese, and Koreans who died in the battle, and other people throughout the world who are deemed refuse, is required for the endless state of war that is life under capitalism.[2] The perversity of the world is that warships, planes, soldiers, anthropologists, engineers, and other instruments of war are deployed to produce mass graves and open-air prisons in the name of freedom, and the very same people take part in looting and desecrating the very same sites to establish even greater control over those who live through the onslaught.[3] At times, bereaved members of aggressor countries get to make their somber return to former battlefields in the name of healing, but that pursuit often produces nothing more than another round of looting and desecration of Indigenous communities who are made to welcome former soldiers and settlers back to the scene of the crime.[4] Records of struggle and domination that I write about in this book, from an institution that continues its own theft from Indigenous people, confirm the impatient stirrings of loved ones gone that weigh upon the lives of the living.[5] I understand these stirrings as refusals of what Dionne Brand calls the "aesthetics of imperialism," or what K'eguro Macharia calls the commonsense of the aesthetic experience of modernity.[6]

Jinah Kim's description of the present as a time "so bloated with dead bodies demanding mourning that their claims threaten to overtake life" sums up the way our vampiric present feeds on the bones of our ancestors—stripped of their flesh, our tears and sweat not abundant enough to enliven them.[7] I continue to think about how I can nourish these remains through exercises of accountability to the people in my life who have passed, and I think about how neither they nor I will be able to be at peace unless I come to terms with my inability to make their demands my own. I understand this inability to be inextricably bound up with the way that the imperatives of the colonial and imperialist present make me—make all of us—complicit in maintaining Brand's aesthetics of imperialism in different ways.[8] Deep mourning is important on a collective level, Kim insists, because it is a necessary precondition for insurgent action that begins from the rejection of the nation-state's declaration of certain deaths and certain people "unworthy of mourning and remembering."[9] Naming helps us to confront how nation-states, often in partnership with other states and capital, label certain peoples' lives and the political struggles they wage as antithetical to the very survival of humanity.[10] Kim warns that the work of mourning is hard because the aliveness of the dead "makes the present melancholy."[11] Our vision is clouded by the weight of generations of grief and fear of stoking the embers precisely because we have not readied ourselves to be engulfed by them.[12] Much of what has accumulated therefore remains in the left-hand ledgers.

Shinjō Ikuo, whose work I write about briefly in chapter 7, reminds us of the fundamental limits of approaching the world of texts as the primary battleground of mourning. His writings show how the demands of the dead sometimes surface suddenly and uncontrollably.[13] He writes about this mainly but not exclusively in the context of Okinawa, where stories, memories, experiences of multiple wars, and other manifestations of colonial and capitalist violence, though repressed, are never too far away—poets, essayists, activists, filmmakers, and survivors refuse to let them be forgotten for too long. Shinjō emphasizes that the connections between bodily manifestations of repressed memories and collective struggle are forged only through praxis, but warns that the first rule of struggling against the forces that keep these memories from seeing daylight or from being appropriated is to "not speak carelessly."[14] He uses the phrase "midari ni shaberanai" to caution against careless speech that places people in danger. In his work, the Japanese intellectual, confident in his ability to speak for Okinawa and treat it as allegory, appears as the primary propagator of careless speech. Shinjō further notes that such intellectuals' discursive mastery over Okinawa—a stepping stone—gives them a new lease on life, what he calls a new "political vantage point," as progressives who can critique Japan and the United States without ever having to turn the gaze back onto themselves.[15]

At first glance, *deluge*, the concept that Shinjō offers to describe the reckoning that is demanded by people who carry unspeakable stories of harm and trauma, and his warning to not speak carelessly appear irreconcilable. However, we can better understand what he is at pains to express when we situate his writing in an intellectual genealogy of other thinkers, like Okamoto Keitoku, who also expressed wariness toward Japanese intellectuals (Okamoto phrased it more broadly as "people who don't live here") who are unwilling to acknowledge their structural position as colonizer researchers. This label is not a personal insult but is a critique of the notion of objective analysis that *Waiting for the Cool Moon* engages. Critique begins from the premise that revolutionary strategizing and praxis, historically and in the present, require us to work across scales by recognizing rather than eliding the potential for intense disagreement and irreconcilability that come from our different positionalities—a concept that, for me, is a demand to continually reassess our place in the world rather than treat it as a fixed place from which we demand accountability from others. Coming together in difference requires a baseline acknowledgement of how each of our positionalities structure our prejudices, our complicities, what we are simply not able to see, and what power we are simply not willing to cede even as we use all the right words. It also requires that we take a side when the moment requires it.

Racialized and colonized people—particularly women—who appear in *Waiting for the Cool Moon* as mourners, organizers, thinkers, mothers, revolutionaries, daughters, lovers, and sisters living through the post–World War I crisis offer us lessons in how to do the difficult work of interrupting the narrative of inevitability that surrounds their premature deaths. In writing about their refusals of Japanese supremacy, born of a realization that the Japanese state and capital's protectionist policies were not meant for them (and, in fact, required their continued domination to be actualized), I refuse the temptation to draw a straight line between the spaces they carved out and collective struggles. Teleology and linearity cannot express the vastness of the dreams that animated each of the actions that enter the historical record. Many of these dreams are withheld by someone akin to Brand's blue clerk, who understands that new warships are always on the horizon, that there is a danger in opening the floodgates because they may enable careless speech.[16]

I grappled with how to write in a manner that could convey the magnitude of their struggles without turning them into fodder for triumphalist narratives of nation-state, empire, or capital. This required that I acknowledge the position from which I write. I had to constantly ask myself how, from my specific place in the North American academy, fueled by its appropriative consumption of the stories, labors, knowledges, and bodies of racialized, colonized, and Indigenous peoples, I should write about the refusals of the women and men who appear in my book as and against Japanese conquistadors as figure, structure, and sensibility without replicating these dynamics. As I explain in the introduction, Dionne Brand's works taught me that a necessary starting point was acknowledging that my own vision was limited by my place in the multiple academic-military-industrial complexes that enable me to do my work. Recognizing that where I stand, however shaky that ground may be, must be the starting point of analysis gives me clarity as I approach the archives as always already sites of contention, withholding, and refusal that can never be faithfully represented. Instead, I approach the right-hand pages I have been given access to as openings that transform me, through my encounters with them, into a sharper critic of the world in which I live.

Encountering Brand's *The Blue Clerk* fundamentally challenged my thinking about the relationship between struggle and the archives, and it put into words the impossibility of the kind of narrative certainty that the historical discipline demands. As much as it has helped me to think about writing about moments of mourning, remembering, and waiting that appear quiet on the surface but simmer with poetic rage, *The Blue Clerk*'s meditations on withholding have been most important for this book. Brand writes about the labor of withholding that she (and her blue clerk, and the blue clerk of the blue clerk) performs, "I have left this unsaid. I have withheld ... I have withheld more than I have written."[17] Withholding and waiting go hand in hand. As the blue clerk steels herself for more cargo of war to be unloaded, she contemplates the shape of new secrets that will have to be guarded. These secrets, she reminds us, have already been vetted by the people who appear in photographs, diaries, and other genres that freeze life into static frames. A conversation between the author and the clerk (the clerk is the author) in verso 16.3, "Museums and Corpses," says as much. To the author, who laments her ability to see her own body as "bags of muscle and fat and bones that are utilized in humanist narrative to demonstrate the incremental ethical development of a certain subject whom is not we," the clerk insists that her ability to see is not unique or particularly avant-garde: "People live that every day."[18] She continues that it is just that they cannot bear to live the consequences of what they see all the time: "It is too lonely there. It is a chasm."[19] I treat the people—many of them unnamed in the archival materials—who appear in this book as those who occupied that chasm and in so doing opened a space from which to see more clearly. Others joined them at times, but comradery was never guaranteed.

While comradery or collective struggle is never guaranteed, possibilities for transformation are pried open only through a willingness to occupy the chasm created by recognizing—by bearing witness, for starters—that liberation or freedom cannot come through the pursuit of imperial aesthetics. Ruth Wilson Gilmore describes the difficult work that people perform to occupy this chasm together as "abolitionist geographies."[20] She values the often messy, rare, and exhilarating moments when people discuss and enact abundance on their own terms. For those of us who want to be transformed through our study of what she calls "rehearsals for revolution," seeing relationships of radical dependency created through acts of place making require that we take critiques of historicism seriously when we craft our narratives. Nothing is guaranteed, and our writing should reflect that. Writing with care requires that we grapple with our own complicities in the here and now.[21]

Cedric Robinson's work similarly teaches us that any effort to draw easy conclusions between consciousness and action are futile, not to mention arrogant. The phrase "revolutionary attack on culture" appears throughout this book to mark subtle shifts in sensibility that preceded intellectuals' identification of detectable shifts in collective consciousness. This phrase comes from Robinson's essay "The First Attack Is an Attack on Culture," which argues that "the leadership always emerges after the mass."[22] When it comes to the direction of what has coalesced into a political movement, he warns, "that visible figure [the leadership] tells you nothing about what is to become, tells you nothing about what will happen." The only thing that charismatic figures can teach us, he writes, is "what already has happened."[23] Maybe the intellectuals that I critique throughout this book have no response to the militant organizing that was taking place before their eyes because they simply could not see what was happening. This is tied to whom they could recognize as comrades and fellow actors in collective pursuits of freedom.

Robinson's understanding of transition is another direct challenge to historians, even historical materialists, whose primary mode of engagement is the textual and whose primary narrative structure remains chronological.[24] We are better equipped to read what is sayable at a particular historical juncture than to make sense of how what is sayable (and, relatedly, imaginable) shifts as a result of forces that are not controlled by leaders or platforms. This makes us especially ill-equipped to apprehend changes to sensibility—the very thing that C. L. R. James and Sylvia Wynter flag as the deep underpinnings of coloniality, whose transformations signal important shifts in the very ground on which mass political consciousness grows. By paying attention to what Robinson calls wars between imperialist and revolutionary attacks on culture that operate on different planes and through multiple temporalities that the tools offered by critiques of political economy cannot apprehend fully, he offers us conceptual tools to think about the link between the lives of ordinary people that can only be glimpsed for a fleeting moment in the archives, shifts in collective understanding that make themselves known through the rise of a charismatic leader, state repression, a strike, or other events that become important historical markers after the fact, and how our own changing presents structure what we are able to see and put into words. Robinson's language of war rather than hegemony expresses the stakes of these often violent struggles over language, logic, land, institutions, and imaginaries, including conceptions of the relationship between pasts, futures, and presents.

What Robinson's and Gilmore's methods have in common is that they push writers and readers to develop their own capacity to imagine, fundamentally challenged by grappling with how others have fought for their freedoms in times and spaces a certain distance from their own.[25] This includes acknowledging that most stories are not accessible to us.[26] Okamoto said something similar on the eve of Okinawa's reversion to Japanese rule in his writings on kindness. He said that kindness was not sympathy or empathy but a political analytic that was guided by a refusal to accept things that may invertedly or indirectly place other people in harm's way during one's pursuit for freedom.[27] To be less complicit in the suppression of other peoples' aspirations for freedom, it is imperative that we acknowledge and grapple with irreconcilability.[28] To do so means being aware of our capacity to place people in harm's way through our careless speech and writing—in other words, through our arrogance disguised as innocence.

By taking the violence inherent in historical research and writing seriously, *Waiting for the Cool Moon* is in part a challenge to the field of Japan studies, which not only seems to have taken comfort in the notion that imperialism needs only to be contemplated as afterlife but continues to write mostly in an extractive, that is to say, colonial, mode.[29] Brand, Kim, Shinjō, Gilmore, Robinson, and others remind us that neither teleologically nor allegorically writing about the so-called past can honor the way that people continue to forge relations of abundance—centrally, with their loved ones who have passed but cannot rest—in the face of dominant colonial sensibilities that demand that they carry on for their own survival.

I have tried to eschew uncritical uses of all-encompassing terms that shut down conversation where it is most needed. I have asked what unexamined notions of *human*, or *Man*, or *Japanese* are taken for granted by those of us who are paid to engage in a study of "Japan." How do we misrecognize these abstractions as universal, and what are the consequences of not historicizing these categories today as we specify our objects of inquiry? Whose lives are made disposable to keep the illusion of a stable Japanese nation alive? In more concrete terms, whose lives, experiences, and struggles risk slipping from the frame when "Japanese fascism," "total war mobilization," or "primitive accumulation"—all markers of a critical historical practice, to be sure, but at this point overdetermined—are defined as discrete moments to be analyzed, problematized, and seen as concepts that are only relevant for illuminating the national past as such? What solidarities are rendered (in)visible and made (im)possible in the act? What life-affirming relations emerged despite the determination of state forces to keep differently racialized people dehumanized, separately? I have kept these questions at the forefront of my own reading practice as antidotes to (my own) careless speech. In this sense, this book is an experiment in history writing of the present.

It is also a book about listening and holding close what poet and filmmaker Shō Yamagushiku calls Uyafaafuji's refusal (the refusal of the ancestors, in Okinawan language).[30] *Waiting for the Cool Moon* aims not to map kernels of a potential future coming together in revolution, but rather to offer glimpses of struggles that people waged from their cramped spaces against a colonial commonsense and imperial, that is to say, anti-Black, anti-Indigenous aesthetics that valorized the Japanese Man-as -human in the heart of empire. As long as the *longue durée* of white supremacy and its Japanese counterpart remain hegemonic, struggles against them that took place in the chasm of loneliness that I write about here remains part of a vast global record of rehearsals for revolution. These and many other struggles continue to shape, nourish, and transform a world that is heavy with the demands of those who have passed to be remembered and mourned even as anxious clerks are kept busy with their work of waiting, witnessing, and withholding.

NOTES

INTRODUCTION

1 Northern California continues to burn, and prisoners-turned-firefighters battle the blaze for a dollar a day. Who will treat their lungs? Tim Arango, Thomas Fuller, Jose A. Del Real, and Jack Healy, "With California Ablaze, Firefighters Strain to Keep Up," *New York Times*, October 28, 2019, https://www.nytimes.com/2019/10/28/us/getty-kincade-fires-california.html.
2 Or to be more precise, as Petero Kalulé has argued in "Being *Right-With*," "human rights law is a paradigm of unfreedom."
3 This is inextricably linked to the allegorical treatment of the plight of certain populations rather than an analysis of how those relations came to be, in much of humanistic scholarship. On the flip side, social scientific scholarship tends to reify these categories as stable units of analysis. See Shinjō, "The Political Formation of the Homoerotics and the Cold War" for a critique of the former in the United States-Japan-Okinawa relation and Patel's "Complicating the Tale of 'Two Indians'" on the relationship between caste oppression, anti-Blackness, and Indigenous dispossession in the Americas and outside of it.
4 Yoneyama, *Cold War Ruins*.
5 Weheliye, *Habeas Viscus*, 1.
6 Trouillot explains, "Whereas the positivist view hides the tropes of power behind a naïve epistemology, the constructivist one denies the autonomy of the sociohistorical process." *Silencing the Past*, 6.
7 Maile Arvin's work, *Possessing Polynesians*, underscores the importance of extending our analysis of whiteness to settler colonial contexts beyond the so-called West.
8 In verso 16.1 of *The Blue Clerk*, Dionne Brand lists the ways that Charles Baudelaire's muse, Jeanne Duval, is represented by Benjamin in *The Arcades Project*. Benjamin characterizes her, among other descriptions, as "the consumptive Negress" who taught Baudelaire the truth about French colonialism. Her clerk says, of the need to include her in this way, "all the bitterness toward Duval and all the jealousies, but most of all the secret architecture of modernity. Of poetry, itself." *Blue Clerk*, 88.

That is what reveals itself in *The Arcades Project*. We have to ask what secret architecture of modernity is contained in his version of historical materialism as well.

9   Benjamin, "Philosophy of History," 257.

10 The rejection of historicism to "seize hold of a memory as it flashes up at a moment of danger" was one of the most important aspects of my own methodology in *The Limits of Okinawa*, 15.

11 Robin D. G. Kelley reminds us of the importance of attending to the genealogies of struggle against capital that Cedric Robinson writes about in *Black Marxism* in the quote he pulls from the text in his foreword: "Marx had not realized fully that the cargoes of laborers also contained African cultures, critical mixes and admixtures of language and thoughts, etc. . . . these were the actual terms of their humanity." Robinson, *Black Marxism*, xiv. How these closely guarded terms of humanity of the living and the dead are incorporated into theorizations of historical transformation in the historical materialist mode is one of the main questions animating this project.

12 See Yoneyama, "Transformative Knowledge," 331, for her presentation of Benjamin's critique of additive modes of universal history.

13 Shona Jackson, in her book *Creole Indigeneity*, explores these dynamics in the context of nation-building in Guyana and settler colonial discourse more broadly.

14 This is all the more puzzling since Lisa Lowe published the essay that preceded her monograph, "The Intimacies of Four Continents," which called for an examination of the connection between Europe, Africa, Asia, and the Americas in the co-constitution of modernity, in 2006.

15 Yoneyama, "Transformative Knowledge," 331.

16 James, *Black Jacobins*; Mariátegui, *Seven Interpretive Essays*; Uno, *Nōgyō Mondai Joron*; Inomata, *Kyūbo no Noson*; and Yamada, *Nihon Shihonshugi Bunseki*. See Harootunian, *Overcome by Modernity*; Endō, *Science of Capital*; Walker, *Sublime Perversion*; Barshay, *Social Sciences in Modern Japan*; and Hoston, *Marxism* for analyses on the debate over Japanese capitalism in the interwar period.

17 Robinson, "First Attack." I explain this in detail in the conclusion, but revolutionary attacks on culture take place against imperialist attacks on culture. The former, he explains, take place before the so-called vanguard declares it to be so.

18 This is not to suggest a strict boundary between theory and poetry, but to simply point out that Brand's poetry is a demonstration of how rich and varied the writing must be because exterminating colonial sensibilities require much more than critiques of structures and processes. Brand discusses the difference between *The Blue Clerk* and *Theory* in an interview with Canisia Lubrin; Lubrin, "Q&A: Canisia Lubrin speaks to Dionne Brand."

19 Macharia, *Frottage*, 37.

20 Macharia, *Frottage*, 37.

21 Michele Mason's "Writing Ainu Out/Writing Japanese In" analyzes one early example of this process through a reading of Kunikida Doppo's "The Shores of the Sorachi River," which was written in 1902.

22   This was especially true after the state's implementation of the rice increase production policy (1920–1934), which directed colonial agricultural departments to prioritize the production of rice with the intention of lowering its price to urban consumers in the metropole. See Doi, "Chōsen Nōkai"; Shin, *Peasant Protest*; and Park, *Proletarian Wave* for more on the impacts that this policy had on local agrarian organizations and the development of organized peasant struggles.
23   Economists and economic historians have questioned the usefulness of the rather simplistic notion of an imperial division of labor by focusing on the relationship between rice and millet production, circulation, and consumption during the colonial period. This analysis, which examines the relationship between the metropole, the peninsula, and southern Manchuria, has shown that things were much more complicated than the proposed triangular structure in which Manchurian millet was sent to Korea, where rice producers consumed it while they cultivated rice for export to Japanese cities. The general structure could not, according to the scholars listed below, get at the specific impacts of imperial agricultural policies that were regionally specific and changed over time. See Tōhata and Ōkawa, *Chōsen Beikoku Keizairon*; Araki, "Foxtail Millet Trade"; and Takeuchi, "Kokumotsu Jyukyū." Neeladri Bhattacharya makes a similar call for regionally specific analyses in debates over the agrarian question in India in *The Great Agrarian Conquest*.
24   Barchiesi and Jackson, "Introduction," 1.
25   Barchiesi and Jackson, "Introduction," 9.
26   Lowe, *Intimacies of Four Continents*, 3.
27   This phrase is from Tiffany Lethabo King, who defines the term: "Rational 'Man,' or the ideal version of the human, was being invented through a construction of the sensuous and irrational Negro and Indian as 'a category of otherness or of symbolic death.' Western European men wrote and represented themselves (through cultural production such as Shakespeare's *The Tempest*) as conquerors in this era." King, *Black Shoals*, 16.
28   Mitropoulos, *Contract and Contagion*, 65–66.
29   Mitropoulos, *Contract and Contagion*, 65–66. Matsumura, "Rethinking Japanese Fascism," discusses the efforts of the Ministry of Agriculture and Commerce to reorganize the household through the standardization of the category of housework from World War I.
30   Davis, *Women, Race and Class*, 300.
31   See Spillers, "Mama's Baby, Papa's Maybe"; and King, "Black 'Feminisms' and Pessimism." King's essay reads Spillers' essay together with Kay Lindsey's "The Black Woman as Woman" as responses to Moynihan's infamous 1965 report, *The Negro Family*, as rare examples of texts that interrogate the category of family itself as a desirable way to organize Black (feminist) relations. In so doing, King illuminates the "violent ways that the family emerges as a category of violent forms of humanism." King, "Black 'Feminisms' and Pessimism," 70.
32   Lisa Lowe's discussion of how this process includes racialized Asian workers through the multiple meanings of intimacy in *Intimacies of Four Continents* also informs my analysis.

33 Haley, *No Mercy Here*, 5.
34 Haley, *No Mercy Here*, 11.
35 Trask, "Settlers of Color and 'Immigrant' Hegemony," 4.
36 On the perils of recognition see Coulthard, *Red Skin, White Masks*.
37 I am thinking here of the ongoing historiographical erasure of Japanese neocolonialism in Asia, as well as an unwillingness to understand the way that new military alliances like the Quad (United States, Japan, Australia, and India) make Japan an active propagator of genocide and settler colonialism throughout the world. See Harsha Walia, *Border and Rule*, chapter 3, on land grabs by Japanese capital on the African continent. Japan is planning to release water from the Fukushima nuclear power plant into the sea, which the Pacific Island Forum (PIF), a bloc of seventeen island nations, is protesting. See, for example, "Pacific Islands Urge Japan to Delay Release of Fukushima Waste over Contamination Fears," ABC, January 18, 2023, https://www.abc.net.au/news/2023-01-18/pacific-islands-japan-delay-release-fukushima-waste-fisheries/101869592.
38 Robin D. G. Kelley's writing provides us with many models of how to do this kind of work while being attentive to the risks that privileging certain actors and certain articulations of struggle can have in reinforcing other modes of erasure. See, for example, *Hammer and Hoe*, as well as "The Rest of Us."
39 Benjamin, "Philosophy of History."
40 Lowe, *Intimacies of Four Continents*; Lowe and Manjapra, "Comparative Global Humanities."
41 Brand, *Blue Clerk*. Barchiesi and Jackson also note the fundamentally compromised nature of archival records in being repositories from which to craft narratives of freedom seeking, writing that "the facticity of slave labor's 'agency' for the historian is tributary to archival records that take notice of black agency as a white problem, while otherwise systematically expunging black voices and experiences as evidence made inadmissible by property status." Barchiesi and Jackson, "Introduction," 4.
42 Brand discusses what this practice looks like through her readings of Gwendolyn Brooks's *Maud Martha* and Wilson Harris's *Palace of the Peacock* and invoking Édouard Glissant's opacity in *An Autobiography of the Autobiography of Reading*: "The event is the event of the colonial, but all elements, all characters, are present and in flux." Brand, *Autobiography*, 43.
43 Brand, *Blue Clerk*, 5.
44 Sharpe, *In the Wake*, 27.
45 I often wonder if this is foreshadowed by the writing of *Fish Story*, which contains two uncritical uses of the n-word (both citations), as well as a complete omission of the transatlantic slave trade in a section titled "Middle Passage" beginning on page 55. Like Benjamin in *The Arcades Project* (see note 8 above), the unintentional slippages are revealing.
46 Sharpe, *In the Wake*, 38.
47 Sharpe, *In the Wake*, 120.
48 Yoneyama, *Cold War Ruins*, and Lutz, "Bureaucratic Weaponry," each discuss how academic understandings of expertise and disciplinary conventions shape the

way that "knowledge" circulates publicly in ways that perpetuate militarism and historical denialism.

49 Wynter elaborates James's *pieza* conceptual frame, which I discuss further in chapter 2, in "Beyond the Categories of the Master Conception." Other scholars take up her theorization in the *Small Axe* issue devoted to a reading of her unpublished opus, "Black Metamorphosis." See also Bedour Alagraa's reading of Wynter's conceptualization in "The Interminable Catastrophe."

50 Teaiwa, *Consuming Ocean Island*.

CHAPTER 1. EMPIRE AND *OIKONOMIA*

1 Wynter, "Beyond the Categories."
2 Notably, it follows that the kinds of events and organizations that we consider to be oppositional or revolutionary need to be rethought. Cedric Robinson addresses this point directly in "The First Attack Is an Attack on Culture."
3 For writings on the *pieza* unit as well as the way that Wynter understands it, see Eudell, "From Mode of Production"; Cunningham, "Resistance of the Lost Body"; Smallwood, "Commodified Freedom"; and Bhandar, "Registering Interests."
4 Eudell, "From Mode of Production," 49.
5 Wynter, "Unsettling the Coloniality of Being/Power/Truth/Freedom," 262. See also Wynter and McKittrick's conversation, "Unparalleled Catastrophe for Our Species?" for a discussion that situates Wynter's work in relation to other anticolonial writers like Césaire and Fanon.
6 Uno Kōzō's *Kyōkōron* theorizes the necessity of crisis. See Ken Kawashima's English-language translation, *Theory of Crisis*; and Kawashima and Gavin Walker's discussion of the text in *Viewpoint Magazine*, "Surplus alongside Excess."
7 Robinson, *Black Marxism*, 28. James and Robinson are also interested in constant refusals that shape this "civilization." See Robinson, *Black Marxism*, from 111, on the profitability question.
8 We see this on full display in, for example, justifications for the establishment of the phosphate industry on Banaba, or Ocean Island, by British and Australian "phosphateers," which I discuss in chapters 5 and 6.
9 *Intimacies of Four Continents*, 15–16.
10 For example, the 1871 Edict Abolishing the Ignoble Classes was justified based on the need to abolish slavery, understood as a remnant of an outmoded form of social organization not befitting a modern nation-state.
11 We see this in Marxist theoretician Yamada Moritarō's definition of Japanese capitalism in *Nihon Shihonshugi Bunseki*. Though he paid careful attention to the kinds of labor relations rooted in the Tokugawa feudal regime that remained important mobilizers of a poorly compensated workforce during what he calls the stage of primitive accumulation and argued that it merged with the massive, state-directed military and heavy industrial projects that formed the "Japanese-style" (*Nihongata*) capitalist development, embedded in his description is a sense of abnormality stemming from national specificity that ultimately reifies nation and capital.

12 Wynter, "Beyond the Categories," 82. When I say *mid-nineteenth century*, this includes the unequal treaties that the Meiji government concluded with Korea prior to formal annexation, starting with the Treaty of Kanghwa (1876) and the Treaty of Chemulpo (1882). Horne argues in *The White Pacific* that the Pacific became a new site of imperialist competition in the mid-nineteenth century, fueled by the impact that the US South's defeat in the Civil War had on the global economy. As slavery was deemed illegal in the South, white settlers moved westward and to the settler states of New Zealand, Australia, and Hawai'i, where they also faced serious labor shortages. Blackbirding emerged during the very same period that the nascent Meiji regime was formulating its first policies regarding emigration. Placing the latter in this history is crucial for understanding how Japanese convict and contract labor fit into a transforming global labor regime that relied on Indigenous Pacific Islanders to mine the raw materials that fueled the imperialist conflicts of the late nineteenth century. Kazumi Hasegawa's dissertation, "Examining the Life of Oyabe Zen'ichirō," traces, through Oyabe, the circulation of racial discourses and policies between the United States, Hawai'i, and Japan during the early Meiji period.
13 Alagraa, "The Interminable Catastrophe." See also her conversation with Wynter: Alagraa, "What Will Be the Cure?"
14 Horne, *White Pacific*, 14. I challenge this narrative in chapter 6.
15 On the place of this incident in the history of blackbirding in the Pacific, see Tokushima, "Abolishonizumu Kenkyū."
16 I elaborate this point through a focus on the dispatch of Okinawan and Japanese workers to Banaba in chapter 6.
17 Quito Swan explains, "Just as Europe fraudulently utilized the suppression of the Atlantic slave trade as an excuse for its imperialism in Africa, Europe used the subduing of blackbirding as a rationale for the colonization of Oceania." *Pasifika Black*, 21. He cites the case of Germany, which acquired its first overseas colony, German New Guinea, in 1884. Japan took over its holdings in Micronesia and the Marshall Islands after World War I as class C mandates and quickly built up extractive industries there. I discuss this in chapter 6.
18 See Jackson, "Colonialism," for a definition.
19 Jackson critiques the materialist tradition in naturalizing Indigenous disappearance in the course of the emergence of a proletarian subject in *Creole Indigeneity*. She cites James's *The Black Jacobins* as one prominent example where the historical narrative is that of "enslaved blacks who clearly evolve into a proletariat." *Creole Indigeneity*, 29. They do so, Jackson explains, without Indigenous peoples: "They literally are not there." *Creole Indigeneity*, 30.
20 I think about witness in relation to Christina Sharpe's "Introduction" to Dionne Brand's *Nomenclature*. Sharpe writes of Brand's commitment to liberation that requires witness: "When, for example, the woman at the center of the long poem *Inventory* (2006) is faced with the choice to watch *Law & Order*'s endlessly reproduced and globally circulated formula of selective crime and punishment, to go to bed, or to bear witness to the wreckage of never-ending atrocities and disasters . . .

what should she choose but to witness, even as that witnessing is, and must be, partial, incomplete, ongoing." Sharpe, "Introduction," xix.
21 Roellinghoff, "No Man's Land," 47.
22 As recent works on Japanese settler colonialism by Eiichirō Azuma and Sidney Lu argue, Japanese intellectuals celebrated the colonization of Hokkaido as they distanced themselves from the colonialism of rival states by describing the Meiji regime's actions as merely doing what was necessary to ward off Euro-American imperialist designs in Asia. This narrative was aided by the exclusionary policies of the US, Canadian, and Australian governments against Japanese and other Asian settlers starting in the 1880s. Calls for an end to exclusionary policies based on the civilizational discourse morphed quickly and predictably into justifications of imperialist policies as soon as the country's military capabilities caught up to capital's need to keep expanding its terrain of surplus value realization. In addition to Azuma, *In Search of Our Frontier*, and Lu, *The Making of Japanese Settler Colonialism*, see writings on race during this period, such as Takahashi Yoshio's 1884 *Nihon Jinshu Kairyōron*.
23 Roellinghoff argues that, in contrast to policies toward the Ryūkyū Kingdom, which had to assimilate a foreign political entity, the treatment of Ainu Mosir was as terra nullius, and Ainu were targeted for collective disappearance. Mason, "Writing Ainu Out/Writing Japanese In," and Komori, "Rule in the Name of 'Protection,'" focus on the discursive erasure of Ainu Mosir by politicians and writers during the first decades of the Meiji regime. As for the state's policies toward the Ryūkyū Kingdom, while I agree with Roellinghoff that the kingdom's foreignness could not be evaded, the "problem" was quite quickly resolved at the discursive level through its enactment of the Preservation of Old Customs Policy. I write about this in chapter 1 of *The Limits of Okinawa*.
24 See Sakata, "Transformation of Hokkaido," 122, for concrete figures. They range from 3,123 in 1897 to 9,659 in 1894.
25 Sakata, "Transformation of Hokkaido," 127. There, they joined Okinawan, Korean, and Pacific Islander workers to labor under the supervision of Japanese military officials and civilian engineers. Yushi Yamazaki traces the movement of convict laborers from Fukuoka, Kumamoto, Nagasaki, and Saga to Hokkaido, as well as the halting of this practice due to rioting. He also discusses the conversion of the system into a different contract labor system called the *naya* or *hanba* system during the mid-1890s. Yamazaki, "Radical Crossings," 125.
26 Roellinghoff, "No Man's Land," 25.
27 Nixon, *Slow Violence*. Anthropologist ann-elise lewallen writes about the ways that Ainu women have asserted their claims to Indigenous rights in the face of these violences in "Ainu Women and Indigenous Modernity in Settler Colonial Japan." See also Sunazawa, "As a Child of Ainu"; and Uzawa, "What Is Left of Us?"
28 For an analysis of this dynamic in Palau, see Cortés, "Land in Trust." I also write about the role Okinawan workers played in this process in chapter 6.
29 While Yamada Moritarō argues in *Nihon Shihonshugi Bunseki* that working conditions that prisoners and others experienced in army munitions depots, Miike

Tankō, Yokosuka Steelworks, etc., were inextricably linked to systems of unfree labor control from the Tokugawa era, he writes about this as a form of primitive accumulation. He specifies that there is a mutual relationship between prison laborers, who enabled the war industries in the early Meiji period to develop; the workers in handicraft who formed the foundation for petty manufacture; and the women and girls who constituted the core of factory-based light export industries like match making. He makes this argument on page 54.

30 The colonial development of Yaeyama was especially intense from the early Meiji period. See Miki, *Yaeyama Kindai Minshūshi*; and Matsuda, *Liminality of the Japanese Empire*. The quoted portion is from a statement made by Kume Kinya, a state representative to a House of Peers session deliberating laws governing state-owned forestlands in Okinawa on January 27, 1907. Matsumura, *Limits of Okinawa*, 164.

31 Okinawaken, *Okinawa no Ringyō*; Nakama, *Okinawa Rinya Seido Riyōshi Kenkyū*; Ōsato, *Jahana Noboru Den*; and Isa, *Jahana Noboru Shū*. It was under Narahara's rule that the first Okinawans left for Hawaiʻi as migrant workers. He was in close communication with the Foreign Ministry to establish a system of contract immigration to Hawaiʻi. While the outflow of Okinawans to North and South America and the Pacific accelerated after his departure from Okinawa, he laid much of the groundwork for its growth, particular during the second decade of the twentieth century. "Gaikō Shiryōkan Shozoku Okinawaken Shusshin Imin no Gaimushō Kiroku," edited by Ishikawa Tomonori, has this official correspondence between Narahara and Foreign Ministry officials, and Hanaki's essay "Meiji Chū-Kō Ki no Okinawaken ni Okeru Imin Gaisha Gyōmu Dairinin no Keireki to Zokusei" presents the various immigration companies that set up shop in Okinawa during the Meiji period.

32 Kinjō, "Meijiki no Okinawa."

33 Though Yushi Yamazaki argues that Jahana, Tōyama Kyūzō, and Taira Shinsuke, not Narahara, initiated immigration from Okinawa as "part of economic and political justice for Okinawans" who were suffering from the governor's enclosure policies, the development of the prefecture into a disproportionate sender of migrant workers outside of Japan was inextricably linked to transformations that mainland sugar capital and politicians made to its socioeconomic relations, in particular, in agrarian villages. Yamazaki makes his argument in chapter 3 of *Radical Crossings*.

34 Lu, *The Making of Japanese Settler Colonialism*, and Azuma, *In Search of Our Frontier*, discuss the translation of these words. As Horne reminds us in *The White Pacific*, the Meiji government was actively trying to increase its influence in Hawaiʻi by leveraging its immigrant labor force in the decade prior to the US annexation of the Hawaiian kingdom.

35 Lu contests this narrativization by pointing out that Fukuzawa Yukichi's encouragement of Japanese migration to the United States was "a direct offspring of the shizoku-based colonial expansion in Hokkaido of the previous years." *Japanese Settler Colonialism*, 58.

36 Roellinghoeff, "No Man's Land," 259.

37 See Itō, "The 'Modern Girl' Question in the Periphery of Empire," and Matsuda, *Liminality of the Japanese Empire*.

38 Park, "Repetition, Comparability, and Indeterminable Nation," 227.
39 Barchiesi and Jackson, "Introduction," 2.
40 Yamamoto, *Shokumin Seisaku Kenkyū*, 133.
41 Yamamoto, *Shokumin Seisaku Kenkyū*, 135.
42 Yamamoto, *Shokumin Seisaku Kenkyū*, 94.
43 Césaire, *Discourse on Colonialism*, 41.
44 Uno, "Nihon Shihonshugi," 392. As he makes clear, one of the reasons why these protectionist policies became politically absolutely necessary, even though they were economically unviable, was the threat that socialism posed to all capitalist countries.
45 See Matsumura, "Triple Exploitation, Social Reproduction, and the Agrarian Question in Japan" for an extended discussion of Uno's work.
46 Uno, "Nōgyō no Kōsei," 463.
47 Uno reiterated that this labor was used mainly as a supplement, quoting Miyazaki Shinichi of the association: "In a country like ours where the employment of labor by the small farm household is not done in order to capture profit through employment of that labor, it is only to fill the lack of family labor power in an effort to maintain the farm household economy." "Nōgyō no Kōsei," 464.
48 Yamada discusses this as semi-serf relationships that continued from the Tokugawa period in *Nihon Shihonshugi Bunseki*. As the next chapter discusses briefly, Inomata Tsunao also problematized long-standing power dynamics in the countryside but, like Yamada, preferred to understand these as stemming from an older era. As the next two chapters take up, buraku studies scholars have debated the meaning of the reconfiguration of the "buraku problem" in the modern nation-state in relation to the agrarian question for decades. A summary of these debates in English is available in Teraki and Kurokawa, *A History of Discriminated Buraku Communities in Japan*.
49 On the formation of the Japan Farmer's Union see Waswo, "In Search of Equity." For a history of peasant struggles in modern Japan, see Mori, *Kindai Nōmin Undō to Shihai Taisei*, and Hayashi, *Kindai Nihon Nōmin Undōshi Ron*. On the Rice Riots inaugurating a new era of women's political activity, see Matsumura, "More Than the 'Wife Corps.'"
50 Hiraga, *Senzhen Nihon*.
51 The full text of the lecture he gave on the first day of the course, "Kosaku Mondai Gaiyō," was republished as a chapter by the Nōrinshō Nōmukyoku in its 1925 publication *Chihō Kosakukan Kōshukai Kōenshū*. According to his figures, membership in tenant organizations, of which the Japan Farmer's Union was the largest, was 163,931 in 1,530 associations at the end of 1922. By 1930, that number had more than doubled.
52 Mitropoulos, *Contract and Contagion*, 65–66.
53 Césaire explains the far-reaching impact of the internalization of the dehumanizing logics of colonialism by the colonizer as boomerang effect: "And I am not talking about Hitler, or the prison guard, or the adventurer, but about the 'decent fellow' across the way; not about the member of the SS, or the gangster, but about the respectable bourgeois." *Discourse on Colonialism*, 47.

54 See Greenberg, "New Economic History"; Folbre, *Greed, Lust, and Gender*; and Blaney, "Provincializing Economics."

55 All the while, projects aimed at increasing labor productivity in agricultural production claimed that women were more productive than men for tedious and backbreaking agricultural tasks. Refer, for example, to the reports issued by the Kurashiki Labor Studies Center, such as number 48, *Taue Sagyō no Gōrika ni Kansuru Kenkyū*, written by Yoshioka Kin'ichi, based on a time study of rice planting conducted in Saga prefecture with the cooperation of the Saga prefecture Nōkai.

56 Eudell, "From Mode of Production to Mode of Auto-Institution," 49, quoting Wynter's "Black Metamorphosis," 890.

57 For more on the way that Tosaka Jun used the family as the basis of his concept of familism (*kazokushugi*) in *The Japanese Ideology* (1935), see Endō, "The Multitude and the Holy Family." For more on familism refer to Tosaka, "Fukkō Genshō no Bunseki." The quote comes from Endō, 313.

58 Nancy Folbre and Marjorie Abel address how government statistics have themselves been plagued with gender biases in "Women's Work and Women's Households." Not only has this led to inaccurate accounting of the quantity of work that women performed; it has also played an active role in reinforcing gendered assumptions about women's work through the categories that it has used in the accounting process. Kate Broadbent and Tessa Morris-Suzuki have addressed similar issues in the context of Japan in "Women's Work in the 'Public' and 'Private' Spheres of the Japanese Economy." For more on the national census in English, see Winther, "Household Enumeration in National Discourse."

59 Nōshōmushō, *Nōka Keizai Chōsa*. Data for 100 households over twenty-one prefectures were included in the annual report. By 1942, the number of households included expanded to 1,400.

60 1 chō = 10 tan, or 0.992 ha. 1 tan = 1,000 meters squared, or 10 are; 1 se = 100 meters squared, or 1 are; 1 bu = 3 meters squared. The category half-owner, half-tenant farmer (*jikosaku*) referred to people who owned part of their land but had to borrow from a different landowner in order to have enough arable land to survive.

61 The work diary of the family I discuss is reproduced in Nōshōmushō, *Nōka Keizai Chōsa*, 121–30.

62 The cow was loaned out to a neighbor on June 1, 1921. There is no record of a cash or in-kind payment for this loan. Nōshōmushō, *Nōka Keizai Chōsa*, 133.

63 One of the earliest usages of *rōdō nōryoku* was in Kawakami Hajime and Kawada Shirō's 1911 translation of Austrian economist Nicolaas G. Pierson's writings on value, which were published in English in 1902 as *The Principles of Economics*. The phrase appears in chapter 6, titled "The Wages of Labour," section 7, "Work and Wages." Pierson countered Adam Smith's idea that wages exercise a great influence on the quantity and quality of labor and favored Alfred Marshall's position that efficiency influences the price of labor but it is not always the case that the efficiency of labor is influenced by its price. Like other neoclassical economists, Marshall's understandings of economic well-being were based on assumptions of human nature and definitions of equality that could only exist via the disavowal

of colonial histories and enslavement and the devaluation of waged and unwaged work performed by women.
64 Ōtsuki, *Book-Keeping System.*
65 Adult men received the highest laboring capacity of 10, which according to Sasaki Jun in his study of the distribution of labor in Kyoto's Tanba district, "1920-nendai Kōhan ni Okeru Tanba Chirimen Nōka no Rōdōryoku Haibun," reflected the labor of someone who performs "full-fledged" work. It should be noted that the application of the labor efficiency index in the 1921 Farm Household Survey was not as intense as what we see from the 1931 survey form, where the concept becomes fleshed out quite a bit, and its applicability becomes limited to agricultural production, which is divided into rice production and "other." In this version, the labor efficiency index is used to convert total work time recorded by a farm household into total number of days worked, which is then used to calculate "normal daily agricultural labor compensation." See 12–13 for the language that is used. An explication of the relationship between the two terms is in Teruoka's 1939 essay, "Manshūkoku Sangyō Kensetsu ni Okeru Rōdōryoku no Igi." "It has already been proven through a variety of projects on the ground that through training that allows humans to achieve 100% of their efficiency, they are able to extend their work capacity." Teruoka, "Manshūkoku Sangyō Kensetsu," 583.
66 The notebook of the family I discuss is reproduced in Nōshōmushō, *Nōka Keizai Chōsa*, 130–39.
67 The daily cash account book of the family I discuss is reproduced in Nōshōmushō, *Nōka Keizai Chōsa*, 141–77.
68 Part of the costs of employing them required feeding them three meals a day that included rice, grains, and side dishes. There is no record in the cash account book of any payment of cash wages.

CHAPTER 2. ENCLOSURE AND THE COMMUNITY OF THE COMMONS

1 For more in English on the meaning of this term and the way that some people mobilized politically around it, see Teraki and Kurokawa, *A History of Discriminated Buraku Communities in Japan*. See also Kobayakawa, "Japan's Modernization and Discrimination."
2 Kalulé, "Being *Right-With.*"
3 See Kurokawa, *Chiikishi no Naka no Buraku Mondai*, for details. Mie prefecture was a leader in national social reformist projects to study the "buraku problem," a project that intensified with the official start of its *buraku kaizen* project, led by Takeba in 1905.
4 Kurokawa, *Tsukurareta "Jinshu,"* 70–71.
5 "Yo ni Somukeru Buraku no Shisatsuki (31)," *Chūō Shimbun*, September 14, 1918, in *Kome Sōdō*, 301. This article, which focuses on Mie prefecture's Aioi in the city of Tsu, asks why there were many rioters despite its recognition as a model district that completed the "special buraku" improvement project. It suggests that constant vigilance is needed to stop them from backsliding.

6 Ōyama, *Mieken Suiheisha Rōnō Undōshi*, 17.
7 Ōyama, *Mieken Suiheisha Rōnō Undōshi*, 11.
8 "Furin Nado Heiki (6)," *Chūō Shimbun*, September 13, 1918, *Kome Sōdō*, 282.
9 *Yamayatoi* worked in the mountains, mainly collecting and transporting lumber and other forestry products. Ōyama, *Mieken Suiheisha Rono Undōshi*, 18. One shō is approximately 1.5 kg of rice.
10 Kurokawa, *Tsukurareta "Jinshu*," 117.
11 Ōyama, *Mieken Suiheisha Rono Undōshi*, 22.
12 Ōyama, *Mieken Suiheisha Rōnō Undōshi*, 26.
13 On the splits within Suiheisha, see Terawaki and Kurokawa, *A History of Discriminated Buraku Communities in Japan*.
14 Loo, "Escaping Its Past," 375.
15 What is state Shintō if not a weapon of Japanese militarism?
16 Totman, *Japan's Imperial Forest Goryōrin, 1889–1945*; Nakama, *Okinawa Rinya*; McKean, "Management."
17 Nakama, *Okinawa Rinya*, 157. Despite their dislocating effects, their significance was and remains underappreciated by many Marxist theoreticians whose stagist understandings of capitalist development relegated enclosure to a single moment of so-called primitive accumulation that ended with the enactment of the land tax reforms in 1873. Uno complicates this a bit, but not explicitly. Uno, "Nihon Shihonshugi."
18 Kikekawa, *Meiji Chihō Seido Seiritsushi*.
19 The 1907 law in its entirety is posted digitally at the National Archives, https://hourei.ndl.go.jp/simple/detail?lawId=0000009459&current=-1.
20 Mieken Sanrinkai, *Mie no Ringyō*, 10.
21 For a study of how pearl cultivators remade the coast of Mie, see Ericson, "Making Space."
22 "Mieken Isekoku Wataraigun Shigōson Ōaza Asama Aza Dake 547-1," Mieken Chiji Yamaoka Kunitoshi to Nōrinshō Daijin Takahashi Korekiyo, October 10, 1924, *Hoanrin Kaijo: Mieken*, 1924.
23 While the point is not explicitly made, this concern for preserving certain parts of a particular plot of land to secure the water sources that fed an area that extended well beyond formal territorial boundaries highlights the strategic concerns that could motivate petitioners or authorities to make strong cases for inclusion or release on lands that at first glance may not seem that valuable or productive.
24 "Wataraigun Shigōson Ōaza Asama Aza Dake 547-1 no Goryō Sanrin," *Hoanrin Kaijo: Mieken*, 1924.
25 This decision was published in the April 9, 1926, *Mieken Kōhō* along with details of all of the land in the village that would be incorporated.
26 "Kokuyūrinya Seiri Riyūsho," April 10, 1926, *Asamachō Rekishi Shiryōshū Kindaihen*, 96.
27 By far the largest area incorporated was plot 547-14 in Dake, Asama, and the smallest was 4 bu in Takao, 149-2, and Nagase, 811-5.
28 *Yamakasegi* refers to a diverse array of tasks, all of which denote dependence on access to the forests for livelihood. Common tasks include cutting down trees, collecting firewood, producing charcoal, and hunting for boar. This is a term for

talking about people whose livelihoods were inextricably linked to their access to nearby forests, who should be distinguished from terms used for waged forestry workers who worked seasonally for forestry companies to cut and transport lumber or make pulp (though they also did *yamakasegi*) and from the forestry capitalists who made their living exploiting human labor and monopolizing raw materials taken from the forests to accumulate capital.

29 "Shigōson Yamakaseginin no Tangansho," April 29, 1926, *Asamachō Rekishi Shiryōshū Kindaihen*, 98.
30 "Shigōson Yamakaseginin no Tangansho," April 29, 1926, *Asamachō Rekishi Shiryōshū Kindaihen*, 98.
31 According to land records, many of the holders of forestland in Asama, including some who signed the second petition, sold some of their land between 1924 and 1926 to the Asamadake Tozan railway company after receiving notice that their properties would be designated "railway lands" (*tetsudo yōchi*) in August 1924. Some, including Sakaguchi Shinemon, held additional land that was designated as protected forestland. It is revealed later in requests for release of protected forestlands made in 1929 that railway construction had led to many local disputes between the company, forestry workers, and landowners in the area because the rail line had disrupted residents' ability to even enter the mountains. See *Hoanrin Kaijo: Mieken*, 1926, for a detailed explanation of these conflicts as well as maps that illustrate the problems that forestry workers constantly had to deal with as development for religious tourism pressed on. Tetsudōshō, *Chihō Tetsudō Menkyo*. This was intended to cover a little over three miles.
32 Since he invoked article 18, no. 1, of the Forestry Law, he did not have to run this through the Chihō Shinrinkai.
33 What is interesting about the signatories on both petitions is that they do not appear to include among their ranks any people whose signatures appear as burakumin representatives of Asama in a document dated August 1930, "Kyōtei Sanka no Daihyōsha e no Iin Chōin," *Asamachō Rekishi Shiryōshū Kindaihen*, 128–30. This is particularly surprising as 80 to 90 percent of villagers who engaged in waged forestry work were from buraku neighborhoods.
34 "Kokuyūrinya Seiri Riyūsho," April 10, 1926, *Asamachō Rekishi Shiryōshū Kindaihen*, 95.
35 "Kuyū Sanrin Kōyūrinya Seiri—Ku no Tōitsu Kyōka," April 10, 1926, *Asamachō Rekishi Shiryōshū Kindaihen*, 94, and "Kokuyūrinya Seiri Riyūsho," April 10, 1926, *Asamachō Rekishi Shiryōshū Kindaihen*, 95
36 Kawamura, "Fashizumu to Buraku Sabetsu," 50.
37 "Kōyūrinya Seiri Ninka Shinseisho: Mura no Tōitsu Ninka," June 15, 1926, *Asamachō Rekishi Shiryōshū Kindaihen*, 106–7. This was approved to take effect on August 14, 1926.
38 On the various categories of compensation for work used in the Tokugawa period, including *temachin*, see Nagashima, "Kinsei Kōki Kyoto."
39 Inomata, *Kyūbo no Nōson*, 77. He concludes the section with a note about the opposition to this kind of construction in a village in Mie prefecture: "They had to construct a road that trucks could not pass through because the impoverished peasantry expressed so much opposition that the village assembly could not do anything."

40 See also Fedman, *Seeds of Control*, for an analysis of how forestry reforms were enacted on the Korean peninsula.
41 Mies, *Patriarchy and Accumulation on a World Scale*.
42 All Farm Household Survey ledgers I mention are kept at the Kyoto University Faculty of Agriculture. Here, and throughout, I have used pseudonyms to protect the privacy of the survey participants. The number provided for each farm household (e.g., no. 251 for the Sasaki household) reflects the number used by the ministry to track it.
43 Jeffrey Bayliss writes in *On the Margins of Empire* about the Ministry of Agriculture's Bunson Imin Hōshin and the *yūwa* immigration policy to Manchuria as part of reducing "surplus populations." There are many sources from the time to confirm this view, but see, for example, the Ministry of Agriculture and Forestry, Keizai Kōsei department's 1939 publication, *Shin Nōson no Kensetsu*, which explains how calculations about which villages had surplus farm households should be made.
44 This included 1 tan 4 se 5 bu of paddy land. For details, see map 150–58 of Mie prefecture, Nyū village's Chiso Kaisei Ezu.
45 The increase came in the amount of paddy land they were able to borrow. They used this to engage in double-cropping.
46 According to the *Kyū Tochi Daichō* held at Tsu Chihō Hōmukyoku, Matsusaka Shikyoku and Kimura Teiichi began to receive paddy lands they had been cultivating since the prewar period from the Ministry of Agriculture and Forestry in 1947.
47 See Maruoka, *Nihon Nōson Fujin Mondai*, for more on the way that work cycles and intensity changed during the prewar period. My reading of proletarian women's writing on the transformations to agrarian village social relations can be found in Matsumura, "More than the 'Wife Corps.'"
48 This analysis preceded the publication of a labor dictionary titled *Musansha Hōritsu Hikkei* edited by the Dōjinsha editorial board in 1932. A section on agriculture-related regulations describes the meaning of the common use rights, or *iriaiken*, and traces the changes to it brought about with the establishment of the Meiji regime. It also preceded the wave of disputes over the commons reported in *Suihei Shimbun* between 1930 and 1930 in Niigata, Fukuoka, and Nagano.
49 "Ichishi gun Tsūshin," *Aikoku Shimbun*, June 10, 1925, in *Mieken Buraku Shiryōshū Kindaihen*, 269.
50 "Ichishi gun Tsūshin," *Aikoku Shimbun*, June 10, 1925, in *Mieken Buraku Shiryōshū Kindaihen*, 269.
51 Yamazaki, "Suihei Undō no Hitobito (7)."
52 Kawamura provides a detailed description of this scene, including the response Kaito representatives received from the assembly members, on page 36 of "Suihei Undō no Hitobito (7)."
53 Yamazaki, "Suihei Undō no Hitobito (7)," 37.
54 As Gilmore writes, "The state's crisis, then, was also a crisis for people whose protections against calamity, or opportunities for advancement, would be made surplus by the state, into which their hard-fought incorporation was only ever partial and therefore contingent." *Golden Gulag*, 84. We can read the new round of enclosures in relation to crisis in this way and also understand that the people,

already hierarchized, had different access to protections that did emerge as concessions.
55 "Asama Kuyū Zaisan Mondai no Shinsō," April 19, 1927, *Asamachō Rekishi Shiryōshū Kindaihen*, 109.
56 "Asama Sanrin Mondai ni Kansuru Hōkokusho," July 15, 1927, *Asamachō Rekishi Shiryōshū Kindaihen*, 112–15.
57 "Asama Sanrin Mondai ni Kansuru Hōkokusho," July 15, 1927, *Asamachō Rekishi Shiryōshū Kindaihen*, 114.
58 Tsumura, "Tennōsei Ninshiki to Suiheisha," "Suiheisha Kaishō Undō Zengo no Koto," and "Tennōsei Nishinki to Suiheisha Undō (Dai Sankai Matome)." Thanks to Tomiyama Ichirō for the suggestion to take a look at *Inomata Kenkyū*, where both of Tsumura's essays have been published.
59 Inomata, *Kyūbo no Nōson*, 72.
60 Daijōsai, which historian Takashi Fujitani translates as "the great food tasting festival," is one of the three important succession rites that coincide with the enthronement of a new emperor. The official ceremonies took place in Kyoto, but villages nationwide held their own festivities. See Fujitani, "Electric Pageantry." On what happened in Maemura, see Ōyama, *Mieken Suiheisha Rōnō Undōshi*, 174.
61 Segregation also existed in Maemura. Unlike in Asama, where the distinction was between north and south, in Maemura it was east-west.
62 Mieken, *Mie Kenshi Shiryōhen Kindai 3*, 853–57. Ōyama also has an analysis of this struggle in Sana village led by the village branch of the Suiheisha in *Mieken Suiheisha Rōnō Undōshi*.
63 "Kyōyuchi Mondai de Tatakatta Mie Kenren," *Suihei Shimbun*, August 5, 1930, *Mieken Buraku Shiryōshū Kindaihen*, 413–14. The petition is "Tangansho," August 28, 1930, *Mieken Buraku Shiryōshū Kindaihen*, 418. Making *ise omote*, straw sandals, was one of the few cash-income-generating industries that buraku households had access to.
64 "Ketsugi," August 28, 1930, *Mieken Buraku Shiryōshū Kindaihen*, 418.
65 "Shakai Undō no Jyōkyō (1936)," *Mieken Buraku Shiryōshū Kindaihen*, 628–31. The area was actually 10 chōbu, but since surface rights on part of the land were held by private parties, the northern side only had rights over 4 chō 5 tan 8 se. The agreement is in "Kyōteisho," August 6, 1930, *Asamachō Rekishi Shiryōshū Kindaihen*, 125–27.
66 Kawamura, "Fashizumu to Buraku Sabetsu," 41.
67 "Kōyūrinya Seiri Ninka Shinseisho: Mura no Tōitsu Ninka," June 15, 1926, *Asamachō Rekishi Shiryōshū Kindaihen*, 106–7.
68 "Mie Kannai ni Okeru Suiheisha no Kenkyū," February 1933, *Mieken Buraku Shiryōshū Kindaihen*, 530–45. This document has a section called "Fūki no Midare," or "entanglement of public morals," that reveals that this idea was entwined in notions of the deviant sexuality of buraku men and women. For example, "so-called illicit meetings at night are very common . . . among men and women, there is no unfreedom in sex. This pursuit of sexual pleasure among men and women may lead to early marriages. In these buraku, there are a lot of people who have entered the family registry recently as illegitimate children." "Mie Kannai ni Okeru," 535.
69 Kawamura, "Fashizumu to Buraku Sabetsu"; Imai, "Washi wa 'Tōtoi' to Omounoya," 109.

70 "Asama Sabetsu Kusei Kyūsan Tōsō Nyūsu," September 5, 1935, *Suihei Shimbun*, *Mie Kenshi Shiryōhen Kindai 4*, 742–46. I use "eXX" here so as to not reproduce the racial slur that people at the time used to denigrate buraku people.

71 He was also known as Ueki Tetsujo. He was an organizer who was sent into Asama by the head of the prefectural Suiheisha, Nitta Hikozō, to aid in rebuilding their cells after the March 13, 1933, roundup of radicals. See Ueki's interview, "Kaihō Tōsō no Omoide." The word that I have rendered "eXX" denotes a category that was formally abolished with the enactment of the aforementioned 1871 Edict. It referred to people who worked as butchers and leather workers and were subject to structural discrimination, as Bakufu regulations imposed differential administrative treatment on them. Chapter 7 in Teraki and Kurokawa, *A History of Discriminated Buraku Communities in Japan* traces these processes.

72 "Kyoin no Sabetsu kara Kusei no Jyōgai Kyūdan e," *Suihei Shimbun*, July 5, 1935, in *Mieken Buraku Shiryōshū Kindaihen*, 603–4. *Suihei Shimbun* describes the latter two as holdovers from the Tokugawa era's systemic discrimination against burakumin. Here, I understand them together to be thoroughly modern attempts to secure a Japanese national community by creating the category of buraku as a supplement that enables the former's self-realization—a process that requires a unitary analysis in the sense defined by Marxist social reproduction feminists.

73 "Asama Sabetsu Kusei Kyūsan Tōsō Nyūsu," *Suihei Shimbun*, September 5, 1935, in *Mie Kenshi Shiryōhen Kindai 4*, 743.

74 "Asama Sabetsu Kusei Kyūsan Tōsō Nyūsu," *Suihei Shimbun*, September 5, 1935, in *Mie Kenshi Shiryōhen Kindai 4*, 744.

75 Kawamura explains that the living standards of the two sides of the district diverged further as the north's access to communal lands was taken away in the midst of a serious unemployment issue.

76 Harry Harootunian and Gabe Masao taught me about the need to attend to subjectification and structure. Neither can be unlinked from these other aspects of social reproduction.

CHAPTER 3. BURAKU WOMEN AGAINST TRIPLED SUFFERINGS

1 A document in Mie prefecture's police archives titled "Watarai Gun Shigō-Son Asama Kusei Sabetsu Jiken" succinctly and matter-of-factly describes the net impact that these conditions had for Asama's residents north of the river: "Northerners had to sell their daughters as prostitutes or entertainers and their homes were left unrepaired." *Mieken Buraku Shiryōshū Kindaihen*, 652.

2 *Shikimi* refers to tree branches that were bunched together and commonly placed atop graves as offerings. The work of collecting these from the commons had been performed by women, including buraku women, for generations.

3 Imai, "Washi wa 'Tōtoi,'" 109. See Ueki, "Kaihō Tōsō no Omoide," for his recollection of the impact that the criminalization of entering the mountain had upon their livelihoods.

4 Kawamura Zenjirō identifies him by name in his article but I will not do so here because I am not sure about consent.

5 "Asama Sabetsu Kusei Kyūsan Tōsō Nyūsu," September 5, 1935, *Suihei Shimbun*, in Mieken, *Mie Kenshi Shiryōhen Kindai* 4, 742.
6 I discuss the concept of sociogeny through K'eguro Macharia's reading of it in chapter 1.
7 Gibson-Graham, *End of Capitalism*.
8 See Suzuki, *Suiheisen o Mezasu*, for more details concerning the start of the Women's Column; and Shindō, "Kyūshū Fujin Suiheisha," for details concerning the formation of the Women's Page at *Suihei Geppō*.
9 "Kei," "Buraku Fujin no Tachiba Kara," *Suihei Shimbun*, August 20, 1924, in Suzuki, *Nihon Josei Undō Shiryō Shūsei* 7, 403-4.
10 "Kei," "Buraku Fujin no Tachiba Kara," *Suihei Shimbun*, October 20, 1924, in Suzuki, *Nihon Josei Undō Shiryō Shūsei* 7, 411.
11 "Kei," "Buraku Fujin no Tachiba Kara," *Suihei Shimbun*, October 20, 1924, in Suzuki, *Nihon Josei Undō Shiryō Shūsei* 7, 412.
12 Suzuki notes in *Suiheisen o Mezasu Onna Tachi* the overlap between many women Suiheisha activists and the zainichi Korean population in Kanehira district, Fukuoka, and argues that an explicit class critique accompanied its stance on buraku women's liberation. This book also has a chapter on Mie prefecture. Bayliss, in *On the Margins of Empire*, reads these texts in the Women's Column but is quite dismissive of the significance of their accomplishments, noting that the energies that fueled the commencement of the column in the early 1920s waned by the latter part of the decade.
13 This language is borrowed from Saidiya Hartman, who uses it in her "speculative history of the wayward," *Wayward Lives, Beautiful Experiments: Intimate Histories of Social Upheaval*.
14 "Only a misreading of the key texts of anarchism could ever imagine a place for wayward colored girls." Hartman, *Wayward Lives*, 466.
15 "Kenshuku Setsuyaku o Kōjitsu ni Rōdō Kumiai no Tataki Tsubushi: Kakushu Hantai no Sōgi Kakuchi ni Hinpan," *Daini Musansha Shimbun*, September 29, 1929, in Naimushō, *Tokubetsu Kōtō Keisatsu Shiryō*, 30.
16 "Matsusaka Momen Kaisha Kōjō no Kyōgi," *Ise Shimbun*, June 16, 1924, in Mieken, *Mie Kenshi Shiryōhen Kindai* 4, 547.
17 "Matsusaka Momen," 546.
18 "Yakusoku Chūcho Suru Kaisha Tsuini Kuppuku," *Rōdō Shimbun*, April 20, 1926, in Mieken Kōseikai, *Mieken Buraku Shiryōshū Kindaihen*, 283-84.
19 "Sanbai, Yonbai to Natta Matsusakachō no Takuchi ka," *Ise Shimbun*, May 27, 1921, in Matsusaka, *Matsusaka Shishi Kindai Shiryōhen* 15, 470.
20 "Kansai Hōmen no Kosaku Shōsō," *Tokyo Asahi Shimbun*, January 10, 1922, http://www.lib.kobe-u.ac.jp/infolib/meta_pub/G0000003ncc_00490178.
21 "Kōkyō ni Mukaeru Matsusaka Momen," *Osaka Asahi Shimbun*, October 2, 1921, http://www.lib.kobe-u.ac.jp/infolib/meta_pub/G0000003ncc_00213243; "Sangyōkai no Susei to Tetsudō Unyū Jyōkyō," *Osaka Jiji Shimpō*, September 16, 1922, to February 6, 1923, http://www.lib.kobe-u.ac.jp/infolib/meta_pub/G0000003ncc_00101427.

22 According to a piece in *Aikoku Shimbun*, in addition to worsening material conditions, an insult that an older woman had received was an important spark for the activation of the Kanbe village Suiheisha branch. It reports that a young woman stood up and said, in response to these insults, "We need a Suiheisha movement." This was followed by an assembly on October 16, 1924, attended by people from Ichishi and Taki. "Kanbeson Kamikawa Suiheisha Taikaiki," *Aikoku Shimbun*, October 28, 1924, in *Mie Nōmin Shimbun Fukkōban*, 188.

23 "Yakusoku Chūcho Suru Kaisha Tsuini Kuppuku," *Rōdō Shimbun*, April 20, 1926, in Mieken Kōseikai, *Mieken Buraku Shiryōshū Kindaihen*, 283–84.

24 See "Iinan gun Kakuson no Sōgi De Denchi o Kuwaen ni Henkō," *Ise Shimbun*, June 7, 1923, in Matsusaka, *Matsusaka Shishi Kindai Shiryōhen*, 433.

25 "Matsusaka Momen Kaibana Kōjō Sōgi Hōkoku," in Mieken Kōseikai, *Mieken Buraku Shiryōshū Kindaihen*, 285.What they meant by *existence* is a matter that can only be incompletely extrapolated by reading into the demands that they made and won concessions to.

26 "Matsusaka Momen Kaibana Kōjō Sōgi Hokoku," 285.

27 "Matsusaka Momen Kōjō Sutoraiki Ōen: Rōdō Kumiai no Daishōri," *Mie Nōmin Shimbun*, April 8, 1926, in Mieken Kōseikai, *Mieken Buraku Shiryōshū Kindaihen*, 283.

28 M-sei, "Mie Ken Matsusaka Sōgi Dayori," *Rōdō Shimbun*, April 20, 1926, in Mieken Kōseikai, *Mieken Buraku Shiryōshū Kindaihen*, 283.

29 See "Shinyagyō o Kyōseishi 12-Jikan mo Kokushi," *Osaka Asahi Shimbun*, July 25, 1930, http://www.lib.kobe-u.ac.jp/infolib/meta_pub/G0000003ncc_00774077; and "Matsusaka Momen no Jokō Dōyō," *Ise Shimbun*, November 15, 1931, in Matsusaka, *Matsusaka Shishi Kindai Shiryōhen* 15, 449.

30 The language used here is that the tenant arbitration law only serves to keep tenant farmers enslaved for eternity. This is in Zen Nihon Nōmin Kumiai Mieken Rengōkai Iinan-gun Kanbe-son Aza Seisei, *Shunki Tōsō Nyūsu Tokubetsugō*, January 25, 1930, held at Ōhara Shakai Mondai Kenkyūjo.

31 Ohno Yoshimi discusses in "Waga Kuni ni Okeru Shitsugyōsha Undō ni Tsuite no Oboegaki (1)" the organizing by and for the unemployed that began to be expressed publicly from around the first May Day held in Japan in 1920. Ohno examines the changes to the unemployed movement alongside the state's unemployment relief policies, including the start of unemployment insurance in the mid-1920s, which was focused in large industrial areas like Tokyo, Osaka, Kobe, and Nagoya. It was at the founding assembly of the Hyōgikai in 1925 where the resolution to eradicate and provide relief for the unemployed was first passed. The "Shitsugyōsha Dōmei" within the Hyōgikai soon proposed a labor struggle that centered the unemployed. From this point, preparations for the establishment of branch alliances began. It should be noted that, while Ohno does not dwell on this here, Suiheisha and Zai Nihon Chōsen Rōdō Sōdomei (Chōsō) and later the Zenkyō Chōsenjin Iinkai were heavily involved in organizing these branches. The formation of the Mie branch followed a regrouping that took place following the state's dissolution of the Hyōgikai in March 1928 and its reorganization as the Nihon Rōdō Kumiai Zenkoku Kyōgikai (Zenkyō).

32 Ōyama, *Mieken Suiheisha Rono Undōshi*, 193.

33 We see landlords' names quite frequently in these pamphlets. For example, see Ichishi Gun Toyota son Niiyano Shibu, *Toyota son Tōsō Nyūsu Daiichigō*, March 1931, held at Ōhara Shakai Mondai Kenkyūjo.

34 These communications are in folders titled "Mie Zennō" that are currently held at Ōhara Shakai Mondai Kenkyūjo. Many, but not all, have been transcribed and republished in Mieken, *Mie Kenshi Shiryōhen Kindai 4*; and Mieken Kōseikai, *Mieken Buraku Shiryōshū Kindaihen*.

35 Toyota son Niiyano Shibu, "Toyota son Niiyano no Tochi Toriage Mondai," 1926, in Mieken Kōseikai, *Mieken Buraku Shiryōshū Kindaihen*, 388.

36 "Mie no Shōgaku Jidō Sabetsu Jiken: Tsui ni Dōmei Kyūkō o Kekkō," *Rōdō Nōmin Shimbun*, October 13, 1928, in Mieken Kōseikai, *Mieken Buraku Shiryōshū Kindaihen*, 337–38.

37 Zennō Mieren, *Niiyano Tōsō Nyūsu*, July 22, 1929, in Mieken Kōseikai, *Mieken Buraku Shiryōshū Kindaihen*, 389.

38 The details of this incident are retold in "Mie no Shōgaku Jidō Sabetsu Jiken: Tsui ni Dōmei Kyūkō wo Kekkō," *Rōdō Nōmin Shimbun*, October 13, 1928, in Mieken Kōseikai, *Mieken Buraku Shiryōshū Kindaihen*, 337–38; and "Toyota son Shōgakkō Sabetsu Jiken," *Suihei Shimbun*, December 1, 1928, in *Mieken Buraku Shiryōshū Kindaihen*, 338. In addition to the public apologies, the authorities agreed to hold an annual public event run by Suiheisha that focused on eliminating discrimination.

39 On the Shōwa panic, the Japanese manifestation of the global depression, see Shizume, "Japanese Economy."

40 Toyota Shitsugyōsha Dōmei Jyunbikai, "Toyota son Hinnō Shokun ni Teisu," September 13, 1930, held at Ōhara Shakai Mondai Kenkyūjo.

41 There are possible points of conflict with Korean workers, who were mainly subcontractors, but we also see that Chōsen Sōdōmei sent a donation of one hundred yen in support of Mie's tenant farmer struggle. Signed by Kawai, dated February 2, 1930, held at Ōhara Shakai Mondai Kenkyūjo (figure 3.2).

42 In the pamphlet "Toyota son Hinnō Shokun ni Teisu," the branch demands the reduction of rents, a 30 percent reduction in electricity costs, extensions on loans, access to low interest rates, and the elimination of regressive taxes like those on transport and bicycles. The opposition to subcontractors again leads us to ask whether they may have clashed with Korean workers, but see previous note regarding demonstrations of solidarity.

43 Similar language is used by the Onoe Shitsugyōsha Dōmei in a short flyer imploring people to join their alliance. The Onoe branch asked their village to provide them with construction jobs like Nakahara and Toyota had, but also included demands for schools to subsidize the cost of school lunches during the annual athletic meet as well as the cost of school trips—and to support each other's organizational activities.

44 It states, "Let us demand that they render a decision on the matter of unemployment relief for us at that meeting, as a resolution of this issue determines whether we go hungry today or not." Toyota son Shitsugyōsha Dōmei, September 1930, held at Ōhara Shakai Mondai Kenkyūjo.

45 Kachō Taisaku Iinkai, "Kayazei wa Ōganemochi kara Dase," in Mieken Kōseikai, *Mieken Buraku Shiryōshū Kindaihen*, 415.
46 Nōson Shitsugyosha Dōmei Renraku Iinkai Jyunbikai, *Shitsugyōsha Tōsō Nyūsu No. 2*, in Mieken Kōseikai, *Mieken Buraku Shiryōshū Kindaihen*, 424.
47 Tanaka Ichirō, "Mie Kannai ni Okeru Suiheisha no Kenkyū," *Shihō Shiryō* 4. Reprinted in Mieken, *Mie Kenshi Shiryōhen Kindai* 4, 532.
48 Nōson Shitsugyosha Dōmei Renraku Iinkai Jyunbikai, *Shitsugyōsha Tōsō Nyūsu No. 1*, in Mieken Kōseikai, *Mieken Buraku Shiryōshū Kindaihen*, 424.
49 "Setsuyaku Day," *Aikoku Shimbun*, May 1, 1924, in *Mie Nōmin Shimbun Fukkōban*, 63.
50 Kaihō Undō Giseisha Kazoku Kyūenkai, "Kyūenkai Nyūsu Daisangō," in Mieken Kōseikai, *Mieken Buraku Shiryōshū Kindaihen*, 410. In Japan the first MOPR (Sekishoku Kyūenkai in Japanese) was organized in late 1928 following Tokuda Kyūichi's return from Moscow. See Tanaka Masato, "Moppuru to Nihon Seikishoku Kyūenkai." The name is also translated as Red Relief Association but I use the English version that appears in their newsletters: International Red Aid.
51 The report mentions that representatives of other branches were also involved in the decision to establish the preparatory committee and were active in collecting funds to support Torakichi's family. Zennō Miekenren Honbu, *Nōmin Nyūsu*, April 10, 1931, held at Ōhara Shakai Mondai Kenkyūjo. Details on the formation of the Niiyano MOPR branch are in the April 10, 1931, edition of *Nōmin Nyūsu*.
52 The report, titled "Matsusaka shi Suihei buraku no Tokuisei," was written by Mieken Tokubetsu Kōtō Keisatsuka and is reprinted in Mieken Kōseikai, *Mieken Buraku Shiryōshū Kindaihen*, 588–93.
53 Details of the most significant suppression, called the 3.13 incident, are recorded in a report by the governor of Mie and police chief, Hayakawa Saburō; see *Chian Ijihō Ihan Higijiken Hōkoku*, in Mieken Kōseikai, *Mieken Buraku Shiryōshū Kindaihen*, 550–76. Their own descriptions of their activities are in Kaihō Undō Giseisha Kazoku Kyūenkai, "Kyūenkai Nyūsu Daisangō," in *Mieken Buraku Shiryōshū Kindaihen*, 410.
54 The Mitsui family got its start as a cotton wholesaler in Matsusaka before expanding its operations to Kyoto and Tokyo. For details about the connection between the conglomerate and the city see "Mitsuike ga Matsusaka e 5-Man Yen Kifu," *Ise Shimbun*, July 19, 1932, in Matsusaka, *Matsusaka Shishi Kindai Shiryōhen* 15, 484.
55 "Chōgiren o Kanzume Keikantai to Rantō," *Osaka Asahi Shimbun*, July 26, 1932, in Matsusaka, *Matsusaka Shishi Kindai Shiryōhen* 15, 451.
56 I am thinking with Okamoto Naomi's discussion of the disturbance of standing water, delivered during an interview about the film *Okinawa no Harumoni* at the April 25, 2018, Kayōkai meeting held at Dōshisha University.
57 "Chōgiren o Kanzume Keikantai to Rantō," *Osaka Asahi Shimbun*, July 26, 1932, in Matsusaka, *Matsusaka Shishi Kindai Shiryōhen* 15, 451.
58 There are also details of how Nichōme became a center of activism in Mie in Kurokawa, "Mie ken ni Okeru." The neighborhood of Hino Nichōme seems to function as a stand-in for the term *burakumin* in official and unofficial texts from around this time much as Suiheisha becomes a stand-in for people from buraku communities who engage in some form of social or political activism.

59 It is in these police documents that we first gain access to the names of the women who were active in organizing Suiheisha-related activities in the prefecture. We see that they were involved in the MOPR, but they were also involved in distributing radical publications and labor organizing in small factories in Mie's cities.

60 *Chian Ijihō Ihan Higijiken Hōkoku*, in Mieken Kōseikai, *Mieken Buraku Shiryōshū Kindaihen*, 561.

61 See *Chian Ijihō Ihan Higijiken Hōkoku*, 571–74, for details of the organizational structures they were part of. The organizational structure of MOPR is on page 574.

62 Mieken Tokubetsu Kōtō Keisatsuka, "Matsusaka shi Suihei buraku no Tokuisei," in Mieken Kōseikai, *Mieken Buraku Shiryōshū Kindaihen*, 588.

63 For details on the arrests, see *Chian Ijihō Ihan Higijiken Hōkoku*. This is also narrated in Ōyama, *Mieken Suiheisha Rōnō Undōshi*.

64 Including but not limited to the "impossibility" that Uno talks about as embedded in the capital-labor relation.

65 Gilmore, *Golden Gulag*, 28.

66 I take the language of contagion from Mitropoulos, *Contract and Contagion*, but the fear that the authorities had of exponential spread is seen in the way that they mapped out the personal relationships between everyone whom they suspected of subversive activity in Mie prefecture. The obsessive mapping out, in what looked like the mapping of terror cells that kept spreading outward, reveals how they understood radical political organizing to take place. What they were unable to map through that form they supplemented with paragraphs of details about people's relationships to each other in the cities that they surveilled.

67 Matsushita, "Buraku Kaihō to Rōdō Undō," 199.

68 On the relationship between one of the groups calling for buraku liberation in the prewar period, Suiheisha, and Japanese labor unions like Osaka Zen Nihon Rōdō Kumiai, the Nihon Rōdō Kumiai, and Zennō Mie, see the section "Kishiwada Bōseki Tsu Kōjō no Sōgi," in Mieken, *Mie Kenshi Shiryōhen Kindai 4*, 699–703.

69 Ōyama, *Mie Ken Suiheisha Undōshi*, 260.

70 The settlement terms are in "Tokkōka no Chōtei de Kishiwada Boseki Ketsu!," *Shakai Undō Tsūshin*, June 21, 1937, in Mieken, *Mie Kenshi Shiryōhen Kindai 4*, 701.

71 The report, "Shōwa Jyūninen Rokugatsu Sanjyūnichi no Katsudō," published June 30, 1937, is reprinted in Asamachō, *Asamachō Rekishi Shiryōshū Kindaihen*, 219–26.

72 "Asamaku Hokubu no Jidō no Dōmei Kyūkō (1)," July 3, 1937, in Asamachō, *Asamachō Rekishi Shiryōshū Kindaihen*, 226–29. A roundup of communist activists beginning in late 1937 led to the arrest of thirty-eight activists from Asama out of a total of eighty-six. They were accused of violating the Peace Preservation Law and the Army Penal Code. These arrests effectively shut down the ability of northern residents to continue their struggle, but resistance reemerged on August 1, 1937, as one of the demands issued in the *Kaihō Shimbun*: equal rights for district-held forestlands. "Jinmin Sensen Jiken Kenkyo," *Ise Shimbun Yūkan*, May 31, 1938, in Matsusaka, *Matsusaka Shishi Kindai Shiryōhen 15*, 459–50; "Mieken Tokkōka Shihō Keisatsukan no 'Ikensho,'" *Mieken Keisatsu Kankei Shiryō*, June 3, 1938, in Asamachō, *Asamachō Rekishi Shiryōshū Kindaihen*, 259–74; "'Asama Jiken' no Gonin wa

Kenkyokyoku Okuri," *Osaka Mainichi Shimbun Mieban*, June 7, 1938, in Asamachō, *Asamachō Rekishi Shiryōshū Kindaihen*, 274.

CHAPTER 4. HOUSEWIFIZATION, INVISIBILIZATION, AND THE MYTH OF THE NEW SMALL FARM HOUSEHOLD

1 Kim, "Mie Ken Kinomoto."
2 The Niigata incident refers to a massacre of more than ten Korean workers who fled their abusive workplace in Nakatsugawa in 1922. The Otaru incident took place at a trade school in Otaru, Hokkaido, where rumors about Korean people, like those that led to the massacre of Korean people during the Great Kanto Earthquake, were circulated during a school's military exercises in late 1925.
3 Zai-Nihon Chōsen Rōdō Sōdōmei Sangatsukai, Zai-Tokyo Chōsen Musan Seinen Dōmeikai Ichigatsukai, "Mieken Bokusatsu Jiken ni Saishi Zen Nihon Musan Kaikyū ni Uttau," February 10, 1926, held at Ōhara Shakai Mondai Kenkyūjo.
4 "Shinsai Tōji o Omowasuru Sxxjin Bokusatsu Jiken," *Musansha Shimbun*, February 20, 1926, in *Musansha Shimbun No. 1*. Also see Yi, "Zainichi Chōsen Josei Undō (ge)"; and Pak, "Zainichi Chōsenjin no Tatakai."
5 Kim Chŏng-mi has also written a critique of the national Suiheisha for its complicity in Japanese imperialism in Asia and for its discriminatory stance toward Koreans. The Japanese title of the piece referenced here is "Wakayama Zainichi Chōsenjin no Rekishi."
6 The concept of self-actualization here is from King, *Black Shoals*. I write about this in the introduction.
7 Manu Karuka's *Empire's Tracks: Indigenous Nations, Chinese Workers, and the Transcontinental Railroad* traces how the inscription of racial and gendered borders was necessary to the establishment of continental imperialism in North America. Naturalizing these bordering practices, he argues, replicates the frontierism of Frederick Jackson Turner, which "trivializes slavery to 'an incident' in American history" and erases Indigenous genocide. Karuka, *Empire's Tracks*, 174.
8 The Ihara farm household's ledgers (like the rest) are stored at the Kyoto University Faculty of Agriculture.
9 We see this in Japanese Marxists' use of data from the ledgers to express the reality of class differentiation in the countryside. See chapter one.
10 Endō, "Multitude."
11 Kawashima, *Proletarian Gamble*; Park, *Two Dreams in One Bed*; Yasuoka, "'Tasha' Tachi no Nōgyōshi." This chapter is indebted to Yasuoka's work but is primarily interested in thinking through what the census documents, ledgers, and reports that he mines to construct a picture of Korean agricultural workers in the metropole occlude through the categories and assumptions of work, especially reproductive labor, that they ossify.
12 See the introduction for my critique of this narrative.
13 As I note in chapter 1, Uno Kōzō uses the data uncritically in his writings on the agrarian question. There was no rigorous debate over the categories used

in the surveys, statistical tables, etc., as we see in Russia, for example. Cox, *Kritsman*.
14 On Okayama city's character as a second city, see Young, *Beyond the Metropolis*.
15 Naikaku, *Shōwa 10*, 48.
16 Tōmin, *Dai Nikai*, 138.
17 Kerry Smith writes about the IRAA in *A Time of Crisis*. He notes that the IRAA, formed in 1940, was meant to replace local civic and governmental associations to extend the reach of the state to the lowest units of political, social, and cultural life. NALP was "voluntarily" dissolved in April 1934 following state repression.
18 Maruyama, *Kōyō son*. In 1940, Maruyama published *Nanyō Kikō*, an account of his travels to the South Seas from Kōa Nipponsha. Naoto Sudō includes him among a group of scholars engaged in colonial literature called Nanyō-Orientalism in *Nanyō-Orientalism*.
19 For details, refer to Zenkoku Nōmin Kumiai Okayamaken Rengōkai, *Zennō Okayama Tōsōshi*.
20 Inomata, "Nōmin to Fashizumu," 347.
21 Maruyama, *Kōyō son*, 67.
22 For one example from this region of Okayama, see a detailed examination of Mizote's expansion in Morimoto, *Kindai Nihon*. A lot of work has been done on the Hosokawa family based in Kumamoto, which established a model village for Japanese settlers in Daejangchon. See Chung, "Model Village."
23 *Kyū Tochi Daichō*, held at Okayama Chihō Hōmukyoku.
24 The Ihara farm household owning 9 tan 2 se 5 bu tells us that they produced for more than their own household consumption and utilized the majority of their land for the production of commodity crops. Of this land, 1 tan 9 se 7 bu was classified as orchard land (*enchi*), on which they had a variety of fruit trees that bore fruit throughout the year. Their main source of agricultural cash income came from these fruits.
25 Nakayama, "Ōhara Shakai Mondai Kenkyūjo to Rōdō Kagaku no Tanjō."
26 Teruoka, "Shochō Nenpō."
27 The ledgers do not tell us how the 28.53 yen payout they received from the *tanomoshikō* in April 1938 was used.
28 For a study of access to modern midwifery services in the countryside, see Terazawa, *Knowledge, Power, and Women's Reproductive Health in Japan*.
29 The ledgers do not include testimonials, interviews, categories, or even space on the paper to gain access into the way that the members of the farm household experienced or understood the changes that they implemented as part of the work of intimate self-management. Feminist journals like *Fujin Sensen*, *Rōdō Fujin*, *Hataraku Fujin*, and *Nyonin Geijutsu* get at these perceptions much more.
30 In the work ledger, we see that the Iharas employed both men and women as seasonal laborers and agricultural helpers (*tetsudainin*) to engage in agricultural production and a total of ninety-nine hours of housework.
31 On the importance of Honam Plain for agriculture, see Matsumoto and Chung, "Japanese Colonizers," and Matsumoto and Chung, "Hosokawa Farm."

32 See Kawashima, *Proletarian Gamble*, for details on the Korean workforce in mainland Japan as day laborers working on public works projects.
33 Fukuoka Chihō, *Nōgyō Oyobi*.
34 Jung, *Coolies and Cane*.
35 Walia, *Border and Rule*, 140.
36 Fukuoka Chihō, *Nōgyō Oyobi*, 2.
37 Yasuoka Kenichi writes about the agricultural trainee project in *"Tasha" Tachi no Nōgyōshi*.
38 Full names and addresses of the trainees as well as heads of household that hired them were listed on pages 6–7 of the report.
39 The Sōaikai was heavily involved in the management of these workers.
40 Fukuoka Chihō Shokugyō Shōkai Jimukyoku, *Nōgyō Oyobi*, 9.
41 Fukuoka Chihō, *Nōgyō Oyobi*, 18. This echoes a report from Nagano prefecture that is a bit more ambivalent about the seasonal nature of the work. "Nagano ken ni Okeru Zainichi Chōsenjin (1927)" includes excerpts from the prefectural governor's office that highlight the instability that Korean workers faced in employment. It explains that Nagano's severe winters required that they plan for a complete stoppage of work in the winter in the power plants or railways that were their main sources of employment during most of the year. Left without work in the winter, Korean workers moved to warmer regions or into agrarian villages, where they engaged in agricultural work or sericulture. It explains that they were only able to move into agricultural work because Japanese workers had moved out of it due to its low pay.
42 There were several brick factories in Mikawa village in the 1920s.
43 Fukuoka Chihō, *Nōgyō Oyobi*, 21. This report does discusses the problem of undercounting.
44 We already see this in Fukuoka Chihō, *Nōgyō Oyobi*, and Kawano, "Yamaguchi Kenka."
45 Folbre and Abel write about this in the US context in "Women's Work and Women's Households."
46 The issue of nationality came up in prefectures like Tokyo, Saitama, Hyōgo, and Yamaguchi. Representatives asked how mixed-race married couples' nationalities should be recorded, how one's nationality should be recorded in the event of a divorce, and how children of mixed-race couples should have their nationality registered. The answers consistently reaffirmed the patrilineal line, but the frequency with which the question appears shows that officials in the metropole had not really had to confront it as a practical issue until this point despite having passed a Nationality Law in 1899. See Lim, *Rules of the House*; Chen, "Gendered Borders," and Kim, "Law and Custom" for detailed studies of the way that these matters were clarified in Taiwan and Korea.
47 "Kokusei Chōsa ni Kanshi Shitsugi no Ken," July 2, 1930, in Jinkōka, *Shōwa Gonen Kokusei Chōsa Shitsugi Ōtō Kankei Tsuzuri*.
48 Determination of possessing "will and ability" was left up to the individual respondents.
49 The latter became targets of paternalistic reform and natalist policies, aided by institutions like the Agricultural Labor Study Center in Okayama. Even if they

worked for wages, their ideological function within the empire was to be good wives and wise mothers.

50 Sonia Ryang said as much when she argued that the massacre of Korean people during the Great Kantō Earthquake was baked into the way that the modern Japanese nation-state was set up. Ryang, "Great Kanto Earthquake."

51 Okayamaken Tokubetsu Kōtō Keisatsu, 335.

52 On these, see Yasuoka, *"Tasha" Tachi no Nōgyōshi*, and the document that discusses them in detail, Fukuoka Chihō, *Nōgyō Oyobi*.

53 See Kawashima, *Proletarian Gamble*, for a detailed discussion of the power that the Sōaikai held. We see a contemporary critique in "Shikibetsu to Doryoku: Jiken Burōkā o Issō Shiyō," *Minshū Jihō*, July 15, 1935, republished in Kim, *Kenshō Maboroshi*, 69–70.

See Kawano Shigeto's 1940 article "Yamaguchi Kenka ni Okeru Sennō no Teichaku Katei" for the process through which Korean agriculturalists came to settle in Yamaguchi prefecture's Magura village. Kawano explains that the earlier arrivals came in 1923 as part of a railway construction project, but that the majority of the thirty-six Korean agricultural families (ten *sumiyaki*, twenty tenant farmers, and six tenant farmers who were also lumber transporters) entered Magura to fill the gap left behind in the village as agricultural crisis led fifteen or sixteen farm households to move to the mandated islands in the Pacific and to Brazil, while others left to Kita-Kyūshū or other cities to find employment in military-related industries. He emphasizes that the path to settlement took place primarily through kinship communities: the vast majority of those who settled, he explains, were from one *myeon* in the peninsula.

54 Seasonal women workers recorded 338 hours and male helpers recorded 37.5 hours in 1934. The ledgers do not tell us how many total people in each category were employed.

55 "Naganoken ni Okeru," 104.

56 Lim, *Rules of the House*. Debates over funerary practices were taking place around this time in the Kinyūkai as well as in terms of burials or cremation, especially with regard to migrant workers from Cheju island. See, for example, "Wareware no Teishō: Kasō o Shinkō Shiyō," *Minshū Jihō*, July 15, 1935, republished in *Kenshō Maboroshi*, 72–73.

57 Wynter writes, "Economic exploitation only follows on, and does not precede, the mode of domination set in motion by the *imaginaire social* of the bourgeoisie. Consequently, the capitalist mode of production is a subset of the bourgeois mode of accumulation which constitutes the basis of middle-class hegemony." "Master Conception," 81. This passage highlights the classed element of the phrase colonial commonsense I use throughout the book.

58 The Hidaka Sōgi that took place in Wakayama is an important exception.

59 Zennō Okayama was aware of this. In Zennō Okayamaken Rengōkai Shibu, *Zennō Okayamakenren Shukisō Nyūsu*, November 23, 1931 (held at Ōhara Shakai Mondai Kenkyūjo), while reporting that their youth division proclaimed solidarity with anti-imperialist struggles, they noted the reason why some prefectures (and

landlords) were interested in bringing in Korean agricultural workers was to serve as strikebreakers in response to tenant farmer radicalism. They mention one particularly egregious example in the report.

60 In her 2023 dissertation "Liberation, Discourses of Liberation, and Liberation from the Discourses of Liberation," Qianqing Huang discusses the Suiheisha's shortcomings regarding solidarity with Korean independence, as well as the pushback that Kim Chŏng-mi experienced when she initially made this critique in 1994.

61 Japanese peasant studies operates from the presumption of settlement as a state of being and boundedness in a community over generations that offers inheritable resources indispensable for survival.

62 I borrow this concept from Ruth Wilson Gilmore.

63 K'eguro Macharia writes about this in terms of Blackness, queerness, diaspora, and intimacies in *Frottage*.

64 Professor Mizuno Naoki's online database of newspaper articles related to Zainichi Korean people at Kyoto University has been an invaluable resource for me. The database is hosted at http://oldwww.zinbun.kyoto-u.ac.jp/~mizna/shinbun/.

65 Saidiya Hartman defines her method of critical fabulation in "The Anarchy of Colored Girls Assembled in a Riotous Manner." She writes, "State violence, surveillance, and detention produce the archival traces and institutional records that inform the reconstruction of these lives; but desire and the want of something better decide the contours of the telling. The narrative emulates the errant path of the wayward and moves from one story to another by way of encounter, chance meeting, proximity, and the sociality created by enclosure. It strives to convey the aspiration and longing of the wayward and the tumult and upheaval incited by the chorus." "Colored Girls," 470.

CHAPTER 5. INTERIMPERIAL KOREAN STRUGGLE IN FERTILIZER'S GLOBAL CIRCUIT

1 "Koibito wa SXXjin," *Kobe Yūshin Nippō*, August 14, 1933.

2 Taki Seihi was consistently second or third in national output but was considered an outsider in the superphosphate industry's cartelization process. Takeda, "Karinsan Dōgyōshakai," 169.

3 Taki Kumejirō Denki Hensankai, *Taki Kumejirō*, 74.

4 Denise Ferreira da Silva's assertion that a focus on the production process of "raw material" inputs can extend Marx's understanding of surplus value realization that destabilizes the centrality of waged factory work from our analyses of capital in favor of one that understands indentured, convict, unpaid, and other forms of gendered, racialized, and colonial manual labor to sustain extractivist projects globally guides my analysis of the full scope of the company's operations. Silva, "1 (life)."

Lisa Lowe makes a similar argument in *The Intimacies of Four Continents*. She writes on page 83, "Marx's formulation of the fetishism of commodities, which focused on British manufactured goods, simultaneously admitted *and* obscured the difference of colonial labor." She continues that what is missing from his formulation is the colonial theft and plunder needed to sustain capital's access to colonial labor and resources.

5 So, "Aru Hansen."
6 So, "Aru Hansen," 3.
7 For Okayama, Korean peoples' occupations in the prefecture in 1925 and 1929 are recorded in Okayama Kenshi, *Okayama Kenshi 28*, 994 and 998. We do see the category "nōgyō tetsudai" but most are men (the ratio of men to women in each year is, respectively, 141:5 and 158:12). There are, in contrast, many more agricultural workers who have been classified as *mushoku* where the ratio is skewed more to women (62:90 and 210:327).

Pak's mother's presence would have been recorded in colonial police records. The association that opened up its own shipping line between Osaka and Cheju island from 1930, Tōa Tsūkō Kumiai, has a brief description of the various ways that Korean workers would have been recorded and subsequently surveilled as they traveled within the empire in a summary of their third assembly of May 1932, *Tōa Tsūkō Kumiai Daisankai Teiki Taikai Gian Sōan*.

8 So, "Aru Hansen," 3.
9 So, "Aru Hansen," 4.
10 So, "Aru Hansen," 5.
11 Mitropolous, *Contract and Contagion*.
12 Kim, "Wakayama Zainichi."
13 Kim, *Kenshō Maboroshi no Shimbun*, 118.
14 As Horiuchi Minoru explains in "Hanshin Shōhi Kumiai ni Tsuite," the consumer association (*shōhi kumiai*) movement among Zainichi Korean communities spread quickly. In the case of Hyōgo, the Hanshin Shōhi Kumiai was founded in March 1931 and had primarily Korean members. Horiuchi explains that these associations played particularly important roles in responding to housing emergencies, especially in the aftermath of flooding and other disasters in the metropole and colony. This particular organization had a women's department by 1933 and were planning on expanding its scope around this time.
15 Kim's *Kenshō Maboroshi no Shimbun* narrates the way some of these spaces formed. It also includes translations from a Zainichi Korean newspaper, *Minshū Jihō*, which circulated between 1935 and 1936. Kim notes that the majority of people who were writing for it were communists and were under constant surveillance by the Japanese police.
16 Yamada Yoshiko examines the life of some of the leaders of the Tokyo branch of Kinyūkai including Pak Hwasŏng. See, for example, "Pak Hwasŏng's School Days in Tokyo." See also Yi, "Kinyūkai Oboegaki," which is a memoir of the times; Yi, "Zainichi Chōsen Josei Undō (jyō)"; and Yi, "Zainichi Chōsen Josei Undō (ge)."
17 Kawashima traces the problem of getting Korean workers to the factory gates as a general problem inherent in the impossibility of capital in *The Proletarian Gamble: Korean Workers in Interwar Japan*.

18 As such, it prefigured the interventions that social reproduction theorists made in mainstream Marxist theory since the 1970s.
19 The entirety of the Tokyo Kinyūkai branch's third assembly in 1929 is reproduced as "Kinyūkai Tokyo Shikai Dai 3 Sōkai Bunken (1929)" in the June 1978 edition of *Zainichi Chōsenjinshi Kenkyū*. This quote is on page 129.
20 Kinyūkai Tokyo Shikai, "Kinyūkai Tokyo Shikai Dai 3," 123.
21 Kinyūkai Tokyo Shikai, "Kinyūkai Tokyo Shikai Dai 3," 127.
22 This and the examples we turn to next were not about affirming Korean familial ties in the metropolitan countryside.
23 For analysis of this on the Korean peninsula, see Lim, *Rules of the House*.
24 Saito, "Bone and Coral," 572.
25 Saito, "Bone and Coral," 574.
26 Kinyūkai Tokyo Shikai, "Kinyūkai Tokyo Shikai Dai 3," 128.
27 Yi, "Zainichi Chōsen Josei Undō (ge)." "Kinyūkai Tokyo Shikai Dai 3 Sōkai Bunken (1929)" also mentions it at the outset.
28 Contemporaneous critiques of the "evil acts" of the Sōaikai appear in *Minshū Jihō* pieces that Kim has translated and compiled in *Kenshō Maboroshi no Shimbun*, 3.
29 Horiuchi outlines this in the context of Hyōgo. What is notable is that even as possibilities for militant action and overt political agitation narrowed considerably in the archipelago, reorganization did take place with the formation of consumer associations. These played extremely important roles in flood relief, housing, and other forms of emergency and mutual aid within Korean communities in the prefecture. Horiuchi, "Hanshin Shōhi Kumiai."
30 Kim, *Kenshō Maboroshi no Shimbun*, 28.
31 "Shiryō: Tonga (Tōa) Tsūkō Kumiai Daisankai Teiki Taikai Gian Sōan," May 27 and 28, 1932; reprint, Tōa Tsūkō Kumiai, "Tōa Tsūkō Kumiai." For details about these other routes see Kō, "Gendai Nicchō Kōro no Naka."
32 Kō, "Gendai Nicchō Kōro no Naka," 14.
33 The piece is "Wareware no Teisho, Kasō o Shinkō Shiyō," July 15, 1935, published in Kim, *Kenshō Maboroshi no Shimbun*, 72.
34 Kim, *Kenshō Maboroshi no Shimbun*, 73.
35 Hyōgoken Chōsen Rōdō Kumiai, which was affiliated with Zainichi Chōsen Rōdō Sōdōmei, was formed in April 1929. Around 80 percent of its membership (as of the end of September 1929, total membership was 450 people) worked in the chemical industries. Horiuchi, "Hanshin Shōhi Kumiai," 30.
36 The development of this relationship is narrated in a biography, *Taki Kumejirō*, 33–43. See Kim, "Shokuminchi Chōsen to Taki Kumejirō," for an analysis of how Taki leveraged his positions in the peninsula and the archipelago to grow his business according to the ideology of Japanese homeland extensionism (*naichi enchōshugi*).
37 Taki Kumejirō Denki Hensankai, *Taki Kumejirō*, 230.
38 Taki Kumejirō Denki Hensankai, *Taki Kumejirō*, 233.
39 Kim, "Shokuminchi Chōsen," 91. As Kim Hyun argues, gaining political power was integral to Taki's ability to expand their business. Lee notes in "Land Utilization and Rural Economy in Korea" that 30 percent of arable land in North Chŏlla was

in Japanese hands (see page 147). As a result, approximately 75 percent of the farmers were tenants See also Kobayashi, *Zainichi Chōsenjin Rōdōsha*.
40 Henshū Taki Kagaku, *Taki Kagaku Hyakunenshi*, 27.
41 Henshū Taki Kagaku, *Taki Kagaku Hyakunenshi*, 59.
42 Henshū Taki Kagaku, *Taki Kagaku Hyakunenshi*, 28. From there its products made its way to Korea, Taiwan, and Hokkaido.
43 Kobayashi, *Zainichi Chōsenjin Rōdōsha*, 96.
44 Henshū Taki Kagaku, *Taki Kagaku Hyakunenshi*, 29.
45 Kobayashi Sueo provides details of where the buraku workers were recruited from. Most came from Kita-Befu and other nearby areas, as well as from Okayama prefecture's Tsuyama region because the factory manager was from there. Kobayashi, *Zainichi Chōsenjin Rōdōsha*, 96.
46 Taki Kumejirō Denki Hensankai, *Taki Kumejirō*, 236.
47 In his dissertation, Chin-Sung Chung notes that these restrictions were loosened and tightened over time, but a significant change seems to have occurred in 1925, when the first police screenings of Korean migrants to Japan began in South Gyeongsang province. Chung, *Colonial Migration*, 49. Kobayashi provides testimony from a former employee who noted that if a Taki Seihi stamp was on their family registry, they would easily be able to travel to Japan. Kobayashi, *Zainichi Chōsenjin Rōdōsha*, 98.
48 Most of this work was performed by the head of household's wife, Tomiko. In total, she and Gisuke worked for 1,541 hours to earn this amount.
49 Henshū Taki Kagaku, *Taki Kagaku Hyakunenshi*, 40.
50 See section 2 of Lowe, *Intimacies of Four Continents*, on Marx's fetishism of the commodities; and Silva, "Reading the Dead."
51 Jairus Banaji describes Jardine Matheson as a "pure emblem of Britain's mercantile capitalism," which had essentially masterminded the First Opium War as a show of force against Chinese authorities. He distinguishes them from vertically integrated industrial capitals that came to control global capital from around World War I, but acknowledges the difficulty of clearly distinguishing the two by the last decade of the nineteenth century. This was the main way that British capital established a dominant position in Asia. Banaji, *Commercial Capitalism*, 67–68.
52 Taki Kumejirō Denki Hensankai, *Taki Kumejirō*, 75. See Schiltz, *The Money Doctors from Japan*, and Metzler, *Lever of Empire*, for analyses of the relationship between currency imperialism and colonial rule. In addition, Hudson, *Bankers and Empire*, illuminates the way that finance capital was inextricably linked to the emergence of racism in the modern world through his analysis of the way that City Bank and other US-based financial institutions expanded their operations to the Caribbean, Latin America, and Asia, especially in times of crisis. The first chapter, which focuses on Jarvis, reminds us of the need to include analyses of the settler colonization of the so-called Midwest even in discussions of the formation of the white Pacific.
53 On the impact of the phosphate industry in Florida on labor and land relations among white settlers, Indigenous peoples, and formerly enslaved Black workers,

see Cattelino, *High Stakes*; Ortiz, *Emancipation Betrayed*; Ware, "The Peace River"; and Brown, *A River of Peace*? For a similar process, in particular, the annexation of Christmas Island and the importation of Chinese indentured workers, see Burstyn, "Science Pays Off." On the use of convict labor in Florida's phosphate industry, see Mancini, *One Dies, Get Another*; and Lichtenstein, *Twice the Work of Free Labor*. Both sites began mining in earnest in the last two decades of the nineteenth century and were main suppliers of phosphorous to Japan.

54 This wording comes from Rivera-Monroy et al., "Life of P," 99. Special thanks to Jessica Cattelino for sharing a copy of "Life of P" with me when library access was limited.
55 Hurston, *Dust Tracks*, 174.
56 Mormino, "A River of Peace?," 57.
57 Caple, "Holocene in Fragments," 38.
58 Caple, "Holocene in Fragments," 42. On efforts to save the Okinawa dugong, see Yoshikawa, "The Plight of the Okinawa Dugong."
59 Teaiwa, *Consuming Ocean Island*, 94.
60 Teaiwa, *Consuming Ocean Island*, 136. As a result of the arrival of the British, residents were moved off of the island to Rabi in the Fiji islands. She defines *te aba* as "that fundamental and corporeally grounded ontological premise linking land and people ... devastated and dismantled at a rapid rate by mining." *Consuming Ocean Island*, xvi.
61 Teaiwa created an art installation, PROJECT BANABA, to commemorate the history of Banaba Island and to share the experiences of its people with the public. https://www.projectbanaba.com.
62 Horiuchi, *Hyōgo Chōsenjin Rōdō Undōshi*, 145.
63 Banshū Gōdō Rōdō Kumiai Honbu, *Sxxjin Rōdōsha no Zanshi*.
64 Banshū Gōdō Rōdō Kumiai Honbu, *Sxxjin Rōdōsha no Zanshi*, 2.
65 The family had already paid 250 yen in funeral expenses. Banshū Gōdō Rōdō Kumiai Honbu, *Sxxjin Rōdōsha no Zanshi*, 4–6.
66 According to Kobayashi Sueo, talks of layoffs had commenced in April of that year. Protests successfully delayed their implementation until July. Kobayashi, *Zainichi Chōsenjin Rōdōsha*, 103. See article on the idling system, 1935. This indicates that the response was to extend furloughs for large numbers of workers even more. "Taki Seihijo Sōgi Kaisetsu," *Shakai Undō Tsūshin*, August 27, 1931.
67 For names of those laid off and details of the dispute, see Kobayashi, *Taki Seihijo Rōdōshi*, 123–24. This is a republication of records of the Osaka branch of Kyōchōkai.
68 Kobayashi, *Zainichi Chōsenjin Rōdōsha*, 100.
69 Kobayashi, *Zainichi Chōsenjin Rōdōsha*, 101.
70 "Taki Seihi Kaisha, Kaiko Hantai ni Danzen Tatsu," *Shakai Undō Tsūshin*, December 22, 1931.
71 One *koku* of rice = 5.12 bushels.
72 Kobayashi, *Zainichi Chōsenjin Rōdōsha*, 108.
73 Taki Seihi Sōgidan, Zenkoku Rōdō Kumiai Dōmei, Banshū Kagaku Sangyō Rōdō Kumiai, Taki Bunkai, *Dōshi Koko ni Saikai o Chikau ni Atatte*, January 11, 1932.

74 Watanabe, "Shisha Nimei o Dashita Taki Seihi Sōgi." *Taki Hiryō Tōsō News No. 1*, December 17, 1931, reprinted in Kobayashi, *Taki Seihijo Rōdōshi*, 41–43.
75 The chemical industry was a central place for Korean worker organizing. Zenkyō's Hanshin branch was especially effective in this regard. Horiuchi, *Hyōgo Chōsenjin Rōdō Undōshi*, 145.
76 Banshū Kagaku Sangyō Rōdō Kumiai held its formation prep meeting at the Aioiza theater in the Nonin neighborhood of Takasago-chō just a few days after Banshū Gōdō Rōdō Kumiai issued its report. A record of their meeting, which started at 6 p.m. on October 24, is in Banshū Kagaku Sangyō Rōdō Kumiai Kessei Taikai Jyunbikai, *Goannai*, October 24, 1931.
77 Kobayashi, *Zainichi Chōsenjin Rōdōsha*, 108.
78 "Ryūketsu no Taki Seihi Sōgi," *Shakai Undō Tsūshin*, January 12, 1932.
79 Kim, "Shataku to Chōsenjin," 27. Some of the photographs included in the paper can be viewed online at https://shimamukwansei.hatenablog.com/entry/20130115/1358223497.
80 See "Hyōgo: Arashi o Haramu Taki Hiryō Sōgi," *Shakai Undō Tsūshin*, December 23, 1931, on Korean women playing this role. Some of them worked in Taki-owned fields in the surrounding areas.
81 Full text can be found in Kobayashi, *Taki Seihijo Rōdōshi*, 49.
82 Kobayashi, *Taki Seihijo Rōdōshi*, 51. Also see "Taki Seihi Kōjō Jikyūsen," *Shakai Undō Tsūshin*, December 24, 1931.
83 Mashiyama Hitoshi, in "Shōwa Shoki Pioniiru Undō no Soshiki to Kyōiku," describes the pioneer movements that emerged between September 1928 and 1936, when they dissolved due to state repression. The Taki Seihi strike pioneer was formed alongside the Kitanaka leather factory strike pioneer that began just before it. Both were supported by Suiheisha because a significant portion of the strikers were from buraku communities.
84 Taki Kumejirō Denki Hensankai, *Taki Kumejirō*, 295.
85 See chapter 2 for a definition of James's public school code.
86 "Han Sōgidan Sōdōin de Mizou no Kanshōburi," *Shakai Undō Tsūshin*, January 12, 1932. The striker's real-time publications contest this narrative.
87 Kim, *Shataku to Chōsenjin*.
88 Ross, *Communal Luxury*. She writes of the Communards who transformed Paris into an autonomous zone in the spring of 1871, "The Communal imagination operated on the preferred scale of the local autonomous unit within an internationalist horizon. It has little room for the nation, or, for that matter, for the market or the state" (5). What she finds notable about this imaginary was enacted through practice and comprised an "expanded temporality" that is prolonged and developed through praxis.
89 Kim explains that residents who lived in the company barracks continued on with life after the war. Included are interviews with Korean residents, including her relatives, who stayed even after they were let go from the company after the war, and also the lawsuit that was filed against them by the company in 1973 for "illegal occupation" for continuing to live there.

90 "Han Sōgidan Sōdōin de Mikaiyu no Kanshōburi," *Shakai Undō Tsūshin*, January 12, 1932. This piece ends with a note that their treatment conjured memories of the massacre of Koreans in the days following the 1923 Great Kantō Earthquake.
91 "Kimje Taki Nōjō: Kosakunin Ichibu Dōyō," *Maeil Shinbō*, December 28, 1931.
92 "Ryōhyō Daihyō ga Kaiketsu e Senryoku," *Maeil Shinbō*, December 31, 1931.
93 According to Morimoto's *Kindai Nihon ni Okeru Jinushi Nōmin Keiei*, the marŭm's role changed significantly under colonial rule. See 113–16.
94 The difficult conditions that Taki Seihi's tenant farmers faced in Kimje are highlighted by this fact. According to Takeuchi Yūsuke, while Manchurian millet remained an important source of food for Korean farmers who could not afford to eat the rice they cultivated, a significant decline in millet imports was recorded in the southern part of the Korean peninsula after 1928 due to improving conditions. Farmers in Kimje who worked on the Taki farm continued to rely on millet as their food source despite these broad trends, likely because of the monopoly power held by the company in setting fertilizer prices, rents, and so on. Takeuchi, "Kokumotsu Jyukyū o Meguru Nihon Teikokunai Bungyō no Saihensei to Shokuminchi Chōsen," 37.
95 "Baeg-yeo Sojagin Nongjang-e tto Swaedo," *Tonga Ilbo*, January 1, 1932.
96 "Taki Nōjō no Kosaku Sōgi Sainetsu," *Kunsan Nippō*, January 20, 1932.
97 Kobayashi, *Zainichi Chōsenjin Rōdōsha*, 106, 209.
98 "Taki Nōjō Shoyū Sōko Hitomune Zenshō," *Maeil Shinbō*, February 6, 1932.
99 "Taki Nōjō no Kosaku Sōgi Sainetsu," *Kunsan Nippō*, January 20, 1932.
100 "Taki Nōjō ni Okeru Kosaku Sōgi no Shubōsha," *Kunsan Nippō*, January 20, 1932.
101 "Futatsu no Sōdō Jiken ni Kyūen Undō Makiokoru," *Shakai Undō Tsūshin*, January 13, 1932. This article provides an interesting insight: that the strikers and the people are closely linked, as made evident by the eruption of the dispute at Taki Nōjō as well as the relief aid that flowed in.
102 "Useless and therefore expendable" returns us to Wynter's *pieza* conceptual frame, discussed in chapter 1.

CHAPTER 6. EMPIRE THROUGH
THE PRISM OF PHOSPHATE

1 The first phase of recruitment was done by Tōyō Imin Gōshi Kaisha beginning in September 1905 and ending in October 1906, with sixty-two people on three-year contracts according to Gaimushō Tsūshōkyoku, *Imin Chōsa Hōkoku*, 14. The second phase, from January 1908 to May 1909, is when Okinawan workers were recruited on two-year contracts from a different immigration company, Nippon Shokumin Gōshi Kaisha. Ishikawa writes briefly on this in "Kaigai Imin no Tenkai," 410–11. The names and hometowns of those recruited from Okinawa are listed in Okinawaken, *Okinawa Kenshi Shiryōhen 6 Kindai 1*.
2 Teaiwa, *Consuming Ocean Island*, 104.
3 Mitsui Bussan entered the Philippines in 1898 and became the primary trading company there by selling coal produced in its Miike mines to the US Navy, its

largest customer. See Viana, "Diversifying Urbanity"; the author cites Watanabe Kaoru, *Philippine-Japan Yearbook and Business Directory*, published in Manila in 1935, as his source. Mitsui Bussan was also the first company to enter Yaeyama to develop its coal mining facilities there in 1885. This garnered a lot of interest from Home Minister Yamagata Aritomo, who recommended that the mine be worked by prisoners. This commenced the following year. The coal that they produced was exported to Fukien and Hong Kong. While the company suspended operations in 1895 due to a malaria outbreak, its experience with the Iriomote mine demonstrated the profitability of state-supported extractive industry. Miki, "Yaeyama Gasshūkoku" no Keifu, 82.

4   See Dixon, "Phosphate Rock Frontiers," on the international division of labor in the phosphate industry.
5   Swan, "Blinded by Bandung?," 61.
6   Phosphate extracted from Banaba was shipped to New Zealand, where it was processed and used in agriculture—an operation acknowledged as costly at the time.
7   Teaiwa, *Consuming Ocean Island*, 9.
8   Banivanua Mar, *Decolonisation and the Pacific*, x.
9   Banivanua Mar, *Decolonisation and the Pacific*, 35.
10 Chantal Ferraro argues that the racialization of Kanaka as not only white, but as a group that had to be disappeared, really came to a head with the 1878 Kanak revolt. See "When Black Is Transparent," 126–28.
11 Gaimushō Tsūshōkyoku, *Imin Chōsa Hōkoku*, 13.
12 Gaimushō Tsūshōkyoku, *Imin Chōsa Hōkoku*, 13. This idea of absolute depletion carried over into their own operations on Fais. According to Hezel, "There were no cultural preserves, no areas off-limits to development as far as Nantaku was concerned." *Strangers*, 199.
13 Gaimushō Tsūshōkyoku, *Imin Chōsa Hōkoku*, 13.
14 Despite these advantages, the Japanese workforce went on strike in November 1919 due to the relative rise in costs at the company store. Macdonald, *Cinderellas of the Empire*, 102. See also Shlomowitz and Munro, "The Ocean Island (Banaba) and Nauru Labor Trade 1900-1940," for where Asian labor recruitment fit into the PPC's broader phosphate labor regime.
15 Okinawan workers also entered New Caledonia starting in 1905 in slightly larger numbers than in Banaba. Tōyō Imin Gōshi Kaisha handled recruitment for Okinawa and worked in close cooperation with Governor Narahara to set up the recruitment system. Ishikawa Tomonori writes about this in "Kaigai Imin no Tenkai."
16 Davis, *Markets of Civilization*, 33–34. On the Code de l'Indigénat in French colonies in West Africa, see Asiwaju, "Control Through Coercion," which emphasizes the importance of the code to secure the system of "forced labour, conscription into the army and payment of capitation tax." It also allowed colonial administrators to "compel the subject peoples' obedience to imposed chieftains and to regulate compulsory agricultural policies and the requisition of both subsistence and cash crops" (95). Davis also emphasizes the code's function

as a tool of multiple forms of extracting, noting, "Punishments led to the extraction of 1,658,958 francs in 1890, which could be paid in cash or forced labor." She concludes, "The Native Code allowed the state to convert certain punishments into forced labor, so that from 1898 to 1910 the state extracted 600,000 days of work from Algerians" (34).

17 Banivanua Mar, *Decolonisation and the Pacific*, 42.
18 Batterbury, Kowasch, and Bouard, "Geopolitical Ecology," 598.
19 According to Ishikawa, early recruitment ads for contract workers to New Caledonia in the local paper in Okinawa in 1905 already indicate that women could be hired if they were accompanying their husbands. "Kaigai Imin no Tenkai," 409. This option was not open to workers from the French colonies.
20 Wilson, Moore, and Munro, "Asian Workers," 87.
21 See Gaimushō, "Nihon Gaikō Monjo" (1961), 434.
22 Teaiwa cites Shlomowitz and Munro on an attempt that was made to hire Japanese boatmen to break the monopoly of Ellice islanders in this position: "In 1911 . . . the use of Japanese boatmen was seen as a corrective to the Kanakas who consider they cannot be replaced." *Consuming Ocean Island*, 81.
23 The commentary on wage rates for phosphate workers in French-colonized Tahiti reveals the very concrete ways that driving down wages in one part of the Pacific enabled similar processes in others.
24 See Gaimushō, "Nihon Gaikō Monjo" (1963), 328.
25 See Gaimushō, "Nihon Gaikō Monjo" (1962), 355–57.
26 For details on the CFPO and its ties to the PPC, see Newbury, *Tahiti Nui*, chapter 9.
27 See Gaimushō, "Nihon Gaikō Monjo" (1963), 327.
28 Gaimushō Tsūshōkyoku, *Imin Chōsa Hōkoku*, 13.
29 "Nanyō no Sangotō," *Ryūkyū Shimpō*, July 5, 1908.
30 As I explain in my conclusion to *The Limits of Okinawa: Japanese Capitalism, Living Labor, and Theorizations of Community*, this recall was initiated by the Okinawa Prefectural Association and affirmed by *Ryūkyū Shimpō*, which published an article providing context for this decision with the title "The Necessity of Reforming Old Customs" the day after the news was reported.
31 "New Order for 150 Riukiu Laborers," March 31, 1908; see Gaimushō, "Nihon Gaikō Monjo" (1961), 434.
32 Immigration records are reprinted in *Okinawaken Shiryō Kindai 6*. We see, for example, that the first 100 workers who departed Okinawa on January 21, 1908 were recruited from fourteen villages on Okinawa and Miyako islands and that the 150 who departed on the next trip on May 12 came from sixteen villages.
33 Ishikawa, "Kaigai Imin no Tenkai." According to the June 1933 *Palau Shichōsei Yōran*, the total population on Angaur was 984 people, of whom 297 were Japanese, 572 were Kanaka, and 110 were Chamorro. Also listed was 1 Korean and 224 "tōmin," a derogatory word used by Japanese authorities and settlers to refer to Indigenous islanders. Of these, 450 were employed in mining. For this history, see Hanlon, *Remaking Micronesia*; Tomiyama, "Colonialism and the Sciences of the Tropical Zone"; and Purcell, "The Economics of Exploitation." The figures are from

August 1, 1933. These can be accessed here: https://u-ryukyu.repo.nii.ac.jp/records/2009574.

The Ministry of Foreign Affairs issued a report on working conditions in Angaur's phosphate industry in 1937, *Nihon Teikoku Itaku Tōchi Chiiki Gyōsei Nenpō 1937 Nendo*. It includes employment contracts, details about the operations of Nanyō Takushoku, and wages. John Decker's book *Labor Problems in the Pacific Mandates*, published in 1940 by the Institute of Pacific Relations, also has an extensive section on labor conditions in the phosphate mining industry.

34   While Allan Lumba focuses primarily on how the formation and exercise of monetary authority in the Philippines facilitated US imperialism by operating as a force of counterdecolonization after 1898, his study *Monetary Authorities: Capitalism and Decolonization in the American Colonial Philippines* is useful in thinking through the way that Japanese merchant capitalists and settlers figured in these processes. Much work remains to situate Okinawan settlers in Latin American countries. See Junyoung Verónica Kim, "Writing Asia-Latin America," for a critique of the way that Okinawan migration has been subsumed analytically into histories of Japanese migration in Doris Moromisato's poetry. Shannon Welch's 2022 dissertation "Transpacific Anomalies and Alterities" reads Medoruma Shun's 1999 short story "Burajiru Ojī no Sake" as a critique of the state's nationalist narrative that interpreted Okinawans as pioneers to Brazil's sugar plantations.

35   Banivanua Mar, *Decolonisation and the Pacific*, 91.
36   Banivanua Mar, *Decolonisation and the Pacific*, 92.
37   Banivanua Mar, *Decolonisation and the Pacific*, 92.
38   According to the figures from *Nanyō Guntō Tochi Chōsasho* (1935), there were 50,573 "islanders." In comparison, there were 51,309 Japanese settlers and 540 Korean settlers. Compared to 1930 figures, the total population increased by 32,911 over five years. The vast majority of this increase was among "Japanese," who numbered 7,430 in 1925. The vast majority of Japanese settlers were from Okinawa prefecture.
39   Mita, "Oral Histories."
40   Mita, "Oral Histories," 152.
41   Mita, "Oral Histories," 71.
42   This is the testimony of Mechas Belenges Oiterong and Mechas Yosko Oiterong (b. 1920 and 1926) in Mita, "Oral Histories," 118.
43   See the testimony of Mechas Tengranger Oiterong (story 39) in Mita, "Oral Histories."
44   Camacho, *Cultures of Commemoration*, 3.
45   Nakano Ryōko writes extensively on Yanaihara's Zionism in *Beyond the Western Liberal Order: Yanaihara Tadao and Empire as Society*. She notes that while he acknowledged that "Jewish people did not have a legal or social right of settlement in Palestine," he asserted that Palestinians did not have "an ultimate right to resist others' access to their land" (54). She notes that he did state that that "the purpose of settlement should not be conquest" (57). John De Boer also analyzes Yanaihara's Zionism in "Circumventing the Evils of Colonialism: Yanaihara Tadao and Zionist

Settler Colonialism in Palestine." Yanaihara wrote "Shion Undō ni Tsuite" after his visit to Palestine and published it in *Keizaigaku Ronshū* in 1923.

46   Yanaihara, "Nanpō Rōdō Seisaku no Kichō," 11.
47   Yanaihara, "Nanpō Rōdō Seisaku no Kichō," 11.
48   Yanaihara, "Nanpō Rōdō Seisaku no Kichō," 11.
49   Yanaihara, "Nanpō Rōdō Seisaku no Kichō," 11.
50   As I explain in chapter 5, this concept comes from Saito, "Bone and Coral."
51   Tellei, Basilius, and Rehuher, "Palau Compact Road Archaeological Investigations," 59.
52   Stephen Murray conducted interviews with village chiefs and elders who discuss the pain they felt when Japanese authorities forbid their use, reportedly because they deemed the practice unsanitary. *Battle over Peleliu*, 37.
53   Sudō Kenichi, "Hijikata Hisakatsu to Nanyō Guntō," 572. Instruction was effective in instilling a sense of comparability between policies imposed by the colonial authorities and existing practices and customs through acts of disingenuous translation. For example, Mechas Katalina Katosang, whose father was from Oikull, Airai, and whose mother was from Ngeremlengui, explained that while her mother taught her Palauan customs, she learned in school that communal work in the villages should be called *kinrōhōshi*, a Japanese term that referred to mutual labor exchange. That said, Rubak Ubal Tellei's testimony from the same batch of interviews shows that not everyone accepted this translation. He explains, "Japanese leaders rather forced their will on the people, and all the people could do was to obey orders. Palauan custom was not like that. Palauan chiefs would order villagers to do some task, but at the same time the chiefs usually served the welfare of the village people; for example, by preparing food while villagers were doing cooperative work." Mita, *Oral Histories*, 88.
54   This is from Peattie's *Nanyō*, but here and throughout the book I hesitate to cite this work, as it reinforces problematic tropes about Pacific Islander populations. Peattie calls the work that Hijikata did for the military advising "on policy toward Indonesian peoples," obfuscating the role that he and others played in informing the implementation of genocidal policies there.
55   Tellei, Basilius, and Rehuher, "Palau Compact Road Archaeological Investigations," 31.
56   Mizuho was the name of another agricultural colony in Airai.
57   Tellei, Basilius, and Rehuher, "Palau Compact Road Archaeological Investigations," 61.
58   *Nanyō, Ngermeskang Gawa o Sakanoborite*, 3.
59   *Nanyō, Ngermeskang Gawa o Sakanoborite*, 2.
60   The labor that Babeldaob islanders performed that made Japanese settlement possible included building roads and schools, working in pineapple cannery development, making charcoal, and constructing military fortifications. Okinawan and Korean workers also performed much of this unacknowledged work. Once bauxite mining commenced in Babeldaob in 1938, former Japanese and Chamorro employees of the Angaur phosphate mines worked the mines in Babeldaob. Hezel, *Strangers*, 199.

61 See Kitazume, "Tamura Hiroshi," for a biography of Tamura including of his time in Okinawa.
62 Tamura, *Okinawa Keizai Jijō*, 121.
63 Tamura, *Okinawa Keizai Jijō*, 122.
64 "Hoanrin Kaijo no Ken," *Hoanrin Kaijo: Okinawaken*, 1924. On the importance of Kin Bay, see Ishii, *Okinawa Bōbi Taisaku*. More on these enemies in chapter 7.
65 "Hoanrin Kaijo no Ken," *Hoanrin Kaijo: Okinawaken*, 1924. Comparing these with the Ippitsu Chōsazu compiled during the US occupation period reveals that these plots of land are now communally owned by villages and municipalities. The following website provides photos and descriptions of this road, now Route 70 connecting Kunigami village's Oku to Higashi village's Taira, as they appear today: http://road.s25.xrea.com/hwy70.html.
66 On the impact of phosphate mining on Peleliu's mesei, see Murray, *Battle over Peleliu*, 62. For the impact that mining in Palau had on communities and the resistance that women showed in a village called Buakonikai, see Katerina Teaiwa, "No More Drinking Water, Little Food: Our Island Is a Field of Bones," *Guardian*, November 2, 2022.

The Okinawaken Shinrinkai rejected some of the areas that Tamura proposed for opening on the basis that they were not necessary for the completion of the repairs and construction projects covered by the request. "Hoanrin Kaijo no Ken," *Hoanrin Kaijo: Okinawaken*, 1924.

67 *Yuta* is translated as "spirit mediums" or "female shamans" and should be differentiated from *noro*, who connected village communities and kinship groups (*munchū*) to the kingdom government through genealogy. Though *noro* held land called *norokumoi* in villages, many of these were lost during Governor Narahara's land reorganization project. Since their official salaries were also revoked during the Meiji period, their authority was weakened and numbers diminished, but they were not completely eradicated. As Tze Loo argues in "Trapped in Text," *yuta* and *noro* are best seen as complementary parts of a spiritual world where authority is held by women, attitudes toward which shifted in important ways first after the annexation of Ryūkyū Kingdom and then in the 1910s with witch hunts. While it is important to acknowledge that *noro* were key to buttressing royal authority and were granted land, salaries, and recognition as part of conferring authority to the *munchū* system in village societies, it is just as important to acknowledge the ways that the social relations that were held together through these institutions and practices went beyond maintaining patriarchal authority and, at times, weakened them.
68 Valerie Barske discusses this as a process that started in 1881, just two years after the Ryūkyū disposition, in "Visualizing Priestesses or Performing Prostitutes?"
69 There are many newspaper articles that contain these references. A convenient, though not comprehensive, volume that has compiled many of these articles is *Okinawa Kenshi Shiryōhen 25*. See, for example, "Karyō," *Ryūkyū Shimpō*, December 1, 1915; "Shidai ni Chōhatsu shi Iku Jyogakusei no Fūki," *Okinawa Nichinichi Shimbun*; Miyagi Shinji, "Dokutoku no Shakai Seido, Naihō ni Arawreta Ryūkyū (12)," *Okinawa Taimusu*, June 12, 1926.

70   The police are ubiquitous in prewar newspapers, in compilations like *Shima no Hanashi*, and in works of fiction. *Officer Ukuma* is an obvious example, but we also see it in "Kunenbo," a short story by Yamagusuku Seichū.

71   Some prefectures were included in 1924 but Okinawa was the only one excluded until 1930. See Nōrinshō Keizai Kōseibu, *Nōka Keizai Chōsa (Shōwa 5-nendo)*, 2.

72   This expanded to six in 1931.

73   See Mukai, *Okinawa Kindai Keizaishi*, for details on the prefecture's policy toward sugar cultivators and its agricultural policy more broadly during the prewar period. Also see Kinjō, *Kindai Okinawa no Tōgyō*, for details on sugar policy specifically.

74   This is not surprising since, in many cases, these roles were held by the same individuals.

75   See Aniya, *Okinawa no Musan Undō*, 87–89, on the Shakai Kagaku Kenkyūkai. See also Arashiro Toshiaki's essay "Gunkokushugi Kyōiku to Yokusan Taisei" for a brief overview of the anarchist and Bolshevik organizations that educators formed during the 1920s and 1930s.

76   It is not listed in the ledgers but they went to Saipan. Thank you to Mori Akiko for this information.

77   Tsuru recorded 189 hours of work in June, 205 in July, and 109 in August, mostly but not exclusively listed under housework.

78   The farm household had to take on large quantities of debt in order to make these purchases.

79   In the farm household composition table where all members' names, occupations, ages, and laboring capacities are listed, we see *bōshiami*, which translates to "hat weaver," next to her name. This clarifies that the task was weaving rather than creating bundles of the adan and other raw material leaves in preparation for weaving, which was a separate task that women performed.

80   Even though the prefecture had encouraged factory-based hat weaving in the prefecture beginning in the late 1890s, by the middle of the 1910s, as it became increasingly associated with work that women in the Tsuji pleasure quarters performed, authorities began to regard hat weaving factories as places of degraded morals where young men and women had inappropriate relations that had corrosive effects on the public. They began to police these spaces on the one hand and encourage a move back to home work (*naishoku*) on the other. See, for example, "Nōson Tsūshin Ginowanson," *Ryūkyū Shimpō*, August 21, 1916, reprinted in Okinawaken, *Okinawa Kenshi Shiryōhen 25*, 393.

81   We gain an understanding of what this work would have required of Sachiko from testimony given by Nakandakari Kamado, who wove panama hats at night in addition to performing agricultural work during the day following the conscription of her husband and eldest son. She notes that it took her approximately one week to complete a hat and she received three to five yen depending on the quality. She did not know what company she was working for, just that someone came around to collect it. Conditions may not have been completely comparable since Nakandakari's testimony was about wartime, but it does help us understand how

strenuous it was to do on top of other work, including domestic labor for social reproduction of the household. Ginowan, *Ginowan Shishi 3 Shiryō 2*, 95.

82 A significant number of people from Okinawa in the fisheries industry went to the Pacific—in particular, to Java, Palau, and Truk—expressly as part of a southward colonization project, so we cannot say that all did so without knowledge of the consequences of their settlement for Pacific Islander communities.

83 This figure was a reduction compared to the 3,100 hours recorded in 1935, but the housework figures for both her and Sachiko seem implausible at a combined 3,122 for the year without an intensification, rationalization, or underreporting of domestic labor time.

84 1 kin = 600 g.

85 "Nōson Fujin to Kazoku Seido" was published in the May 1926 edition of *Mirai* following Yamagami's appearance as a speaker at the fifth Nichinō (Japan Farmer's Union) general assembly in March. She writes of how little women agriculturalists are allowed to rest: "In addition to being tired after the day's work, her body is also tired after working late at night. Her body has not recovered from the fatigue even when morning comes." She argues for the liberation of the proletariat, including the destruction of the "feudalistic tradition, the family system."

86 There is no record of this payment in the 1938–1939 ledgers even though they completed the forms.

87 The split, according to the ledgers, was 239 hours devoted to panama hat weaving and 713 hours for housework.

88 There are no significant expenditures on medicine or health until early August in the hygiene expenditures (*eiseihi*) ledgers.

89 Tamura Hiroshi used the phrase "primitive communism" in *Ryūkyū Kyōsan Sonraku no Kenkyū*.

90 *Refuse* is the term that Sylvia Wynter uses to describe older men and women being "thrown in a job lot" as though they had nothing of value to contribute. Wynter, "Master Conception," 81.

91 "Kenmin o 30 man ni Hangen," *Okinawa Shimpō*, February 12, 1945, in Ginowan, *Ginowan Shishi 6 Shiryō 5*, 617.

92 On the way that the war devastated life in Palau and Babeldaob, see Murray, *Battle Over Peleliu*, chapters 4 and 5.

CHAPTER 7. WATER STRUGGLES IN A COLONIAL CITY

1 Yoneyama, "Decolonial Genealogy."

2 "The clerk would like a cool moon but all the weather depends on the left-hand pages. All the acridity in the salt air, all the waft of almonds and seaweed, all the sharp, poisonous odour of time." Brand, *Blue Clerk*, 5.

3 While Stoler's work is valuable for identifying and analyzing the occlusions created by imperialist archives in order to arrive at a more complex understanding of colonial rule through, for example, the fostering of intimacies, it is still problematic in my view because it ultimately places the ability to analyze, explicate,

and problematize in the hands of the researcher rather than acknowledging that some things are not for us to know (or to be able to know). This is a fine line that we have to walk, especially if we believe that intimacy and colonialism go hand in hand. In addition to seeing only dead people in the archives, the method I am critiquing does not acknowledge those I have called clerks, following Brand, as the archives' most skilled readers, shapers, and interpreters.

4 Brand, *Blue Clerk*, 5.
5 These processes are articulated by Brand in three places in *Blue Clerk*: verso 1, "The Back of a Leaf"; verso 33; and verso 5.
6 Appropriation of Okinawan cultural practices as Japanese (and as Okinawan) accelerated during the 1930s and rendered decisions around disclosure and withholding matters of life and death. I discuss cultural appropriation of Okinawa's music (*minyō*) in "Uneven Development." On Japanese intellectuals absorbing Okinawan culture as a way of naturalizing the colonial relation, see also Christy, "The Making of Imperial Subjects in Okinawa"; and Loo, *Heritage Politics*. Brand writes about the violence of nation, particularly for women, in *Blue Clerk*, versos 5, 5.1, and 5.5.
7 Tuck and Yang remind us that "there are some forms of knowledge that the academy does not deserve.... Academe is very much about the generation and swapping of stories, and there are some stories that the academy has not yet proven itself responsible enough to hear. We are writing about a particular form of loquaciousness of the academy, one that thrives on specific representations of power and oppression, and rarefied portrayals of dysfunction and pain." "R-Words," 224, 232.
8 See verso 3.3 on bigotries and palimpsests: "The old city resurfaces. Its old self, barely concealed, lifts its figure off the page, heaves deep sighs of bigotry." Brand, *Blue Clerk*, 26.
9 Shinjō, "Mizu no Kioku."
10 Katsukata=Inafuku Keiko has written about a similar problem of reification that she ties to the need to recognize the need for those who theorize about Okinawan women to grapple with the challenges that Black feminists in particular have posed to white bourgeois feminist theorizations in "Unaiism Manifested in the Denoument of *Syushin-Kaneiri*." Katsukata=Inafuku proposes Unaiism as a fluid concept that emphasizes the performative aspect of crystallizations of Okinawan womanhood against notions of womanhood rooted in colonial epistemologies. In his review of an Okinawa studies textbook, *Okinawagaku Nyūmon*, coedited by Katsukata=Inafuku and Maetakenishi Kazuma, Inoue Mayumo similarly discusses efforts that scholars have made to attend to the structural and psychic violences of multiple colonialisms in Okinawa while rejecting reifications of the category. Inoue also discusses challenges posed by the entry of Okinawa studies into Japanese university curriculums in a manner akin to the institutionalization of ethnic studies in US academia. Inoue, review of *Okinawagaku Nyūmon*.
11 In his dissertation, "Kichi to Seichi no Okinawa shi," Yamauchi Kenji makes clear that water sources connected places like communal wells, natural caves, irrigation ditches, and reservoirs. That it is possible to draw water from one source and keep that measure separate from all other aspects of village society was something that

only bureaucrats from the outside could argue. The devastation that the loss of one source would have on the community was understood by all who lived there.
12 *Noro hinukan* refers to the *hinukan* (place where the god of the hearth is worshipped) of the *noro*'s home. *Noro dunchi* refers to the *noro*'s home, which is visited during important annual ceremonies by districts and *munchū*. For more detailed definitions of these terms, see *Okinawa Daihyakka Jiten Ge*.
13 See, for example, "Ōjana no Mizu," told by Ishikawa Eiho of Ōyama (b. 1907) in Ginowan, *Ginowan Shishi 5 Shiryō 4*, 630–31.
14 Kinjō, "Nōson no Keizai." Tze Loo examines the relationship between this project and changes to policies around shrines in Okinawa in her forthcoming work.
15 On changes to official policies to noro, see *Okinawa no Noro no Kenkyū* by Miyagi Eishō.
16 Even these disappear in the 1941 ledgers, which only record the types of things that the farm household spent money on as ceremonial expenditures. Most entries were for sake, konbu, and incense that year.
17 As Tze Loo argues, the degree to which the appearance of noro and yuta in the Farm Household Survey ledgers was transgressive or not depends on the broader societal context. She argues that in places like Takamine, where Nanzan Jinja was located, there was an uneasy incorporation of noro in the enthronement ceremony that did not indicate their enduring power, but state efforts to assimilate them into state Shintō.
18 Tamura, *Ryūkyū Kyōsan Sonraku*.
19 The Hypothec Bank was also instrumental in enabling the postwar US military enclosure of Okinawa's lands. According to *Castles in the Far East*, a report by the U.S. Army Corps of Engineers, the Corps contracted with the Hypothec Bank in order to assist the OED in determining land ownership, since prewar governmental records had largely been destroyed during the Battle of Okinawa. Senaga Kamejirō discusses this in speeches from the early 1950s.
20 Sakishima refers to the outer islands under the jurisdiction of Ōkinawa prefecture. On the military fortification of these islands and the construction of "comfort stations," or *ianjo*, see Hong's chapter in *The Battle of Okinawa and "Comfort Stations" in Memory*, which focuses specifically on the Daitō islands.
21 Mori, "Senjiki Nanyō," 17.
22 One concrete project to forward this kind of development was a plan to build an amusement park in the middle of the city in order to attract tourists. This was to be built in Gusukudake/Jōgaku, also known as Naha's Sobe district. This plan actually came to fruition in the postwar period with the construction of Shinsekai. "Nahashi ni Yūenchi o Mōkeru," *Osaka Asahi Shimbun Furoku Kyūshū Asahi*, June 3, 1930.
23 A couple of disputes over rent were taking place in Naha around this time, one in the Tsuji pleasure quarters area and one in nearby Asahi-machi. Both were close to the area being proposed for the development of an amusement park, Gusukudake/Jōgaku. See "Tsuji Yūkaku no Jyōshōren ga Yachin no Nesage Undō," *Osaka Asahi Shimbun Furoku Kyūshū Asahi*, August 29, 1930; and "Kenyūchi Shakuchiryō Nesage o Chinjō," *Osaka Asahi Shimbun Furoku Kyūshū Asahi*, September 23, 1930.

24 See the proceedings for December 17, 1930, of the Okinawa Prefectural Assembly, "Tsūjō Okinawa Kenkai Giji Sokkiroku, dai 8 gō," in *Okinawa Kenkai Gijiroku*. Ikemiyagi Kiki, a centrist from Naha's Wakasa district, advocated for construction to begin as soon as possible because the completion of the project could develop the prefecture's industry and alleviate some unemployment problems by creating jobs in construction.

25 Ice makers, people who questioned the lack of facilities in the women's school, those who were concerned about Naha-centrism, and others did raise objections in the prefectural assembly and in the newspapers. The obstacles that various mayors from different parties faced as they tried to pass similar proposals to bring tap water facilities to Naha are outlined in chapter 4 of Naha Shigikai, *Naha Shigikaishi*, "Ippan Shisei to Chōsonsei," 78–113.

26 A description of Ōyama's demographics is available on pages 29–32 of Ginowan, *Ginowan Shishi 5 Shiryō 4*. Figures on population, number of farm households, and area under cultivation in 1925 are on page 152.

27 See the conclusion of this chapter for more.

28 Kamata, Yamamoto, Urayama, and Nakama explain in *"Hōgo" to Okinawa* that records are pretty complete in Ishigaki but that there are almost no records left on Okinawa island. This edited volume only includes male authors.

29 "Suigenchi Shiyo Mondai de Nahashi, Ken ni Sugaru," *Osaka Asahi Shimbun*, August 16, 1929, in *Ginowan Shishi 6 Shiryō 5*, 100.

30 See *Limits of Okinawa*, chapter 2, for details on Narahara's enclosure project.

31 "Naha Jyōsuidō Iyoiyo Shokushin Saru," October 10, 1930, in Ginowan, *Ginowan Shishi 6 Shiryō 5*, 133. Yasuda Gen'emon was also an executive of Okinawa Kidō, a streetcar that connected Yonabaru and Awase, established in 1914 as Okinawa Jinsha Kidō. It became Okinawa Kidō in 1929. It was primarily used to transport raw sugarcane to the sugar factories. See page 47 in *Nahashi Suidō Gojūnenshi* for the announcement.

32 "Okinawa Kokutō o Mitsui ga Chokuyunyū," *Osaka Asahi Shimbun*, November 8, 1921, in Ginowan, *Ginowan Shishi 6 Shiryō 5*, 111. This article notes that Kagoshima-based merchants had long served as intermediaries between the prefecture's producers and that mainland Japanese and Hokkaido consumers would be negatively impacted by this development; Tainansha, which had been trying to secure steady supplies of cane that it could process from small brown sugar producers, would also feel the blow.

33 "Jigyōkai ni mo Kinshaku Kaze Ugokidasu," *Osaka Asahi Shimbun*, September 10, 1929, in Ginowan, *Ginowan Shishi 6 Shiryō 5*, 106.

34 These figures are as of December 31, 1925, and appear in Fukuokaken Naimubu, *Okinawaken Kosaku*, 95.

35 Higa Kamejirō was one of the leaders of the strike. He explains, "They are a large organ of exploitation of the colony of Taiwan and their history is full of this kind of exploitation." Higa, "Okinawa no Bokutachi."

36 "Totsujo Kōjō o Chūshi shi 200-mei ga Shitsugyōhi Chingin Neage no Yōkyū kara Tainan Seitō Kadena Kōjō Sōgi," *Osaka Asahi Shimbun*, July 9, 1930, in Kadenachō,

36 *Kadena Chōshi Shiryō 4*, 45. To put this in perspective, Okinawan workers' daily wages in mainland spinning factories were between 1 yen 20 sen and 1 yen 50 sen.
37 Higa, "Okinawa no Bokutachi," 75.
38 "Chingin to Jikan Mondai de Shōmen Shōtotsu shi Sūshūkan ni Watari Sōgi Makihara Kōsei Kumiai Jinfu," *Osaka Asahi Shimbun*, July 15, 1930, in Kadenachō, *Kadena Chōshi Shiryō 4*, 46.
39 Higa, "Okinawa no Bokutachi," 76.
40 "Nōka no Sonshitsu wa 20 man en ni Agaru?," *Osaka Asahi Shimbun*, October 11, 1930, in Ginowan, *Ginowan Shishi 6 Shiryō 5*, 134. The paper also reported that the heads of municipal assemblies relayed their decision to appeal to Governor Ino Jirō to compel Tainansha to raise its purchase prices of cane. "Tainan Seitō no Genryō Hikiage o Yōbō," *Osaka Asahi Shimbun*, October 25, 1930, in Ginowan *Ginowan Shishi 6 Shiryō 5*, 137.
41 "Kōwan Shūchiku Kōji ni Kansuru Ken," 1934.
42 Ishii, *Okinawa Bōbi Taisaku*, 1,128.
43 Ishii notes, for example, that even the hardest-working farm households only work an average of three hours a day, that the *mōasobi* is a practice that happens throughout the year where dance and music continue into the middle of the night, after which men and women sneak into each other's homes and do not wake up until well after sunrise, that young men have brought back sexually transmitted diseases and tuberculosis from the cities, and so on. See *Okinawa Bōbi Taisaku*, 1135–37.
44 Ishii, *Okinawa Bōbi Taisaku*, 1130. Ishii does note that they became part of the empire in name only (and did so relatively recently) so does not completely disavow the colonial aspect of Japanese rule.
45 This is outlined on pages 1157–59 of Ishii, *Okinawa Bōbi Taisaku*. Ishii expresses many concerns about communist activities in Yaeyama and the northern part of Okinawa island.
46 According to chapter 7 of Hong, *The Battle of Okinawa and "Comfort Stations" in Memory*, even though northern Okinawa (except Iejima) was not suitable for the development of air bases, Motobu became a place where Thirty-Second Army forces concentrated in the north. People were recruited to engage in work on the Iejima air base and its schools and other public facilities were seized to construct barracks.
47 Murray outlines the impact that military construction had on village life in *The Battle over Peleliu*.
48 David Hanlon discusses the way that phosphate extraction on Anguar by Japanese interests and the disposal of its mines by the United States after surrender inflicted damage on the people and lands there in *Remaking Micronesia.*.
49 Mori, "Senjiki Nanyō," 23.
50 Mori, "Senjiki Nanyō," 22.
51 Vicente Diaz writes about how memories of military sexual violence can only circulate in Guam through gossip in what he calls narratological misfits that cannot be conscripted into contemporary discourses about liberation. Diaz, "Liberation Day," 159.

In "Chamorro Warriors and Godmothers Meet Uncle Sam," Miyume Tanji writes about how theater has been a site for interrogating Okinawan complicities and for breaking the silence of these wartime atrocities among Chamorro audiences. She cites the writing of Julius Sotomayor Cena, who discusses playwright Peter Onedera's work *Ai Hagå-hu!* which traces how a Chamorro woman who was forced into military sex slavery survived and is based on the stories of a survivor. Cena's piece is online at https://www.guampedia.com/theater/.

52 "Mizu no Setsumei ga Futettei," *Okinawa Mainichi Shimbun*, July 26, 1930, in Ginowan, *Ginowan Shishi 6 Shiryō 5*, 129. A few days later, Miyagi was fired for not following prefectural orders to hold new elections following the firing of an assembly member. See "Miyagi Ginowan Sonchō Teishoku o Meizeraru," *Okinawa Asahi Shimbun*, August 2, 1930, in Ginowan, *Ginowan Shishi 6 Shiryō 5*, 129–30.

53 "Suigenchi Shiyō no Zettai Hantai o Tōshin Su," *Osaka Asahi Shimbun*, October 22, 1930, in Ginowan, *Ginowan Shishi 6 Shiryō 5*, 135.

54 The order contained nine regulations that limited the amount of water that could be drawn from each of the four rivers, the length of use, and assurances that they would make changes if damage to crops were detected. "Naha shi Jyōsuidō no Suigenchi, Shiyō Kyōka saru," *Osaka Asahi Shimbun*, November 6, 1930, in Ginowan, *Ginowan Shishi 6 Shiryō 5*, 140.

55 He did so even as he fielded accusations of corruption and bribery around the bidding process. "Komine Naha Shichō no Shūwai, Oshoku Jiken Hakkaku," *Osaka Asahi Shimbun*, July 16, 1931, in Ginowan, *Ginowan Shishi 6 Shiryō 5*, 174.

56 For details refer to Nahashi Suidōkyoku, *Naha-shi Suidō Gojūnenshi*, 399–405.

57 Nahashi, *Nahashi Suidōshi*, 339; "Mizu ga Seimei to Ginowan Sonmin Ken e Hantai Chinjō," *Osaka Asahi Simbun*, December 10, 1932, in Ginowan, *Ginowan Shishi 6 Shiryō 5*, 205–6.

58 Bhandar describes the "complex layers of forms of ownership and possession" that the British installed in Palestine as the "fragmented and recombinant nature of property law in the settler colony," which required the "maintenance of non-capitalist rationales for the appropriation of indigenous lands." "Possession," 121. Her analysis, which understands property law as "fragmented and recombinant," allows us to understand that the Meiji regime's maintenance of the commons, framed as primordial, could not only remain intact until the second decade of the twentieth century in the Japanese metropole without any damage to capital's self-realization, but could be incorporated as such into the modern private property regime, and that this was not exceptional to the Japanese case but was a common practice among Western imperialist powers.

59 "Suigenchi oyobi Yōchi ni Shuyōhō o Tekiyō," *Osaka Asahi Shimbun*, March 25, 1932, in Ginowan, *Ginowan Shishi 6 Shiryō 5*, 201.

60 "Iyoiyo Saigo no Shudan to Shite Tochi Shuyōhō o Tekiyō Suru," *Osaka Asahi Shimbun*, April 10, 1932, in Ginowan, *Ginowan Shishi 6 Shiryō 5*, 201.

61 In the Kitty Lundy lecture "What we saw," delivered on March 11, 2021, Dionne Brand mentioned Jose Saramago's *Seeing*, which talks about elections where people returned blank ballots and then resumed life after the politicians left.

62 Ginowan, *Ginowan Shishi 5 Shiryō 4*, 32.
63 Kinjō, *Kindai Okinawa*.
64 Many of these opened alongside the prefectural road during the Taishō era. For locations refer to Ginowan, *Ginowan Shishi 5 Shiryō 4*, 218–22.
65 For details on this, as well as the locations of communal springs, see Ginowan, *Ginowan Shishi 5 Shiryō 4*, 31.
66 These areas are viewable in the maps of 1944 reproduced in Ginowanshi Kyōiku Iinkai, *Tsuchi ni Umoreta Ginowan*.
67 Nahashi Suidōkyoku, *Naha-shi Suidō Gojūnenshi*, 58.
68 Rinyachō, *Hoanrin Kaijo: Okinawaken*.
69 While the imperial relations were created anew, Naha's centrality to an imperial project remains intact.
70 For details on how the stops on the Kadena railway line changed after the war, see the following website, which locates in the present-day terrain where the prewar line ran: http://www.hotetu.net/haisen/Kyushu/090531kadenasen.html.
71 "Basu ni Hikare Sokushi," *Okinawa Taimusu*, March 9, 1957; "Shojo Hikarete Sokushi," *Ryūkyū Shimpō*, March 9, 1957.
72 "Ginowan son Kyūna Kakku Omizu Sama no Oiwai," *Ryūkyū Shimpō*, July 22, 1957, in Ginowan, *Ginowan Shishi 7 Shiryō 6*, 817.
73 I use *premature* here in the sense used by Ruth Wilson Gilmore to define racism's relation to capitalism "as state-sanctioned or extralegal production and exploitation of group-differentiated vulnerability to premature death." *Golden Gulag*, 28.
74 Shinjō's essay in *Okinawa no Kizu to iu Kairo*, chapter 4, "Kokyō de Kyakushi Suru Koto," is on the poet Nakaya Kōkichi, who had been at the University of Ryūkyūs at the time of the crash but was so affected by seeing his niece's burned body at the scene of the incident that he took a leave of absence, returned in 1960, and then died by suicide in 1964. Shinjō reads his poetry throughout the book but provides an analysis of the line between suicide and murder that Nakaya explored in his poems. On the Miyamori elementary school incident, also see a piece that appeared in the *Ryūkyū Shimpō* to commemorate anniversary of the crash, including video footage: https://ryukyushimpo.jp/tag/宮森小ジェット機墜落事故/.
75 This has been one basis of internationalist solidarity against US military bases in recent years. See, for example, a statement by the International Women's Network for Genuine Security (started in 1997), Cachola et al., "Resistance, Resilience and Respect for Human Rights." In addition to CHamoru women who were forced to serve in the military sex venues that were built on Guam, around five hundred Korean women were sent to Palau in that capacity (as well as approximately six thousand forced laborers). Murray, *Battle over Peleliu*, 241.
76 See Horiba, *Inaguya Nanabachi*, and Miyagi, "Kasōba Secchi Undō no Saishuppatsu." This issue is explicitly addressed on page 19 of a transcript of a meeting published by the Okayama District Court's public prosecutor's office: Okayama Chihō Saibansho Kenjikyoku, *Okayamaken ni Okeru Hanamushiro ni Tsuite*. Here, piecework at home (*naishoku*) was advocated as a way to circumvent factory laws that restricted nighttime work. It states, "During the period of handweaving, it

did not matter if it was day or night. The wife, the husband, and the children would weave, taking turns eating to do so. The loom would only be at rest when the farm household was occupied with agricultural production."

77 On infrastructure, see Mezzadra and Neilson, *Politics of Operation*.

CONCLUSION: WAITING, WITNESSING, WITHHOLDING

1 Maia Hibbet, "In Okinawa, the US Military Seeks a Base Built on the Bones of the War Dead," *Nation*, February 18, 2021.
2 Saito argues in "Bone and Coral" that state efforts to control Indigenous peoples' remains is a central part of perpetuating colonial rule. I also think about the University of California, which continues to hold the remains of over one thousand Native American people. Finally, I think about Kashmir, where neighborhood playgrounds were turned into cemeteries, Kashmiri Muslim survivors of the 1990s genocides are fearful of even showing their face at commemorations, and activists who have uncovered evidence of mass graves and arbitrary killings like Khurram Parvez have been imprisoned by the Indian government. On the University of California, see Logan Jaffe, Mary Hudetz, Ash Ngu, and Graham Lee Brewer, "America's Biggest Museums Fail to Return Native American Human Remains," ProPublica, January 11, 2023, https://www.propublica.org/article/repatriation-nagpra-museums-human-remains. On Kashmir, refer to a report from January 29, 2022, submitted by various working groups and special rapporteurs to the United Nations, Ref.: AL IND 6/2022, July 29, 2022, https://spcommreports.ohchr.org/TMResultsBase/DownLoadPublicCommunicationFile?gId=27424.
3 Verso 16.3, "Museums and Corpses," reminds us that the living are also saddled with the weight of the world that requires the desecration of the dead. Brand, *Blue Clerk*, 92.
4 Murray, citing Wakako Higuchi's work on the way that Japanese bone collecting expeditions ended up damaging sacred Chamorro sites and excavating the remains of native Chamorros, notes, "The caves contain not only Japanese history but a priceless Palauan history that can be lost forever through a single act of carelessness." Murray, *Battle over Peleliu*, 25.
5 ProPublica's investigation of university and museum holdings of Indigenous peoples' remains has a searchable database that contains the figures of UCSD's holdings. Ash Ngu and Andrea Suozzo, "Does Your Local Museum or University Still Have Native American Remains?," ProPublica, January 11, 2023, https://projects.propublica.org/repatriation-nagpra-database/.
6 In verso 16.3, Brand defines the aesthetics of imperialism as "the world where certain bodies signify certain immovable qualities, deployed like lampposts along a route." *Blue Clerk*, 93. Macharia, *Frottage*, 37.
7 Kim, *Postcolonial Grief*, 1.
8 I write a bit about this context in the preface to the Japanese-language translation of my first book, *The Limits of Okinawa*, published by Hōsei University Press in 2023 under the title *Ikita Rōdō e no Tatakai*. I am extremely grateful to the book's transla-

tors, Masubuchi Asako, Kohagura Kei, and Mori Akiko, all excellent researchers in their own right, for allowing me the opportunity to think with them. On questions of complicity and what is urgently needed in this political moment, I am also grateful for Shō Yamagushiku's reminders that our thinking should challenge the space-time horizons of capitalism that keep us alienated from those who are precious to us and, crucially, that prevent us from creating those ensembles that go beyond nation, state, and capital.

9 Kim, *Postcolonial Grief,* 1.
10 Kim settles on not mourning (meant to be a temporary journey) or grief (a self that must learn to replace a loss and thus let go), but on melancholia to express the way that the "refusal of the dead to leave" infuses the present with a melancholy that, through artistic production, unsettles efforts by nation-states to settle the past through political performance, official reparations, and so on. She writes, "Melancholia and loss constitute an unsettling and insurgent cultural force across the transpacific," noting that the Pacific is a watery grave that is "full of unclaimed dead souls" that cannot be parceled out for nation-states to try to manage. *Postcolonial Grief,* 110, 112.
11 Kim, *Postcolonial Grief,* 10.
12 "These bales try to set fire to themselves and that would be fine if it could be done but all they do is smoulder." Brand, *Blue Clerk,* 138.
13 He writes, "Only water fights against history and brings forth the fragments of memory that lie in its shadows." Shinjō, *Okinawa ni Tsuranaru,* 103.
14 Shinjō, "Preface," in *Okinawa no Kizu,* 15.
15 Also see Shinjō's reading of Oe Kenzaburō's *Okinawa Note,* "The Political Formation of the Homoerotics and the Cold War," for a devastating critique of Oe and other Japanese scholars' use of Okinawa to "reconstruct themselves actively as part of the whole, namely, Japan(ese)." Shinjō, "Political Formation," 98.
16 From verso 3.6, "The clerk expects a sloop of war from across the water. Always." Brand, *Blue Clerk,* 31.
17 Brand, *Blue Clerk,* 3.
18 Brand, *Blue Clerk,* 91.
19 Brand, *Blue Clerk,* 93.
20 Gilmore, "Abolition Geography."
21 See Patel, "Talking Complicity, Breathing Coloniality"; and Baik, "From "Best" to Situated and Relational," who discuss the imperative that we critique our own practices and are aware of our own complicities as we teach and engage in the act of critiquing settler colonialism, capitalism, militarism, and so on.
22 Robinson, "First Attack," 74.
23 Robinson, "First Attack," 74.
24 In fact, even the statement "what has already happened" that Robinson puts forth requires careful consideration.
25 Brand's distinction between the clerk and the author is one that warns me against fetishizing place or positionality. To Lubrin, who says, "Why don't we start with time and place," Brand responds, "*The Blue Clerk* is an attempt to observe time and

not place. Therefore, the materials that the clerk excavates and collects are not hinged to place. The clerk lives in nowness. The clerk lives in the continuum of the present. The author is stuck in place." What happens in those moments when the author, who is stuck in place as reader and witness to what the clerk makes visible, is also the clerk, for whom, as Brand says in her interview with Canisia Lubrin in *Quill and Quire*, "records are always undone, always changing"?

26 Gilmore, "Abolition Geography," 329.
27 Okamoto, "Yasashii Okinawajin."
28 Shaista Patel and Dia Da Costa explain the limits of writing together across caste lines and the cover that collaborative writing often provides to white settler colonialism in the North American academy. While the piece is specifically about cross-caste collaborative writing, it is a powerful reminder of the need to foreground colonial power relations that structure who gets to speak about and for the communities that I discuss in this monograph. Patel and Da Costa, "We Cannot Write About Complicity Together."
29 Perhaps this requires some explanation. By writing in an extractive, colonial mode, this refers to both to the disavowal of Japan's settler colonial and imperialist presents that dominates at least English-language work in the field as well as the perspective that sees the Euro-America based scholar as being a purveyor of knowledge about Japan or Asia rather than as someone who is shaped by the politics of knowledge production in which they are implicated. The latter would require an interrogation of complicity like the one that Yoneyama calls for in her essay "Toward a Decolonial Genealogy of the Transpacific."
30 Yamagushiku's film with yana-imi, *Uyafaafuji's Refusal: An Ode to the Yanbaru*, makes connections between our present and the times of his great-grandfather/my grandmother, insisting that those who left their islands behind "for this land of lines" are still here with us.

BIBLIOGRAPHY

Alagraa, Bedour. "The Interminable Catastrophe." Offshoot, March 1, 2021. https://offshootjournal.org/the-interminable-catastrophe/.
Alagraa, Bedour. "What Will Be the Cure? A Conversation with Sylvia Wynter." Offshoot, January 7, 2021. https://offshootjournal.org/what-will-be-the-cure-a-conversation-with-sylvia-wynter/.
Aniya Masaaki. *Okinawa no Musan Undō*. Naha: Hirugisha, 1990.
Araki Hitoshi. "Foxtail Millet Trade between Korea and Manchuria in the Interwar Period through the Customs Records of Sinuiju: One Aspect of Japan's Food Supply System." *Japanese Journal of Human Geography* 68, no. 1 (2016): 44–65.
Arashiro Toshiaki. "Gunkokushugi Kyōiku to Yokusan Taisei." In *Okinawa Kenshi* 5, edited by Okinawaken Kyōiku Iinkai, 525–44. Itoman: Henshū Kōbō Tōyō Kikaku, 2011.
Arvin, Maile. *Possessing Polynesians: The Science of Settler Colonial Whiteness in Hawai'i and Oceania*. Durham, NC: Duke University Press, 2019.
Asamachō Rekishi Shiryōshū Henshū Iinkai. *Asamachō Rekishi Shiryōshū Kindaihen*. Iseshi: Asamachō Rekishi Shiryōshū Henshū Iinkai, 1996.
Asiwaju, A. I. "Control through Coercion; A Study of the Indigenat Regime in French West African Administration, 1887–1946." *Journal of Historical Society of Nigeria* 9, no. 3 (December 1978): 91–124.
Asō Yawata. *Rinkō Jijō: Tōyō oyobi Nanyō Hōmen*. Tokyo: Tōyō Seitō Tokyo Shucchōjo, 1925.
Azuma, Eiichirō. *In Search of Our Frontier: Japanese America and Settler Colonialism in the Construction of Japan's Borderless Empire*. Berkeley: University of California Press, 2019.
"Baekyŏ Sojagin Nongjang-e tto Swaedo." *Tonga Ilbo*, January 1, 1932.
Baik, Crystal Mun-hye. "From 'Best' to Situated and Relational: Notes toward a Decolonizing Praxis." *Oral History Review* 49 (2022): 3–28.
Banaji, Jairus. *A Brief History of Commercial Capitalism*. Chicago: Haymarket, 2020.
Banivanua Mar, Tracey. "'Boyd's Blacks': Labour and the Making of Settler Lands in Australia and the Pacific." In *Labour Lines and Colonial Power: Indigenous and Pacific Islander Mobility in Australia*, edited by Victoria Stead and John Altman, 57–73. Canberra: ANU Press, 2019.

Banivanua Mar, Tracey. *Decolonisation and the Pacific.* Cambridge: Cambridge University Press, 2016.
Banivanua Mar, Tracey. *Violence and Colonial Dialogue: The Australian-Pacific Indentured Labor Trade.* Honolulu: University of Hawai'i Press, 2007.
Banshū Gōdō Rōdō Kumiai Honbu. *Sxxjin Rōdōsha no Zanshi Kara Taki Seihi o Yattsukero to Tatakai: 500 no Kyōdai o Shōsero.* October 20–21, 1931. Ōhara Shakai Mondai Kenkyūjo. Reference code G-77.
Banshū Kagaku Sangyō Rōdō Kumiai Kessei Taikai Jyunbikai. *Goannai.* October 24, 1931. Ōhara Shakai Mondai Kenkyūjo. Reference code G-77.
Barchiesi, Franco, and Shona N. Jackson. "Introduction." In "Blackness and Labor in the Afterlives of Racial Slavery." Special issue of *International Labor and Working Class History* 96 (Fall 2019): 1–16.
Barshay, Andrew. *The Social Sciences in Modern Japan: The Marxian and Modernist Traditions.* Berkeley: University of California Press, 2007.
Barske, Valerie. "Visualizing Priestesses or Performing Prostitutes? Ifa Fuyū's Depictions of Okinawan Women, 1913–1943." *Series IV* 3, no. 1 (March 2013): 65–116.
Batterbury, Simon, Matthias Kowasch, and Séverine Bouard. "The Geopolitical Ecology of New Caledonia: Territorial Re-ordering, Mining, and Indigenous Economic Development." *Journal of Political Ecology* 27, no. 1 (2020): 594–611.
Bayliss, Jeffrey. *On the Margins of Empire: Buraku and Korean Identity in Prewar and Wartime Japan.* Cambridge, MA: Harvard University Press, 2013.
Benjamin, Walter. "Theses on the Philosophy of History." In *Illuminations: Essays and Reflections*, translated by Harry Zohn, 253–64. New York: Schocken, 1987.
Bhandar, Brenna. "Possession, Occupation and Registration: Recombinant Ownership in the Settler Colony." *Settler Colonial Studies* 6, no. 2 (2016): 119–131.
Bhandar, Brenna. "Registering Interests: Modern Methods of Valuing Labour, Land and Life." In *Searching For Contemporary Legal Thought*, edited by Justin Desautels-Stein and Christopher Tomlins, 290–311. New York: Cambridge University Press, 2017).
Bhattacharya, Neeladri. *The Great Agrarian Conquest: The Colonial Reshaping of a Rural World.* Ranikhet: Permanent Black, 2018.
Blaney, David. "Provincializing Economics: Jevons, Marshall and the Colonial Imaginaries of Free Trade." *Review of International Political Economy.* https://doi.org/10.1080/09692290.2020.1794929.
Brand, Dionne. *An Autobiography of the Autobiography of Reading.* Edmonton: University of Alberta Press, 2020.
Brand, Dionne. *The Blue Clerk: Ars Poetica in 59 Versos.* Durham, NC: Duke University Press, 2018.
Brand, Dionne. "What we saw. What we made. When we emerge." Kitty Lundy Memorial Lecture, York University, Toronto, March 11, 2021.
Broadbent, Kate, and Tessa Morris-Suzuki. "Women's Work in the 'Public' and 'Private' Spheres of the Japanese Economy." *Asian Studies Review* 24, no. 2 (June 2000): 161–73.
Brown, Canter, Jr. *A River of Peace? The Southern Florida Frontier in the Nineteenth Century.* Orlando: University of Central Florida Press, 1991.

Burstyn, Harold. "Science Pays Off: Sir John Murray and the Christmas Island Phosphate Industry, 1886–1914." *Social Studies of Science* 5 (1975): 5–34.

Cachola, Ellen-Rae, Gwyn Kirk, LisaLinda Natividad, and Maria Reinat Pumarejo. "Resistance, Resilience and Respect for Human Rights: Women Working across Borders for Peace and Genuine Security." The International Women's Network against Militarism, 2009. http://iwnam.org/wp-content/uploads/2015/09/16_womenworkingacrossborders.pdf.

Camacho, Keith. *Cultures of Commemoration: The Politics of War, Memory, and History in the Mariana Islands*. Honolulu: University of Hawai'i Press, 2011.

Caple, Zachary. "Holocene in Fragments: A Critical Landscape Ecology of Phosphorous in Florida." PhD diss., University of California, Santa Cruz, 2017.

Cattelino, Jessica. *High Stakes: Florida Seminole Gaming and Sovereignty*. Durham, NC: Duke University Press, 2008.

Cena, Julius Sotomayor. "Theater." Guampedia, n.d. https://www.guampedia.com/theater/.

Césaire, Aimé. *Discourse on Colonialism*. New York: Monthly Review, 2001.

Chayanov, A. V. *The Theory of Peasant Economy*. Edited by Daniel Thorner, Basile Kerblay, and R. E. F. Smith. Madison: University of Wisconsin Press, 1986.

Chen, Chao-Ju. "Gendered Borders: The Historical Formation of Women's Nationality under Law in Taiwan." *positions: asia critique* 17, no. 2 (Fall 2009): 289–314.

Christy, Alan. "The Making of Imperial Subjects in Okinawa." In *Formations of Colonial Modernity in East Asia*, edited by Tani E. Barlow, 141–70. Durham, NC: Duke University Press, 1997.

Chung, Chin-Sung. "Colonial Migration from Korea to Japan." PhD diss., Columbia University, 1984.

Chung Seung-Jin. "Model Village of Daejangchon: The Image of Imperial Japan in the Eyes of Rural Korea." *Review of Korean Studies* 16, no. 2 (2013): 127–39.

Cortés, Antonio L. "Land in Trust: The Invasion of Palau's Land-Tenure Customs by American Law." *Asian-Pacific Law and Policy Journal* 14, no. 3 (2013): 167–240.

Coulthard, Glen Sean. *Red Skin, White Masks: Rejecting the Colonial Politics of Recognition*. Minneapolis: University of Minnesota Press, 2014.

Cox, Terry, and Gary Littlejohn, eds. *Kritsman and the Agrarian Marxists*. New York: Routledge, 1984.

Cunningham, Nijah. "The Resistance of the Lost Body." *Small Axe* 20, no. 1 (49) (March 2016): 113–28.

Davis, Angela Y. *Women, Race and Class*. New York: Random House, 1981.

Davis, Muriam. *Markets of Civilization: Islam and Racial Capitalism in Algeria*. Durham, NC: Duke University Press, 2022.

De Boer, John. "Circumventing the Evils of Colonialism: Yanaihara Tadao and Zionist Settler Colonialism in Palestine." *positions: asia critique* 14, no. 3 (Winter 2006): 567–95.

Decker, John. *Labor Problems in the Pacific Mandates*. New York: AMS Press, 1978.

Diaz, Vicente M. "Deliberating 'Liberation Day': Identity, History, Memory, and War in Guam." In *Perilous Memories: The Asia-Pacific War(s)*, edited by Takashi Fujitani, Geoffrey M. White, and Lisa Yoneyama, 155–80. Durham, NC: Duke University Press, 2001.

Dixon, Marion. "Phosphate Rock Frontiers: Nature, Labor, and Imperial States, from 1870 to World War II." *Critical Historical Studies* 8, no. 2 (Fall 2021): 271-307.

Doi Hirotsugu. "Chōsen Nōkai no Soshiki to Jigyō: Keitō Nōkai Taisei Seiritsu kara Senji Taiseiki o Chūshin ni." *Kobe Daigaku Shigaku Nenpō* 22 (2007): 40-67.

Dōjinsha Hensanbu. *Musansha Hōritsu Hikkei*. Tokyo: Dōjinsha, 1932.

Endō, Katsuhiko. "The Multitude and the Holy Family: Empire, Fascism, and the War Machine." In *Tosaka Jun: A Critical Reader*, edited by Ken Kawashima, Fabian Schäfer, and Robert Stolz, 274-96. Ithaca, NY: Cornell University Press, 2013.

Endō, Katsuhiko. "The Science of Capital: The Uses and Abuses of Social Sciences in Interwar Japan." PhD diss., New York University, 2004.

Ericson, Kjell. "Making Space for Red Tide: Discolored Water and the Early Twentieth Century Bayscape of Japanese Pearl Cultivation." *Journal of the History of Biology* 50, no. 2 (2017): 393-423.

Eudell, Demetrius L. "From Mode of Production to Mode of Auto-Institution: Sylvia Wynter's Black Metamorphosis of the Labor Question." *Small Axe* 20, no. 1 (49) (2016): 47-61.

Fedman, David. *Seeds of Control: Japan's Empire of Forestry in Colonial Korea*. Seattle: University of Washington Press, 2020.

Ferraro, Chantal. "When Black Is Transparent: French Colonialism in New Caledonia, 1878-1914." In *Wansalawara: Soundings in Melanesian History*, edited by Brij Lal, 119-56. Honolulu: Pacific Island Studies Program, Centers for Asian and Pacific Studies, University of Hawai'i at Manoa, 1987.

Folbre, Nancy. *Greed, Lust, and Gender: A History of Economic Ideas*. New York: Oxford University Press, 2010.

Folbre, Nancy, and Marjorie Abel. "Women's Work and Women's Households: Gender Bias in the US Census." *Social Research* 56, no. 3 (Autumn 1989): 545-69.

Fujitani, Takashi. "Electronic Pageantry and Japan's 'Symbolic Emperor.'" *Journal of Asian Studies* 51, no. 4 (November 1992): 824-50.

Fukuchi Hiroaki, ed. *Okinawa Jokō Aishi*. Haebaru, Okinawa: Naha Shuppansha, 1985.

Fukuoka Chihō Shokugyō Shōkai Jimukyoku. *Nōgyō Oyobi Saisekigyō Naisenjin Rōdō Jijō*. Fukuoka: Fukuoka Chihō Shokugyō Shōkai Jimukyoku, 1928.

Fukuokaken Naimubu. *Okinawaken Kosaku ni Kansuru Chōsa*. Fukuoka: Fukuokaken Naimubu, 1930.

"Futatsu no Sōdō Jiken ni Kyūen Undō Makiokoru." *Shakai Undō Tsūshin*. January 13, 1932. National Diet Library, Tokyo.

Gaimushō. "Nihon Gaikō Monjo." *Documents on Japanese Foreign Policy* 41, no. 2. Tokyo: Nihon Kokusai Rengō Kyōkai, 1961. National Diet Library, Tokyo.

Gaimushō. "Nihon Gaikō Monjo." *Documents on Japanese Foreign Policy* 43, no. 2. Tokyo: Nihon Kokusai Rengō Kyōkai, 1962. National Diet Library, Tokyo.

Gaimushō. "Nihon Gaikō Monjo." *Documents on Japanese Foreign Policy* 45, no. 1. Tokyo: Nihon Kokusai Rengō Kyōkai, 1963. National Diet Library, Tokyo.

Gaimushō Tsūshōkyoku. *Imin Chōsa Hōkoku*. Tokyo: Gaimushō Tsūshōkyoku, 1908.

Gibson-Graham, J. K. *The End of Capitalism (As We Knew It): A Feminist Critique of Political Economy*. Minneapolis: University of Minnesota Press, 2006.

Gilmore, Ruth Wilson. "Abolition Geography and the Problem of Innocence." In *Futures of Black Radicalism*, edited by Gaye Theresa Johnson and Alex Lubin, 225-40. New York: Verso, 2017.

Gilmore, Ruth Wilson. *Golden Gulag: Prisons, Surplus, Crisis, and Opposition in Globalizing California*. Berkeley: University of California Press, 2007.

Ginowan Shishi Henshū Iinkai. *Ginowan Shishi 3 Shiryō 2*. Ginowanshi: Ginowan Shishi Henshū Iinkai, 1982.

Ginowan Shishi Henshū Iinkai. *Ginowan Shishi 5 Shiryō 4*. Ginowanshi: Ginowan Shishi Henshū Iinkai, 1985.

Ginowan Shishi Henshū Iinkai. *Ginowan Shishi 6 Shiryō 5*. Ginowanshi: Ginowan Shishi Henshū Iinkai, 1987.

Ginowan Shishi Henshū Iinkai. *Ginowan Shishi 7 Shiryō 6*. Ginowanshi: Ginowan Shishi Henshū Iinkai, 1988.

Ginowanshi Kyōiku Iinkai. *Tsuchi ni Umoreta Ginowan*. Ginowan: Ginowanshi Kyōiku Iinkai, 1989.

Greenberg, Michael. "The New Economic History and the Understanding of Slavery: A Methodological Critique." *Dialectical Anthropology* 2, no. 131 (1977): 131-41.

Haley, Sarah. *No Mercy Here: Gender, Punishment, and the Making of Jim Crow Modernity*. Chapel Hill: University of North Carolina Press, 2016.

"Han Sōgidan Sōdōin de Mikaiyu no Kanshōburi." *Shakai Undō Tsūshin*. January 12, 1932. National Diet Library, Tokyo.

Hanaki, Hironao. "Meiji Chū-Kō Ki no Okinawaken ni Okeru Imin Gaisha Gyōmu Dairinin no Keireki to Zokusei." *Okinawa Chiri* 13 (2013): 1-16.

Hanlon, David. *Remaking Micronesia: Discourses over Development in a Pacific Territory, 1944-1982*. Honolulu: University of Hawai'i Press, 1998.

Harootunian, Harry. *Marx after Marx: History and Time in the Expansion of Capitalism*. New York: Columbia University Press, 2017.

Harootunian, Harry. *Overcome by Modernity: History, Culture, and Community in Interwar Japan*. Princeton, NJ: Princeton University Press, 2000.

Hartman, Saidiya. "The Anarchy of Colored Girls Assembled in a Riotous Manner." *South Atlantic Quarterly* 117, no. 3 (July 2018): 465-90.

Hartman, Saidiya. *Scenes of Subjection: Terror, Slavery, and Self-Making in Nineteenth-Century America*. New York: Oxford University Press, 2010.

Hartman, Saidiya. *Wayward Lives, Beautiful Experiments: Intimate Histories of Social Upheaval*. New York: W. W. Norton, 2019.

Hasegawa, Kazumi. "Examining the Life of Oyabe Zen'ichirō: The New Formation of Modern Japanese Identity at the Turn of the Twentieth Century." PhD diss., Emory University, 2013.

Hayashi Yūichi. *Kindai Nihon Nōmin Undōshi Ron*. Tokyo: Nihon Keizai Hyōronsha, 2000.

Henshū Taki Kagaku Hyakunenshi Henshū Iinkai. *Taki Kagaku Hyakunenshi*. Kakogawa: Taki Kagaku Kabushiki Gaisha, 1985.

Hezel, Francis. *Strangers in Their Own Land: A Century of Colonial Rule in the Caroline and Marshall Islands*. Honolulu: University of Hawai'i Press, 1995.

Higa Kamejirō. "Okinawa no Bokutachi mo Tatakatta Zo." *Senki* (September 1930): 74–76.

Hiraga Akihiko. *Senzhen Nihon Nōgyō Seisakushi no Kenkyū: 1920–1945*. Tokyo: Nihon Keizai Hyōronsha, 2003.

Hong Yunshin. *The Battle of Okinawa and "Comfort Stations" in Memory*. Translated by Robert Ricketts. Leiden: Koninklijke Brill, 2020.

Horiba Kiyoko. *Inaguya Nanabachi: Okinawa Joseishi o Saguru*. Tokyo: Domesu Shuppan, 1991.

Horii, Mitsutoshi. *The Category of "Religion" in Contemporary Japan: Shūkyō and Temple Buddhism*. New York: Palgrave Macmillan, 2018.

Horiuchi Minoru. "Hanshin Shōhi Kumiai ni Tsuite: 1930 Nendai." *Zainichi Chōsenjinshi Kenkyū* 7 (December 1980): 1–16.

Horiuchi Minoru. *Hyōgo Chōsenjin Rōdō Undōshi 8.15 Kaizōhen*. Kobe-shi: Mukuge no Kai, 1998.

Horne, Gerald. *The White Pacific: US Imperialism and Black Slavery in the South Seas after the Civil War*. Honolulu: University of Hawai'i Press, 2007.

Hōsei Daigaku Ōhara Shakai Mondai Kenkyūjo, ed. *Musansha Shimbun No. 1*. Tokyo: Hōsei Daigaku Shuppankyoku, 1975.

Hoston, Germaine. *Marxism and the Crisis of Development in Prewar Japan*. Princeton, NJ: Princeton University Press, 1987.

Huang, Qianqing. "Liberation, Discourses of Liberation, and Liberation from the Discourses of Liberation: Buraku Dreams of Love-Politics and Migration from late 19th to mid-20th Century." PhD diss., University of California, Los Angeles, 2023.

Hudson, Peter James. *Bankers and Empire: How Wall Street Colonized the Caribbean*. Chicago: University of Chicago Press, 2017.

Hurston, Zora Neale. *Dust Tracks on a Road: An Autobiography*. New York: Harper Collins, 1996.

"Hyōgo: Arashi o Haramu Taki Hiryō Sōgi." *Shakai Undō Tsūshin*, December 23, 1931. National Diet Library, Tokyo.

Hyōgo no Naka no Chōsen: Aruite Shiru Chōsen to Nihon no Rekishi. Tokyo: Akashi Shoten, 2001.

Ichishi Gun Toyota son Niiyano Shibu. *Toyota son Tōsō Nyūsu Daiichigō* (March 1931). Ōhara Shakai Mondai Kenkyūjo. Reference code 農 24-3.

Iida Akiko, Ōsawa Satoshi, Ishikawa Mikiko. "Nanyō Guntō Kyū Nihon Itaku Tōchiryō ni Okeru Kaitaku no Jittai to Genjyō ni Kansuru Kenkyū: Palao Kyōwakoku Baberudaobu Tō no Nōchi Kaitaku to Bōkisaito Sakkutsu no Jirei." *Toshi Keikaku Ronbunshū* 46, no. 3 (October 2011): 319–24.

Imai Hiroko. "Washi wa 'Tōtoi' to Omounoya: Mie Ken Asama Tōsō o Sasaeta Kokoro, Interview of Yamamoto Heijū." *Buraku Kaihō* 342 (June 1992): 106–15.

Infante, Chad, Sandra Harvey, Kelly Limes Taylor, and Tiffany King. "Other Intimacies: Black Studies Notes on Native/Indigenous Studies." *Postmodern Culture* 31, nos. 1–2 (September 2020–January 2021). https://doi.org/10.1353/pmc.2020.0022.

Ino Jirō. *Chiji Jimu Hikitsugisho*. 1935. Okinawa Prefectural Archives, P00013259B.

Inomata Tsunao. *Kyūbo no Nōson—Chōsa Hōkoku*. Tokyo: Iwanami Shoten, 1982.

Inomata Tsunao. "Nōmin to Fashizumu." *Chūō Kōron* 75, no. 12 (June 1935): 339-51.
Inoue Mayumo. Review of *Okinawagaku Nyūmon: Kūfuku no Hōhō*, edited by Katsukata=Inafuku Keiko and Maetakenishi Kazuma. *International Journal of Okinawan Studies* 2, no. 1 (2011): 74-78.
Isa Shinichi. *Jahana Noboru Shū*. Tokyo: Misuzu Shobō, 1998.
Ishii Torao. *Okinawa Bōbi Taisaku Sōfu no Ken*. 1934. Rikugun Senjō Shiryō. Cabinet Office, Government of Japan. Reference Code B03-4-149. https://www8.cao.go.jp/okinawa/okinawasen/document/b03_4/b03_4_17.html.
Ishikawa Tomonori, ed. "Gaikō Shiryōkan Shozoku Okinawaken Shusshin Imin no Gaimushō Kiroku (2): Meijiki no Jirei." *Imin Kenkyū* 13 (August 2017): 105-20.
Ishikawa Tomonori. "Kaigai Imin no Tenkai." In *Okinawa Kenshi* 7, edited by Okinawaken Kyōiku Iinkai, 205-420. Naha: Ryūkyū Seifu, 1974.
Itō, Ruri. "The 'Modern Girl' Question in the Periphery of Empire: Colonial Modernity and Mobility among Okinawan Women in the 1920s and 1930s." In *Modern Girl around the World: Consumption, Modernity, and Globalization*, edited by Alys Eve Weinbaum, Lynn Thomas, Priti Ramamurthy, Uta Poiger, Madeline Yue Dong, and Tani Barlow, 240-62. Durham, NC: Duke University Press, 2008.
Ivy, Marilyn. *Discourses of the Vanishing: Modernity, Phantasm, Japan*. Chicago: University of Chicago Press, 1995.
Jackson, Shona. "Colonialism." In *Keywords for African American Studies*, edited by Erica R. Edwards, Roderick A. Ferguson, and Jeffrey O. G. Ogbar, 51. New York: NYU Press, 2018.
Jackson, Shona. *Creole Indigeneity: Between Myth and Nation in the Caribbean*. Minneapolis: University of Minnesota Press, 2012.
James, C. L. R. *The Black Jacobins: Toussaint L'Ouverture and the San Domingo Revolution*. New York: Vintage, 1989.
Jinkōka. *Shōwa Gonen Kokusei Chōsa Shitsugi Ōtō Kankei Tsuzuri*. National Archives of Japan. Reference code: Tsukuba Shoko 5 5-58 149.
Jung, Moon-Ho. *Coolies and Cane: Race, Labor, and Sugar in the Age of Emancipation*. Baltimore, MD: Johns Hopkins University Press, 2006.
Kadenachō Kyōiku Iinkai. *Kadena Chōshi Shiryō 4*. Kadenachō: Kadenachō Kyōiku Iinkai, 1998.
Kalulé, Petero. "Being *Right-With*: On Human Rights Law as Unfreedom." *Feminist Legal Studies* 31 (2022): 243-64. https://doi.org/10.1007/s10691-022-09500-x.
Kamata Seishi, Yamamoto Takatsugu, Urayama Takakazu, and Nakama Yūei, eds. *"Hōgo" to Okinawa no Sonraku Kūkan: Dentoteki Chiri Shisō no Kankyō Keikangaku*. Tokyo: Fūkyōsha, 2019.
Karuka, Manu. *Empire's Tracks: Indigenous Nations, Chinese Workers, and the Transcontinental Railroad*. Berkeley: University of California Press, 2019.
Katsukata=Inafuku, Keiko. "Unaiism Manifested in the Denoument of *Syushin-Kaneiri*: Feminist Ethnography in Okinawa." *International Journal of Okinawan Studies* 1, no. 1 (2010): 111-22.
Kawamura Minato. "Popular Orientalism and Japanese Views of Asia." Translated by Kota Inoue. In *Reading Colonial Japan: Text, Context, and Critique*, edited by Michele M. Mason and Helen J. S. Lee, 271-98. Stanford, CA: Stanford University Press, 2012.

Kawamura Zenjirō. "Fashizumu to Buraku Sabetsu: Mie ken Asama Buraku no Tatakai." *Buraku* 20, no. 3 (March 1968): 34-52.

Kawano Shigeto. "Yamaguchi Kenka ni Okeru Sennō no Teichaku Katei." *Nōgyō Keizai Kenkyū* 16, no. 1 (1940): 170-71.

Kawashima, Ken. *The Proletarian Gamble: Korean Workers in Interwar Japan*. Durham, NC: Duke University Press, 2009.

Kawashima, Ken, and Gavin Walker. "Surplus alongside Excess: Uno Kōzō, Imperialism, and the Theory of Crisis." *Viewpoint Magazine*, February 1, 2018. https://viewpointmag.com/2018/02/01/surplus-alongside-excess-uno-kozo-imperialism-theory-crisis/.

Kelley, Robin D. G. Foreword to *Black Marxism: The Making of the Black Radical Tradition*, by Cedric J. Robinson, xi-xxvi. Chapel Hill: University of North Carolina Press, 1983.

Kelley, Robin D. G. *Hammer and Hoe: Alabama Communists during the Great Depression*. Chapel Hill: University of North Carolina Press, 1990.

Kelley, Robin D. G. "The Rest of Us: Rethinking Settler and Native." *American Quarterly* 69, no. 2 (June 2017): 267-76.

"Kenyūchi Shakuchiryō Nesage o Chinjō." *Osaka Asahi Shimbun Furoku Kyūshū Asahi*. September 23, 1930.

Kikekawa Hiroshi. *Meiji Chihō Seido Seiritsushi*. Gannendō Shoten: Tokyo, 1967.

Kim Ch'anjŏng. *Kenshō Maboroshi no Shimbun "Minshū Jihō": Fashizumu no Taitō to Hōdō no Genten*. Tokyo: Sangokan, 2001.

Kim Chŏng-mi. "Mie Ken Kinomoto ni Okeru Chōsenjin Shūgeki, Gyakusatsu ni Tsuite." *Zainichi Chōsenjinshi Kenkyū* 18 (October 1988): 102-46.

Kim Chŏng-mi. "Wakayama Zainichi Chōsenjin no Rekishi." *Zainichi Chōsenjinshi Kenkyū* 14 (November 1984): 49-106.

Kim Hyun. "Shokuminchi Chōsen to Taki Kumejirō: Chōsen ni Okeru Jigyō Kiban to Saiseiken Mondai." *Kaikō Toshi Kenkyū* 4 (March 2009): 77-95.

Kim, Jinah. *Postcolonial Grief: The Afterlives of the Pacific Wars in the Americas*. Durham, NC: Duke University Press, 2019.

Kim, Junyoung Verónica. "Writing Asia-Latin America." In *Asian American Literature in Transition, 1996-2020*, 56-74. New York: Cambridge University Press, 2021.

Kim, Marie. "Law and Custom under the Chosŏn Dynasty and Colonial Korea." *Journal of Asian Studies* 66, no. 4 (November 2007): 1067-97.

Kim Rihyang. "Shataku to Chōsenjin—Taki Seihijo Shataku no Zainichi Seikatsushi." Undergraduate thesis. Kansai Gakuin Daigaku, 2013.

"Kimje Taki Nōjō: Kosakunin Ichibu Dōyō." *Maeil Sinbo*, December 28, 1931. National Library of Korea Digital Reading Hall.

King, Tiffany Lethabo. "Black 'Feminisms' and Pessimism: Abolishing Moynihan's Negro Family." *Theory and Event* 21, no. 1 (January 2018): 68-87.

King, Tiffany Lethabo. *The Black Shoals: Offshore Formations of Black and Native Studies*. Durham, NC: Duke University Press, 2019.

Kinjō Isao. *Kindai Okinawa no Tetsudō to Kaiun*. Naha: Hirugisha, 1983.

Kinjō Isao. *Kindai Okinawa no Tōgyō*. Naha: Hirugisha, 1985.

Kinjō Isao. "Meijiki no Okinawa no Tōgyō." In *Kindai Okinawa no Rekishi to Minshū*, edited by Okinawa Rekishi Kenkyūkai, 111-42. Rev. ed. Tokyo: Shingensha, 1977.

Kinjō Isao. "Nōson no Keizai Kōsei Keikaku ni Tsuite." *Okinawa Shiryōshitsu Henshūjo Kiyō* 6 (March 1981): 25–72.

Kinyūkai Tokyo Shikai. "Kinyūkai Tokyo Shikai Dai 3 Sōkai Bunken (1929)." *Zainichi Chōsenjinshi Kenkyū* 2 (June 1978): 118–138.

Kitazume Masao. "Tamura Hiroshi to Okinawa." In *Chiiki Keisei no Shisō*, edited by Ōtsubo Shōichi and Uchida Masaki, 59–78. Chōfu: Āban Puro Shuppan Sentā, 2007.

Kō Seong-Bong. "Gendai Nicchō Kōro no Naka no Osaka-Jejutō Kōro." *Hakusan Jinruigaku* 12 (2009): 7–33.

Kobayakawa, Akira. "Japan's Modernization and Discrimination: What Are Buraku and Burakumin?" *Critical Sociology* 47, no. 1 (2021): 111–32.

Kobayashi Sueo. *Taki Seihijo Rōdōshi: Buraku, Chōsenjin Rōdōsha Danketsu no Tatakai*. Okayama-shi: Okayama Buraku Mondai Kenkyūjo, 2003.

Kobayashi Sueo. *Zainichi Chōsenjin Rōdōsha to Suihei Undō*. Kyoto: Buraku Mondai Kenkyūjo Shuppanbu, 1974.

"Koibito wa Sxxjin." *Kobe Yūshin Nippō*, August 14, 1933, 6.

Kome Sōdō to Buraku Mondai. Edited by Fujino Yutaka, Watabe Tōru, and Kurokawa Midori. Tokyo: San'ichi Shobō, 1985.

Komori Yōichi. "Rule in the Name of 'Protection': The Vocabulary of Colonialism." Translated by Michele M. Mason. In *Reading Colonial Japan: Text, Context, and Critique*, edited by Michele M. Mason and Helen J. S. Lee, 60–76. Stanford, CA: Stanford University Press, 2012.

Kurokawa Midori. *Chiikishi no Naka no Buraku Mondai: Kindai Mie no Baai*. Osaka: Kaihō Shuppansha, 2003.

Kurokawa Midori. "Mie ken ni Okeru Suihei Undō no Seiritsu." *Chihōshi Kenkyū* 32, no. 3 (June 1982): 79–96.

Kurokawa Midori. *Tsukurareta "Jinshu": Buraku Sabetsu to Jinshushugi*. Tokyo: Yūshisha, 2016.

Lee, Hoon K. *Land Utilization and Rural Economy in Korea*. Chicago: University of Chicago Press, 1936.

lewallen, anne-elise. "Ainu Women and Indigenous Modernity in Settler Colonial Japan." *Asia-Pacific Journal: Japan Focus* 15, no. 18.2 (September 2017). https://apjjf.org/2017/18/lewallen.html.

Lichtenstein, Alex. *Twice the Work of Free Labor: The Political Economy of Convict Labor in the New South*. New York: Verso, 1996.

Lim, Sungyun. *Rules of the House: Family Law and Domestic Disputes in Colonial Korea*. Berkeley: University of California Press, 2019.

Loo, Tze M. "Escaping Its Past: Recasting the Grand Shrine of Ise." *Inter-Asia Cultural Studies* 11, no. 3 (2010): 375–92.

Loo, Tze M. *Heritage Politics: Shuri Castle and Okinawa's Incorporation into Modern Japan, 1870–2000*. Lanham, MD: Lexington, 2014.

Loo, Tze M. "Trapped in Text: The Changing Place of Female Ritualists in Taisho Okinawa." *Journal of Asian Studies* 83, no. 2 (2023): 184–205.

Lowe, Lisa. *The Intimacies of Four Continents*. Durham, NC: Duke University Press, 2015.

Lowe, Lisa. "The Intimacies of Four Continents." In *Haunted by Empire: Geographies of Intimacy in North American History*, edited by Ann Laura Stoler, 191–212. Durham, NC: Duke University Press, 2006.

Lowe, Lisa, and Kris Manjapra. "Comparative Global Humanities after Man: Alternatives to the Coloniality of Knowledge." *Theory, Culture, and Society* 36, no. 5 (September 2019): 23–48.

Lu, Sidney. *The Making of Japanese Settler Colonialism: Malthusianism and Trans-Pacific Migration, 1868–1961*. New York: Cambridge University Press, 2019.

Lubrin, Canisia. "Q&A: Canisia Lubrin Speaks to Dionne Brand about Her Two New Books, *The Blue Clerk* and *Theory*." *Quill and Quire* 13 (2018). https://quillandquire.com/omni/qa-canisia-lubrin-speaks-to-dionne-brand-about-her-two-new-books-the-blue-clerk-and-theory/.

Lumba, Allan. *Monetary Authorities: Capitalism and Decolonization in the American Colonial Philippines*. Durham, NC: Duke University Press, 2022.

Lutz, Catherine. "Bureaucratic Weaponry and the Production of Ignorance in Military Operations on Guam." *Current Anthropology* 60, no. S19 (February 2019): 108–21.

Luxemburg, Rosa. *The Accumulation of Capital*. Translated by Agnes Schwarzchild. New York: Routledge, 2003.

Macdonald, Barrie. *Cinderellas of the Empire: Towards a History of Kiribati and Tuvalu*. Canberra: Australian National University Press, 1982.

Macharia, Keguro. *Frottage: Frictions of Intimacy across the Black Diaspora*. New York: NYU Press, 2019.

Mancini, Matthew. *One Dies, Get Another: Convict Leasing in the American South, 1866–1928*. Columbia: University of South Carolina Press, 1996.

Mariátegui, José Carlos. *Seven Interpretive Essays on Peruvian Reality*. Translated by Majory Urquidi. Austin: University of Texas Press, 1971.

Maruoka Hideko. *Nihon Nōson Fujin Mondai: Shufu Boseihen*. Tokyo: Ōzorasha, 1997.

Maruyama Yoshiji. *Kōyō son: Okayama ken Akaiwa gun (Mura no Chōsa Hōkoku)*. Tokyo: Taisei Yokusankai Bunkabu, 1942.

Maruyama Yoshiji. *Nanyō Kikō*. Tokyo: Kōa Nipponsha, 1940.

Mashiyama Hitoshi. "Shōwa Shoki Pioniiru Undō no Soshiki to Kyōiku." *Jinbun Gakuhō. Kyōikugaku* 11 (March 1976): 91–138.

Mason, Michele M. "Writing Ainu Out/Writing Japanese In: The 'Nature' of Japanese Colonialism in Hokkaido." In *Reading Colonial Japan: Text, Context, and Critique*, edited by Michele M. Mason and Helen J. S. Lee, 33–54. Stanford, CA: Stanford University Press, 2012.

Matsuda, Hiroko. *Liminality of the Japanese Empire: Border Crossings from Okinawa to Colonial Taiwan*. Honolulu: University of Hawai'i Press, 2019.

Matsumoto Takenori, and Chung Seungjin. "Japanese Colonizers in the Honam Plain of Colonial Korea." *Sungkyun Journal of East Asian Studies* 15, no. 2 (October 2015): 263–89.

Matsumoto Takenori, and Chung Seungjin. "On the Hosokawa Farm and the History of Daejangchon, a Japanese-Style Village in Colonial Korea." *Korea Journal* 49, no. 3 (2009): 121–50.

Matsumura, Wendy. *The Limits of Okinawa: Japanese Capitalism, Living Labor, and Theorizations of Community*. Durham, NC: Duke University Press, 2015.

Matsumura, Wendy. "More than the 'Wife Corps': Female Tenant Farmer Struggle in 1920s Japan." *International Labor and Working-Class History* 91 (Spring 2017): 127–55.

Matsumura, Wendy. "Rethinking Japanese Fascism from the Politics of the Household." *Marxism 21* 13 (2016): 146–80.

Matsumura, Wendy. "Triple Exploitation, Social Reproduction, and the Agrarian Question in Japan." In *The SAGE Handbook of Marxism*, edited by Beverley Skeggs, Sara R. Farris, Alberto Toscano, and Svenja Bromberg, 1373–88. London: SAGE, 2022.

Matsusaka Shishi Hensan Iinkai. *Matsusaka Shishi Kindai Shiryōhen 15*. Tokyo: Sōjinsha, 1983.

Matsushita Matsuji. "Buraku Kaihō to Rōdō Undō—Kindai Bōsekigyō to Hisabetsu Buraku—Kishiwada Bōseki Gaisha o Chūshin to Shite." *Buraku Kaihō* 190 (December 1982): 193–202.

McKean, Margaret. "Management of Traditional Common Lands (Iriaichi) in Japan." In *Proceedings of the Conference on Common Property Resource Management*, edited by National Research Council, 533–89. Washington, DC: National Academy Press, 1986.

McKittrick, Katherine. *Demonic Grounds: Black Women and the Cartographies of Struggle*. Minneapolis: University of Minnesota Press, 2006.

Metzler, Mark. *Lever of Empire: The International Gold Standard and the Crisis of Liberalism in Prewar Japan*. Berkeley: University of California Press, 2006.

Mezzadra, Sandro, and Brett Neilson. *The Politics of Operation: Excavating Contemporary Capitalism*. Durham, NC: Duke University Press, 2019.

Mie Nōmin Shimbun Fukkōban. Tokyo: Fuji Shuppan, 1990.

Mieken. *Chiso Kaisei Ezu (Mieken, Nyū son)*. Held at Tsu Chihō Hōmukyoku, Matsusaka Shikyoku.

Mieken. *Kyū Tochi Daichō*. Held at Tsu Chihō Hōmukyoku, Matsusaka Shikyoku.

Mieken. *Mie Kenshi Shiryōhen Kindai 3*. Mie: Mieken, 1983.

Mieken. *Mie Kenshi Shiryōhen Kindai 4*. Mie: Mieken, 1991.

Mieken. *Mieken Kōhō*, no. 1364, April 9, 1926.

Mieken Kōseikai, ed. *Mieken Buraku Shiryōshū Kindaihen*. Tokyo: San'ichi Shobō, 1974.

Mieken Sanrinkai. *Mie no Ringyō*. Edited by Sai Ryōsuke. Tsu: Mieken Sanrinkai, 1940.

Mies, Maria. *Patriarchy and Accumulation on a World Scale: Women in the International Division of Labour*. New York: Zed 1998.

Miki Takeshi. *"Yaeyama Gasshūkoku" no Keifu*. Ishigaki: Nanzansha, 2010.

Miki Takeshi. *Yaeyama Kindai Minshūshi*. Tokyo: San'ichi Shobō, 1980.

Mita, Maki. "Oral Histories of Palauan Elders." *Senri Ethnological Reports* 87 (October 2009): 21–274.

Mitropoulos, Angela. *Contract and Contagion: From Biopolitics to Oikonomia*. London: Minor Compositions, 2012.

Miyagi Eishō. *Okinawa no Noro no Kenkyū*. Tokyo: Yoshikawa Kōbunkan, 2013.

Miyagi Etsu. "Kasōba Secchi Undō no Saishuppatsu." In *Okinawa Onna Tachi no Sengo: Shōdō kara no Shuppatsu*, 327–67, Naha: Hirugisha, 1986.

Morgan, Jennifer. *Laboring Women: Reproduction and Gender in New World Slavery*. Philadelphia: University of Pennsylvania Press, 2004.

Mori Akiko. "Senjiki Nanyō Guntō ni Okeru Shigen Kaihatsu Yōsaika to Sono Kiketsu: Kyōkai o Ikita Okinawa no Hitobito ni Chakumoku Shite." *Nōgyōshi Kenkyū* 48 (2014): 15–27.

Mori Takemaro. *Kindai Nōmin Undō to Shihai Taisei: 1920-nendai Gifu-ken Seinō Chihō no Nōson o Megutte*. Tokyo: Kashiwa Shobō, 1985.

Morimoto Tatsuaki. *Kindai Nihon ni Okeru Jinushi Nōmin Keiei: Okayamaken no Jirei*. Tokyo: Ochanomizu Shobō, 2007.

Mormino, Gary. "A River of Peace? The Southern Florida Frontier in the Nineteenth Century." *Florida Historical Quarterly* 70 (July 1991): 55–68.

Mukai Kiyoshi. *Okinawa Kindai Keizaishi*. Tokyo: Nihon Keizai Hyōronsha, 1988.

Murray, Stephen C. *The Battle over Peleliu: Islander, Japanese, and American Memories of War*. Tuscaloosa: University of Alabama Press, 2016.

"Naganoken ni Okeru Zainichi Chōsenjin." *Zainichi Chōsenjinshi Kenkyū* 12 (September 1983), 102–14.

Nagashima Yūki. "Kinsei Kōki Kyoto ni Okeru Shōke Hōkōnin no Koyō to Saiseisan: Hiranoya Endōke o Jirei to Shite." *Jinbun Chiri* 67, no. 1 (2015): 1–19.

Naha Shigikai Jimukyoku Gikaishi Hensanshitsu. *Naha Shigikaishi* 1. Naha: Naha Shigikai, 2011.

Nahashi. *Nahashi Suidōshi*. Naha: Nahashi, 1935.

"Nahashi ni Yūenchi o Mōkeru." *Osaka Asahi Shimbun Furoku Kyūshū Asahi*, June 3, 1930. Okinawa Prefectural Library.

Nahashi Suidōkyoku, ed. *Naha-shi Suidō Gojūnenshi*. Naha: Nahashi Suidōkyoku, 1983.

Naikaku Tōkeikyoku. *Shōwa 10 nen Kokusei Chōsa Hōkoku: Okayama ken*. Tokyo: Tōkyō Tōkei Kyōkai, 1937.

Naimushō Keihokyoku. *Tokubetsu Kōtō Keisatsu Shiryō* 9 (April 1930).

Nakama Yūei. *Okinawa Rinya Seido Riyōshi Kenkyū: Yama ni Kizamareta Rekishizō o Motomete*. Naha: Hirugisha, 1984.

Nakano Ryōko. *Beyond the Western Liberal Order: Yanaihara Tadao and Empire as Society*. New York: Palgrave Macmillan, 2013.

Nakayama Eiji. "Nettai ni Okeru Rōdō Nōritsu." In *Nanpō Kyōeiken no Rōdō Mondai*, 171–206. Tokyo: Kyōchōkai Shuppanbu, 1942.

Nakayama Izumi. "Ōhara Shakai Mondai Kenkyūjo to Rōdō Kagaku no Tanjō." *Journal of the Ōhara Institute for Social Research* 591 (February 2008): 4–9.

Nanyō Keizai Kenkyūjo. *Ngermeskang Gawa o Sakanoborite*. Tokyo: Nanyō Keizai Kenkyūjo Shuppanbu, 1943.

"New Order for 150 Riukiu Laborers." Mitsui Bussan Kaisha to Nippon Shokumin Gōshi Kaisha, March 31, 1908. *Nippon Shokumin Gōshi Kaisha ni Oki Taiyōtō Iki Imin Toriatsukai Ikken*. Ministry of Foreign Affairs, Diplomatic Archives, 3.8.2.242.

Nihon Gaikō Monjo (Documents on Japanese Foreign Policy) 41, no. 2. Ministry of Foreign Archives, Diplomatic Archives, Tokyo, Japan.

Nixon, Rob. *Slow Violence and the Environmentalism of the Poor*. Cambridge, MA: Harvard University Press, 2011.

Nōrinshō Keizai Kōseibu. *Nōka Keizai Chōsa (Shōwa 5-nendo)*. Tokyo: Nōrinshō Keizai Kōseibu, 1932.

Nōrinshō Keizai Kōseibu. *Nōka Keizai Chōsa (Shōwa 6-nendo)*. Tokyo: Nōrinshō Keizai Kōseibu, 1934.

Nōrinshō Keizai Kōseibu. *Shin Nōson no Kensetsu: Tairiku e Bunson Daiidō*. Tokyo: Tokyo Asahi Shimbun, 1939.

Nōrinshō Nōmukyoku. *Chihō Kosakukan Kōshukai Kōenshu*. Tokyo: Teikoku Nōkai, 1925.

Nōshōmushō Nōmukyoku. *Nōka Keizai Chōsa: Taishō 10-nendo*. Tokyo: Nōshōmushō Nōmukyoku, 1925.

Ohno Yoshimi. "Waga Kuni ni Okeru Shitsugyosha Undō ni Tsuite no Oboegaki (1)." *Shakai Rōdō Kenkyū* 23, no. 2 (February 1977): 55–112.

Okamoto Keitoku. "'Yasashii Okinawajin' to Iu Koto." *Okinawa Keiken*, May 1972.

Okayama Kenshi Hensan Iinkai. *Okayama Kenshi 28*. Okayama-shi: Sanyō Shimbunsha, 1987.

Okayamaken. *Kyū Tochi Daichō*. Held at Okayama Chihō Hōmukyoku.

Okayamaken Chihō Saibansho Kenjikyoku. *Okayamaken ni Okeru Hanamushiro ni Tsuite*. Shihōshō Chōsabu, 1939.

Okayamaken Tokubetsu Kōtō Keisatsu. *Okayamaken Tokubetsu Kōtō Keisatsu Jyōsei*. In *Senzenki Keisatsu Kankei Shiryōshū 6*, edited by Hirohata Kenji, 297–349. Tokyo: Fuji Shuppan, 2006.

Okinawa Daihyakka Jiten Kanko Jimukyoku. *Okinawa Daihyakka Jiten Ge*. Naha: Okinawa Taimususha, 1983.

Okinawa Shishi Henshū Iinkai. *Okinawa Shishi 5*. Okinawashi: Okinawa Shishi Henshū Iinkai, 1986.

Okinawaken Bunka Shinkōkai Kōbunshokan Kanribu Shiryō Henshūshitsu, ed. *Okinawa Kenshi Shiryōhen 6 Kindai 1*. Naha: Okinawaken Kyōiku Iinkai, 1998.

Okinawaken Gikai Jimukyoku, ed. *Okinawaken Gikaishi*. Vol. 4. Naha: Okinawaken Gikai, 1984.

Okinawaken Kyōiku Iinkai. *Okinawa Kenshi Shiryohen*. Vol. 25. Naha: Okinawaken Kyōiku Iinkai, 2015.

Okinawaken Nōkai. *Keizai Chōsa Kara Mita Honken Nōka Keizai no Dōkō*. Naha: Okinawaken Nōkai, 1938.

Okinawaken Nōkai. *Nōka no Keizai*. 1931.

Okinawaken Sanrinkai. *Okinawa no Ringyō*. Naha: Okinawa ken Sanrinkai, 1938.

Onoe Shitsugyōsha Dōmei. "Untitled." October 1930. Ōhara Shakai Mondai Kenkyūjo. Reference code 農 24-3.

Ortiz, Paul. *Emancipation Betrayed: The Hidden History of Black Organizing and White Violence in Florida from Reconstruction to the Bloody Election of 1920*. Berkeley: University of California Press, 2005.

Ōsato Kōei. *Jahana Noboru Den: Okinawa Jiyū Minken Undō no Kiroku*. Tokyo: Okinawasha, 1957.

Ōtsuki Masao. *Book-Keeping System for Family Farm*. Kyoto: Institute of Farm Accounting, College of Agriculture, Kyoto University, 1958. https://rcisss.ier.hit-u.ac.jp/Japanese/introduction/tss/tss071.pdf.

Ōyama Shunpō. *Mieken Suiheisha Rōnō Undōshi*. Tokyo: San'ichi Shobō, 1977.

Pak Kyŏng-sik. "Zainichi Chōsenjin no Tatakai." *Sanichi* 9 (February 1980): 3–16.

Park, Hyun Ok. "Repetition, Comparability, and Indeterminable Nation: Korean Migrants in the 1920s and 1990s." *boundary 2* 32, no. 2 (2005): 227-51.

Park, Hyun Ok. *Two Dreams in One Bed: Empire, Social Life, and the Origins of the North Korean Revolution in Manchuria*. Durham, NC: Duke University Press, 2005.

Park, Sunyoung. *The Proletarian Wave: Literature and Leftist Culture in Colonial Korea, 1910-1945*. Cambridge, MA: Harvard University Press, 2015.

Patel, Shaista Aziz. "Complicating the Tale of 'Two Indians': Mapping 'South Asian' Complicity in White Settler Colonialism Along the Axis of Caste and Anti-Blackness." *Theory and Event* 19, no. 4 (2016). muse.jhu.edu/article/633278.

Patel, Shaista Aziz. "The 'Indian' of Four Continents: Reading for Horizontal Relations of Violence, Complicity, and the Making of White Settler Colonialism." PhD diss., University of Toronto, 2018.

Patel, Shaista Aziz. "Talking Complicity, Breathing Coloniality: Interrogating Settler-Centric Pedagogy of Teaching about White Settler Colonialism." *Journal of Curriculum and Pedagogy* (2021). https://doi.org/10.1080/15505170.2020.1871450.

Patel, Shaista Aziz, and Dia Da Costa. "'We Cannot Write about Complicity Together': Limits of Cross-Caste Collaborations in Western Academy." *Engaged Scholar Journal: Community-Engaged Research, Teaching, and Learning* 8, no. 2 (Spring 2022): 1-27.

Peattie, Mark. *Nanyō: The Rise and Fall of the Japanese in Micronesia, 1885-1945*. Honolulu: University of Hawai'i Press, 1992.

Pierson, Nicolaas G. *The Principles of Economics*. Translated into Japanese by Kawakami Hajime and Kawada Shirō as *Kachiron*. Tokyo: Hōbunkan, 1911.

Purcell, David. "The Economics of Exploitation: The Japanese in the Mariana, Caroline, and Marshall Islands, 1915-1940." *Journal of Pacific History* 11, no. 3 (1976): 189-211.

Rinyachō Sanrinkyoku. *Hoanrin Kaijo: Mieken*. 1924. National Archives of Japan. Reference code 47 3A 3-2 67.

Rinyachō Sanrinkyoku. *Hoanrin Kaijo: Mieken*. 1926. National Archives of Japan. Reference code 47 3A 4-1 136.

Rinyachō Sanrinkyoku. *Hoanrin Kaijo: Okinawaken*. 1924. National Archives of Japan. Reference code 47 3A 4-1 78.

Rinyachō Sanrinkyoku. *Hoanrin Kaijo: Okinawaken*. 1934. National Archives of Japan. Reference code 47 3A 4-2 224.

Rinyachō Sanrinkyoku. *Hoanrin Kaijo: Okinawaken*. 1934. National Archives of Japan. Reference code 47 3A 4-2 225.

Rivera-Monroy, Victor, Jessica Cattelino, Jeffrey Wozniak, Katrina Schwartz, Gregory Noe, Edward Castaneda-Moya, and Gregory Kochi. "Life of P: A Biogeochemical and Sociopolitical Challenge in the Everglades." In *The Coastal Everglades: The Dynamics of Social-Ecological Transformation in the South Florida Landscape*, edited by Joseph Boyer and Stephen Davis, 99-128. New York: Oxford University Press, 2019.

Robinson, Cedric J. *Black Marxism: The Making of the Black Radical Tradition*. Chapel Hill: University of North Carolina Press, 1983.

Robinson, Cedric J. "The First Attack Is an Attack on Culture." In *Cedric J. Robinson: On Racial Capitalism, Black Internationalism, and Cultures of Resistance*, edited by H. L. T. Quan, 69-74. London: Pluto, 2019.

Roellinghoff, Michael. "No Man's Land: De-Indigenization and the Doctrine of *Terra Nullius* in the Japanese Colonization of Hokkaido, 1869-1905." PhD diss., University of Toronto, 2020.

Ross, Kristin. *Communal Luxury: The Political Imaginary of the Paris Commune*. New York: Verso, 2015.

Ryang, Sonia. "The Great Kanto Earthquake and the Massacre of Koreans in 1923: Notes on Japan's Modern National Sovereignty." *Anthropological Quarterly* 76, no. 4 (Autumn 2003): 731-48.

"Ryōhyō Daihyō ga Kaiketsu e Senryoku." *Maeil Sinbo*, December 31, 1931. National Library of Korea Digital Reading Hall.

"Ryūketsu no Taki Seihi Sōgi." *Shakai Undō Tsūshin*, January 12, 1932. National Diet Library, Tokyo.

Saito, Nozomi (Nakaganeku). "Bone and Coral: Ossuopower and the Control of (Future) Remains in Occupied Okinawa." *American Quarterly* 74, no. 23 (2022): 567-89.

Sakata, Minako. "The Transformation of Hokkaido from Penal Colony to Homeland Territory." *International Review of Social History* 63, no. 26 (August 2018): 109-30.

Sasaki Jun. "1920-nendai Kōhan ni Okeru Tanba Chirimen Nōka no Rōdōryoku Haibun." *Ryūkoku Daigaku Keizaigaku Ronshū* li, no. 9 (February 2012): 105-26.

Satō Masahiro. "Taiwan ni Okeru Nōka Keizai Chōsa: Hikakushiteki Shiten Kara." In *Nōka Keizai Chōsa no Shiryōron Kenkyū—Saitō Mankichi Chōsa Kara Ōtsuki Kaisei Made (1880-1940 Nendai)*, edited by Satō Masahiro, 197-242. Tokyo: Hitotsubashi Keizai Kenkyūjo Fuzoku Shakai Kagaku Tōkei Jōhō Kenkyū Sentā, 2009.

Schiltz, Michael. *The Money Doctors from Japan: Finance, Imperialism, and the Building of the Yen Bloc, 1895-1937*. Cambridge, MA: Harvard University Press, 2012.

Sekula, Allan. *Fish Story*. Dusseldorf: Richter Verlag, 2002.

Sharpe, Christina. *In the Wake: On Blackness and Being*. Durham, NC: Duke University Press, 2016.

Sharpe, Christina. Introduction to *Nomenclature: New and Collected Poems*, by Dionne Brand, xvii-li. Durham, NC: Duke University Press, 2022.

Shin, Gi Wook. *Peasant Protest and Social Change in Colonial Korea*. Seattle: University of Washington Press, 1996.

Shindō Toyoo. "Kyūshū Fujin Suiheisha to Kyūshū Rōdō Fujin Kyōkai—Fujin Rōdō sha no Dokuji Yōkyū to Sono Undō." *Rekishi Hyōron* 327 (July 1977): 87-92.

Shinjō Ikuo. "Kokyō de Kyakushi Suru Koto." In *Okinawa no Kizu to iu Kairo*, 91-115. Tokyo: Iwanami Shoten, 2014.

Shinjō Ikuo. "Mizu no Kioku no Dansō." In *Okinawa ni Tsuranaru: Shisō to Undō ga Deau Tokoro*, 93-107. Tokyo: Iwanami Shoten, 2018.

Shinjō Ikuo. "The Political Formation of the Homoerotics and the Cold War: The Battle of Gazes at and from Okinawa." Translated by Nitta Keiko. In *Trans-Pacific Imagination: Rethinking Boundary, Culture and Society*, edited by Hyon Joo Yoo and Naoki Sakai, 97-106. Singapore: World Scientific, 2012.

Shizume Masato. "The Japanese Economy during the Interwar Period: Instability in the Financial System and the Impact of the World Depression." *Institute for Monetary and Economic Studies* (May 2009): 1-10.

Shlomowitz, Ralph, and Doug Munro. "The Ocean Island (Banaba) and Nauru Labour Trade 1900–1940." *Journal de la Société des Océanistes* 94 (1992): 103–17.

Shōji Shunsaku. "Shōwa Kyōkō no Kosaku Tōsō: Wakayama-ken Gobō Sōgi ni Sokushite." *Shakai Kagaku* 32 (February 1983): 201–82.

Silva, Denise Ferreira da. "1 (life) ÷ 0 (blackness) = ∞ − ∞ or ∞ / ∞: On Matter Beyond the Equation of Value." e-flux. https://www.e-flux.com/journal/79/94686/1-life-0-blackness-or-on-matter-beyond-the-equation-of-value/.

Silva, Denise Ferreira da. "Reading the Dead: A Black Feminist Poethical Reading of Global Capital." In *Otherwise Worlds: Against Settler Colonialism and Anti-Blackness*, edited by Tiffany Lethabo King, Jenell Navarro, and Andrea Smith, 38–51. Durham, NC: Duke University Press, 2020.

Silva, Denise Ferreira da. *Toward a Global Idea of Race*. Minneapolis: University of Minnesota Press, 2007.

Smallwood, Stephanie. "Commodified Freedom: Interrogating the Limits of Anti-Slavery Ideology in the Early Republic." *Journal of the Early Republic* 24, no. 2 (Summer 2004): 289–98.

Smith, Kerry. *A Time of Crisis: Japan, the Great Depression, and Rural Revitalization*. Cambridge, MA: Harvard University Press, 2003.

So Pok-hŭi. "Aru Hansen Shibyō Zainichi Chōsen Josei no Aruitekita Michi." *Zainichi Chōsenjinshi Kenkyū* 13 (April 1984): 1–13.

Spillers, Hortense. "Mama's Baby, Papa's Maybe: An American Grammar Book." *Diacritics* 17, no. 2 (Summer 1987): 64–81.

Sudō Kenichi. "Hijikata Hisakatsu to Nanyō Guntō." *Kokuritsu Minzokugaku Hakubutsukan Chōsa Hōkoku* 89 (2010): 567–82.

Sudō Naoto. *Nanyō-Orientalism: Japanese Representations of the Pacific*. Amherst, NY: Cambria, 2010.

Sunazawa Kayo. "As a Child of Ainu." In *Beyond Ainu Studies: Changing Academic and Public Perspectives*, edited by Mark J. Hudson, ann-elise lewallen, and Mark K. Watson, 92–98. Honolulu: University of Hawai'i Press, 2014.

Suzuki Yūko, ed. *Nihon Josei Undō Shiryō Shūsei 7*. Tokyo: Fuji Shuppan, 1993.

Suzuki Yūko. *Suiheisen o Mezasu Onna Tachi: Fujin Suihei Undōshi*. Tokyo: Domesu Shuppan, 2002.

Swan, Quito. "Blinded by Bandung? Illuminating West Papua, Senegal, and the Black Pacific." *Radical History Review* 131 (May 2018): 58–81.

Swan, Quito. *Pasifika Black: Oceania, Anti-Colonialism, and the African World*. New York: NYU Press, 2022.

Takahashi Yoshio. *Nihon Jinshu Kairyōron*. Tokyo: Ishikawa Hanjirō, 1884.

Takeda Haruhito. "Karinsan Dōgyōshakai." In *Ryōtaisenkanki Nihon no Karuteru*, edited by Hashimoto Jurō and Takeda Haruhito, 169–218. Tokyo: Ochanomizu Shobō, 1985.

Takeuchi Yūsuke. "Kokumotsu Jyukyū o Meguru Nihon Teikokunai Bungyō no Saihensei to Shokuminchi Chōsen: Testudō Yusō ni Yoru Chiikinai Ryūtsū no Kentō o Chūshin ni." *Shakai Keizai Shigaku* 74-5 (January 2009): 25–45.

Taki Kumejirō Denki Hensankai. *Taki Kumejirō*. Kakogawa: Taki Kumejirō Denki Hensankai, 1958.

"Taki Nōjō ni Okeru Kosaku Sogi no Shubōsha." *Kunsan Nippō*, January 20, 1932. National Library of Korea Digital Reading Hall.

"Taki Nōjō no Kosaku Sōgi Sainetsu." *Kunsan Nippō*, January 20, 1932. National Library of Korea Digital Reading Hall.

"Taki Nōjō Shoyū Sōko Hitomune Zenshō." *Maeil Sinbo*, February 6, 1932. National Library of Korea Digital Reading Hall.

"Taki Seihi Kaisha, Kaiko Hantai ni Danzen Tatsu." *Shakai Undō Tsūshin*, December 22, 1931. National Diet Library, Tokyo.

"Taki Seihi Kōjō Jikyūsen." *Shakai Undō Tsūshin*, December 24, 1931. National Diet Library, Tokyo.

"Taki Seihijo Sōgi Kaisetsu." *Shakai Undō Tsūshin*, August 27, 1931. National Diet Library, Tokyo.

Taki Seihi Sōgidan, Zenkoku Rōdō Kumiai Dōmei, Banshū Kagaku Sangyō Rōdō Kumiai, Taki Bunkai. *Dōshi Koko ni Saikai o Chikau ni Atatte*, January 11, 1932. Ōhara Shakai Mondai Kenkyūjo. Reference code G-77.

Tama Shinnosuke. "Uno Kōzō no Nihon Nōgyōron." *Hirosaki Daigaku Nōgakubu Gakujutsu Hōkoku* 58 (1994): 74–96.

Tamura Hiroshi. *Okinawa Keizai Jijō*. Tokyo: Nantōsha, 1925.

Tamura Hiroshi. *Ryūkyū Kyōsan Sonraku no Kenkyū*. Tokyo: Oka Shoin, 1927.

Tanaka Masato. "Moppuru to Nihon Seikishoku Kyūenkai." *Kirisuto Kyō Shakai Mondai Kenkyū* 17 (December 1978): 134–69.

Tanji, Miyume. "Chamorro Warriors and Godmothers Meet Uncle Sam: Gender, Loyalty and Resistance to US Military Occupation in Postwar Guam." In *Conflict Transformation: Essays on Methods of Nonviolence*, edited by Emiko Noma, Rhea A. DuMont, and Tom H. Hastings, 98–117. Jefferson, NC: McFarland, 2013.

Teaiwa, Katerina. *Consuming Ocean Island: Stories of People and Phosphate from Banaba*. Bloomington: Indiana University Press, 2014.

Tellei, Julita, Umai Basilius, and Faustina K. Rehuher. *Palau Compact Road Archaeological Investigations, Babeldaob Island, Republic of Palau, Phase 1: Intensive Archaeological Survey*. Vol. 3, *Oral History Documentation*. Honolulu, HI: International Archaeological Research Institute, 2005.

Teraki Nobuaki and Kurokawa Midori. *A History of Discriminated Buraku Communities in Japan*. Translated by Ian Neary. Folkstone, UK: Renaissance, 2019.

Terazawa, Yuki. *Knowledge, Power, and Women's Reproductive Health in Japan, 1690–1945*. New York: Palgrave Macmillan, 2018.

Teruoka Gitō. "Manshūkoku Sangyō Kensetsu ni Okeru Rōdōryoku no Igi." *Rōdō Kagaku* 16, no. 8 (August 1939): 577–86.

Teruoka Gitō. "Shochō Nenpō (1935 nendo)." Kurashiki Rōdō Kagaku Kenkyūjo.

Teruoka Shūzo, ed. *Nihon Nōgyōshi: Shihonshugi no Tenkai to Nōgyō Mondai*. Tokyo: Yūhikaku, 1981.

Tetsudōshō. *Chihō Tetsudō Menkyo: Tōhō Denryoku (Moto Asama Tozan Tetsudō)*. 1919 to 1929. National Archives of Japan. Reference code 3B 13 1536.

Tōa Tsūkō Kumiai. "Tōa Tsūkō Kumiai Daisankai Teiki Taikai Gian Sōan." *Zainichi Chōsenjinshi Kenkyū* 7 (December 1980): 140–52.

Tōhata Seiichi and Ōkawa Kazushi. *Chōsen Beikoku Keizairon, Beikoku Keizai no Kenkyū 1.* Tokyo: Yūhikaku, 1939.
Tokushima Tatsurō. "Abolishonizumu Kenkyū: Taiheiyō ni Tenkai suru Blackbirding." *Ekonomikusu* 6, no. 1 (September 2001): 47–69.
Tōmin Kyōkai. *Dai Nikai Yūryō Kōsei Nōson Hyōshōroku.* Osaka: Tōmin Kyōkai, 1935.
Tomiyama Ichirō. "Colonialism and the Sciences of the Tropical Zone: The Academic Analysis of Difference in 'the Island Peoples.'" *positions: asia critique* 3, no. 2 (1995): 367–91.
Tomiyama Ichirō. *Gendai Nihon Shakai to Okinawa-jin: Nihon-jin ni Naru to Iu Koto.* Tokyo: Nihon Keizai Hyōronsha, 1997.
Tosaka Jun. "Fukkō Genshō no Bunseki—Kazoku-shugi no Anarojii ni Tsuite (1935)." In *Tosaka Jun Zenshū* 2, 309–15. Tokyo: Keisō Shobō, 1966.
Totman, Conrad. *Japan's Imperial Forest Goryōrin, 1889–1945.* Kent: Global Oriental, 2007.
Toyota Shitsugyōsha Dōmei. "Untitled." September 1930. Ōhara Shakai Mondai Kenkyūjo. Reference code 農 24-3.
Toyota Shitsugyōsha Dōmei Jyunbikai. "Toyota son Hinnō Shokun ni Teisu." September 13, 1930. Ōhara Shakai Mondai Kenkyūjo. Reference code 農 24-3.
Trask, Haunani-Kay. "Settlers of Color and 'Immigrant' Hegemony: 'Locals' in Hawai'i." *Amerasia Journal* 26, no. 2 (2000): 1–24.
Trouillot, Michel-Rolph. *Silencing the Past: Power and the Production of History.* Boston: Beacon, 1995.
Tsumura Takashi. "Tennōsei Ninshiki to Suiheisha." *Inomata Kenkyū Tsūshin* 3 (1975): 1–3.
Tsumura Takashi. "Tennōsei Nishinki to Suiheisha Undō (Dai Sankai Matome)." *Inomata Kenkyū Tsūshin* 6 (1975): 5–8.
Tuck, Eve, and K. Wayne Yang. "R-Words: Refusing Research." In *Humanizing Research: Decolonizing Qualitative Inquiry with Youth and Communities*, edited by Django Paris and Maisha T. Winn, 223–47. Thousand Oaks, CA: SAGE, 2014.
Ueki Tetsujo. "Kaihō Tōsō no Omoide." *Buraku* 18, no. 8 (August 1966): 52–61.
Uno Kōzō. *Kyōkōron.* Tokyo: Iwanami Shoten, 1953.
Uno Kōzō. "Nihon Shihonshugi no Tokushu Kōzō to Nōgyō Mondai." In *Uno Kōzō Chosakushū 8*, 152–63. Tokyo: Iwanami Shoten, 1974.
Uno Kōzō. "Nōgyō Mondai Joron." In *Uno Kōzō Chosakushū 8*, 9–21. Tokyo: Iwanami Shoten, 1974.
Uno Kōzō. "Nōgyō no Kōsei." In *Uno Kōzō Chosakushū. Bekkan*, 436–88. Tokyo: Iwanami Shoten, 1974.
Uno Kōzō. *Theory of Crisis.* Translated by Ken Kawashima. Leiden: Brill, 2021.
[U.S. Army Corps of Engineers, Japan Engineer District]. *Castles in the Far East: The U.S. Army Corps of Engineers Okinawa and Japan Districts, 1945–1990.* Report. 1990.
Uzawa Kanako. "What Is Left of Us? The Living Story of the Ainu in Japan." *The Funambulist* 41 (April 2022). https://thefunambulist.net/magazine/article/what-is-left-of-us-the-living-story-of-the-ainu-in-japan.
Viana, Augusto Vicente de. "Diversifying Urbanity: The Japanese Commercial Community of Prewar Manila." In *The Asian Conference on Cultural Studies 2015, Kobe, Japan: Official Conference Proceedings*, 209–23. Nagoya: International Academic Forum, 2015.

Walia, Harsha. *Border and Rule: Global Migration, Capitalism, and the Rise of Racist Nationalism*. Chicago: Haymarket, 2021.

Walker, Gavin. *The Sublime Perversion of Capital: Marxist Theory and the Politics of History in Modern Japan*. Durham, NC: Duke University Press, 2016.

Ware, Lynn. "The Peace River: A Forgotten Highway." *Tampa Bay History* 6 (Fall/Winter 1984): 19-30.

Waswo, Ann. "In Search of Equity: Japanese Tenant Unions in the 1920s." In *Farmers and Village Life in Twentieth-Century Japan*, edited by Ann Waswo and Nishida Yoshiaki, 79-125. New York: Routledge Curzon, 2003.

Weheliye, Alexander. *Habeas Viscus: Racializing Assemblages, Biopolitics, and Black Feminist Theories of the Human*. Durham, NC: Duke University Press, 2014.

Welch, Shannon. "Transpacific Anomalies and Alterities: Decolonial Possibilities through Japanese Brazilian Literature." PhD diss., University of California, San Diego, 2022.

Williams, Maslyn, and Barrie Macdonald. *The Phosphateers: A History of the British Phosphate Commissioners and the Christmas Island Phosphate Commission*. Victoria: Melbourne University Press, 1985.

Wilson, Margaret, Clive Moore, and Doug Munro. "Asian Workers in the Pacific." In *Labour in the South Pacific*, edited by Clive Moore, Jacqueline Leckie, and Doug Munro, 78-107. Townsville, Australia: James Cook University of Northern Queensland, 1990.

Winther, Jennifer. "Household Enumeration in National Discourse: Three Moments in Modern Japanese History." *Social Science History* 32, no. 1 (Spring 2008): 19-46.

Wynter, Sylvia. "Beyond the Categories of the Master Conception: The Counterdoctrine of the Jamesian Poiesis." In *C. L. R. James's Caribbean*, edited by Pajet Henry and Paul Buhle, 63-91. Durham, NC: Duke University Press, 1992.

Wynter, Sylvia. "Unsettling the Coloniality of Being/Power/Truth/Freedom: Towards the Human, After Man, Its Overrepresentation—An Argument." *CR: The New Centennial Review* 3, no. 3 (Fall 2003): 257-337.

Wynter, Sylvia, and Katherine McKittrick. "Unparalleled Catastrophe for Our Species? Or, to Give Humanness a Different Future: Conversations." In *Sylvia Wynter: On Being Human as Praxis*, edited by Katherine McKittrick, 9-89. Durham, NC: Duke University Press, 2015.

Yamada Moritarō. *Nihon Shihonshugi Bunseki: Nihon Shihonshugi ni Okeru Saiseisan Katei Haaku*. Tokyo: Iwanami Shoten, 1977.

Yamada Yoshiko. "Park Hwa Sung's School Days in Tokyo." *Kenritsu Niigata Jyoshi Tanki Daigaku Kenkyū Kiyō* 45 (2008): 305-13.

Yamamoto Miono. *Shokumin Seisaku Kenkyū*. Kyoto: Kōbundō, 1920.

Yamagami Kimie. "Nōson Fujin to Kazoku Seido." *Mirai* 3 (May 1926). Reprinted in *Nihon Fujin Mondai Shiryō Shūsei 8*, edited by Maruoka Hideko, 578-80. Tokyo: Domesu Shuppan, 1976.

Yamagushiku, Shō, dir. *Uyafaafuji's Refusal: An Ode to the Yanbaru*. Canada, 2021. 11 min.

Yamauchi Kenji. "Kichi to Seichi no Okinawa shi" [Ethnography of Forced Relocation Villages and Sacred Places within and Surrounding US Military Bases in Okinawa]. PhD diss., Meiji University, 2020.

Yamazaki Satoshi. "Suihei Undō no Hitobito (7): Iriaiken Tōsō no Rekishi o Iseshi Asama chō ni Saguru, Yamazaki." *Buraku* 24, no. 9 (August 1972): 57–61.

Yamazaki, Yūshi. "Radical Crossings: From Peasant Rebellions to Internationalist Multiracial Labor Organizing Among Japanese Immigrant Communities in Hawaii and California, 1885–1935." PhD diss., University of Southern California, 2015.

Yanaihara Tadao. "Nanpō Rōdō Seisaku no Kichō." In *Nanpō Kyōeiken no Rōdō Mondai*, edited by Kyōchōkai, 3–16. Tokyo: Kyōchōkai Shuppanbu, 1942.

Yanaihara Tadao. "Shion Undō ni Tsuite." *Keizaigaku Ronshū* 2, no. 2 (1923): 25–76.

Yasuoka Kenichi. *"Tasha" Tachi no Nōgyōshi: Zainichi Chōsenjin, Sokaisha, Kaitaku Nōmin, Kaigai Imin*. Kyoto: Kyoto Daigaku Gakujutsu Shuppankai, 2014.

Yi Sun-ae. "Kinyūkai Oboegaki." *Zainichi Chōsenjinshi Kenkyū* 1 (December 1977): 33–41.

Yi Sun-ae. "Zainichi Chōsen Josei Undō (ge): Kinyūkai o Chūshin to Shite." *Zainichi Chōsenjinshi Kenkyū* 4 (June 1979): 30–41.

Yi Sun-ae. "Zainichi Chōsen Josei Undō (jyō): Kinyūkai o Chūshin to Shite." *Zainichi Chōsenjinshi Kenkyū* 2 (June 1978): 29–44.

Yoneyama, Lisa. *Cold War Ruins: Transpacific Critique of American Justice and Japanese War Crimes*. Durham, NC: Duke University Press, 2016.

Yoneyama, Lisa. "For Transformative Knowledge and Postnationalist Public Spheres: The Smithsonian *Enola Gay* Controversy." In *Perilous Memories: The Asia-Pacific War(s)*, edited by Takashi Fujitani, Geoffrey M. White, and Lisa Yoneyama, 323–46. Durham, NC: Duke University Press, 2001.

Yoneyama, Lisa. "Toward a Decolonial Genealogy of the Transpacific." *American Quarterly* 69, no. 3 (September 2017): 471–82.

Yoshikawa Hideki. "The Plight of the Okinawa Dugong." *Asia-Pacific Journal: Japan Focus* 18, no. 16.2 (August 2020). https://apjjf.org/2020/16/YoshikawaOEJP.html.

Yoshioka Kin'ichi. *Taue Sagyō no Gōrika ni Kansuru Kenkyū*. Tokyo: Nihon Rōdō Kagaku Kenkyūjo, 1939.

Young, Louise. *Beyond the Metropolis: Second Cities and Modern Life in Interwar Japan*. Berkeley: University of California Press, 2013.

Young, Louise. *Japan's Total Empire: Manchuria and the Culture of Wartime Japan*. Berkeley: University of California Press, 1998.

Zai-Nihon Chōsen Rōdō Sōdōmei Sangatsukai, Zai-Tokyo Chōsen Musan Seinen Dōmeikai Ichigatsukai. *Mieken Bokusatsu Jiken ni Saishi Zen Nihon Musan Kaikyū ni Uttau*, February 10, 1926. Ōhara Shakai Mondai Kenkyūjo. Reference code T1-3.

Zen Nihon Nōmin Kumiai Mieken Rengōkai Iinan-gun Kanbe-son Aza Seisei. *Shunki Tōsō News Tokubetsugō*, January 25, 1930. Ōhara Shakai Mondai Kenkyūjo. Reference code 農 24-2.

Zenkoku Nōmin Kumiai Okayamaken Rengōkai. *Zennō Okayama Tōsōshi*. Okayama: Doi Shoten, 1936.

Zennō Miekenren Honbu. *Nōmin Nyūsu*, April 10, 1931. Ōhara Shakai Mondai Kenkyūjo. Reference code 農 24-3.

Zennō Okayamaken Rengōkai Shibu. *Zennō Okayamakenren Shūki Nensō Nyūsu*, November 23, 1931. Ōhara Shakai Mondai Kenkyūjo. Reference code 農 33-5.

INDEX

3.13 incident, the, (March 13, 1933), 79–80

abundance, 177, 189, 191; of narrative, 13
ableism, 30
abolitionist geographies, 189
administrative village, the, 42
Agriculture Labor Study Center, 92, 95; kitchen modernization requirements of, 93fig., 94fig.
Ainu Mosir, 24, 26; colonization of, 4, 22; as a site of internal colonization, 25
Alliance of the Unemployed, the, 69, 73, 76; pamphlets from, 72fig.
allowances, 34, 98
ancestor time, 175
ancestor worship, 113, 149
anti-Blackness, 3, 7, 141, 191; in language, 144; logic of, 11–12; and modernity, 5; and nation formation, 22; in Okinawa, 163; and temporality, 2
anticapitalism, 30, 105
anti-imperialism, 5, 28, 122
anti-Indigeneity, 3, 7, 137, 141, 191
archives, 160, 162–163, 188, 190; of imperialism, 10, 12, 107; of the state, 120; of struggle, 11; visibility in, 65, 79, 104
Arimatsu Hideyoshi, 38
Asama, 37, 58; customary rights in, 53; land sale and reorganization, 47, 52, 55, 57; protected forestland in, 43–44, 44map, 47–48; river in, 37, 57, 61, 82; struggle in, 38, 40, 50–51, 54, 56–61, 66, 81–82
Asama Tozan Railway Company, 41fig., 46

austerity, 90; state conditions of, 48, 75, 88, 165
autarky, 26–27, 36

Babeldaob island, 146, 159; Asahi plantation in, 147; as terra nullius, 148
Banaba Island, 109, 135, 150; conditions of labor in, 125, 136–138; as seascape, 122; transport of laborers to, 14, 134, 139–140, 175
Banshū Gōdō Rōdō Kumiai Honbu, 122–123, 126
barley, 31, 71, 82, 125, 168
barracks, 84, 125–129, 133, 184. See also *hanba*
Battle of Okinawa, the, 143, 159, 171, 180, 183, 185. See also genocide
Befu-chō, 108–109, 127; factory in, 116–118; Taki Seihi strike in, 122, 126, 132; workers' experiences in, 123, 129, 133
Black Jacobins, The (James), 5, 198n19
blackbirding, 20–21, 135, 198n12
Blue Clerk, The (Brand), 11, 162–163, 188
body politic, the: expulsion from, 10; of Japan, 14
bone cleaning, 183
boomerang effect, the, 29, 35, 201n53
bourgeoisie, the, 19, 217n56; in Japan, 69, 84; and Japanism, 88–90; narratives of, 2, 4; in white societies, 20, 22; women of, 64
Brand, Dionne, 5, 162, 186, 188; *The Blue Clerk*, 11, 162–163, 188
Buraku Liberation Movement, the, 38, 54. See also the Suiheisha

buraku women, 12, 66; activism of, 62, 65, 77–78, 82, 129; criminalization of, 61, 80; and potential solidarity with non-buraku, 63. *See also* the Suiheisha

burakumin, 37; activism by, 57, 59; burdens on, 74–75; conflicts with ippanmin, 14, 42, 50, 55; discrimination against, 38–40, 51, 69; expulsion from Asama, 54, 60, 62; households of, 9. *See also* harmonization

capitalism, 19, 80, 121, 186; and class, 75; and development, 5, 8, 43, 47; and extraction, 12; global, 86; and imperialism, 4; in Japan, 26, 120, 183; and neoliberalism, 2; and socialism, 201n44. *See also* monopoly

care, 48; barracks as sites of, 127; of the collective, 106; and forced intimacy, 104; by Korean women, 114–115

caretaking, 32, 35

censuses, 87–88, 100, 107; forms of, 31; Korean women's erasure from, 101, 110–111, 127

ceremony, 167–168; as expression of kinship, 156, 165–166, 178; as intimacy, 104; religious, 58

Césaire, Aimé, 26, 36, 61. *See also* boomerang effect, the

Chamorro/CHamoru, 141, 144, 146

chattel slavery, 18, 21, 135, 173

Cheju Island, 115

child rearing, 64

childbirth, 92

Code de l'Indigénat, the, 137–138

colonial wage markets, 120

colonialism, 3, 29, 109, 120; erasure of, 5, 7; logic of, 1; and *pieza* conceptual frame, 19, 113; and primitive accumulation, 24; Yamamoto Miono on, 25. *See also* "miracles and magic"; settler colonialism

comfort stations, 174. *See also* comfort women

comfort women, 182–183

commodity, the, 3; phosphate as, 120, 133; value of, 18

Commodore Perry, 25

commons, the, 47–48, 57; access to, 51, 67, 82, 103, 105; reorganization of, 52, 61. *See also* burakumin; enclosure

commonsense, 11–12, 28, 36, 159, 191; and accumulation, 104; ; in agrarian villages, 9; colonial concept of, 5–6; and derogatory language, 144; expulsion and confinement as, 86; of ippanmin, 82; and Japanism, 90; and modern aesthetics, 186; white supremacist norms as, 8

communal luxury, 128, 133

communism, 159, 168

Compagnie Française des Phosphates de l'Océanie (CFPO), 139

condolences, 104, 113–114, 116, 123

Confucianism, 113

conquistador humanism, 22, 27, 37, 110, 188; and colonialism, 91; criteria for, 28; definition of, 7; and ippanmin, 61; small farm households as sites of, 13, 14, 26, 85, 97

consciousness, 28, 189–190; of class, 27, 173; of self, 173

consensus, 9–10, 86, 114; desire for, 62; power of, 37–38, 53–54. *See also* ippanmin

consumption, 184; in the home, 35, 101, 152; state attempts to control, 75

contract labor, 115, 138; conditions of, 124, 134; as island colonial violence, 143, 145; as modernist, 21. *See also* Korean agricultural trainee system; Mitsui Bussan

convict labor, 109, 120, 137, 175; in Bone Valley, Florida, 121, 122, 125; of the Tokugawa regime, 23, 199–200n29

cooking, 127, 178

coolie system, the, 97; in Okinawa, 138, 141, 142fig., 143fig.

corporations, 42, 43, 91, 116

credit associations, 118

deluge, 180, 184; concept of, 164; and stories, 165

democracy, 12, 64

Edict Abolishing Ignoble Classes (1871), 37, 58

elderly, the, 30

elections, 6, 73fig.

enclosure, 151, 156, 176, 184; logics of, 10; practices of, 19, 24, 60, 177; repercussions of, 47, 50, 87; and settler colonialism, 22. *See also* the commons

enslavement, 13, 25; of African peoples, 4, 18, 120; enduring effects of, 8; erasure of, 19, 29

eugenics, 30, 39

expropriation, 22, 36, 127, 148, 167; mechanisms of, 28, 116

extrafamilial labor, 27–28

Fanon, Frantz, 5
fascism, 2–3, 14, 28; common use rights and, 57; in the countryside, 88; Katsuhiko Endo on, 86. *See also* Japanese fascism
feminism, 113, 156; and Black radical thought, 8; in Japan, 62; and labor struggles, 5;
fertilizer, 91, 118, 120, 124; prices of, 56, 71, 129; synthetic, 110; *See also* Shikishima (brand)
feudalism, 19, 24, 26
feudality, 27, 38. *See also* feudalism
First Sino-Japanese War, 116, 134
fishing, 34, 42, 183
forestry, 43, 47–48, 73fig.; products of, 46, 50; protected status of, 42; workers in, 23, 44–45, 57–59
Forestry Law, the, 44; 1907 revision of, 42

gathering, 165, 173; act of, 65–66
gender, 32, 35, 102, 153; and accumulation, 3; in buraku relations, 39; dynamics in Black households, 8; exploitation based on, 101, 104; expulsions from, 10; in the Farm Household Survey, 48, 95; and household relations, 29; norms of, 79, 109. *See also* gendered-racial-sexual order
gendered-racial-sexual order, the, 9
General Federation of Labor, the, 40
genocide, 1, 19; commonsense as a legitimating idea for, 9; of Indigenous peoples, 4–5, 21, 22, 90, 141, 173; Japan as perpetrator, 10, 120; understandings of, 3. *See also* Battle of Okinawa; slow violence
ghosts, 40, 180, 182, 184
Ginowan (town, Okinawa), 170; activism in, 165, 179, 183; significance of water sources in, 178; as strategic colonial node, 171; women in, 180, 182. *See also* water struggle (Ginowan)
Great Kantō Earthquake, the (1923): anti-Korean massacres during, 83–86

Haitian earthquake (2010), 12
Haitian Revolution, the, 4
hanba, 84–85, 102, 110–112
harmonization policies, 40, 57, 61, 69, 71
Hawai'i, 9, 12, 20, 152, 170; remittances from, 155, 157, 167
health, 49, 169, 175; of buraku communities, 39; of women, 92–93

hegemony, 19, 85, 190, 192; in the Pacific, 169
heteropatriarchy, 90, 101, 184; and anti-Blackness, 5; in the household, 129; through immigration, 138. *See also* family
Hino Nichōme, 40, 64, 76, 78–82
historical materialism, 2, 190
Hokkaido, 147; colonization of, 14, 22, 24, 173, 199n22; as a site of internal colonization, 25;
Home Ministry, the, 7, 38, 42, 87, 176–177
Horne, Gerald, 20; *The White Pacific*, 9, 20, 198n20, 200n34
housewifization, 14, 95, 96
housework, 8, 64, 75, 93, 101; as survey category, 32–35, 48, 50, 154, 156–157
humanism, 63; economic, 4; liberal conception of, 1, 19; narratives of, 189. *See also* conquistador humanism

ideology, 54; of the "local nation," 9
idol worship, 113
illegality, 66
immigration, 118; of Korean agricultural workers, 97; in mainland Japan, 22; Okinawan policy, 24–25, 138, 141; and white supremacy, 136
imperialism, 2–4, 110, 191; aesthetics of, 186; circuits of, 135; and competition, 20–22, 26, 141; of Japan, 12, 19, 113, 120, 161, 163; of the United States, 162. *See also* enclosure; feudalism; *kanaka*
inclusion, 15, 159, 161; of buraku, 61; of buraku women, 62, 64–65; and enclosure, 43; in Okinawa, 151; politics of, 1
indentured servitude, 4, 122, 137, 218n4; of Chinese laborers, 120; conditions of, 97–98; differences with slavery, 11; of Korean laborers, 85
intellectuals, 30, 145, 187, 189; and acts of translation, 24; on the Battle of Okinawa, 159; of the imperial universities, 6; limitations of, 7, 12, 19, 162; in the Meiji era, 150
Intimacies of Four Continents, The (Lowe), 10, 19, 194n14, 218–219n4
intimacy: assimilative, 109–110, 113; forced, 86, 98, 104–106
International Red Aid (MOPR), 76, 80; women's divisions of, 77. *See also* Matsusaka city

ippanmin, 37–38, 50, 60, 62; and colonial commonsense, 82; as conquistador humanists, 61; and corruption, 52; discrimination by, 53. *See also* burakumin
Ise Grand Shrine, 40, 43, 46fig., 54; route to, 41fig., 84
Ishiguro Tadaatsu, 28–29
invisibilization of labor, 90. *See also* housework

James, C. L. R., 5, 17, 18, 29, 190; *The Black Jacobins*, 5, 198n19. *See also* the *pieza* conceptual frame; public school code
Japan Farmer's Union, the, 28, 40, 50, 68, 92, 105
Japanese Communist Party, 84
Japanese fascism, 35, 59, 191
Japanese Imperial Navy, the, 146
Japanese language, 100, 132, 135, 146
Japanese settler ascendancy, 9
Japanese supremacy, 9, 136, 145, 162, 188, 192
Japanism, 89–90
journalism, 109, 145, 183, 185

kanaka, 136–137, 145
Kimje, 116, 123, 132–133; plantations in, 117, 129, 160
Kinomoto incident, 84, 86
kinship, 1, 62, 105, 113, 165, 176; and heteronormativity, 106; state attempts to control, 147; understandings of, 8. *See also* ceremonies
Kinyūkai, 6, 28, 112–116
Kise railway project, 55, 70
Kisekishugi. See "miracles and magic"
Kishiwada Spinning Factory's Tsu factory no. 1, 81
Kobayashi Kenichirō, 136–137, 140–141
kōgakko, 146
Korea, 24, 91, 109–110, 116, 123, 126, 133, 160, 198n12; colonies in, 25–26; Governor General's office in, 97, 99, 115; migrant workers from, 14, 85–87, 103, 111–112, 116; struggles for independence in, 28, 113, 118
Korean agricultural trainee system, the, 97, 100, 102, 104, 109; eligibility criteria of, 98
Korean agriculturalists, 85, 87, 96, 118; conditions of labor for, 86, 98–99, 105; invisibilization of women, 100–102, 113; in the *pieza* conceptual frame, 104; as a solution to labor shortages, 97

Koror, 144, 147
Kōyō village, 88, 90–92, 102, 118, 135, 160
Kumamoto Imperial Agricultural Association, 97, 99

labor efficiency index, the, 29, 30, 86, 153; of agricultural work, 93; definition of, 13; of housewives, 92
laboring capacity, 29, 33, 35, 86; definition of, 13, 30, 32
laissez-faire. *See* monopoly
Land Expropriation Law, the, 171, 176
land registration system, the, 38, 49, 91, 177
landlords: access to land of, 58; power of, 28, 55, 57, 177; tenant disputes with, 56, 60, 69, 76, 77fig.
landscape, 122, 180; manufacturing of, 40, 43; preservation of, 42
language, 2, 65, 120; of austerity, 75; colonial violence in, 5, 175; of economic rationality, 66; of harmonization, 57; of protest, 26; of war, 190. *See also* Japanese-language
law, the: as a concept, 2, 10; and the police, 177; power of, 58, 69
loneliness, 189, 192
Lowe, Lisa, 4, 7, 118; *The Intimacies of Four Continents*, 10, 19, 194n14, 218–219n4

machiya, 178
Maemura, 54–57, 60, 76, 78
"Man-as-human," 11; concept of, 8; in Japan, 20, 101, 110, 191
Manchuria, 85, 129; and divisions of labor, 86
March First movement, the, 28, 118
Maria Luz incident, the, 21
Mariana Islands, the, 14, 144, 157
Marxism, 2, 5, 24, 194n11; limitations of, 4; and territorial fixity, 6, 99
Matsusaka city, 40, 65, 70, 77; labor activism in, 66, 71, 78. *See also* Alliance of the Unemployed; International Red Aid (MOPR)
Matsusaka Momen Company, 65–66, 68
matriarchal authority, 150
May Day demonstrations, 69, 75, 210n31
May Fourth movement, the, 28
mechanization, 47
medicine, 2, 49

Meiji regime, the, 21, 134; economy during, 23, 116; foundations of, 9, 22; policies of, 24, 26, 38, 149, 167

metropole, the, 9, 31, 118, 135: agriculture in, 26, 97; antagonisms in, 6; conquistador humanism in, 14, 91; difference with the colony, 116–117; Korean migrant workers in, 84–87, 96, 104, 106; Korean women in, 101, 107, 110–115; protectionism in, 27. *See also* Korean agricultural workers; religious tourism

Micronesia, 144

Middle Passage, the, 2–4, 10, 14, 18

midwifery, 49, 92–93

Mie Rōdō Gōdō Kumiai, 67, 78–79

militarization, 143, 160, 168, 174. *See also* total war

mining, 91, 222n60; labor of; 23, 103, 112, 121, 137; of nickel, 137; of phosphate, 121–122, 137, 139, 150; rights to, 121

Ministry of Agriculture and Commerce, the, 13, 31, 149, 168; in Asama, 53; heteropatriarchy under, 151; on housework, 153; and self-management, 48. *See also* Model Revitalization Village; oikonomic policy; shared genealogical existence; the Home Ministry

"miracles and magic," 88, 90–91

miso, 70

Mitsui Bussan, 110, 120, 135, 140, 171; recruitment by, 138–139

Model Revitalization Villages, 88

modernity, 135; 194n14; aesthetics of, 186; colonial, 6; conditions of oppression under, 3, 5; European conceptions of, 22

monopoly, 19, 168; and capital, 23, 30, 169; and corporations, 125, 135

Mount Asama, 43, 45, 59

mourning, 164–165, 167, 186–188; practices of, 106, 109, 156, 166, 187; state control over, 114, 122

munchū, 165, 168, 183. *See also* kinship

Musansha Shimbun (newspaper), 84

mushoku, 99, 101, 111

mutual aid, 49, 72fig., 75, 131fig., 149, 159; spaces of, 62; systems of, 27, 76, 112, 131fig., 152, 183

Naha, 12, 165, 173–176, 178–180, 183–184; after Allied forces' attack, 182fig.; City Museum of History in, 166fig.; cultural transformation in, 169; port of, 169, 173, 179–180; water systems in, 169–172, 175, 178, 180, 181fig.

Nakazato Hatsuno, 78–79, 81

Nanyōchō, 141, 143, 146–147

Narahara Shigeru, 23, 24, 171

nationalism, 5, 19, 30; of the military, 89; provocation of, 115

nationality, 100, 216n46

New Caledonia, 137–138

"News on the Struggle against Political Customs of Asama Discrimination" (newspaper report), 58, 61, 81–82

nickel mining, 137–138, 141

Nōka Keizai Chōsa (Farm Household Survey), 13, 35, 179; devaluation of women in, 50; entries in, 33fig., 86, 92, 97, 151, 152, 158, 165. *See also* housework

noro, 150, 160, 166–168, 178, 229n67

oikonomic policy, 10, 111; definition of, 8; of the Japanese Ministry of Agriculture and Commerce, 9, 29, 35, 86, 104; tools of, 31, 48

Okinawa, 6, 12, 24, 141, 169; complicity in settler colonialism, 144–148, 161, 179; customs of, 150–151; immigration policy in, 25; migrant workers from, 9, 135, 137, 143, 155, 175; privileges of those from, 138–139; recruitment of labor from, 14, 140; survey project in, 159–160. *See also* Battle of Okinawa; enclosure

Okinawa Labor Farmer Party, 28

Okinawa's Economic Conditions (text), 148–150

Ortiz de Retez, Yñigo, 135, 136

Ōyama, 169–170, 176–179, 182, 184

Pacific Phosphate Company (PPC), the, 14, 120, 134; recruitment by, 136, 138, 140–141, 175; wage policy of, 139

Palau, 146, 160, 169, 175

Palau Resources Institute, the, 146, 148

pamphlets, 72fig.; as organizing tools, 69–71, 73, 76, 94fig.; publication of, 123

panama hats, 154–158, 230; production of, 151

patriarchy, 7, 19, 30, 77, 96, 113, 177

patriotism, 89, 159

Peace Preservation Law, the, 78

peasantry, 113, 172; dispossession of, 91, 96; organizations of, 40, 115, 150; struggles of, 5

"Peasantry and Fascism," 88

INDEX • 265

penal transport, 23
Perry, Matthew C. (Commodore), 25
persimmons, 90, 92, 103–104
pieza, 3, 20, 104, 135; conceptual frame, 13, 19, 113; definition of, 18; and labor, 30. *See also* Wynter, Sylvia
pioneer: discourses about American, 22; in fairy tale, 90; as revolutionary organization, 128, 223n83
"Plan for Okinawan Defense" (military plan), 173
pleasure quarters, 150, 169
police, 38, 78, 91, 151, 183; and anti-Korean sentiment, 83, 85, 127; and harmonization, 61; and land ownership, 177; suppression of labor organizers, 76, 115, 125–126, 129, 132; surveillance by, 64, 112; of Uji Yamada, 52, 57. *See also* 3.13 incident, the
pollution, 2
PPC Wage Policy, the, 139
"primitive accumulation," 24, 191, 197n11
proletariat, the: organizations of, 29, 68, 79, 124; and the subject, 22; women's movement of, 63–65, 81, 114
promiscuity, 39, 173
property, 38, 137; Japanese conception of, 22, 85; laws of, 53, 177; of private, 24, 31
protectionism, 7, 87; small farmer, 27, 35; state policies of, 9, 188, 201n44
public school code, 17, 29, 36, 128

reading, act of, 5, 162–164, 191
race-making, 97, 102
racism, 2, 7, 26, 177; and blackbirding, 135; and valorization, 80
religious tourism, 40, 43
remittances, 71, 141, 146, 152–153, 155, 157, 167
rent, 49, 67, 105, 154
reproductive labor, 8, 111, 214n11
rice, 34, 68, 125, 131fig., 156, 167–168; prices of, 39, 56; plantations of, 91, 117; production of, 31, 49, 92, 95, 152. *See also* Rice Riots (1918)
Rice Riots (1918), 39, 52, 80
Ryūkyū Kingdom, 25, 134, 152; colonization of, 4, 14, 26, 199n23; overthrow of, 23

sake, 70
Sanyō railway system, the, 117

seascapes, 122
secrets, 11, 164, 179, 189
sedimentation, 120
self-management, 48, 56, 159, 215n29
settler colonialism, 2, 9, 196n37; and immigration, 2; in the Pacific, 14, 26, 135
sewage systems, 43, 180
sex, 151; venues for, 35, 174–175, 183
sexual autonomy, 47
sexual slavery, 9, 102, 184
sexual violence, 174
sexuality, 151; of burakumin, 207n68
shared genealogical existence, 103, 164
Sharpe, Christina, 2–3, 11–12
Shigō village, 37, 44–45, 47, 52, 58
Shikishima (brand), 118, 120, 124
Shiratsuka Daisaburō, 66
Shishido Sajirō, 147
Shōwa panic, the, 70
silkworms, 34, 71
slow violence, 23
sociogeny, 24, 62
solidarity, 54, 85, 128–129, 140; between buraku and non-buraku farmers, 56; of class, 53, 84; organizations in, 40, 68–69, 76, 172; spaces of, 14, 62
sovereignty, 19, 22, 114, 185
soy sauce, 70
"special buraku," 38
Special Higher Police, the, 76, 79, 81
subjectivity, 54
sugar, 173, 180; capital from, 159, 177; centrifugal, 151, 171; plantations of, 21; production of, 24, 150, 152, 155, 167. *See also* Tainansha
sugarcane, 171, 173
Suihei Shimbun (newspaper), 55, 58, 62–65
Suiheisha, the, 6, 28, 59; national policy of, 54; organizing by, 40, 50, 78; women's activism in, 62, 64, 69, 114
surplus labor, 151; extraction of, 8, 29
surveillance, 2, 39, 64, 137, 174; corporate control through, 64, 97, 105; of Okinawan women, 151

Tainansha, 150, 152, 171, 175, 178; disputes against, 151, 172
Taiwan, 6, 172–173; as a "formal" colony, 24–26
Taki Kumejirō, 109–110, 116, 117, 120, 123, 127, 132

Taki Seihi Kabushikigaisha, 14, 108, 116, 119fig.; exploitation by, 109, 118, 135, 160; Korean women workers at, 127; labor at, 110; strike against, 122–126, 129–132
Tamura Hiroshi, 148, 159, 168
tattoos, 140
tax reform, 22, 204n17
taxes, 34, 56, 71, 74
tea, 31; production of, 34
teachers, 56, 152
temachin, 47
tenancy rights, 28, 51, 69, 105
tetsudai, 27. *See also* extrafamilial labor
textile factories, 65–66, 81, 112, 126; strikes in, 62
total war, 3, 35, 164, 173; mobilization for, 175, 191
"Treasure Island," 155

unemployment, 73, 77, 100, 150. *See also* mushoku
United States military occupation, 171, 183
Uno Kōzō, 5, 26, 86

vigilante violence, 83–85, 102, 105, 112, 127; of youth, 126

waged labor, 9, 34, 101; and legitimacy, 111; low, 87, 92, 99; opportunities for, 74, 97; relations of, 7; reliance on, 49; as supplemental income, 118, 160; in textile factories, 81; working hours of, 156
wages, 34, 63, 96, 103, 156; discrepancy between promised and real, 155, 172; discriminatory, 126; in ledgers, 92, 94, 105, 158; reductions of, 65, 68, 71, 75, 99, 124, 139; social, 61; spending of, 98; struggles over, 67, 70, 81, 124–125, 129, 152; withholding of, 98

wasteland, 49
water sources (Okinawa), 165–166, 169, 170–171, 175–177, 179, 182, 184, 204n23, 232n11; during Allied occupation, 180, 182; and expropriation law, 177, 179; as gathering places, 165, 166fig., 178
water struggle (Ginowan), 164, 165, 169, 171–172, 175–76, 184
White Pacific, The (Horne), 9, 20, 198n20, 200n34
white supremacy, 1, 6, 192; logic of, 2; in the Pacific, 20, 135–136; and vulnerability, 9. *See also* commonsense; Japanese supremacy
whiteness, 22; and commonsense, 6; logic of possession through, 20
withholding, act of, 153, 169, 179, 189, 192; in archives, 188; of secrets, 164
womanhood, 64, 232n10; white conceptions and denial of, 8
World War I, 9, 28, 66, 117; economic recessions following, 10, 26, 188; and protectionism, 31, 56, 61, 86; state reactions to, 141
World War II, 49, 87, 112, 146, 180; and US imperialism, 162
Wynter, Sylvia, 5, 17, 86, 144, 190; on Man-as-human, 8, 20. *See also pieza* conceptual frame

Yamaoka Kunitoshi, 43
youth, 73, 141; groups, 83, 89; and vigilantism, 126, 159
yuta, 150, 160, 168, 229n67

Zainichi Chōsen Rōdō Sōdōmei, 84
Zenkoku Rōdō Kumiai Hyōgikai, 66, 67
Zennō, 73fig., 76–78, 124

STUDIES OF THE WEATHERHEAD EAST ASIAN INSTITUTE

COLUMBIA UNIVERSITY

SELECTED TITLES
(Complete list at weai.columbia.edu/content/publications)

Rejuvenating Communism: Youth Organizations and Elite Renewal in Post-Mao China, by Jérôme Doyon. University of Michigan Press, 2023.

From Japanese Empire to American Hegemony: Koreans and Okinawans in the Resettlement of Northeast Asia, by Matthew R. Augustine. University of Hawai'i Press, 2023.

Building a Republican Nation in Vietnam, 1920–1963, edited by Nu-Anh Tran and Tuong Vu. University of Hawai'i Press, 2022.

China Urbanizing: Impacts and Transitions, edited by Weiping Wu and Qin Gao. University of Pennsylvania Press, 2022.

Common Ground: Tibetan Buddhist Expansion and Qing China's Inner Asia, by Lan Wu. Columbia University Press, 2022.

Narratives of Civic Duty: How National Stories Shape Democracy in Asia, by Aram Hur. Cornell University Press, 2022.

The Concrete Plateau: Urban Tibetans and the Chinese Civilizing Machine, by Andrew Grant. Cornell University Press, 2022.

Confluence and Conflict: Reading Transwar Japanese Literature and Thought, by Brian Hurley. Harvard East Asian Monographs, 2022.

Inglorious, Illegal Bastards: Japan's Self-Defense Force During the Cold War, by Aaron Skabelund. Cornell University Press, 2022.

Madness in the Family: Women Care, and Illness in Japan, by H. Yumi Kim. Oxford University Press, 2022.

Uncertainty in the Empire of Routine: The Administrative Revolution of the Eighteenth-Century Qing State, by Maura Dykstra. Harvard University Press, 2022.

Outsourcing Repression: Everyday State Power in Contemporary China, by Lynette H. Ong. Oxford University Press, 2022.

Diasporic Cold Warriors: Nationalist China, Anticommunism, and the Philippine Chinese, 1930s–1970s, by Chien-Wen Kung. Cornell University Press, 2022.

Dream Super-Express: A Cultural History of the World's First Bullet Train, by Jessamyn Abel. Stanford University Press, 2022.

The Sound of Salvation: Voice, Gender, and the Sufi Mediascape in China, by Guangtian Ha. Columbia University Press, 2022.

Carbon Technocracy: Energy Regimes in Modern East Asia, by Victor Seow. The University of Chicago Press, 2022.

Disunion: Anticommunist Nationalism and the Making of the Republic of Vietnam, by Nu-Anh Tran. University of Hawai'i Press, 2022.

Learning to Rule: Court Education and the Remaking of the Qing State, 1861–1912, by Daniel Barish. Columbia University Press, 2022.

Printed in the USA
CPSIA information can be obtained
at www.ICGtesting.com
LVHW021950020724
784520LV00002B/117